MAGDALENE MYSTERIES

"Please do yourself the great favor of exploring this wisdom-filled and transformative book—full and alive as a pregnant mother's womb! It will answer so many questions, fill in so many blanks, and offer much more than one could have imagined about the awakening of our sacred wombs. Grounded in a vital feminine spiritual lineage that extends back through all human time, *Magdalene Mysteries* opens wide the door not only to essential lineages of the past but also to the present and future of our own personal lives and empowerment. Much more than your mind is engaged here: your body and soul and connection to the womb of Gaia and the Great Mother, birther of all. Stepping into our loving, vital feminine power is profoundly important to reclaim our embodied place on our Mother, Lady Gaia."

BROOKE MEDICINE EAGLE, EARTHKEEPER, WISDOM TEACHER, AND AUTHOR OF *BUFFALO WOMAN COMES SINGING* AND *THE LAST GHOST DANCE*

"Beautifully written and illustrated, this extensively researched book restores Mary Magdalene to her rightful place as a spiritual leader from the lineage of womb shamans. Offering sacred rituals, the teachings in this book guide us effortlessly to follow the left-hand path of Christ."

CHRISTINE PAGE, M.D., AUTHOR OF *THE HEALING POWER OF THE SACRED WOMAN* AND *THE HEART OF THE GREAT MOTHER*

"*Magdalene Mysteries* is a remarkable book that awakens the deep spiritual knowing that Mary Magdalene was a sacred priestess who has so much to teach us and that also sheds new light on the wild feminine. This exceptional book is a deep and rich immersion into the sacred feminine mysteries of Mary Magdalene and reveals a lost knowledge that needs to be reclaimed today. Seren and Azra wrote a truly exquisite book."

SANDRA INGERMAN, M.A., SHAMANIC TEACHER AND AWARD-WINNING AUTHOR OF *THE BOOK OF CEREMONY*

"Seren and Azra are two brilliant souls dedicated to diving deeply into the wisdom hidden within the ancient mystery schools to retrieve the sacred keys that will restore and give new life to the sacred womb initiation mysteries. In their new book, *Magdalene Mysteries,* the teachings they have discovered and returned to us may well be a profound step toward co-creation of an archetypal soul return for the sacred feminine and sacred masculine on Earth during these times that have been predicted throughout millennia. The information in this book is profound and tantalizing, brimming with life-force energies and preparing humanity for a time of rebirth."

LINDA STAR WOLF, PH.D, VISIONARY TEACHER, SHAMANIC GUIDE,
COAUTHOR OF *VISIONARY SHAMANISM,* AND
AUTHOR OF *SHAMANIC BREATHWORK*

"Controversial and intriguing! This well-researched, passionately written book is a journey into a time in human history where women were treated as an expression of the Goddess of All Life. This is not only the aspect of the Great Mother but also the sexual goddess whose tantric arts affirmed humanity in the divine dance of sacred love. A powerful and enlightening take on the celebration of the Divine Feminine."

TRICIA MCCANNON, AUTHOR OF
RETURN OF THE DIVINE SOPHIA AND
THE ANGELIC ORIGINS OF THE SOUL

MAGDALENE MYSTERIES

The Left-Hand Path
of the Feminine Christ

SEREN BERTRAND & AZRA BERTRAND, M.D.

Bear & Company
Rochester, Vermont

Bear & Company
One Park Street
Rochester, Vermont 05767
www.BearandCompanyBooks.com

Bear & Company is a division of Inner Traditions International

Cataloging-in-Publication Data for this title is available from the Library of Congress

ISBN 978-1-59143-346-0 (print)
ISBN 978-1-59143-347-7 (ebook)

Printed and bound in China by Reliance Printing Co., Ltd.

10 9 8 7 6 5 4 3

Text design and layout by Virginia Scott Bowman
This book was typeset in Garamond Premier Pro, Gill Sans, and Legacy Sans with Trajan Pro and Avenir used as display typefaces

Illustrations on pages xviii, 45, 47, 49, 59, 81, 90, 135, 151, 178, 186, 195, 200, 225, 240, 250, 301, 332, 339, 351, 357, 367, 387, 391, 394, 403, 410, 422, 436, 440, 445, 450, 455, 457, 466, 470, 473 by Natvienna Hanell; pages vi, 12, 24, 48, 54, 128, 206, 215, 336, 341, 362, 400 by Helen Claira Burt; page 335 by Ssolbergj, CC BY-SA 3.0; page 337 CC BY 3.0, webstockreview.net

To send correspondence to the authors of this book, mail a first-class letter to the authors c/o Inner Traditions • Bear & Company, One Park Street, Rochester, VT 05767, and we will forward the communication, or contact the authors directly at **www.SerenBertrand.com**.

Honi Soit Qui Mal y Pense

This book is dedicated to
Mary Magdalene,
Mother Mary,
And to Mnemosine,
The Goddess of Memory,
Mother of the Nine Muses.

And to all the Mothers,
Including our own,
Margaret and Jean.
And to our beloved daughter,
Orphea Rose.

Naked I came from my mother's womb,
And naked I shall return.

Job 1:21

CONTENTS

PORTAL ONE

MAGDALENE CHRONICLES

Mary Magdalene's Lineage, Her Lifetime, and Her Legacy

MAGDALENE'S LINEAGE: THE DRAGON PRIESTESSES

PORTAL TWO

MAGDALENE CODEX

The Ghent Altarpiece—Art and Symbols of the Holy Grail

PORTAL THREE
MAGDALENE VISION QUEST

Pilgrimage Path: Stories, Oracles, and Personal Rituals

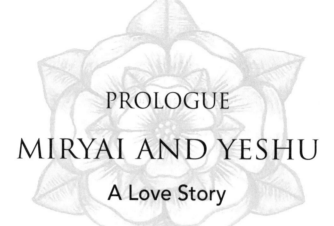

PROLOGUE
MIRYAI AND YESHU
A Love Story

When the rose is gone and the rose garden fallen to ruin,
Where will you seek the scent of the rose?

RUMI

DEAR ROSE PILGRIMS,

We open the prayer circle of this book and invite you to take your seat. Red rose petals are scattered at your feet, and the harpist strikes a note. We have a tale to tell.

Before we turn to the world of facts and suppositions, let us first immerse ourselves in the imaginal world of storytelling, allowing a weaving of words to lure us in. This story is a magical key to unlock the secrets held within this book and the vision it unfolds for you:

Two thousand years ago there existed a man whom we will call Yeshu and a woman named Miryai who lived together near a curiously shaped "lyre lake"—the Sea of Galilee—where the ancient goddess was once a mermaid. Their native language was Aramaic, the language of provincial Samaria and Galilee, which had, by their time, become an extraordinary cultural melting pot.

For thousands of years the region had been the tribal homeland of the moon-revering Canaanites, who worshipped Asherah and her consort Ba'al. But over time, Asherah, Ashtoreth, and other native goddesses would slowly be degraded, sidelined, and pushed underground by the increasingly patristic sentiments in Roman, Greek, and Judaic cultures.

However, the goddess was not forgotten by the Syrian-Phoenician people, who still flourished intact at the dawn of the first millennium CE, just a few dozen miles north of the Sea of Galilee. The Syrian-Phoenicians drew from far-ranging spiritual influences—from the Canaanite Asherah, the Assyrian-Babylonian Ishtar (Astarte), the Syrian Atar-Gatis, the Anatolian Kybele, the Hellenic pantheon that had by this time adopted Artemis, Aphrodite, and other west Asian deities, and the most widespread ecstatic religious cults of the day—the Mystery religions—in their various forms that included Isis/Osiris, Kybele/Attis, Astarte/Tamuz, and Demeter/Dionysus. During Yeshu and Miryai's time, the Great Mothers Kybele and Atar-Gatis—the Star-Fish goddess—still sat prominently on their lion thrones, representing the ancient wisdom of the goddess, the power and mystery of the Great Womb, whose unmistakable and alluring mana still resided in the female priestesses who had not abandoned the old ways.

Miryai and Yeshu's homelands were also closely connected to the Egyptian port city of Alexandria, the foremost center of Hellenic culture in the Roman empire, home to mystical and gnostic Jews, the temples of Isis, the ascetic Therapeutae, all manner of mystery religion cults, as well as the Mayagi (Magi) magical traditions of Persia. The scholars of Alexandria also maintained connections with Indian tantric, Buddhist, and Vedic masters, linked by the vast web of Eastern trade routes created by Alexander the Great, setting the stage for a mystical education.

YESHU'S STORY

Yeshu was born into a high-ranking family. His adoptive father, Yosef, was politically connected to the rabbis, priests, and sages as well as the Hellenized leaders and businessmen of the time; he was well educated and heavily involved in Jewish-gnostic mysticism and the Jewish nationalist cause. The open secret was that Yeshu's mother was a priestess, educated and trained in the goddess temples from a very young age, as the sacred feminine tradition had not disappeared completely in northern Israel and Syria.

The wisest of the zealot mystics knew that it was the priestesses who held the power of magical conception. Only they knew how to birth a messiah—an anointed king—as did Bath-Sheba, the pagan priestess-wife of King David and mother of King Solomon. She, like Yeshu's mother, Miriam, was recruited to birth an heir to the royal line of the lion and dragon.

By the first century BCE, the people of Israel desperately needed a messiah.

For generations they had suffered terrible oppression at the hands of various self-serving parties: the Roman armies and tax collectors, the tyrannical vassal-governor Herod and his family, and the wealthy Sanhedrin collaborators. Though the zealot leaders found the goddess traditions distasteful, this was the time to set aside the law in the name of the greater good.

The young priestess Miriam was selected by the mystic-spiritual political movement to be the vessel. *She was sought after for her maternal bloodline, woven into the millennia-old magical tapestry of the sacred goddess traditions. Miriam was trained in the esoteric rites of* hieros gamos—*the sacred marriage—so that she might conceive and give birth to the messiah-king who would lead Israel out of Roman bondage. She was the chosen "harlot," the* qedesha, *who at the age of sixteen was arranged to mate with a* panthera, *a "panther" or "lion" priest—an initiated adept of the Mysteries, who himself was charged with magical mana. Though the secret rites were considered terribly taboo by the greater Jewish community of the day, it had been arranged beforehand that Yosef, who was already the father of four children, including Ya'cov (later called "James the Just"), and who was recently a widower, would take Miriam and her child into his family for the good of the nation, even though he still had mixed feelings about her pagan roots.*

Shortly after the birth, Miriam and Yeshu were sent to Alexandria, Egypt, along with several other family members, so that Yeshu could study with the best teachers and scholars in the known world. Tremendous resources were passed to him, so that he did not have to take common work, in order to study, train, and prepare for his mission. His curriculum included intensive tutoring with the most well-respected rabbis and sages of the day, in both the Therapeutae community native to Alexandria as well as with a very prominent rabbi and high priest of the Jerusalem Temple who was brought in specifically to mentor Yeshu.

He also studied the magical arts of the Egyptian and Persian masters, including in the temples of Isis and Osiris, as well as Greek and Vedic-tantric philosophy. His practices included fasting, ritual cleansing, and meditation. He took the initiations of the Mystery Schools of Isis and Osiris. When he came of age he was sent to India to learn the philosophies of the Brahmins, Buddhists, and tantrics of Odisha. From both the mystical Kabbalist practice and the Eastern ways he learned the arts of sacred sexuality necessary for a mystical king-priest.

But the path was not always easy or clear. In time, Yeshu's rabbinic mentor excommunicated him from the temple community. Yeshu felt the rabbis were too narrow-minded and patriarchal in their perspectives—they could not tolerate the magic of the left-hand path and ancient goddess mysteries. At the age of twenty-

nine, after completing his studies, he returned to his family in Palestine with a new vision.

Even though he was so clearly accomplished, Yeshu was still a mystery to his family. Though he was a brilliant scholar of the pagan Greek philosophies and Mosaic law, a bold leader, an anatomist and healer, a charismatic speaker who knew how to hold power and work with crowds, he was also extremely sensitive and introspective at times. He liked spending time alone in nature, so that he could hear himself think, away from the politically intense environs of his family. Everyone but himself was convinced of his destiny as a king and political leader who would save the Jewish nation. Yet, in his heart, he knew he did not fit in with his father and eldest brother Ya'cov's world.

Yeshu needed a spiritual renewal, and announced to his family, to their great concern, that he would retreat for a time to the wilderness camp of his cousin on his mother's side, John the Nasoraean (the Baptizer), to fast, pray, and have some time away from politics. John was considered radical, heretical, and terribly fringe even to the mystic zealots, but he was impeccably disciplined, bursting with righteous fire and fiercely ascetic—commanding all people to repent and revoke their materialistic ways so they could be prepared for the end of days, the coming of the Kingdom of God-Goddess. John, known by his people as Yochanan, attracted a massive following that came to hear his impassioned preaching, as he denounced the wicked Romans, the incest-ridden Herods, and the corrupt Sanhedrin.

MIRYAI'S STORY

The priestess Miryai was named the Magdalene to honor her calling to the sacred work of the Divine Mother. Miryai was, like Miriam the mother of Jesus, a highborn priestess of the goddess traditions. Her father, Cyrus Eleazer, was of Syrian-Phoenician kingly blood. He converted to Judaism in name only, to wed her mother who hailed from a wealthy Hellenized family in Tiberias, closely related to the Herodian family. Miryai was trained in the both the Canaanite-Phoenician religions of Tyre as well as the mystical feminine aspects of the Torah.

Miryai was a stunning young woman—brilliant in her studies, big-hearted and devoted, but bold, fiery, and unwilling to fulfill the role of a submissive Jewish wife, even within the wealthy and Hellenized world she lived in. She was mystically inclined, a trained temple dancer, a musician and poet, and a prized potential bride. Her father received marriage proposals beginning when Miryai first came upon her moontime as a thirteen-year-old girl, but he held her in reserve, waiting for the perfect match for his beloved daughter. She, however, had other plans for her life.

The most exciting man of that day was Yochanan the Baptist, considered by all to be a prophet. The rumor was that he was starting a revolution and that he may have been the Messiah foretold by scripture. John was filled with wisdom and spiritual power. He promised entry for all people into the queendom of heaven through prayer, sacred ritual immersions, self-discipline, and renouncing worldly corruptions; it was said that he even taught the secrets of the greater mysteries, reserved for his inner circle of disciples.

Most important, in his camp, women held equal status to men. They could be priestesses and oracles and live a life of spiritual mystery unavailable in the repressive world of temple and palace. Ignoring the warnings of her parents, the bold and fiery Miryai scandalously fled to John's desert camp. Her family never forgave her, calling her a harlot and prostitute, deeply ashamed that Miryai, as an unwed woman, took company with a mixed-sex community of wild mystics—led by a man who dared to openly criticize her relative and the governor of Galilee, Herod Antipas. Her father, in his anger, began to drum up support for his campaign to eradicate John the Baptist. John was an embarrassment to Herod and a shame to his family. Herod, in his cunning, knew that the people of Galilee would be angered to the point of violence if anything happened to their beloved prophet. He needed to move slowly, carefully.

Cyrus Eleazer went with a gang of men to John's camp, threatening to stone Miryai for her supposedly sinful behavior. Miryai denied all wrongdoing—her intents were pure, her mission spiritual. She could not believe that her father would turn on her in this way, and she shouted at him to leave. John mobilized his followers to drive them away from the camp, and he took Miryai under his wing.

John's central practice was a daily purifying baptism in the Jordan's waters of life—fully naked, whole-body immersions for all men and women of the community, in the mother river of the Yardana—along with a prayer of rebirth to the Mother-Father deity, called Abwoon in Aramaic. His camp included both male and female disciples, a controversial position in the eyes of the greater Judaic community but a precedent that had already been set by the respected mystical sects of the Therapeutae and Essenes. John taught the old secrets of the moon and Eastern Mysteries. He had grown up in the greater Essene community, which tolerated dissidents and sects of many varieties, but he himself had been profoundly influenced by the goddess religions, and the Kabbalist-gnostic philosophies that taught the secrets of solar-lunar alchemy at a spiritual, and also sexual, level.

Miryai immediately fell in love with the wild and ecstatic practices and preaching of John; it felt that with him she had found her place. John for his part recognized her brilliance and spiritual power and knew that he had found his queen and goddess. He called her many beautiful names: Ama'gadala, "Great Mother Goddess" in Aramaic; Migdal, "the Tower" in Hebrew, the one to whom the Messiah would first be revealed, as foretold by prophecy. He called her Ella, the Hebrew name meaning "goddess," and Elena (Helen), the Greek name for "spiritual light." He lifted her up, enthroned her as the goddess incarnate, and made her his wife, opening her to the esoteric practices of sacred union and the Mysteries of the Moon.

Miryai shortly became pregnant and gave birth to a boy, also named John, her little "beloved." But life in the desert camp was not easy—John the Baptist was harsh and terribly difficult to live with. His infamous temper scorched the land. No flower or feminine softness could bloom in his rigid field of discipline and asceticism. John felt Miryai's growing distance, but he would not bend from his rigid and righteous position. The Queendom of God was at hand—all must be sacrificed to prepare for this. Nothing else mattered.

THEIR LOVE STORY

Yet, as the mysteries taught, the moon must be balanced with the sun. A male prophet, in order to be in the fullness of his power, must work together with a female prophetess and soulmate. This was the greatest secret. A prophetess in her years of fertility also held the power of the sacred menstrual blood, the sacred-taboo flow—a living mystery that across so many cultures of the world was understood to be so powerful as to be potentially dangerous. These rites were kept secret to all but the most trusted inner circle.

Yeshu now returns to the story—arriving at John's camp, weary of the politicking of his family, and quickly weaving into the lives of John the Baptist, Miryai, and several other members of the community who would become key disciples and friends: Andrew, Philip, Thomas.

John the Baptist instantly recognized Yeshu's bright spirit from his dreams. For many years he had dreamed a man would come who would help take his message out to the world. He baptized Yeshu and saw the descent of the Holy Spirit, the dove of the Divine Goddess into Yeshu—and was humbled at the signs. Yochanan was a renunciate prophet, not a worldly man, but Yeshu was of both Spirit world and the world of men. At the same time Yeshu, more than any other, shared John's brilliance, discipline, and commitment. Quickly Yeshu became his lead teacher and cohead of the community—second in command of the wilderness camp.

But in this paradise, a terrible problem arose. Over time, Yeshu fell in love with John's beautiful wife and prophetess Miryai, the Magdalene, and she with him. They kept their distance from each other, painfully, and never violated John's trust, but John felt their hearts and was driven mad with jealousy and anger. He became reckless. His tirades against Herod, the Sanhedrin, and the Saducees grew more and more vicious, to the point of treason. Yeshu felt that he was the cause of this disturbance—and that John's Mystery School, and his life, were at risk—so he left for Alexandria to try to give John and Miryai peace.

But things only grew worse. Herod sent his men to arrest John, and they brought him to prison in the hilltop palace at Machaerus. John, in a letter from prison, announced his divorce of Miryai. He ordered her out of his camp. She did not need any further prompting. Her time with him was over. She was older, wiser now—she could not be with a man she no longer loved.

THEIR ROSE TEACHINGS

So Yeshu and Magdalene consummated their sacred union, in love and trust. Magdalene's womb opened and merged with her heart and the entire world shook and warped around them. A magical power and wisdom was at play, flowing through them in a way they had never experienced. Nothing would ever be the same. They had, without their full advance knowledge, embodied the true teachings of the syzygy. The mythical and ancient rites of the bridal chamber, the inheritance of Solomon and the Queen of Sheba, were truly real. Miryai and Yeshu were soulmates, born to be together, separated at birth somehow but now reunited. This was the Great Revelation. Together they were the Unified Pillar; the Standing One, the Tree of Life that emerged from the earth and sheltered and fed all, and from those deep roots reached up into the heavens like a miracle, transcending the bounds of nature. In Hebrew, the name for such a miracle and sign is SIMN.

Some in the wilderness community of Nasoraean Baptists blamed Yeshu and Magdalene for the demise of their leader, while others remained loyal to Yeshu and Magdalene and followed them as they set off to create a new school, to leave the desert for the small cities and towns of Galilee and Samaria, to form a new brother- and sisterhood that dived even deeper into the practices of feminine magic of the left-hand mysteries.

Yeshu also lost the support of his Jewish, patristic family, as he abandoned his political role as messiah, but he found companionship in the group of people that gathered around him and Magdalene, including many female disciples. These women were often refugees from the goddess temples and hidden moon mysteries, whose incredible wisdom could find no place in conventional society. Together, as a circle of initiates, they founded a ministry of love, traveling, teaching, and practicing the mysteries. Their legacy was intended to bring together many wisdom traditions and to restore the true union of heaven and earth.

But eventually, the Church of Rome would raise up one of Jesus's more conservative disciples, whom they called Simon Peter, to become a "puppet pillar." Peter represented the consolidation of worldly power. He set about to spread his own version of the story and to undo and discredit Yeshu and Magdalene's true left-hand teachings of magic. There were other divisions within Yeshu and Magdalene's disciples—between the mystical gnostics (such as Philip and Thomas) and the more literal disciples, and between those who wanted to include women and those who didn't (such as Simon Peter). Few could ever truly understand the mysteries of the left-hand path and accept Mary Magdalene for who she truly was.

Yeshu and Magdalene wrote a great book, divided into four quartets, one for each direction of the world, called The Great Revelation. *The church, uncomfortable with Mary Magdalene's elevated position as a founder, would fabricate their own, upside down and inverted version of the Revelation—*Apocalypsis, *added as the final book of the New Testament—creating a divided ideal of the Virgin Mother, pure and controllable, as the goddess, while obscuring and defaming the "Great Whore" Magdalene; the great light-bearer who "knew the all." And so the oracle priestess and her magical lineage were sidelined and lost, along with her sacred teachings.*

This is the story whispered by tale-weavers since time out of mind, told around fires, passed through caravans of travelers, encrypted in illuminated manuscripts and secret alchemical works, along with the prophecy that the true Revelation would awaken once more.

INTRODUCTION

VISIONS OF THE ROSE

Left-Hand Path
of the Feminine Christ

Footfalls echo in the memory
Down the passage which we did not take
Towards the door we never opened
Into the rose-garden.

T. S. Eliot, Grail Poet,
"Burnt Norton," *Four Quartets*

OUR JOURNEY INTO THE *Magdalene Mysteries* is first and foremost a Vision Quest—a descent into the unknown, placing ourselves at the mercy of Spirit to be humbled, opened, astounded, and initiated by something greater than our minds could imagine. By approaching the presence of Magdalene with this grounded, sacred curiosity, with a genuine thirst from within our hearts, we honor her true spirit, and open the doorway to the hidden truths about her teachings.

Like any riddle of the mysteries, Magdalene can never be fully *known* or contained by the "facts"; as she impudently wriggles free of any solid definition of who she once was, who she now *is,* and who she might become, with a wink and a forbidden smile. Because of the scant evidence of her life, lived over two thousand years ago, we will never be restricted to one version of her life—instead it is constantly expanding into new dimensions. We have the biblical Magdalene of religion, the historical Magdalene of scholars and academics, and the mystical Magdalene of visionaries and oracles. And even these understandings are constantly revised and rebirthed in this *living tradition*.

Maybe she always intended it this way? Or maybe the sheer voluptuous radiance of her presence had to be forbidden, hidden, and written away by a patriarchal world that could not handle her power, until—like a treasure text—she emerged for a new age, a new era, that could bear the enlightened presence of an embodied feminine.

As we gather together in the circle of this book, we are going to explore a radical, forbidden version of Mary Magdalene (MM) as a priestess of the Womb Mysteries who holds within her memory an entire lineage of women, lacing right down into the prehistoric realms of the Neanderthal womb shamans of lunar consciousness, and weaving upward through the red thread of the Cathar priestesses of the Holy Spirit, and into your hands, as you rediscover the wisdom thread that you are now holding.

We will learn how MM holds the secrets of the original Eve, and how she became heralded as the New Eve—who, in her sacred union with Jesus, rebirthed the world. This mysterious and long-forbidden story of the sacred union of Jesus and MM, with the alchemy of their deep love bond, has called out to humanity through the ages—a cry that still resounds deep within the secret chambers of our innermost heart. Within this union MM is a *Christed Grail Priestess* of the feminine mysteries—an anointed and awakened teacher of the Way of Love, the feminine counterpart of Jesus and the fulfillment of the prophecy. She is also a wild woman, a bride, a lover, and a mother, and the lineage-holder of a sect of ancient dragon priestesses.

During our journey together, we will remember the Holy Womb mysteries of the feminine medicine path of Sophia, which became rewritten as whoredom and sin. In this remembrance, we will discover the old priestess wisdom and how it was overturned, degraded, and then shunned. This wisdom is now rising and calling out to be reclaimed.

Magdalene the Christ

Many apocryphal and gnostic gospels portray Magdalene as the leading disciple, the true inheritor of Jesus's teachings, and the one whom Jesus loves most. Of course the canonical gospels give Magdalene the most important roles aside from Jesus—she is present at the crucifixion, anoints him for burial, and is the first witness to his resurrection. She was such a key figure in the movement that the anti-Christian historian Celsus felt compelled to denounce her in his book *The True Word*—an honor he gave to no other woman in Christianity. Celsus also mentioned that at the time of his writings, around 170 CE, there were sects of Christians devoted to the teachings of "Mariamne," referring to Mary Magdalene.[1] By the fourth century, devotees had already begun making pilgrimage to Magdalene sites, and soon after, Christian churches would begin battling over claims to her relics.

There has been an underground stream of worship of Mary Magdalene for almost two thousand years spread across the Near East, Egypt, and Europe, supported by secret orders of initiates. These occult left-hand path traditions often explicitly name Mary Magdalene as a priestess-shaman and revere her as the Holy Womb—recognizing her as the wisdom keeper for a lineage of female magicians and oracles, and the birth portal of Christ Consciousness.

Rather than just modern "wishful thinking," these secret teachings were clearly encoded in the Middle Ages by famous artists, philosophers, and alchemists, often in plain sight for those who could "see"—and we can still peer through this magical mandorla, this doorway of wisdom, kept open by the alchemists, even today.

There is a revelation underway, as something lost and veiled is returning to us. Can you sense the fragrance of the lost rose garden, calling out once again?

Magdalene the Great Womb Goddess

Mary Magdalene is a talismanic name—*it has magic within it*. Before we start our quest, we should pause a few moments at the temple gates and really drink in the essence of this name. How much can fit within two simple words? Entire worlds it seems; a new dreaming, a renewed holy matrimony of the universe. A forbidden *herstory* of such magnitude it could melt entire worldly structures. This name is a deep, spiraling, serpentine power portal; play with it on your lips, feel its thrilling, enchanting, alluring, disturbing call. *Mary Magdalene, Marie Madeleine, Miriam of Magdala, Miryai e Mara. The Magdalene, Maria, Our Mary, Mari, Maryam.* This name is truly a secret and dangerous invocation; it belongs on hidden manuscripts of lost incantations and alchemical formulas. It is a lost promise, now remembered.

Jesus gave his disciples and cohorts spiritual names that reflected their essence. He called Peter "the Rock," he called Judas "the Knife"—and he called his beloved spiritual partner Mary, "the Portal"—meaning mystic yoni* gateway. *Magdalene* is a word of great feminine power: it derives from the Hebrew name of the ancient mother goddess *'ma-gadala* (אסא גדלא), meaning "Great Mother," as well as the Aramaic *magdala* and Hebrew *migdal,* both meaning "elevated, magnificent, or tower."[2] In the Semitic languages, *mag* and *dal* are among the oldest primitive roots, signifying "great, powerful, magical" and "portal, doorway," respectively.[3] They are shared across other language families: the Latin *maga* is a female magician—the feminine version of *magus* or *mage.* The biblical Greek *amygdale* derives from the same roots and means "almond" or "almond tree." The primary mother goddess of the gnostic sacred serpent sects was called *Amygdalus*—representing the almond tree, the feminine Tree of Life, the first tree to flower in the spring: "[the almond tree] is the wakeful tree (Hebrew *shaqed*), that is, the early blooming, the first to wake from the winter's sleep, sprang from the blood of the mother of the gods."[4] It is also the vulva-shaped *mandorla*† or "magic doorway," portal of the goddess. In ancient Sumerian, the language of Inanna, who we will meet later in our story, the phrase *mug-dalla* means "shining vulva gateway."[5] The name *Magdalene* at its origin means magic doorway of the Great Mother, the primordial goddess, the Tree and Source of Life. It held the secrets of a primeval "cunt theology" that became encoded as the "Mandorla of Mary."

Even to this day, iconography of Mother Mary is often held within an almond mandorla, a coded wink for those who know that there is a secret "Mary Mystery" waiting to be revealed. This symbolism of the *Magdala* encompasses both the sacred doorway of the woman's womb, and the mystical womb of consciousness sought out by all the great alchemists, shamans, and initiates. This divine gateway was also symbolized by the rose; and those who followed the Magdalene Mysteries were known as initiates of the Rose Line.

This mandorla, or Mystic Rose, also suggests the amygdala region of the brain, the intuitive, feminine "feeling" center in all human beings, which is a portal to the cerebellar cosmic mother consciousness and can initiate profound awakenings. Using this lunar wisdom, priestesses initiated others into the intuitive, visionary, divine love of the Christ Mysteries.

Yoni is a Sanskrit word for vulva, vagina, and womb—the sacred passageway—used throughout the book to convey the sacred dimensions of these physical gateways.

†*Mandorla* is the almond-shaped "glory" or aureola frame that symbolizes the womb and vulva. It is derived from the *vesica piscis* sacred geometry, formed by the intersection of two circles with the same radius.

The Grail Witch

Across heretical and alchemical art Magdalene is depicted bearing her magical ala-bastron (the holy vessel of anointing oil), held suggestively open like the mandorla of her sacred womb, to bestow the initiatory blessings of her anointing elixirs. The priestess tradition of the alabaster jar, flowing with its sacred unguents and perfumes, was passed down to Mary Magdalene through the lineages of the Sumerian love goddess Inanna, as well as the Egyptian Bast—cat goddess of sacred sexuality, and the erotic soul of Isis—who both used the talismanic alabastron in their ritual craft. Magdalene is imbued with the fragrance of these, and even more ancient priestess lineages dating back in a continuous tradition to the female shamans of prehistory.

The earliest shamans in the archaeo-anthropologic record were *shamankas;* they were women. They were adorned in the color red, with mineral paints. Their figures were carved on cave walls with hands raised up in the *orans* and *ka* prayer positions of magico-spiritual invocation. Their vulvas featured prominently in paleolithic art, with *V* and *M* vulvic symbols engraved on stone and bone, later called "witch marks" in medieval times. Their womb-vulvas were considered the

Samarran dancing womb shaman with "omega birthing hips," ca. 5000 BCE.

Phoenician/Canaanite "womb on altar" scarab stamp seal, ca. 1000 BCE.

Greek omega womb symbol, ca. 600 BCE.

AVE MARIA GRACIA PLENA

The modern-day combined *M*/omega symbol of Mary, at St. Marie Cathedral of Sheffield and the Mary Chapel at Glastonbury Abbey.

The omega womb/priestess symbol as it has evolved over time, eventually merging with the Christian *M* symbol of Mary.

greatest source of their *mana,* their spirit power. Over time, this ancient lineage of womb shamans would gradually shapeshift into priestesses of Mary, worshippers of the goddess, woven into the garland of her red thread of sexual and menstrual womb wisdom.

Mary is a title that means "sea, beloved or awakened," and the first symbolic art created by humans was an *M,* along with wavy waterlines, engraved on a sea shell on the islands of Indonesia 500,000 years ago, showing us the ancient spirit of the Mermaids of Magdalene.[6] The mysterious letter *M* is a doorway of primeval sea magic, our original mother matrix.

Medieval Magdalene engraving, drawing emphasis to her sacred womb.
Hendrick Goltzius, 1585.

Magic of the Left-Hand Path

A crown of olive over her white veil,
A woman appeared to me; beneath her green
Mantle she wore a robe of flaming red....
I turned round to the left with the blind trust
Of a small child who races toward his mother.

DANTE ALIGHIERI, *DIVINE COMEDY,*
PURGATORIO, CANTO 30

A key to our journey into the Magdalene Mysteries is to understand the *true* left-hand path of the goddess; and that Mary Magdalene, in her priestess robes of red and green (see color plates), was the lineage holder for this sacred tradition. Red was the symbolic color of a womb priestess, a witch-shaman of the feminine. Green was the color of the wild fertility of the forest and the Earth Mother's body. These alchemical "color codes" reveal Mary Magdalene as an elemental witch, sexual maga, and herbal adept in the left-hand medicine path of Sophia.

The left-hand path *is* the feminine mysteries. Left equals feminine, moon, lunar, yin, night. Right equals masculine, sun, solar, yang, day. Together they form the perfect balance of the universe. Achieving this alchemical union is the heart of the Magdalene Mysteries.

This can also be described as the *ascending Christ* (of the right hand) and the *descending Christ* (of the left hand), the Feminine Christ, embodied in Magdalene. Jesus descended through the path of the left-hand Feminine Christ for resurrection. We have to first descend before we can ascend. Darkness comes before the light. Then, in the Christ Mysteries the *two become one,* and heaven and earth entwine.

Records reveal that Jesus was an adept of these mysteries. According to a gnostic text found at Nag Hammadi: "The Lord . . . did everything in a mystery, a baptism and a chrism and a eucharist and a redemption and a bridal chamber" (Gospel of Philip 67:27–30).

Of all these rites, the chrism (anointing) is one of the most important, as it creates the Christ: *"The chrism is superior to baptism. . . . He who has been anointed possesses everything"* (Gospel of Philip 74:12–20). And if Jesus is the Christ, then Magdalene is the chrism that makes him so. She is the *source* of Christ, she is the light-force that brings illumination. She is the anointer, the illuminatrix, the redemptrix, the Feminine Christ of our supernal origins, "of the left." In her chrism, her elixirs of love, comes a light that dispels our fallen consciousness.

This is the ancient left-hand path of the Feminine Christ—rebirth through the Mother, and resurrection through the Bride. One gives birth to the man, and one to the "Son of God/dess"—a term for an alchemist, magician, and awakened avatar. The alchemical means for this transfiguration is the left-hand path—to lunarize our soul and subtle body with the magical essence of the *feminine sinistrum.* Carl Jung says that in gnostic writings Sophia *Prounikos*—Sophia the Whore—is known as *Sinistra,* the left.[7] The twentieth-century gnostic scholar and translator G. R. S. Mead affirms the Mother is "She of the Left Hand," the Sinistra.[8]

Sinister literally means "left" in Latin—and refers to the lunar feminine Womb Mysteries.

Sinister is beautiful, luscious, dark, and mysterious—rich with fertility and possibility. It revolves with the "round dance" of the moon in dark-light rites. By reclaiming the Moon Mysteries and the Womb of Christos, we remember the original primordial wisdom teachings.

As the left hand and right hand of god/dess merge, the heart-womb enters an infinity sigil of matrimony, catalyzing an etheric supernova of primordial Shakti that emits out as dazzling spiritual radiance, known as *tiphareth* in Kabbalah, the beauty of the descent of God. This is the Magdalene door, the ancient *daleth,* where the virgin mother and sexual initiatrix merge into wholeness. Never truly separate or dual, these qualities come from the mysterious circle of the Divine Mother, and are united within her divine *pleroma,** in the sacred flow of life.

Mary Magdalene, as a sacred priestess of the Womb Rites, knew how to embody the wisdom of light and dark (known as the "dark bright" or "black light") and how to dissolve, cleanse, and resurrect the soul. Over the past two thousand years many initiates—with various levels of understanding and integrity—knew of the left-hand path of Christ, led by the figurehead of Mary Magdalene and the lineage of womb shamans she hailed from.

By revealing the lost word of the Magdalene Mysteries, we allow MM and the priestesses of Mary to once more take their seat in the wisdom circle of the Ancient Mothers, who hold a womb-web of mitochondrial DNA linking us back to the Garden of Eden of human consciousness, and hold the keys to our returning home.

---

*A gnostic term meaning "the fullness"—the infinite container of the heavens or divinity.

This original matrilineal bloodline is more accurately described as the *menstrual bloodline*—as it is only the womb blood that can grow and nurture a baby, and each mother down the ages is created from the menstrual blood of the mother who came before her. This generates an unbroken magical "red thread" of primordial wisdom; the Holy Sophia. Messianic blood is matrilineal womb blood. A Eucharist of Sophianic blood links communities in an unbroken red thread to the Holy Family, and beyond to the Ancient Mothers: "Thy mother is like a vine in thy blood, planted by the waters; she was fruitful and full of branches" (Ezekiel 19:10).

Magic Doorway of Love

I thought of the soul as resembling a castle, formed of a single diamond or a very transparent crystal, and containing many rooms, just as in Heaven there are many mansions.

SAINT TERESA OF AVILA

Mary Magdalene herself has become a "mansion of possibility" for the rebirth of the world soul and the remembrance of our sacred roots in the primal Motherworld of creation. Ultimately, through communion with Mary Magdalene, we connect to a magic door within ourselves where we activate, initiate, and awaken our own Magdalene essence. With this we step through a gateway of the feminine Holy Spirit—called Sophia, Tara, Isis, Yemoja,* Kali, Kwan Yin, Changing Woman, Brighid—or many other names of the Divine Mother throughout time.

This creative Spirit lives at the foundation of our universe, as the eternal Birthing Womb of God, and embraces both the male and female, every spectrum in between, and all expressions of life. *Magdalene* is a title, meaning the "Initiator," and *Christ* is a title for the Anointed One. We all have the potential to be a Magdalene and a Christ, as this story is archetypal. Through the love story of one woman, we discover a universal story for humanity. We can all invoke and embody this essence of love and deep heart-womb wisdom.

In this book, we sometimes speak of Mary Magdalene in her personal incarnation as a woman from an order of priestesses that she trained within and also initiated others into. Other times we refer to her essence as an embodiment of

---

*The Yoruban goddess Yemoja is also known as Yemaya or Yemanja in the Americas.

Sophia, the mystical Aeon who emanated from the galactic womb to become the World Mother. Allow yourself to weave between the personal and the eternal to receive inspiration.

This book is our vision birthed from the Magdalene path that has called us, and the research we have undertaken. It is by no means the only story, nor should it be. Allow it to be a space to birth your own vision of the Magdalene Mysteries, from your unique experience and perspective, weaving in your own knowings of the path.

This work is created as a mystical mansion with many chambers and rooms. It is not linear, reasonable, or logical. Its aim is to mystify, evoke, and provoke. Please explore any chamber of this book as you feel called, in whatever order you choose. You do not have to take a linear path through its many rooms. Follow your own way toward the Rose.

Together, we light a candle and begin a pilgrimage into the spiral or labyrinth path—we send out our prayers to bring forth the perfect ensouled questions, not the perfect answers. At the center of this spiral path, you will find wisdom we have not written but that has lain dormant, coiled as a serpent, in the womb of your soul.

Always remember: you are an incredibly important thread in this visionary weaving.

The book is divided into three portals to help you navigate this pilgrimage. The first portal is called the "Magdalene Chronicles," and is a journey into herstory to discover MM's lost priestess lineage, her lifetime, and her legacy, which is rich in historical detail and background.

The second portal explores how the secrets of this lost lineage of the Magdalene Mysteries were encoded in art and symbol by the medieval alchemists in one of the greatest paintings of all time—the *Ghent Altarpiece*—a living manuscript that you can see in color plates 14 and 15 and view online in detail (see the Closer to Van Eyck website).

The third and last portal is the "Magdalene Vision Quest," where personal stories and oracles are included alongside a comprehensive initiatory map and set of rituals called the *Magdalene Mandala,* where you can undertake your own journey into these mysteries. These rituals are designed to evoke the living path of the Magdalene Mysteries *within you.* They can be practiced alone in your own home, with your beloved, or in your circles, connecting you directly to the Holy Spirit. Feel free to weave with them in your own practice in whatever way feels good. Everyone, no matter what their gender identification, is held within the red thread of the Magdalene and the Ancient Mothers, and everyone has a spiritual womb within.

This visioning focuses mainly on the male-female sacred union of Mary Magdalene and Jesus, and the specific teachings and pathway of practice birthed from this. But the sacred union of all sexual orientations and love-pod configurations are holy and bring unique wisdom. The alchemical union of the cosmic yin and yang at the heart of the journey is within everyone.

Mary Magdalene is calling out to us, like a divine torchbearer, emerging from a dark tunnel of almost two thousand years of fundamentalist religion, to light up *The Way* again.

This is an audacious soul retrieval for the world, a renewal of our cosmic destiny. With her holy anointing cup, she pours out the secrets of the Holy Grail.

As prophesized, the Feminine Christ awakens.

The Rose Path unfolds its mystic petals.

The Order of the Magdalene returns.

Shall we unlock the Magic Doorway?

It is time.

OUR LOVE LETTER

ROSE PILGRIMS

Meeting Mary Magdalene

By Seren Bertrand

AM I LOOKING FOR MARY MAGDALENE, or is she searching for me?

My soul senses that it is the latter. For how could I search for this icon, this "Saint," this presence, this *magical doorway,* when I do not truly know who or what she is?

Yet there is the uncanny feeling that *she* knows exactly who *I* am. And more than that—who I am meant to become. This Magdalene essence knows the parts of me that are lost and need to be rediscovered, that I unknowingly have so veiled that I do not even know to search for them. So together we embark on this quest, this inner journey to reassemble the parts of my feminine soul, like a cosmic jigsaw of redemption. The great unveiling of the lost feminine.

For me, Mary Magdalene is an *instinctive* force as well as spiritual essence. The more I read about her with my logical mind, the less tangible she becomes. Yet, as twilight falls, a sudden sweep of a thick, red velvet cape appears to the left of my eye, moving quickly out of sight, around a corner, and I must follow and find her there in the darkness.

In this magic world of MM, her true gospel is written on soft skin and in the stars. Her parables are shared by lover's eyes, and in the in-between spaces of silence. Her true gospel breathes down the back of my neck, hot, subtle, mysterious, and laughing.

I cannot find her within scrolls and scholar's arguments, remote and historical, or in dualistic theologies of bodily hatred, held in the inquisitorial records of her legacy. She does not sing to me of crucifixions, or of Catholic, gnostic, or Cathar priesthoods.

Instead, I find her seated by the fire in the desert, laughing, her body warm against that of her lover, as they melt into the mystery of the two in flesh becoming one. Or I meet her in a wild old woodland at the foot of the Pyrenees, with the Cathar priestesses of the Holy Spirit, preparing herbs, as red moon blood seeps into wild green moss.

In moments, I see her like a rare crystal jewel, shining light across all dimensions, sitting on a golden throne at the very heart of the earth, illuminating the soul of matter. I glimpse beyond the doorway of life, into the great mystery of the Womb of God.

Yet I must also be in this body, in this life, in this world.

She comes to meet me here.

I must also find her in the small details of my own childhood, my own struggles, my own heartbreaks. When I am weeping, I discover her weeping right by my side.

When I am shining, celebrating, loving, ecstatic, she is born again within me.

Her life, like my life, is full of contradictions and it is important to include it all.

So I search for her, as she is searching for me—as she is searching for all of us.

Birthing a New Way

Although I was baptized into the Christian Church, and my grandfather considered the priesthood, the nature of my birth meant I never felt an affinity with mainstream religion. When my mother labored in agony, surrounded by "sisters of mercy," who had never known motherhood, the nuns told her that her pain was God-mandated, and that women were destined to toil in pain to create life. My heartbeat stopped at those cursed words, and I was torn from my mother's body by surgical forceps.

My mother was a quietly stubborn rebel, and she subtly and determinedly set about deauthorizing the religion she inherited from her father, and living by the feminine folklore of her mother, and her mother's mother, that celebrated Life's holy power. She sprinkled my childhood with the magic of the dreamtime, educating me with percolations, questions, and spiritual explorations such as "where is the edge of the universe"—and what then lives beyond this infinity? She asked me to imagine our world as a dream within a dream, and our universe as a living, breathing, dreaming being (a dreaming-womb) who holds and births other infinite dreaming universes. Often we would have to stop our visioning and make a cup of tea, in order to reassemble our atoms, which were in danger of floating away into that vast, unknowable, dark ocean of infinity; a witches cauldron of wild quantum soup.

One day a local vicar paid a visit to our house to meet my family. A decision he would soon regret. On a dark, foreboding, rainy Yorkshire night, my mother barred his entrance, looming over him as he stood on the doorstep, making him account for the death of thousands of wise women during the Inquisition. The vicar looked embarrassed and flustered, standing in the rain, politely apologizing for his religion. After ten minutes she relented and let him in for the supreme unction of a cup of tea.

Like a chastised schoolboy, rather than give his intended religious proselytizing, he listened politely to my mother's folk wisdom. Whilst pouring the sacramental tea, she let him know that hell was what people (and religions) did to each other through hate—and that heaven was the beauty of love and the wisdom of nature.

So I did not grow up in a religious household, and I rarely got to read much Christian scripture, or hear the stories of this mysterious "sinner" and saint, Mary Magdalene. Yet her Feminine Christ path, full of deep mystery, called me like a siren.

Visions of Saint Marie

My first emissary of Mary was the land herself, with its witchy feminine ways. The wild moors and peaks of Yorkshire wore their conversion to Christianity lightly, carrying on its ancient pagan goddess-worshipping rituals and ceremonies as usual, with past vicars leading labyrinth dances, and right up to the modern day where iPhones capture the May Queen in all her glory. The new religion of Jesus was neatly tucked, like a suckling babe, into the old religious traditions dating back at least three thousand years, with sermons etched in the stones.

Within the craggy contours of Yorkshire and the nearby Pennine Way, ruined castles, darkened caves, fallen abbeys, and old churches, all flowed with the same essence, forming a magical landscape. I loved visiting churches, just like I loved visiting castles; in fact, I liked churches more. Often set upon old pagan power sites, with old mossy stones, rugged graveyards, and fantastical beasts carved as guardians, inside it was like entering a *mysterium*.

Stained-glass windows cast light beams of vivid jewel colors, the silence throbbed with peace, and old wood groaned under its memories, sometimes carved with mermaids or other relics of a forgotten faith. The altar was adorned by rich red velvet drapes, crisp white satin cloth, scented flowers from local meadows, tall candles in thick brass holdings, and in the center, a dramatic, sturdy gold cross. In this world, Christianity took on the hue of old-time fairy tales, encoding the memory of a hidden spiritual feminine DNA, waiting to share its forgotten wisdom.

Then, one day, shortly after my coming of age—around age thirteen, the traditional time of rites of passage into young adulthood, often menarche in women—this spiritual DNA transmitted into me: I had a rapturous vision of an unknown woman, whose name had never been spoken to me, and who I knew nothing about. I was walking through my hometown, when a presence called out to me. Literally, this force of energy turned my feet and walked them into a cathedral. I had no idea what was happening and I had never before entered this gothic building.

It was as if some deeper part of my feminine soul was impelling me to search for it. I was instantly guided to a small white pamphlet on an unknown saint called Mary Magdalene. I knew I had to have this booklet on her—that it was calling out to me. As I turned the first page open, the sharp edge of the paper cut my finger, and a flow of crimson-red blood infused into the crisp white paper, awakening a mystical infusion of Red and White magic. My consciousness was melting into waves of energy, and my entire perceptual range was focused on the book. As if an ancient incantation had been made, I was ushered into a timeless, oracular sphere.

Over three days, I received a vision of Mary Magdalene, representing a lineage of divine feminine beings, who had embarked on an audacious journey of initiation, to awaken a cosmic love consciousness and embody it here on earth. I later discovered it paralleled the gnostic story of the Goddess Sophia. This cosmic resurrection would restore a spiritual-sexual wholeness to the world and bring back balance, ushering in a new cycle of divine feminine love and magic.

Shortly after the vision, I began creating striking paintings and artwork of women with "divinized wombs" glowing with light, or magical trees bearing fetuses within them—which many years later I discovered was the symbol of Mesoamerican womb shamans. Of course, at the time I had no idea what it all meant, and my mom humored me by creating a gallery of this artwork pinned to the entryway of our home, no doubt causing a scandal among the neighbors!

Many years later, on returning to the St. Marie Cathedral, the original site that had initiated my visionary journey with Magdalene, I was stunned to find that the entire church appears as a temple to the feminine principle—with images of Mary Magdalene and the Black Madonna, and a specific chapel dedicated to female saints.

Most incredulous of all, in the center of a magnificent stained-glass window that occupies an entire face of the cathedral is a powerful—and unusual—image of Mary. She is holding her hands in the traditional "womb shaman" mudra of the ancient yogini and dakini lineages, placed in a heart shape over her sacred womb space, revealing the seat of her power (see color plate 1).

She is the awakened Womb of Christ.

The Cave of the Feminine Christ

Tehom el-tehom qore.
Deep calls unto the deep.

PSALM 42:7

Over the years, the mystery deepened. As the labyrinth of my path unfolded, it became populated with the fertile mysteries of the Divine Mother, encrypted spiritually in the womb of earth, and also the wisdom of the Black Madonna, the universal womb of the Cosmic Mother.

I made a pilgrimage to Marseilles to sit with the Black Madonna there, perched regally, deep within her underground crypt, near the sea. Walking through cobbled streets, I peered through the windows of bakeries selling "navette" breadcakes, shaped like the vulva cakes once used in ancient goddess worship, and used as body sacraments to the Virgin Mary by heretical priestesses. Winding up the hill to the great cathedral, dedicated to ships, I entered a forgotten temple of Isis, the Queen of Heaven, savior of all those who sailed upon the seas.

What was this long-forgotten religious faith calling out to me since childhood?

Every step I took, a secret revealed itself with a wink and a new rabbit hole. Expectantly, I made the sacred journey taken by pilgrims for over a thousand years, including Anne Boleyn, to the mystical sacred cave of Saint Baume—the "balm." My driver, who escorted me up the steep hill through the aromatic scents of the countryside, was named Delphine—meaning "of the Womb," like the oracle of Delphi.

I stayed in the convent, in a simple pilgrim's room, facing out onto the cave.

At night I dreamed of an old sage, and I sat with him as he was dying, crying out to him—Issa! Later on, I discovered that *Issa* is the Islamic and Indian name for Jesus, which I did not know. Inside the cave, dripping with the tears of earth, I melted into Magdalene.

Legends say that Mary Magdalene meditated alone in this holy cave for thirty years, like a tantric yogini. The cave had originally been dedicated to Diana Lucifera, the goddess of the witches, light-bearer of the Moon Mysteries. It was likely sacred to our Neanderthal ancestors.

After hours sequestered in the primordial consciousness of the cave, I received the impulse to keep climbing higher, to find the spot high on the cliffs where Mary Magdalene supposedly ascended and was lifted bodily by angels into the heavens.

It was a steep climb over the white chalk cliffs, and at the top I was alone—circled only by beautiful white and orange butterflies, who followed me along the rocky path. There was a shimmering stillness, as if time had stopped to rest. It was as if an energy was dancing through me in subtle yet exotic waves. I found the small chapel, perched high on the cliff with a dramatic view outward across the valley of Provence. Inside it was cool with white marble, small bench seats, and a beautiful white statue of Mary Magdalene with the skull of the initiate at her feet.

The energy was palpable, an undulating softness, a soul kiss of the deep and high. I sat in the silence and the softness, as if it were the center of the universe. After a while I reached for my notebook and pen, and a message wrote itself out: *Write my lost love story. MM.*

It was as if Magdalene and the divine wisdom of Sophia were placing magical rose petals at my feet, like dimensional stepping-stones of awareness, calling me to their story.

I would soon discover that my visionary communion with Mary Magdalene had told, in a magical, holographic form, the story of the Fall of the Sophia and her return to the throne.

It was a "feminine apocalypse"—a revelation of the fall and restoration of the goddess. *Apocalypse* is derived from the womb root word *cal/kal,* related to the word *chalice,* or the Holy Grail. It means "unveiling or revealing."

It has begun.

You have seen my descent, now watch my rising.

RUMI

Sacred Masculine Vision

By Azra Bertrand

IF YOU ARE READING THIS BOOK, you likely already *know* in your body, heart, and soul that we live in extraordinary times, at a *mythic edge* where an old story meets a new one. A five-thousand-year-old, male-oriented worldview is now receding. In its place a deeply interconnected feminine cosmology, with ancient roots, is birthing.

Like the Celtic myth of Taliesin, it is from the great feminine cauldron of inspiration where all the new myths, poetry, beauty, and cycles of transformation originally emerge. A feminine worldview is naturally ecological. A guiding principle of permaculture is that life flourishes at these edges—*on the cusps, at the wild margins, at the boundaries of all that is familiar.* Diversity and creativity naturally bloom where two different realities touch, their intimate roots connecting and interweaving as they move, dance, take shape.

My story and humble place in the co-creation of this book begins here, as I find myself in the great shifting of the worlds, as a supporter of the return of the Divine Feminine. Like many of you, much of my life has been dedicated to asking questions about the great religions we have inherited, and seeking to understand the deeper meanings, lost histories, and secrets they contain. In the living of these questions, I have long been aware of the compelling tide that, in the midst of a solar world, has always drawn me toward the "moon" of feminine wisdom.

My background is the "logic" of science. I was born to a family of doctors, scientists, and healers stretching back many generations—some of them include physicians to the late Renaissance German royal courts, as well as André Michaux, explorer and botanist to King Louis XVI of France. Many others quietly worked in the fields of medicine, cellular biology, theoretical physics, and the like, dedicating themselves to incrementally advancing the understanding of the body and laws of nature.

These are the deep roots of the ancestral tree that birthed me. As I have come to understand more and more, a family lineage is like a living entity—it has a mind of its own, with its own proper agendas, its own plans for us, and its own *very strong* pull. I, as a young apple, fell not far from the tree, but then rolled down the hillside a considerable way it seems, beyond the other apples on my tree, into the lush and misty valley of the feminine where I would lay new roots.

In the professional world I trained in—in research biochemistry, in medical school and residency, in a neuroendocrinology research group at the National Institutes of Health—I longed for the marriage of science and spirit, a world that understood that physical health was deeply interconnected with relationships and was inseparable from the health of our natural world. In my personal spiritual path, I craved direct experience of the sublime and mystical beauty inherent in matter, in relationships, in sexuality, here on the earth, in the world of form. These longings were at odds with the cultures around me, who were dancing to a different tune. Something was missing in the worlds of science and medicine, and that piece was the sacred feminine. Without it, our story and our cosmology could not be whole.

So I looked deeper for inspiration, to the scientist-mystic-philosophers of old, like Pythagoras who apprenticed with the Pythia, the high priestess and Oracle of Delphi. He soaked in the underground wisdom streams of the feminine cosmologies for a decade before beginning to share his work. Isaac Newton, Carl Jung, and so many others modeled a blend of science and mysticism, of inner knowledge and alchemy. These men drew from a deep well of knowledge that originated in the feminine spiritual traditions and had been encoded in ancient mystery schools.

The ancient priestesses, who are rarely mentioned, were the keepers of a vital knowledge that somehow the world has forgotten, to our great peril. How often, in school, do we hear that the men who brought us mathematics were taught by great women?

Or that Paracelsus, considered the father of modern medicine, said on the subject of pharmaceuticals that he had "learned from the sorceresses all he knew."[1] These are the stories that need to be told now, to bring back balance.

The Grail—A Way of Love

In old traditions, wisdom had been envisioned as a garden—and as feminine. And over time I began remembering this "gardener" archetype, which is obliquely mentioned in the story of Jesus's resurrection, and dates all the way back to ancient Sumeria. If the modern world we live in is a wasteland, it is because we have not been successful as gardeners—of the earth, of the feminine, of the body, of spirit.

Just as the culture of science ignored feminine qualities such as intuition, vision, and interconnectivity, so the popular spiritual paths I found my way to cut out relationship and romantic love. Despite the fact that almost every modern model of spirituality champions the individual's journey to God, or solitary enlightenment, the carefully guarded secret is that the romantic, sexual, spiritual relationship between two individuals is the hidden heart of Christianity and Tibetan Buddhism. And, if you looked further, you could trace this path of sacred union back to many other traditions.

My understanding of this came through a striking meeting with a respected philosopher and author, who gave me a new blueprint as to how I might see the world. As a twenty-three-year-old medical student, I was a member of a small circle that would meet up weekly to discuss different spiritual traditions, meditating on the pearls of wisdom from each path, and how we might actually live these truths. At the time, back in 1997, the spiritual climate was distinctly masculine. My own personal practice involved meditating for hours and seeking to free myself from the illusions of the world. Feelings, romance, and sexual desire were never mentioned by any of the mentors that I studied with, or were classed as obstacles to flight.

One day, the leaders of our spiritual circle—two Zen Buddhist teachers— invited the renowned mystic and philosopher Joseph Chilton Pearce to come and speak to our group. Joseph had experienced an intense spiritual awakening in the 1960s, and was the author of several books, including *The Crack in the Cosmic Egg, The Magical Child,* and *The Biology of Transcendence.* Beyond that, he was a man who exuded a contagious energy of open-hearted love.

Around fifteen of us gathered together one winter evening, in a small, uninspiring college meeting room at Duke University, to meet this famous author. The atmosphere was electric. At the time Joseph was the voice merging science, spirituality, and a vision of our true human potential, and we felt honored to have an intimate and frank spiritual dialogue with him. A young couple in love were sitting together, holding hands. They asked how their relationship could fit into a spiritual path. Before Joseph could reply, the Zen teachers stepped in to say that romantic relationship was an illusion and a distraction to deep spiritual realization—advising that it was better to let the relationship go and "seek first God."

A look of heartache and despair passed between the young lovers, who for a moment doubted the truth of their own hearts. I glanced over at Joseph Chilton Pearce, wondering if he would agree. What I saw was riveting—Joseph was listening incredulously, his increasingly red face betraying his outrage. Finally, he could hold his tongue no longer. He proceeded to pour forth the most incredible teaching on the Path of Love. He lit up the room with a scintillating and passionate impromptu dissertation on the supernova of spiritual and psychic energy that accompanies romantic love—the meeting of the eyes; the soul kiss; the dissolution of the state of separation into fields of unified consciousness; the remembering of our shared past lives, future lives, and our destiny; and the undeniable and astounding impact of the well-known spiritually pioneering lovers and troubadours who have come before us. He looked round the room, meeting all our eyes, and reminded us how precious this seed of love is, and how human biology is wired for the bonding, connection, and intimacy of deep soul love. He addressed the couple, saying they should stay true to Great Love at all costs.

The transmission that came through Joseph Chilton Pearce was extraordinary. He was radiant. His heart was on fire. The room shook. All else seemed dim in comparison to the light streaming forth from him. It was an unforgettable moment. And it came from his own devotion to the spiritual path of romantic love. The Zen teachers were shocked, stuttering that love was just an illusion generated by base, hormonally driven instinct. Joseph roared back that this young couple was touching a thread of a Great Love that—if fully committed to—would lead them down the path all the great lovers have walked, and to a new evolutionary cycle.

I was also shocked, but ecstatically so. This remarkable man had opened a precious doorway to the Path of Love for me. I had met a shower of the Way, and Love was calling.

Romantic relationship as an authentic spiritual path has always been known as a fast track for those prepared to enter the crucible. Sacred lovers such as Yeshua and Magdalene remind us of the enormous spiritual potency of those who alchemize themselves in love's fire. The "peace that passeth all understanding" is the divine child of the "passion that passeth all understanding." It is an initiatory journey full of wildness, joy, pain, ecstasy, fear, and the commitment and devotion to keep opening through any and all obstacles. This is the beauty of the dance of love. It is full of vulnerability, humility, and chaos that become the fuel for rapid growth. As the philosopher Nietzsche says, "One must still have chaos in oneself to be able to give birth to a dancing star" (from *Thus Spoke Zarathustra*).

The Mother Calls

At the age of twenty-eight, Mary Magdalene appeared to me in a vision. She let me know I needed to begin a period of deep service to the sacred feminine. Through this I would bloom in a new way, but it would take courage, it would take hard work and dedication. I would need to let go of some long-held beliefs and identifications I had with the patriarchal structures I had clung to for safety.

It was once common knowledge that men could only be truly reborn through a profound integration with the feminine, through a process of unification, apprenticeship, and descent through the womb. All of us are born through the womb of a human mother, our bodies are made in hers. At a greater level it is the "womb" of the earth that holds us, feeds, nurtures us. These nested mothers, this realm of womb consciousness, is our true spiritual home, though many have forgotten.

Some time later, I was called to visit the Black Madonna of Le Puy-en-Velay, France, one of the oldest Black Madonna pilgrimage sites in Europe. The cathedral there is built on an ancient puy—a rocky hill outcropping sacred to the feminine and earth-worshipping religions indigenous to Europe for many thousands of years before the coming of Christianity. An old megalithic dolmen once stood on the hill, and its solid stone roof piece was preserved and built into a sanctuary within the cathedral, because of the magic it held, an extremely unusual event in Catholic churches.

Le Puy-en-Velay is also a starting point of the Way of Compostela pilgrimage, and in the neighboring monastery I stayed in, I was surrounded by many pilgrims. Although I wasn't walking the Compostela way, I was on my own pilgrimage.

For a week I made daily visits to the Dark Mother, sitting on a simple wooden pew in front of her, crying and crying and crying. I couldn't have explained why. Something within me softened, something let go and opened. I was initiated by her in that time. A doorway in my heart opened, clearing the way for the next level of my "apprenticeship," seven years of study, research, mystical experiences, and openings of love as an ally, supporter, husband, and "gardener" of my beloved wife, Seren, as she channeled and expressed her vision of the Sophia. Together we remembered, through the portal of her womb, a lost feminine cosmology, and grew in it and with each other. I committed to opening, learning, trusting, and of course putting in the long hours of research and writing along with her, so the many details of this lost history could be shared in a grounded and practical way in this book, with its story of Mary Magdalene, and in our previous book, *Womb Awakening: Initiatory Wisdom from the Creatrix of All Life*.

The feminine is rising again, with a new voice, and a new vision, to restore balance to our world. The story of Mary Magdalene and the Goddess Sophia is a key part of this restoration.

MARY MAGDALENE

Holy Whore of Sophia

*And behold, a woman in the city, which was a sinner, when she knew
that Jesus sat at meat in the Pharisee's house, brought an alabaster
box ointment, And stood at his feet behind him weeping, and began
to wash his feet with tears, and did wipe them with the hairs of her
head, and kissed his feet, and anointed them with the ointment. . . .
And he said unto her, "Thy sins are forgiven."*

LUKE 7:37–48

OUR CURRENT ERA IS PERCOLATING on this: Is Mary Magdalene
really a whore and sinner?

Before you rush to answer, be warned: it is a trick question. We invite you to
reserve your answer until we have unfolded the petals of our Rose Quest.

Likely, if you are reading this book your immediate response might be *no*.

You might already know that in 1969 the Catholic Pope Paul VI quietly declared
that MM was *not* a prostitute, and that the liturgy read out on MM's feast day was also
changed from the passage quoted above to the resurrection scene where she becomes
the first to see the risen Christ, and hence the first female pope. You might be fully
aware that nowhere in the Bible does it ever say MM was a prostitute, and that this
doctrine was first established in 594 by Pope Gregory the Great, who first preached
about Magdalene's "sexual sins"; you may have rejoiced when the church officially
declared her Apostle of the Apostles in 2016 on July twenty-second, MM's feast day.

In the past fifty years there has been a great movement, both within the
Catholic Church and the "heresies" of new age spirituality, to redeem Magdalene

of her whoredom. In the Catholic decree to upgrade Mary Magdalene's feast day, the missive says that Mary can be seen as "the paradigm of the ministry of women in the Church." It is beautiful and heartening to see MM acknowledged and celebrated at last. But is this truly Magdalene's ministry? One where her forbidden wild erotic power has been "cleansed"? Truth be told, we cannot tolerate the sin of a whorish woman. We must purify her; we must take her to the light; we cannot meet her wildish darkness.

True, there was a sense that unfairly burdening MM with the sexual sins of the world, and then making her "repent," was done to deliberately obscure the truth of her spiritual power. But have we not diminished her yet again? In the recent reevaluation of MM, she is no longer a whore or sinner; instead she emerges as a "good girl" of the Bible, an "Apostle of the Apostles," a spiritual leader, the brightest and shiniest disciple, the "model for all women in the church."

Of course, MM *is* a great spiritual leader and luminary. But this is not *all* she is. There is wild magic in her sacred sexual power, waiting to be reclaimed.

On one hand we decry the split of the feminine into the "Virgin" (the light) and the "Whore" (the dark), yet on the other we avoid and judge the wildish, erotic aspect of the feminine nature. In recoiling from the fertile darkness, we cannot find union.

The secrets of the Holy Grail live on the dark, left-hand side of the Magdalene.

Secret Religion of the Magdalene

For two thousand years Mary Magdalene has carried the sexual sins of the world, while at the same time bearing the hidden seeds of possibility for our sexual salvation. As we enter this next cycle, her magic seeds of truth are spilling out into the fertile soil of an emerging womb consciousness, ready to birth a new feminine awakening.

First though, we have to face the Grail Wound that has imprisoned our Rose Lady.

The intriguing, disturbing, and perplexing nature of this split was never more present than in the grand theater and intense environs of the medieval ages, where Mary worship reached an all-time peak, while human women were persecuted as evil witches. The feminine was both revered and annihilated. Male priests, bishops, and mystics looked more than ever to their visions of the Marys for wisdom, while heretic priestesshoods of women lived in caves and woodlands in France, hunted by a church who threatened to burn them at the stake for their magical womb wisdom.

Within a five-hundred-year span, from the time of the Cathars in the 1100s to the late Renaissance of the 1500s and beyond, fantastical legends and teachings arose around MM. While the hierarchies of men who produced theology clearly decried her, the public, the mystics, and the lay clergy embraced her in the wantonness of her sin.

Hippolytus of Rome recorded that astrologers, magicians, pagan priests and priestesses, and prostitutes were forbidden from entering the church. However, prostitutes who repented could enter the church—and were known as "Magdalens" or "Maddelonettes." Also in France, a prostitute's race was run on Mary Magdalene's feast day, July 22, in the late fifteenth century as part of an annual fair at Beaucaire in Languedoc. Monasteries were set in up Magdalene's name to house former prostitutes. Author Susan Haskins describes the Italian female mystic Catherine of Siena's ravishing vision of Magdalene, saying: "The sorrowing Magdalene, repenting of her sins, red-cloaked, and with long loose hair, clasping the cross . . . as the weeping lover."[1]

In 1515, Leonardo da Vinci, or perhaps his student Giampietrino, paints a bare-breasted, Venuslike image of Mary Magdalene, which is described as conveying the spirit of the "Red feminine": "She is entirely frank about her sensuality; her smile is a promise, and soon her fingers will let her robe fall away entirely. There is not an ounce of repentance in this MM."[2]

Secret orders, including the Knights Templar and Rosicrucians, worship her and make her the centerpiece of a forbidden religion concurrent with Catholicism. Immense womb cathedrals, such as Chartres, based on the feminine womb and vulva are crafted with breathtaking audacity as barely hidden Sophia Temples.

Fabulous stained-glass windows reveal MM wearing the red robes of the witch-shaman and womb priestess, also adorned with the greening power of Gaia, and surrounded by symbols of the goddess—fleur-de-lys, dragons, elemental crosses. Black Madonnas are enthroned in crypts reigning over the hearts of the public and become the sites of great wealth because of the devotion they evoke. Pilgrims of the Camino Way wear vulva-shaped badges to bring them good luck as they walk the ancient sacred ley lines of the land, under the emblem of the scallop—symbolic for thousands of years of the sacred Yoni of the Great Mother of creation.

Mystery plays are enacted in towns and villages throughout Europe, where the rapturous MM is clearly billed as the vivacious leading lady, with Jesus her consort and costar; revealing a deep archetypal need for the priestess of the mysteries.

Paradoxically, MM's reputation as a redeemed sinner and the patroness of prostitutes allows her to be an incredible channel for the forbidden feminine mysteries.

The Magdalene that emerges in the medieval folklore and heresies is a wild, flamboyant chalice of sexual potency and enraptured earthly and divine love. Her weepings and lamentations over Christ lend themselves the taste of a lover. Their reunion in the garden of Gethsemane, illuminated with the birth light of resurrection, becomes the ecstatic merging of a new Adam and Eve—with the subtle hint of a sexuality that brings the serpent of wisdom's alchemical union, not "the fall."

The picture of Magdalene that emerges is vivid and compelling, with her scarlet hair, green eyes, alabaster or ebony skin, and rich wine-red hooded cloak. This is a woman who has become a "low priestess"—who is on her knees, weeping with the world, yet infused with the rich, abundant fertility of the soil; she can be ecstatic and enraptured with love, the one who loves "too much," or she can be found walking among the fallen and forgotten, in the taverns and inns of ill repute, suffering alongside the wounded, sobbing and lamenting for the losses of humanity.

She is wildish, instinctive, irrepressible, and truly *hamartolos*—an outsider, one who exists beyond the conventional bounds of society, who is forbidden, and "other." In this otherness she belongs completely to the world; she is One with everything.

Please, do not let us not banish this Vision of Magdalene.

Let us not prematurely "sanctify" our radiant Saint of Sin.

Let her be utterly *unrepentant* in her wild female power.

Let us celebrate her forbidden sacred feminine essence.

Mary, Priestess of the Mysteries

The great Queen of Heaven is at hand; the Lord's power is Hers. . . .
Before two full moons shall have shone in the month of flowers, the
rainbow of peace shall appear on the earth. The great Minister shall
see the Bride of his King clothed in glory. Throughout the world a
sun so bright shall shine as was never seen since the flames of the
Cenacle until today, nor shall it be seen again until the end of time.

NOSTRADAMUS (MESSENGER OF "OUR LADY")

As we progress along our Rose Path, a fascinating realization dawns: the same qualities that emerged in medieval times as the hallmark of Magdalene place her directly in an ancient tradition and lineage of sacred women, including the priestesses of Isis and Inanna.

These female spiritual orders were known for their oracular nature, their redemptive sexuality, their ability to anoint and initiate a man into his spiritual kingship, and their power to grieve and lament so deeply that the world reconfigured into a more blessed shape.

The priestesses held holy titles such as Whore, Harlot, Harine, Hathor, Horae, and Houri, meaning "the pure and immaculate ones"—the wisdom keepers.

What if Mary Magdalene *was* a whore and sinner—and the only thing that needs to be changed or redeemed is our perspective of what those two words really mean? In modern times the word *whore* is used as an insult. But in ancient times, the word *whore* referred to a priestess of the mysteries. We can begin to see how the esteemed and ancient traditions of the sacred feminine were demeaned and insulted, their languages stolen and reversed.

The Great Mother—birther of Creation—was once known as the Great Whore. In the Semitic languages of the Middle East *hor* meant "cave" and "womb." The titular word *harlot* also meant "womb of Light," suggesting an awakened womb. Interestingly, the word most commonly used for MM in medieval times is the ancient priestess title of harlot.

Feminist researcher Barbara Walker writes of ancient Babylon: "As Mother of Harlots, Ishtar was called the Great Goddess HAR. Her high priestess the Harine was spiritual ruler of 'the city of Ishtar.'"[3] In both Sumeria and Babylon, Inanna and Ishtar were called the Harlots of Heaven. The earliest appearance of this sacred title is in the writings of ancient Sumeria. In the Sumerian language, *hur** is a word of the primordial and sacred womb (as in whore, har, or hor). The *hur* is holographic, fractal, multidimensional. Its spirit resides in the womb of every living woman, as well as the underworld womb of the earth, and in the primordial energies that birth and shape creation, which across culture and time have been envisioned as dragons. The *hur* dragon stirs, shapes, rumbles, and moves the great tectonic plates from within the womb of our planet. She is a birthing dragon, a womb of creation.

When we see the root word *hor/har/whore* we descend into the feminine cave, and know we are in the presence of an honorary title of a divine feminine priestess. The title of Holy Whore celebrates a woman's embodiment of an "awakened womb"—the magical, creative, cosmic kundalini power. Emma Restall Orr, druidic priestess, author, and poet, writes:

[Whore's] etymology could be sourced in the horae, divine maidens who danced the turning of time in Greek mythology, mellowing the souls of men with

---

*Pronounced with a guttural *h* sound, as in Hebrew *challah* or Scottish *loch*, written in older texts as *kur,* and sounded as *w-hur* or *w-hor.*

their beauty and their touch. The word is linked to the Babylonian harine, the Semitic harlot, the Persian houri, temple prostitutes who brought pleasures of life to humankind. Yet far from a bringer of delight, the word now describes a woman who deals in sexuality. Used as an insult, the whore is definitively a woman who degrades herself. Yet does she? Each one of us are whores.[4]

Here are the cultural homes of some of the ancient priestess titles in the Near East:

Hathors (Egypt)
Harine (Babylon)
Horae (Greece)
Houri (Islamic Near East)
Harlot (Babylon/Canaan)

In Hebrew the word *horaa* also meant "instruction" and the word *hor* meant "light." In fact, it was from related holy *hor* word roots that the Torah (the *whorah*), the Hebrew Bible (Old Testament), took its name. The Great Mother, and her Womb of Light, was always known as the light bearer. *Horasis*—another "whore" word—was the ancient Greek word for womb enlightenment, often bestowed through the sexual union of man and woman. In the Bible, *horasis* was used to describe an oracular, ecstatic vision.

Often it was priestesses and prophetesses who were famous for their sexual oracular vision, with their womb-centric, erotic religion of sensual salvation. And the expression *whoring* is used in the Bible to chastise those people who return to worshipping the ancient goddesses and consulting her "Holy Whore" oracles.

HOLY WHORE

I was sent forth from the power,
and I have come to those who reflect upon me.
and I have been found among those who seek after me.
Look upon me, you who reflect upon me,
and you hearers, hear me.

You who are waiting for me, take me to yourselves
And do not banish me from your sight. . . .
For I am the first and the last,

I am the honored one and the scorned one,
I am the whore and the holy one. . . .

I am the silence that is incomprehensible
and the idea whose remembrance is frequent.
I am the voice whose sound is manifold
and the word whose appearance is multiple.
I am the utterance of my name.

EXCERPTS FROM "THE THUNDER, PERFECT MIND,"
NAG HAMMADI CODEX

Medieval engraving of Magdalene boldly displaying her feminine power.
Master of the Die, ca. 1530–1560.

Originally, the priestesses of the goddess were sexually liberated and sovereign women, considered to be living embodiments of the Womb of God. They were also spiritual leaders and secular rulers at times, and held in the highest societal esteem. So, to be clear, by the honorary term *Whore* we do not refer to a prostitute, either a secular or sacred one (who exchanges sex for money that is donated to a temple). Whore is a title of spiritual sexual power, whispering back to a time when the feminine was revered as the Creatrix.

"As free agents commanding respect for their sexuality, the priestesses of Sophia, the Whore of Wisdom, were beyond approbation and condemnation alike. They modeled woman's autonomy in the gylanic (sexually and spiritually balanced) social systems they helped to establish," writes gnostic researcher John L. Lash, author of *Not in His Image*.[5]

So we don't need to divest MM of her whoredom—*we need to help reclaim it,* and to remember its true meaning, so the Holy Whore of the feminine can be rebirthed.

This is the remembrance of our true *whorethority.*

Mary of the Moon, Priestess of Sin

Similarly, within the Magdalene Mysteries we renegotiate the meaning of *Sin.*

The etymology of this psychologically loaded word is by no means clear, and the word evokes the terrifying vibration of "sinners burning in hell." No wonder most nonreligious folk shy away and wish to bury it underground. It also brings to mind the "original sin" of Eve—who fundamentalist religions say was seduced by the serpent, effectively dropping humanity on its head and breaking it. Within this concept of the original sin of Eve, every woman is also culpable, also a "sinner." Even the miraculous event of birth is tainted by this word, as birthing mothers are no longer the divine emissaries of the Great Mother, but rather the agents of sin.

In recent times, with the attempted cleanup of some of the more unpalatable aspects of religion, the word *sin* has been dropped in favor of the Greek word *hamartia,* used in the New Testament, which is said to mean "to miss the mark."

Yet . . . let us not let go of the word *sin* too soon, because it holds a secret mystery.

Sin was the ancient Akkadian name for the moon and the moon god/dess.*

---

*At times we refer to Sin as the moon *goddess,* as her original identity was likely female, and at other times as the moon *god,* because by the time of the Sumerian culture "she" had been transformed into a male god, and the symbolic consort of the high priestess.

In the days of old the moon goddess was the center of the feminine mysteries of menstruation, renewal, and rebirth. She had many honorary names, and the name Sin specifically refers to her aspect as the new moon: the time of menstruation for women.

The concept of Shabbat, a "holy rest day," comes from the menstrual rites of the goddess Ishtar. The word derives from the Sumerian *Sha-bat,* "womb rest," where the entire community rested every full moon, to honor the menstrual lunar rhythms, which waxed and created then waned and released. In the old lore, when God rested after birthing creation, it was for *her* menstruation.

Sin refers to the lunar cycles, and to the process of death, rebirth, and purification through menstruation, which not only clears away the old, but renews our creativity and fertility. Sin is the left-hand path of the feminine Moon Mysteries. It is the women's womb wisdom of the ancient prehistoric shamankas—female womb shamans and moon magicians.

A "sinner" was a moon priestess who practiced the menstrual mysteries of rebirth. It was believed that every moon cycle a woman's womb had the ability to cleanse any sins/burdens/negative imprints, not only from her own body and soul *but also* from her beloved and community. This monthly cycle of renewal and rebirth was considered a holy gift of the feminine. In the same way it was believed that the body of Mother Earth received and cleansed the burdens and negative emotions of her human children.

In a sad case of mistaken transmission down the ages, the true meaning of sin and its origins in the feminine menstrual arts has been inverted—or deliberately demonized—to suggest an unforgivable crime against god. In fact, sin was the goddess's gift of healing, forgiveness, and renewal.

Many religious ideas, such as "going to hell" and "cleansing sin," originally come from the old feminine womb religion and menstrual rites. For instance, "going to hell" once described the ancient path of shamanic descent into the Earth Womb for rebirth. From there the shaman could travel out into the vulva of the Milky Way (the Great Rift) and into the galactic womb (the galactic center). "Cleansing sin" referred to the sacred menstrual rites of purification of the womb and soul. For thousands of years, sin was celebrated as a mystical, feminine shamanic journey. A "Sin Woman"—*a sinner*—was once holy.

The idea of sin as a sacred cleansing extended to the Aztec tradition. Ritual confessions were made to the earth goddess Tlazolteotl, who in her Christlike redemptive role would "eat the filth" of the soul to cleanse it before its onward soul journey. Similar practices of confession were practiced throughout Mesoamerica—

in the Zapotecs, Maya, and other groups. This later transformed into the idea of "sin-eaters" and "eating the humble pie" of earth.[6]

Sin-eaters might also eat a ritual meal to magically take on and cleanse the sins of another person—a form of spiritual community service, rooted in the Old Magic. In nineteenth-century England, Shropshire legends held that a sin-eater would sit by the graveside to eat a simple meal of bread and ale, saying the phrase "I give easement and rest now to thee . . . and for thy peace I pawn my own soul. Amen."* After the ritual meal was eaten, the bowl would be burnt. In those times, a sin-eater was often feared and lived a solitary life of exclusion.

Jesus is an archetype of a collective sin-eater, offering his body to atone for the sins of everyone—in the form of a cosmic and shamanic world-soul menstruation of all sin.

Yet the original sin-eaters were menstruating women in their Red Temples.

Sin-Ishtu: Moon Woman, Moon Mother

In the Akkadian language, the word for woman, *Sin-ishtu,* literally means "Sin Woman," "Moon Woman," or "Moon Mother," paying reverence to the cyclical womb nature of woman, who through her resonance with the moon's cycles can conceive, birth, and rebirth life.

Some four thousand years ago in ancient Sumeria and Akkad, midwives would sing an incantation called "The Cow of Sin" to pregnant women to ease their childbirth. In the hymn, the moon god Sin impregnates his beloved consort, a divine cow named Sin Woman. During her birth pains, the Moon hears her cries and sends celestial spirits down to earth who perform a ritual to help her give birth. Part of ancient midwifery lore, the metaphor is that all pregnant women are also Sin Women or Moon Women, passing through the same initiatory journey of birth undertaken by the goddess herself, the Cow of Sin. The Moon, the Sin Mother, blesses them on this incredible journey of giving life.

A "sinner" is literally a sacred woman who cycles with the moon. To be "born in sin" is to be created in the light of the moon, born from the inner light of the womb goddess, as all humanity is. The creative luminosity of *Sin* is the great feminine generative principle that births us, yet it has been shamed and

---

*This tradition was made popular by the early twentieth-century British novelist Mary Webb, as quoted in her book *Precious Bane,* 36.

defamed in the patriarchal era. In ancient times the concept of the sacredness of Sin was central to the feminine mysteries of the lunar goddess. *Sin-ishtu* not only meant "woman," it was an epithet of Ishtar, the Lady of the Left, and is the probable origin of the Latin word *sinister*.

Honorific titles of the Moon, Moon Women, and Womb Mysteries:

◊ *Shag-munus*—"womb woman," womb shaman (Sumerian)

◊ *Shag-zu*—"womb doctor," midwife, also "house of god," "womb of god" (Sumerian)

◊ *Noor sin*—moonlight, luminosity, inner light (Aramaic)

◊ *Sin, Sinu*—woman, goddess, moon, crescent moon (Akkadian)

◊ *Sin-ishtu, Sinnishtu*—woman, "moon woman," origin of Latin word *sinister* (Akkadian/Assyrian)

◊ *Malkatu shemaya*—"Queen of Heaven," Ishtar, goddess (Akkadian, similar in Aramaic)

◊ *Inbu*—new moon, fruit, flower, menstrual blood offerings, sex appeal (Akkadian)

Blood of Salvation— Passion of Christ

In the new religion, a male god—Jesus Christ—was given the menstrual powers to redeem us of sin, replacing the sacred renewing womb power of the priestess. Now it is his life, his passion, his sacrifice of blood that heals and renews the world. This switch-around where the feminine power of his consort, Mary, as a "Magdalene of the Moon," is attributed to him, tears apart their role as a Divine Christ couple, with deep spiritual consequences.

For as a man, without a womb, the magical, life-generating, life-healing blood had to be replaced with the blood of sacrifice and death—either human or animal. In Christianity this was symbolized as a Mystic Lamb, bleeding into a sacred chalice—which we will investigate later on our Rose Path, as we explore the secrets of the Holy Grail.

The knowing that menstruation was the "blood of salvation" was passed down through secret teachings, or was understood intuitively by mystics. Originally, the menstrual blood of the goddess was a salvic substance that was *physical and spiritual,* to cleanse body and soul, and was administered as a sacrament of Sophia, through the wombs of all women, until it was eventually called the "blood of Christ."

Christian mystic Julian of Norwich, who wrote *Revelations of Divine Love* in the fourteenth century, instinctively (or heretically) describes this blood magic. She uses masculine form to describe her vision, but if read from a feminine perspective a deeper meaning opens. In her fourth revelation, she describes how "it pleases God better to wash us from sin in [her] blood rather than in water, for [her] blood is most precious."[7] She goes on to describe this mystical menstrual magic, saying of the blood of Christ, "for there is no liquid created which [she] likes to give us so much; it is plentiful as it is precious by virtue of [her] holy [Godwomb]."[8]

This rhapsody on the spiritual powers of the divine menstrual blood, and the elucidation of the blood mysteries continues, "And it shares our nature and pours over and transports by virtue of [her] precious love. The precious plenty of [her] beloved blood descended into hell and burst their bonds. . . . The precious plenty of [her] beloved blood overflows the entire earth."[9]

She goes on to share how this "precious blood of salvation" flows through the heavens, and eternally bleeds as a way of intercession between God and wo/man.

The Passion of Christ is a symbolic divine menstruation that cleanses and heals. Every month, by the cycle of the moon, a menstruating woman experiences her own "Passion of Christ" to menstruate all that does not serve, and shed the womb lining of "sin." This is a soul release: letting go of accumulated hurts, mistakes, and old energies, and then rebirthing the stem cells of original innocence and creative potentiality again, rebirthing spiritual fertility.

Yet this essentially female experience, undertaken as a spiritual service to self and community as part of the Womb Mysteries, is then given to a male god.

The ferocity of feeling associated with the word *sin*— "moon woman"—reveals the toxic hatred toward women and the feminine at the heart of our culture, and also directs our gaze back to an ancient time when the feminine mysteries were revered, then persecuted. But we can heal, re-language, and remember the true healing power it once held.

Sinister is Latin for the left-hand side or path—that of the feminine. A priestess of Sin was a practitioner of the left-hand path of the Feminine Christ. In the tantric traditions of eastern India it is said that the indigenous people of the original ancestral mother religions sit on the left-hand side of god and are actual blood relations of the deity (through the matrilineal menstrual bloodline)—while the newer masculine traditions sit on the right-hand side of god with no deep blood bond. Often it is only those on the left-hand side that can partake in death-rebirth rituals.

So, truth be told, MM *is* both a sinner and a whore. She belongs to a sacred lineage of women who, throughout time, have practiced the Womb, Moon, and Menstrual Mysteries, and who have embodied the Holy Feminine.

It is time to reclaim their sacred legacy, with no apologies and nothing to repent.

Rape Consciousness— The Bible's Hidden Secret

As long as the root of evil is hidden, it is strong.
But if it becomes known, it dissolves.

GOSPEL OF PHILIP

We must also invoke MM's archetypal communion with the over-lighting principle of Sophia, the Holy Spirit of Creation, Wisdom incarnated in heaven on earth.

Heretical mystics, known as gnostics, taught the parable of Sophia as the "Lost Sheep"—who the Christ reunited with to restore unity to earth. In this gnostic philosophy, the Great Feminine is divided into the Higher and Lower Sophia: one the eternal Cosmic Womb, and the other the "fallen goddess" who birthed out from the cosmos into form to become the womb of earth, and the womb of the divine woman—the heavenly body of the goddess on Earth.

This earthly Sophia, the planetary mother and the sacred wombs of women, was wrenched apart from her Cosmic Mother by an abusive energy that enslaved her. Her epic journey of restoration is to return to the wholeness of her divine origin, crowned and enthroned.

Womb Curse—Cast for Disobedience

We are all threaded on a maternal ancestral loom, a vast matrilineal womb-web of life that hangs ornamented by great lights of souls throughout the timelines of earth. This "Fairy Tree of Life" was cursed as the powers of the womb and the feminine came under attack.

Jesus and Magdalene came to undo, reverse, and heal this curse on the womb—for though it was written in the Old Testament, it was *not* made in the name of their god of love, the Holy Sophia.

It was cast by an abusive energy—the Great Deceiver—the Archon of Patriarchy, who, masquerading as a god, said, "All these curses will come on you. They will pursue you and overtake you until you are destroyed, because you did not obey the Lord your God" (Deuteronomy 28:45). And, he continued:

> The fruit of your womb will be cursed
>
> You will be cursed when you come in and cursed when you go out.
>
> You will be pledged to a woman, but another will take her and rape her.
>
> I will multiply your pain in childbearing; in pain you shall bring forth children.
>
> Your desire shall be contrary to your husband, but he shall rule over you.
>
> The Lord will afflict you with boils and with tumors.
>
> You will become a thing of horror, a byword and an object of ridicule.
>
> (DEUTERONOMY 28 AND GENESIS 3:6)

Yet with the spirit of the Holy Sophia—whose regenerative life force lives within each being—this spell can be broken. Sophia is pouring down in celestial waters from the Cosmic Womb. She is rising up as flames from within Mother Earth, with awesome velocity, into our own center. Our awakened wombs are the Blessing Way, the Fountain of Life, and the Holy Grail. This wise creative power within the soul-womb is the fire of the Feminine Christ.

The gnostic myth of Sophia can be read symbolically, or it can be read more literally, as an encoding of our lost and forbidden history, which birthed the foundations of patriarchy and the fall of consciousness.

The Bible is replete with references to rape and fathers "selling their daughters," and chronicles a terrifying time in herstory when the feminine principle herself was being dismantled, demonized, discarded, and her women raped or prostituted.

Magdalene—More Sinned Against

The apocryphal stories surrounding MM hint at a hidden secret at the heart of her life, often veiled under the convenient meme of prostitution, which reveals that—like Sophia—she has suffered at the hands of the fallen consciousness that wishes to hurt the feminine.

One gnostic legend tells the story of how Mary Magdalene is promised as a bride to a wealthy Babylonian merchant. But on her way to Babylon she is raped and sold into sex slavery and prostitution. She becomes trapped in Babylon. Author Cynthia Bourgeault summarizes the tale: "After a time she managed to regain her outer freedom, but inwardly she was still held hostage by hatred, rage, and darkness. At length a dream came to her telling her that she must return to the land of her birth and seek out the Anointed One, who would deliver her—she left immediately."[10] When she finds the Anointed One, he is also waiting for his Anointrix to initiate him. The redemption is mutual; their love becomes a chalice of resurrection.

According to Saint Augustine and Honorius Augustodunensis, the wedding of Cana was actually held to celebrate the marriage of Mary Magdalene with John the Evangelist. However, on seeing Jesus perform the miracle of turning water into wine, John jilts Magdalene and leaves to become a disciple. Heartbroken and rejected, MM flees to Jerusalem where she becomes a "common prostitute" who founds a brothel of sin, and it is in this "temple of demons" that the seven demons (that are later exorcised by Jesus) enter into her. It is notable that this story holds the energy signature of the "Bride" being mistreated and abandoned by the masculine, and that this Sophianic theme is associated with a temple of demons.

The healing and exorcism of these seven demons, which is more accurately described as the initiatory alchemical healing of the wounds of love of the traumatized feminine, takes place in the intimate holy temple of the redemptive love that unfolds between MM and Jesus.

This healing also calls for the uniting of the Higher Sophia, the Cosmic Womb, with the Lower Sophia, the earthly womb, which precipitates the mystical marriage of the feminine and masculine in the "bridal chamber" of the *pleroma,* "infinite womb consciousness."

As with Sophia's myth, in the Jewish Kabbalistic tradition Shekinah creates the world but is then exiled after the fall of consciousness. The reunification of Shekinah and God is the purpose of the mystical and alchemical path, said to heal the broken heart of Creation.

This journey is Magdalene's descent into the Underworld, a profound feminine mystery school initiation, in which she becomes one with the primordial fertility of Wisdom—she becomes the embodiment of Sophia's return, the resurrected feminine.

Magdalene the Savior

This reading and visioning of the Magdalene legend brings us deep medicine. She is both the fallen *and* the redeemer. She is the Holy Whore who has lost her throne. She is not only the Light of the World, but she has known the darkness of the world. We cannot tear her apart into a pure side and a fallen side; she is whole unto herself. With this, she inspires our most innocent love, and weeps with our deepest wounds. She is both that which saves us and that which needs saving. This is Sophia's Salvation.

MM's story resonates with the story of the feminine—and of all people— especially the ancient lineages of priestesses, medicine women, elders, wise witches, and womb shamans throughout the ages whose sacred medicine has been stolen, who have been defamed, cut out, shunned, and judged for their feminine power.

We can meet her in intimacy, confide in her, trust her, and be consoled by her. She has walked and wept and suffered among us. She does not judge us or turn away. Within her presence is a maternal white light *and* a magnetic red light. She does not ask us to choose between them—instead she reveals the way to unite within them.

Jesus—Sage of the Sacred Masculine

We can also vision Jesus from an alternative perspective, as a man who chooses love and who makes an escape from the rigid patriarchal structures—both inner and outer—of his own strict father culture, to liberate the true divine masculine within, and to enter as an initiate into the feminine mysteries, to heal and help restore them and himself.

When Christ is teaching in the temple, the Pharisees bring before him a woman accused of adultery who is sentenced to be stoned to death as punishment, according to Jewish law. The Pharisees ask him if this is the correct penalty, hoping to trick him into recommending they break the law. Instead, he writes in the sand, "He who is without sin among you, let him first cast a stone at her" (John 8:7). Ashamed of themselves, they free her.

In another vignette from his life, Jesus meets a Samarian woman by a well and asks to "drink from her cup" (symbolic of the feminine mysteries) and shares about "everlasting water"—despite the fact that she is a foreign woman who is living out of wedlock, thus "unclean." He is clearly a man well versed in the ancient feminine religion and welcoming of its women. Interestingly, he never names himself a follower of Yahweh, and the Aramaic name of his "god" is Maryah Alaha or Abwoon (Great Birther).

Jesus emerges not as a religious fanatic or macho warrior but as a clever, car-ing, free-thinking, and loving embodiment of the sacred masculine—completely at odds with the traditional image of the heart-armored, power-thirsty masculinity of the times. Historian Michael Haag says about him: "Jesus was no ascetic like John the Baptist or the Essenes; he was relaxed about ritual washing and diet; he loved food and drink and good talk; he was witty and sharp; he was at ease with women; and he was self-deprecating but had an intensity and aura about him that was very attractive."[11]

Jesus himself was likely from a wealthy family, and the names he is called in the gospels—*rabbi, naggar,* and *tekton* (often mistranslated as "carpenter")—refer to an educated man who is a spiritual teacher, master, and scholar. This explains the high esteem and respect ordinary people hold him in, as they seek him out for wisdom. In fact, Zechariah, the father of his cousin John the Baptist, held the position of high priest at the Temple of Jerusalem.

But eventually both Jesus and John rebel against their family legacy.

Encoded in Talmudic stories, we learn that "Yeshu" (Jesus) was a favorite student of the foremost Jewish sage and teacher of the law, named as Rabbi Joshua ben P'rachyah, who lived in Alexandria, Egypt, along with Yeshu. In time, however, a rift developed between the two. Yeshu also studied mysticism and magic, and found the community of priests too narrow in their thinking. His mentor excommunicated Jesus for teaching the inner mysteries of the left, symbolized by the dark goddess Gevurah, which is later reflected in the way he included women in his ministry. The Talmudic commentary reads: "The left should always be repelled, and the right on the other hand drawn nearer. But one should not do it . . . as R. Joshua ben P'rachyah, who thrust forth Jesus with both hands . . . and put him under strict excommunication. Jesus oftentimes came and said to him, 'Take me back.'"[12] The rabbi refused.

After his break with the orthodox priestly community, the Talmud states that Jesus set up "the foundation stone" of his own teachings, no doubt traveling to study the many left-hand paths that flourished elsewhere, such as the Temples of Isis and Ishtar, and the tantric temples.

In ancient Israel, just like in the modern world, although many people never left their villages, the offspring of wealthier families often traveled internationally for their studies—visiting notable world centers of learning such as Egypt, Greece, India, and Britain. For instance, Apollonius of Tyana, born circa 3 BCE, a contemporary of Jesus, had an in-depth spiritual education across many traditions, eventually becoming famous as a neo-Pythagorean gnostic philosopher, who even appeared on Roman coins. His primary biographer, Philostratus the elder, writing in 170 CE, records that during his life Apollonius traveled to study with the Brahmins in India, studied with the naked sages of Egypt, and studied with the Persian magi—called Zoroastrians. Plotinus, a Greek philosopher born a few hundred years later, studied in Alexandria for eleven years, then traveled to study with the magi and holy men of Persia and India.

It is likely that both John the Baptist and Jesus also traveled these study circuits. Then, after a comprehensive spiritual education and multidisciplinary initiation, rather than follow in the footsteps of the Jewish temple law, they turned to a more direct and rapturous direct connection with the Holy Spirit, to found new schools.

Their wisdom was unified in the oral Kabbalistic wisdom teachings of the embodied Shekinah, a native tradition of initiation into the holy marriage of spirit and form.

What Was Jesus's True Name?

Aramaic was the common spoken language in Palestine at the time of Jesus and Mary Magdalene, particularly in their home province of Galilee. Greek was the international language of arts, culture, and scholarship, and was a second language spoken by all educated people of the Middle East after Alexander the Great conquered and Hellenized the whole of the region in 334 BCE. Most of the New Testament, for example, was originally written in Greek. Many scholars believe that by Jesus's day Hebrew had already begun to decline as a common spoken language. It was still used by the priestly and scholarly class, and in Jewish religious services, but Aramaic gradually replaced Hebrew among the common people.

Jesus's proper Hebrew name was *Yeshua* or *Yehoshua*, but in Aramaic, the language he and Magdalene spoke, it was *Yeshu*, sometimes written *Isho*. In the related language of Arabic, as well as in India, he was known as *Issa*. In Greek books of the New Testament his name was written as *Iesous*, and was translated in Latin as *Iesus*, or Jesus. In old Gaelic it was *Isa* or *Iosa*.

But most importantly, what was the name his loved ones called him? In all likelihood, Magdalene would have whispered to him, "Come *Yeshu*," in their native tongue of Aramaic.

The Redemption of Sacred Union

Son of Man consented with Sophia, his consort, and revealed a great androgynous light. His male name is designated "Savior, Begetter of All Things." His female name is designated "All-Begettress Sophia." Some call her "Pistis."

THE SOPHIA OF JESUS CHRIST,
NAG HAMMADI CODEX III

When we pull together the many pieces of the puzzle, what emerges is an epic, redemptive Sophianic story, embodied in the union of MM and Yeshua, which brings the healing and reunification of the masculine and feminine, restoring Magdalene to her throne as the embodied holy feminine queen on earth. This is reflected in the medieval heresies that MM, the anointrix, had restored the true Garden of Eden and become the New Eve, birthing a new cycle on earth.

The lasting power of the Magdalene Mysteries is forged in the sacred heart of love, which spills open with the sacred anointing oil of divine rapture and erotic balm. It is not something that comes from religious judgment or moral repentance. MM awakens into the Shekinah, the sacred bride, the anointrix, through true union.

She sings to us through time, provocatively, of the secrets held behind the veil of King Solomon's Song of Songs—"How fair is thy love, my sister, my spouse! How much better is thy love than wine! And the smell of thine ointments than spices!"

Ultimately, the spiritual message of MM reveals that this "Christ" essence lives within all of us—waiting to be reclaimed. It cannot be harmed or removed; it is eternal.

The return of Mary Magdalene to consciousness is also the return of the wild sacred feminine medicine and of a remembrance of the immortal beauty of the Womb of Creation.

She gives us hope on long dark nights—just as she lit up the dark ages.

Let her be a prostitute, a sinner, a whore. For she is always Holy.

Merged in a cosmic union with her beloved Christ-consort, she dwells within the mystery of "I and the Mother are One"—the unified Black Rose—and invites us to join her in this Love.

Reclaiming Our Holy Whorethority

I know that what you call "God" really exists, but not in the form
you think; God is primal cosmic energy, the love in your body.

WILHELM REICH

Mary Magdalene without her whoredom has no authority. Her sacred womb magic is the source of her true *whorethority*.

A vision of Mary Magdalene dispossessed of her sexual magic has no power to anoint, to *Christen,* thus cannot bestow upon a man true kingship and sovereignty.

Mary Magdalene separated from her lust has no luminosity, no luxuriance, no *lust*er, no phosphorescence, no fluorescence. Her Christing is sensual, wild, erotically alive.

Mary Magdalene cut off from the Original Innocence of her sexuality, the Red River of her sensual delight, has no balm for our wasteland, no new Life to offer.

MM denied access to the potency of her numinous, fecund cunt, her cunning vulva, is a slave to the archonic, antilife forces. Opening this mystic gateway is her liberation.

MM stripped of her divine harlotry is a pawn of the patriarchal agenda, a symbol of the oppression and disempowerment of all women. This is a counterfeit of the true feminine, a deviation of the original, reversing and inverting the original power of the *anthropos.*

Jesus and MM taught the power of reclaiming our original blueprint as *true humans,* our inner Shakti, our primal life force—wild and free, to become a shimmering Light of the World.

So we invite you through the magic doorway of the left-hand path of the Feminine Christ, into a sacred mystery of harlotry, whoredom, sexual mystique, elemental magic, and a mythic cosmologic love story—where the lustrous, awakened serpent of divine Sophianic wisdom leads us back through a labyrinth rose path into the inner Garden of Eden.

Mary Magdalene is everyone.

You, I, we are all Mary Magdalene.

Her fate is our fate.

Her destiny, our destiny.

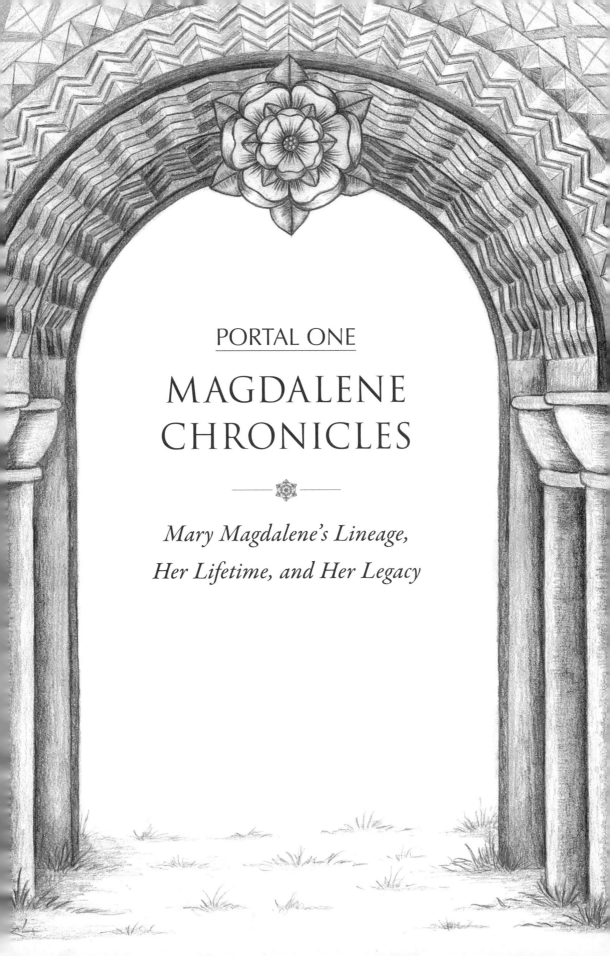

PORTAL ONE

MAGDALENE CHRONICLES

❖

Mary Magdalene's Lineage,
Her Lifetime, and Her Legacy

Pilgrim's Guide

Loe where a Wounded Heart with Bleeding Eyes conspire.
Is she a Flaming Fountain or a Weeping Fire?

RICHARD CRASHAW, "THE WEEPER"

BEAR WITH US AS, LIKE SCRIBAL SPIDERS, we spin a web for you, drawing a pattern together. *Myth* as a living energy is inherently creative, *story* is inherently creative, because whatever collective vision or cosmology we hold, we birth that reality onto the earth, and it becomes our world. A new story, then, is a womb of sorts; it has the power to birth new worlds.

We now enter into the chronicles of Mary Magdalene, the *herstory of the Feminine Christ,* where we explore MM's deep roots in the spiritual lineage of the feminine mysteries; the stories and secrets from her own lifetime as recorded in the Bible and gnostic texts; and the incredible spiritual legacy she left behind that spread into Europe, creating a "Rose Line."

To discover the lost secrets of Magdalene, we also explore the jewels of wisdom transmitted to us through ancient symbols, such as dragons, serpents, scorpions, scallop shells, and chalices, that are often associated with Magdalene and the Mary lineage, and which originate with an ancient lineage of priestesses who used these symbols as magical talismans to communicate a left-hand gnosis of sexual alchemy. Their forgotten left-hand faith of uterine magic and the unification of the womb worlds went on to birth gnostic, Sufi, and Kabbalistic mystic paths, before flowing secretly, like an invisible elixir, into the mystic heart of Christianity. This primordial feminine wisdom became known as "Sophia" in Greek.

Our search for the lost heritage of the Magdalene begins in ancient Sumeria. Some of the first words ever written, which birthed human civilization over four thousand years ago, were lovingly etched into clay tablets in ancient cuneiform

Cylinder seal from Ur, Sumeria, 3000 BCE.
(From Legrain, *Ur Excavations,* vol. 3, fig. 268)

by high priestesses of Inanna—real flesh and blood women, scholars, holy womb shamans, spiritual leaders, and the earliest poets.

Those words, which launched our current world of letters and lore, were these:

"Behold my wondrous vulva."

This is the secret inheritance of Mary Magdalene.

MAGDALENE'S LINEAGE
THE DRAGON PRIESTESSES

CHAMBER 1

DRAGON MOTHERS

Ancient Elemental Magic

We call forth the red roots of the ancient mother tree
Of dancing serpent, eagle priestess and cave by the sea
Dressed in the scarlet robes of the old and sacred ways
Visions of dragon, of bear, of lioness blaze
Through body, through spirit, through shining eyes we see
A new flower blooms on the ancient mother tree

A. AND S. BERTRAND

The Whorestory of the Dragon Priestesses

The root of the Magdalene Mysteries lives within the divine wombs of the Ancient Mothers, who were called the *Elohim* in Hebrew, a word whose oldest meaning was "birth goddesses": the original mothers of humanity who once lovingly spun the web of life into being.* In Sumeria these birth mothers were originally known as Dragons.

---

*Elohim is most commonly translated as "god" in the Bible but is also used to describe the goddess Ashtoreth: "For Solomon worshipped Ashtoreth the goddess [*Elohim*] of the Sidonians" (1 Kings 11:5). *Elohim* is plural in its form and can refer to feminine or masculine deities.

Nammu and Hur:
Twin Dragons of Sumeria

The creation story of Sumeria, like so many ancient cultures, is deeply intertwined with dragons and serpents. They are the primary archetype of feminine power, primal energy, and cosmic intelligence. Dragon Mothers were known as the birthers and creators. They represent the most ancient and primordial forces of creation, the unseen powers that move the cosmos and the inner workings of the Earth. The dragons of Creation are linked at a cosmologic level to the invisible flows of dark matter and dark energy that make up 94 percent of the known universe, that knit together every galaxy, black hole, galactic supercluster, and superstructural filaments of creation—the structure of the universe on the grandest scale, the "great feminine weaving"—that somehow remain entirely mysterious to modern physics. From the deep womb of the ocean comes the elemental Dragon Mother, *Nammu*—keeper of the sacred waters of life. From within the belly of the sacred mountain arises the elemental Dragon Mother *Hur*—the stoker of the sacred kundalini fires within earth.

These elemental goddesses, with their magic of fire and water, are the matrilineal parentage of the embodied consciousness of humanity, birthed from the flowing lava of earth's volcanoes, and the dark fertility of soil, baptized with the living waters emerging from earth's inner worlds, and the rivers of lactating spirit flowing downstream from the cosmic vulva of the black night goddess. This is the work of the mythic dragons; connected to the birthing power of women's wombs.

These elemental dragons of fire and water created the lineage of priestess-whores and grail-mermaids that are the bedrock of the spiritual traditions Magdalene inherited.

Genesis of the Dragon World

The oldest Sumerian myths say that, in the beginning, there was Mother Nammu, the first, the formless, the one who gave shape to all of creation. She was ancient, before time, space, before the universe. She was a water dragon of the deep, the most primordial ancestress.

Nammu lived deep in the *Abzu*, the primordial freshwater lake under the surface of the earth, from which all life was birthed. The veins and channels of the underground Abzu lake are the source of all the sacred wells, lakes, springs, rivers, and oases of the world—forming a flowing and interconnected network of life-giving waters across the planet. Life cannot exist without her.

Although Nammu was never depicted in image or form, because she existed *before* form, she was a primordial water dragon of Creation, closely linked with the saltwater creatrix dragon *Tiamat* of Babylonia. Together, their breath of life stirred the vortex of the ancient birthing seas. All creation, including the earth and the living creatures, emerged from her sea. The Genesis story of the Old Testament, scribed thousands of years after Nammu, borrowed the essence of her original story: "And the earth was without form, and void; and darkness was upon the face of the deep [*tehom*]. And the Spirit of God moved upon the face of the waters" (Genesis 1:2).

The abyss is a central theme in Jewish lore. The word *abyss* derives from the Sumerian word *abzu,* just as the Hebrew word *tehom,* "the deep," comes from the same word root as *Tiamat.* The mystery of the abyss is the mystery of creation itself that emerges from the dark, swirling feminine vortex, the dazzling darkness, the deep ocean of unmanifest potential that births all from its waters. Emergence from the primordial waters is the most common story of creation across time and culture. "The deep" is the essence of the primordial feminine.

Nammu was a prehistoric deity, and by 3500 BCE she was already ancient history in the Sumerian world. But Nammu gave birth to a daughter, the Sumerian mother goddess *Nin-hur-sag,* whose name meant "Queen of the Sacred Hur," the primeval womb dragon of the Underworld. In feminine lore, she symbolized the elements of fire and earth. The *Hur* dragon was imagined to live deep inside the Earth Womb of the holy mountains, within the fiery lava at its center. As Queen of the Hur, Ninhursag was also the first "Queen Whore." She became the birth portal for the Holy Whores of Fire and priestesses of the Underworld.

Of Dragon and Moon

The ancient dragons are the grandmothers of the love goddess Inanna, and the great-grandmothers of Mary Magdalene and the Moon priestess line she belongs to. The ancient priestesses of the Near East claim descent from the primordial forces of nature, as well as the moon, the stars, and the venerable dragons. They knew that to honor and remember these connections was to open the doorway to the deepest magic. We must understand and *feel* the enchantment and lost wisdom of this lineage to truly know Magdalene.

The dragons also appear in Christian iconography, with Mother Mary traditionally depicted standing on the back of a dragon or serpent, or a crescent moon, symbolizing that she too was originally a dragon priestess of this ancient lunar lineage.

This feminine shamanic tradition is over 300,000 years old. Stone Age art reveals the evidence of shamanic, goddess-worshipping humans across the globe, including the remarkable 73,000-year-old red ochre art in the Blombos caves in South Africa, the striking crimson-red handprints, mainly made by women, in El Castillo cave in Spain, more than 40,000 years old, and the red "Jacob's ladder" found in a nearby Spanish cave, dating to 65,000 years ago. At Cueva de los Aviones, a cave in southeastern Spain, researchers also found perforated seashell beads and pigments that are at least 115,000 years old. South African artists were already working with red ochre, which archaeologists believe symbolized fertility, death, and menstruation, over 160,000 years ago.[1]

The ancient womb shamans and dragon priestesses were artistic, intuitive, *feeling beings,* connected to the sacred web of life. Theirs was a cerebellar intelligence rather than a cerebral thinking one. They were spiritually and emotionally awakened, through a more developed amygdala and neural network of the cerebellum— the feminine brain and portal of cosmic mother consciousness, which philosopher Emanuel Swedenborg described as the gateway to the angels.

The womb shamans weaved with the old root magic of the instinctual world. They merged with bird, serpent, scorpion, wild bull, lion, fish, and dragon in the magical process of a spirit-journey communion undertaken by the shaman-priestesses. To become animal, to call in their spirit power, they would ritually dress themselves in animal costumes. They would move like the creature, dancing in darkened womb chambers or under the moonlight. They would fast, pray, make animal sounds, swirl and spin to the rhythm of the animal-skin moon drums, until they *became* serpent-women, scorpion-women, dragon-women. The primordial powers channeled by the priestesses heightened their ability to interpret dreams, to read the omens, to receive spirit messages, and to magically minister between the gods and peoples of earth.

The primacy of the psyche, the potency of the mythic imagination, the magic of sign and sigil, of totemic animal communion around the midnight fire, of memories stored in stone, land, and water—these were the domains of the ancient womb shamans. They tapped into the vast field of creative potential and ancestral memory to give birth to structures of spirit, building majestic mythological landscapes the way modern architects build cities of concrete and steel. The shaman priestesses of old knew what forces propel, fertilize, and animate *life,* and the cycles that rise and fall over time. They reached for these powers, brought them down into form, and whispered them forward across time.

Mary Magdalene inherited this legacy; she was a priestess of the four elements, mistress of the *elemental mandala of creation*. She ministered to Yeshu the four elemental baptisms of water, fire, air, and earth, which awakened him into his *anthropos,* his divine human potential.

She was not just a priestess; *she was a dragon priestess*. As we will soon discover, her role as chalice bearer, a water priestess, traces back to the mermaid lineage of the ancient Water Dragon Nammu. But Magdalene was also a priestess of earth and fire, a red-robed Holy Harlot descended from the spiritual lineage of the Fire and Earth Dragon *Hur,* the source of the womb words *whore* and *harlot*. The spiritual legacy of Sumeria was built upon the backs of dragons and through the priestesses that invoked their magic.

Twin dragon and serpent sacred libation vessel,
carved from green chlorite. Lagash, Sumeria, 2120 BCE.
(Louvre, photo by Claude Valette, CC BY-ND 2.0 via Flickr)

As time and culture evolved, elemental dragons became elemental shamans, who became elemental priestesses. Worship moved from cave and stone circle to the temples of the newly forming cities. The priestesses of the ancient world straddled wilderness and civilization, spoke to the stars as well as large assemblies of people, shapeshifted into animal as needed—serpent, dragon, scorpion, eagle—while at other times sat enthroned next to kings in great palaces, wearing the finest fabrics and jewels. They were the living link between the human and divine, between the ancestors and those of this world, heirs to a talismanic craft, where symbol held power, where it altered and structured consciousness. They were priestesses of the mother world, mistresses of all creation.

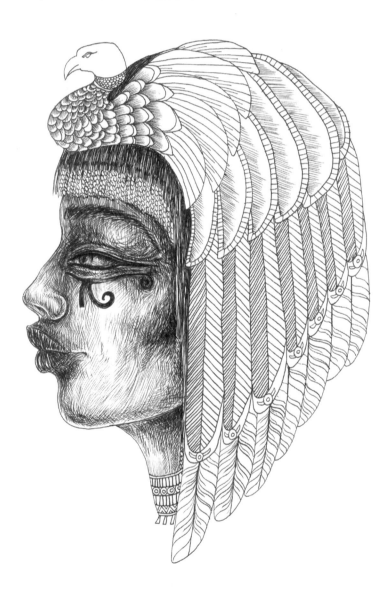

Fall of the Dragon Mothers

Yet, similar to stories across the world, a tale is told of a fall in creation, when the collaborative forces of creation were disrupted, and the sacred union of masculine and feminine split. The powers of earth, fire, water, air, spirit lost their fructifying partner as the king forgot his place in the dragon world and sought to become its lord and master.

Between 3500 BCE and 300 CE, stories of the displacement of the goddess abounded. Female deities such as Nammu, Tiamat, Inanna, Nanna, and Ninhursag fought to keep their power—and Sumerian lore tells of both Ninhursag and Inanna's "run-ins" with Enki, the male god of wisdom and magic, who would eventually replace their feminine magic.

As one story goes . . .

THE MYTH OF ENKI AND NINHURSAG

Enki and Ninhursag were once united in love and sexual union deep in the primordial birthing waters of the Abzu. From their union they gave birth to a daughter. By the time their daughter came of age Enki became sexually fascinated with her. Mistaking her for Ninhursag, he impregnated his daughter, and continued in the same way with several more generations of his granddaughters. In the process some of his seed fell to the ground and grew into the first eight plants of the world. When Enki saw them, he was delighted. He named the plants, decreeing their divine fate, and greedily ate them. Unfortunately, the plants continued to grow larger within his belly—he bloated, swelled, and became very sick—but he had no womb and no yoni, so he couldn't birth them out as a goddess could!

The dragons thought Enki a fool, and Ninhursag was outraged by his inappropriate behavior on all accounts, particularly his arrogance in trying to claim power over her domain of birthing and naming. Enki begged and pleaded for her help, but she refused.

In his desperation Enki called on the clever fox to help negotiate with Ninhursag, so that she would birth the plants with the authority and birth-light power of the true Mother. Finally, she relented. She grabbed the "pregnant" Enki and, before he could protest, swiftly stuffed him into her divine yoni-womb where he and the plants could have a proper gestation.

After a time, she safely birthed Enki and the eight plants back into the world. Enki should have learned his lesson: never try to steal the power of procreation from the feminine.

This old, old story has been shared over time, finding whispers of similarity in the stories of the Welsh goddess Cerridwen, who eats Taliesin, and gestates him inside her womb-cauldron, as a form of apprenticeship, so he can receive his second birth into wisdom. It also has hints of the Sophia story, and the male demiurge who tries to create his own world. It tells a "slant" story of both a stealing of womb power *and* an initiation into it. It reminds us that the Great Mother always presides over these rites and is the birth power.

From this old Sumerian story, we eventually find Christ gestating inside the womb-tomb of the Divine Mother, the Holy Spirit, to receive his second birth into resurrection.

It is the elemental dragon magic that initiates, births, and rebirths the world.

PRAYER OF THE DRAGONS

There is no beginning of time, and no end, only cycles of birth, dissolution, and rebirth, eternal spirals of becoming that inevitably return us to the fecund womb of darkness, where we quietly gestate the next phase of our journey. We wax, we wane, we wax again. Ours is a lunar womb world.

Mother Night, the Great Shepherdess of the dark birthing sea, presides over her queendom, along with her numinous, luminous divine children—the moon, the imperishable stars, and the fertilizing sun.

The song of creation sounds forth, rising up from her nethermouth, the Great Hor of the Cosmos.

Let there be moonlight over the primordial oceans.

Let the earth and her creatures be born.

The she-dragon Nammu, Hur, Tiamat—creatrix of many names—stirs in the deep.

We know her by her birth bellows—her volcanic eruption and earthshake. New land pours out with her lava. Valleys rise into mountains, hills sink back into the seas.

There are forces older than human that shape us, that we must learn to live with, that we must summon and evoke, that we must have faith in.

Our spirits fly with the soul birds, our thighs are strong like the bounding gazelle. We spit and kick with the vigor of wild asses. We mate like lions. We roar.

The power in the wildness is ours to remember.

The serpents coil around each other to sexually conjoin, pulsating, mesmerizing, magical. As do the two strands of our human DNA. New life arises.

Woman's blood comes monthly, with the moon. It is the gift of the goddess, the gift of life, and the measure of time. From the mother's blood our bodies are formed, from the milk of her breasts we are nourished. From her womb we are born. All culture arises from this foundation. May we never forget.

Male and female, masculine and feminine, god and goddess come together. Infinite form is birthed. One becomes two, two becomes one. We are interwoven everywhere.

The microcosm reflects in the macrocosm, the mundane in the celestial. As in the heavens, as in the earth; as in the wild creatures, so it is in us.

The fruit of the date palm nourishes us; her fronds shade us. The reeds of the marshes become shelter. The dry land is watered, the field plowed, the furrow seeded. Green shoots of wheat and barley rise each spring. We celebrate their return with the esh-esh New Moon temple festivals and the rites of sacred marriage. In turn we celebrate each new moon, her golden crescent crown like the horns of the wild cow, reminding us of all that nourishes us, our many mothers.

The garden of earth and spirit must be cultivated with song, with prayer, with craft, with ritual, with the waters of life. We weave the world into being. Every movement, every word, every item of beauty we adorn ourselves with is its own magic.

Let the Gate of Horn be thrown open, let us step across time into another world, let what is ancient be remembered and be born again into fresh forms.

Love becomes itself.

CHAMBER 2

MERMAID PRIESTESSES

Chalice of Holy Waters

Nammu, Holy Mother of Creation,
Mother of the Ancient Deep,
Your sweet waters are the waters of life.
May they nourish, cleanse, renew,
May they make us fertile, wet, dark, deep
Like the mystery of your ancient womb.
You are the Mother of All Living
Form—giver, matrix, giver of shape.
The power of your name sounds again and again
Whispered by every river, every spring, every well and oasis.
With every offering of milk from your breast
May all remember and drink deeply from your well.

A. AND S. BERTRAND

THE STORY OF THE MERMAIDS emerges from this ancient lineage of the primeval water dragon and her elemental forces, first encoded in art and lore from around 6000 BCE.

A *mer-maid* is not just a mythical fish-woman, she is a priestess of the *mer-line* that traces back to the Motherline of the Neanderthal womb shamans. Known as ancient feminine divinities, mermaids represented a priestesshood that served as the water bearers, ladies of the chalice, and protectors of the living waters of earth and womb. The left-hand path of mystical Christianity began with this priestess-hood of "Grail Mermaidens" and their feminine rites, as it was the mermaids who became the "Mary" line of Magdalene.

Mary, Mari, Mar, or *Mer* are words that mean "mother, beloved, sea, or feminine light" in many of the oldest languages of the world, including the ancient Egyptian, Sumerian, Semitic, and Indo-European languages. They are not ordinary

names; they are *priestess titles*. In Egypt, Hathor was called Mari-Hathor, "Beloved and Honored Hathor," and Isis was called Mari-Isis, "Beloved and Honored Isis," as were their priests and priestesses.

The mer-maid shamankas worked with the element of water and the power animals of the primordial waters of creation—the fish, whales, dolphins, and serpent-dragons—the creatures that remind us of our fertile, wet, amniotic beginnings. Life on earth first emerged from the salty seas, from the waters of life, just as human life emerges in a splash of birth blood and amniotic fluid that is similar in composition to the great saltwater oceans.

What we now call *mer-maids* and *mer-men* were once the initiated priestesses and priests of the water dragon. Mermaids were mistresses of the water rituals, and ceremonially tended to the watery womb of creation. In Babylonia they were called *ku-lullu* "fish-man" and *ku-liltu* "fish-woman." Mermaids administered the rites of the water blessings, the most ancient rituals of Sumeria. Their temple, the *E-engur,* "House of the Abyss," was located in the southern Sumerian city of Eridu, the oldest settlement of Sumeria that likely began with Neanderthals and other Stone Age peoples who hunted and gathered shellfish along the coast of southern Iraq.

Mermaid Religion: Mesopotamian mermaid (with horns of divinity) and merman approaching Tree of Life for prayer offering, with Apkallu fish priest on left. Babylonian cylinder seal, ca. 700 BCE.

(British Museum, illustration © Stéphane Beaulieu)

The Abzu, the Womb of Creation, was said to lie directly underneath Nammu's temple. The sign for the Abzu is the "Stargate in the Womb"—illustrating the mystical belief of the left-hand path that there exists a creative, cosmic portal within the womb of every woman.

In the figure below, we can see the Abzu, and other sacred glyphs, revealing sacred feminine symbols in ancient Sumeria. The pictogram of the Abzu is the eight-pointed star cross, held in the square that represents the underworld womb. Next to it is the *An* sign meaning Venus, Inanna, star, goddess, god, heaven. To the right is the symbol *Ama* for mother—the star represents both the stargate in her womb as well as breast milk, the mystical "food of life" of the mother, and the surrounding "house" is simultaneously her womb, body, temple, earth. The symbols on the top row are variations of the female pubic triangle and sacred chalice, equated with woman. In the middle we see the vulva seated upon a throne and altar to represent the esteemed queen, goddess, or high priestess. The symbol in the upper right shows the link between food and the sign of the female—in early Sumeria, food was conceived of as a sacrament or eucharist of the Mother.

Thousands of carp bones were found buried deep in the foundations of

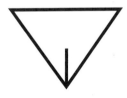

Sal, also pronounced *munus,* meaning "woman, vulva." Pictograph of female vulva/pubic triangle.

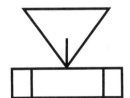

Nin, meaning "queen, lady, princess, mistress." Pictograph of vulva on throne and altar.

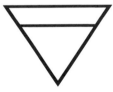

Sha, "womb, chalice, heart," a variation of the vulva symbol, also called *nin-da,* meaning "bread" or "nourishment."

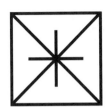

Abzu, underworld. "Stargate in the Womb," star cross contained in temple or womb.

An, meaning "star, Inanna, Venus, heaven, goddess, god, also milk."

Ama, "mother," containing symbols for star, goddess, Venus, inside a house or temple. Also a breast with milk.

Archaic Sumerian glyphs, the earliest written language.
From Inanna's temple at Uruk, Sumeria, ca. 3400 BCE.

(Illustration © Stéphane Beaulieu, modeled on Labat, *Manuel D'Épigraphie Akkadienne*)

Nammu's temple, which dated back to 5000 BCE. The fish were offerings given to the goddess and were also ceremonially eaten by the priestesses in honor of Nammu, to merge with her through the eucharistic act.

This tradition of mermaid priestesses and divinities existed all across the world, showing that the original "Water Dragon Mother" who birthed creation was a global mystical phenomena. In China, mermaids were renowned craftswomen, and the fabric they wove was described as "dragon yarn." Legends also say that their tears turned into pearls. Mami Wata, an African water spirit, is portrayed as a mermaid and a snake charmer. Yemoja, a water goddess from the Yoruba tradition, is often depicted as a mermaid and, as the "Mother of the Orishas," is linked to the Christian Virgin Mary in later times. Her ritual items include seashells and fishnets, and she is associated with deep wisdom, the moon, and the waters of creation poured from the primordial womb. She is considered the mother of humanity, and her name means "Mother Whose Children Are Like Fish." She also holds a white jar—reminiscent of Magdalene.

In Wales, where wells were considered sacred portals, salmon were eaten as a holy sacrament. Female oracles and priestesses protected the wells and the "wisdom fish" within. Fish were also held sacred in the Eleusinian Mysteries, whose ultimate rite was the direct gnostic revelation of the Holy Sophia.

The Judaic and Christian practice of eating fish on Friday evening, part of the *Shabbat* in the Jewish tradition, evolved from the original rites of Nammu, as they were passed down into ancient Babylon, Assyria, Canaan, and Israel. The Hebrew word *Shabbat* is related to the Babylonian *sabatu,* meaning both "seven" and "the menstruation of the goddess Ishtar." On the days of Ishtar's menstruation, originally on the three days of the dark moon, the whole community would stop working and observe this feminine religious rite. The Shabbat eating of fish is traditionally followed by lovemaking between husband and wife, and associated with the arrival into the home of the Shekinah, the Bride and feminine Holy Spirit. The ritual fish meal has its origins deep in the goddess tradition.

The mer-people are linked to this long tradition of sacred fish symbolism. Jesus, a *mer-man* and lover of the goddess, was well known as a "fisher of men," symbolized by the *ichthys* fish symbol, derived from the sacred geometry of the vesica piscis, which represented the female vulva. This ancient yoni symbol can still be seen on the back of cars today, reminding us of the vulvic power, and the great sense of humor of the goddess. For many thousands of years fish— and the water rites of the mermaid priestesses—have been associated with the

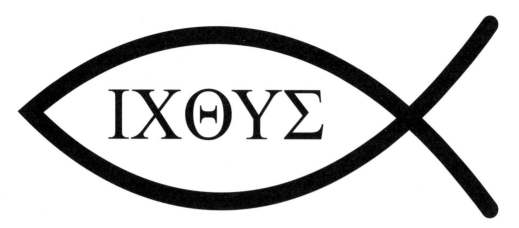

The "Jesus Fish" (Greek *Ichthys*), acronym for Jesus Christ, Son of God(dess).

feminine, fertility, the vulva, female sexuality, and our deep origins at the watery root of creation.

Alabaster Jar—The Holy Grail

This legacy of Nammu, as the holy womb–water mother, was later passed on to Inanna's priestess-mermaids. The principal symbol of this lineage across the ages is the *Sacred Vessel—the Grail Cup*. For Mary Magdalene, it is the alabaster anointing jar, and, as with all sacred vessels, it symbolizes the multidimensional feminine womb, source of the waters of life, source of magic, and source of conception, creation, and birth.

The shape and form of the sacred vessel varied over time and culture, but its magical essence and symbolic power has remained constant. It was the Sacred Basket, the Holy Grail, the Sacred Gourd, the Sparkling Chalice, the Sacred Cup, the Sampo of the Fins, the gold and silver libation vessels of the Temple of Jerusalem, the carved stone dragon and lion flasks of Sumeria, the cup of the *dergflaith,* the dragon drink of Sovereignty of the Celts, and an infinite variety of others. The sacred vessel was not merely symbolic; it was the everyday magical tool essential to the priesthood.

Some of the oldest written records of holy water rituals come from ancient Sumeria. The most ornate sacred vessels of Mesopotamia were made of gold and silver, but others were crafted of copper and bronze, or beautiful cut alabaster, lapis lazuli, calcite, chlorite, or steatite. They might be set with jewels or semiprecious stones, or they might be very simple clay vessels in more humble settings.

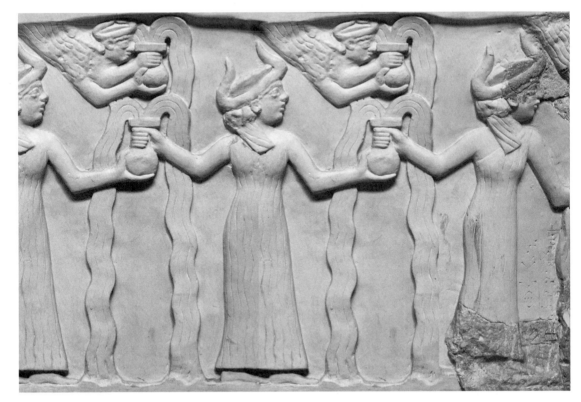

Water priestesses of Sumeria, holding vases of the flowing waters of life, with lunar horned tiaras of divine radiance. Reconstructed detail of an "abzu" baptismal basin from Lagash, Sumeria, 2040 BCE.
(Museum of the Ancient Orient, Istanbul, ©Radish | Dreamstime.com, adaptation)

The most important sacred vessels were *divinized*—they were given names and considered to be divine beings. Divinized vessels were stored in the darkened, innermost womb chamber of the temple, the house of the god or goddess herself, the "holy womb of holies." Their making was a ritualistic process, with every detail of production accompanied by prayers, chants, incense, and astrological calculations.

The practice of ritual anointing and libation dates back thousands of years into prehistory. The earliest shrines in Mesopotamia, from around 5000 BCE, already contained primitive stone altars, with evidence that libation fluids were poured across them and onto the earth around them. Libation rituals involved the pouring of fragrant oils, water, honey, milk, wine, beer, and date-nectar syrups over stone altars, omphalos "navel" stones, or into the earth. Libations could also be given to the ancestors. The temples of ancient Sumeria contained hollow pipes that led down deep into the earth, so priest/esses could pour libations through them to reach the ancestors who rested in the underworld Earth Womb.

These feminine water rites—based on the magical blood, milk, and sensual elixirs of the feminine—were also a key part of the temples of Isis, Hathor, and Bast in Egypt. Bast, the cat goddess, was one of the most beloved goddesses in Egypt. She was the lunar face of the lioness Sekhmet, associated with sensuality, playfulness, erotic pleasure, and love. She could be open and surrendered but also activated and energized. Bast's magical art was beauty, fragrance, and adornment; her name in hieroglyphs was written with the symbol of a jar of anointing oil or perfume. She was the ancient Egyptian archetype of the anointrix Mary Magdalene and her alabaster jar, which became MM's primary symbol for over two thousand years—revealing her as a mer-maid.

For Mary Magdalene, and other *myrrhophores,* or "myrrh bearers," the anointing jar was used to carry the sacred myrrh and frankincense oils traditionally used in the anointing rites at birth, death, rebirth, kingship, queenship, investiture in the priesthood, and sacred marriage, symbolizing the sacred womb elixirs. This precious alabaster jar, and the secrets it holds, has been passed down, metaphorically, by many lineages of priestesses, housing the fragrance of their rites.

The Disappearance of the Mermaids

Over time the mermaids retreated from the foreground of this primordial womb religion, to be replaced by male priests of Enki and his mermen descendants who wore the sacred fish hat. (The pope still wears this headdress, called a miter, to this day.) They called themselves Lords of the Fish and Fisher Kings, and performed the water baptism rites. A version of Nammu's "eucharist of the fish" was still regularly performed thousands of years later by the male priesthood of Atargatis, the mermaid fish-goddess of Syria, even through the lifetime of Magdalene and Jesus. Her priests believed that the fish represented her body; to eat fish was to embody the goddess.[1]

The Fisher King and the Holy Grail

The Celtic cultures have a similar lore to the mermaid-priestesses of Sumeria. Both traditions tell of the eventual abuse of the grail womb of the mermaids. One of the oldest Grail myths, from Wales and Ireland, is *Elucidation: Voices of the Wells.* It encodes the story of how the Well Maidens, who served food on a golden platter and elixirs from a golden cup at sacred water sites, were raped by a king and his men. After the desecration, the sacred life-giving waters of the otherworld no longer flowed through the wombs of the Well Maidens. A curse came upon the land and its people, birthing the wasteland.

In the later Grail stories, the memories of the original enchanted Grail maidens and their queens and priestesses—the Ladies of the Fish and the Fisher Queens—disappeared entirely, to be replaced by an impotent Fisher *King,* wounded in "the thigh," a euphemism for genitals. His court was somber and his lands barren, as the feminine fountain of life, the Fisher Queen of "the deep," was displaced and her magical roses no longer bloomed.

Across the world legends abound of the temple priestesses, holy whores and sacred harlots of the global sisterhood of Sophia, who had once given blessed eucharists from their grail wombs, but who had been attacked or raped in the patriarchal era. The holy wells of Nammu the water dragon were enslaved and her living waters dammed up. For more than a thousand years, the mermaids would all but disappear in European and Near Eastern art.

Yet even in the darkest times, it was known by the prophets and prophetesses that one day the mermaids and Grail maidens would return, and the wasteland would be restored to wholeness. The balm would come through the honoring, respect, empowerment, and sexual liberation of the feminine, bringing balance once again to the masculine and feminine energies

Twin-Tailed Mermaids, Sheelas, and Frog Goddesses

After many centuries of absence through the Dark Ages, we witness the most curious development in the artwork of medieval Christianity—the sudden reappearance of mermaids. This magical symbol of the Magdalene lineage had been secretly preserved by the Cathars and underground Magdalene heretics, used as a hidden code in their illuminated manuscripts and correspondence. With the blossoming of the mystical Magdalene stream, mermaids became a favorite image used by alchemists of the mysteries, and, inspired by Templar architects, they began to appear in churches across Europe.

The mermaids of medieval Christian churches are evidently womb shamans, with their twin tails spread to expose the V of their sacred doorway, their ancient

Left: Twin-tailed siren from the Duomo of Modena.

(Photo by Sailko CC BY 3.0)

Right: Mermaid of the Clonfert Cathedral, Ireland,
with mirror over her womb and comb in her right hand.

(Photo by Trounce, CC BY-SA 2.5)

Left: Twin-tailed siren from the Ceiling of the Demigods, painted by the
Italian master Pinturicchio, 1490, in the Palazzo dei Penitenzieri of Rome.

(Photo by Sailko CC BY-SA 3.0)

Right: Twin-tailed mermaid wearing an equal armed cross of the Cathars
and Templars in Porcia Castle, Austria.

cunt wisdom, sometimes with founts of water gushing from the sacred center of their holy vulva. They share features with the Celtic Sheela-Na-Gigs, who also appeared on churches, exposing their wise yonis for all to see and touch, as was traditional before entering the "womb" of the old Celtic church.

Churches also bore mysterious talismanic images of squatting nude women, with legs in an M position, exposing their majestic moongate, similar to the Sheelas and mermaids. Church officials insisted they were meant as a warning to prevent lascivious behavior, or to scare away evil spirits, but the M symbol of fertility had a long history, related to the Sheela-Na-Gigs.

The M was associated with the Neolithic image of the sacred frog and birth goddess with her open legs, who represented the regenerative power of the womb, and was also associated with the traditional squatting position of childbirth. Examples of the M-legged female shamans of birthing and sacred sexuality are found across the cultures of the world (see page 276), and form the hidden centerpiece of the alchemical artwork of the *Ghent Altarpiece,* which we will visit later.

In Egypt the frog goddess was known as Heket; her symbol was the M, which was related to the Egyptian hieroglyph for "water." In the old European tradition, the Greek goddess Hekate was also called *Baubo,* meaning "frog." The frog goddesses were represented as a face with big frog eyes, over an M symbol. Frogs were associated with gestation in amniotic waters and represented fertility—legend had it that if a frog crossed a woman's path she would soon be pregnant. Frogs could live on land as well as in water, symbolizing the two realms of the logical and intuitive mind, and the union of solar and lunar consciousness.

The symbolism of the fertile frog goddess was passed along to the Celtic Sheela-Na-Gig—a froglike female figure squatting down and holding open the gates of her supernatural vulva. The origin of the name Sheela-Na-Gig has long been a mystery, as it is unrelated to any language used in the Celtic lands. Yet, in Sumeria, temple priestesses who held the high office of "sacred harlot" were called *nu-gig,* meaning "the pure and immaculate ones," suggesting that Sheela-Na-Gigs are an echo of this ancient womb priestess tradition.

A red thread of connection links the mermaids, Sheelas, and chalice bearers, and their sexual talismanic symbolism, across time and culture. These women, and this Rose Line, are the priestesses of the Holy Grail.

CHAMBER 3

MOON SHAMANS
Serpent Daughters of Fire

NOW WE MEET THE GREAT-GRANDMOTHER of the Magdalenes, the Sumerian Dragon Mother of earth and fire, *Nin-hur-sag*. She is the namesake of all whores and harlot priestesses, the grandmother of the Great Whore of Babylon, Ishtar, the mother of the Moon and her sacred cult of priestess-sinners. She was known as *Shassuru*, the Womb Goddess, the Mother of All Living, the Mother of the Gods. Sumerian kings claimed descent from her; fierce warriors proudly boasted that they suckled at her divine breasts. As Lady of the Diadem she presided over the crowning of Sumerian and Babylonian kings. She was also known as *Ge*, the living Earth, a name that transfigured over time into a name we are more familiar with—*Gaia*. Like the gnostic Sophia, she was both goddess and the Earth itself, her divine spark infused throughout Creation.

Ninhursag's name holds tremendous power and is key to understanding her crimson lineage of whore priestesses. *Hur* is a name of the multidimensional womb, from which *whore, harlot,* and related words are derived. To perceive its meaning, we must step back from our logical mind and begin to think intuitively, as the shaman-priestesses did many thousands of years ago. The ancients conceived of the world axis, the *axis mundi,* as a vertical line that connected the underworld Earth Womb, located at the center of the earth, to the Sacred Mountain that sat on top of it, from which all life first emerged, and extended out to the Cosmic Womb in the heavens above. Inside the earth's womb lived the great and fiery dragon of creation, who spat out the lava from volcanoes and shook the earth with flicks of her mighty tail.

Ninhursag's name translates as "Queen of the Sacred Hur" (*nin*, "queen"; *sag,* "sacred," "great"), where the Hur is the Underworld, the World Mountain, *and,* in its most ancient form, the dragon that lived beneath them. So the name of the goddess Ninhursag means "Queen of the Sacred Mountain" but also "Queen of the Underworld," "Queen of the Dragon," and "Queen Whore." In archaic memory, she is a *triple queen,* a queen of multiple realms.

The Sumerian underworld dragoness Hur/Whore is ancient of days. She is deep, magical, beyond thought and time. She is a dragon of the fire and earth elements—a heavy, pregnant weaver of "mother matter," the physical form and substance of the universe that arises from invisible, rich dark-matter webs, and the unseen swish of dragon tails. Hur is beyond this world but helped give shape to it, controlling the deep earth and fire energies, awakening the fiery pathways of volcanic births as well as the entry and exit of all souls from the Earth Womb portal.

In ancient times, sacred words such as *Hur* were powerful magic; they were not spoken superficially but were sounded through the body as a resonant vibratory field. When toned in this way *HUR* is a deep, primal birthing sound that extends down and opens the womb, making the guttural *whore* sound. It is a universal sound that transcends language, made by birthing mothers in the throes of their womb surges since time immemorial. This same word was transliterated in the Semitic languages as *hor* and *har,* and gave rise to the English *whore* and *harlot.* A Hur Dragon is also a Hor Dragon and a Whore Dragon. And a priestess of the Holy Whore and Holy Harlot is a priestess of the Holy Dragon—the primordial, birthing mother of the earth and cosmos.

This same connection is seen in the priestess title of the Delphic Oracle, the *Pythia,* whose name means "dragoness" or "serpentess." This dragon/whore title conveyed such prestige in the ancient world that the famous philosopher and mathematician Pythagoras, who was a student of the Delphic Pythia, took on a dragon name (*pyth,* "dragon" + *agora,* "meeting place") to honor her as his teacher and muse.

Hur and Hor—Origins of Whore

Let us take a closer look at the hidden language of the womb to see the shared origin of *hur, har, hor,* and related words in many languages. We just need to apply two simple etymology tricks to reveal the connections. The first is that vowels were often interchangeable. The second is that the consonant sounds H and K were also easily interchanged. So, for example, the Hebrew *hor-* is related to the Arabic *har-* and Greek *kor-.* When we look at the list of womb words below, the pattern becomes clear: we see HR and KR words that are all linked to the womb, sexuality, pregnancy, birthing goddesses, and underworld Earth Womb.

HuR—(Sumerian) underworld Earth Womb, dragon, and Sacred Mountain of birth

HoR/HuR—(Hebrew) hole, cave, pit, sacred mountain, crevice of the serpent, round vessel, cauldron; all are womb symbols

HoRon—(Phoenician) underworld, Earth Womb deity

*HaRah**—(Hebrew) pregnant, to become pregnant; cistern, well, cave

HaRem—(Arabic) sacred female consorts or concubines, originally female sexual priestesses with awakened wombs

HaRimtu—(Akkadian) a class of priestesses of Inanna, originally connected to sacred sexual rites; later a term for a prostitute

HeRa—(Greek) Womb Mother, goddess of birth

HieRos—(Greek) sacred, relating to the birth goddess Hera, the sexual union rite of *hieros gamos*

HaRlot—(English) priestess and "holy whore," used in English translations of the Bible to describe the sexually "immoral" goddesses Ishtar of Babylon or Asherah of Canaan, or their priestesses

HaRa—(Japanese) womb, and the analogous energy center in men

wHoRe—(English) originally a title of a womb goddess or womb priestess, and eventually a derogatory word meaning "prostitute or loose woman" in English

HoRtus—(Latin) garden, a common metaphor for the womb and sexuality

ishHaRa—(Babylonian) scorpion goddess of sexuality and sacred union, aspect of Ishtar

KoRa—(Arabic) gourd, a sacred symbol of the womb

Kar/Ka—(Indo-European) proposed root of "whore," meaning to love, desire; word family also includes heart (French *coeur*), Sanskrit *kama* ("love, sex"), Sanskrit *garbha* ("womb")

KoRe—(Greek) virgin goddess and queen of the underworld Womb, equivalent to Persephone; also maiden or virgin

Kora/ChoRa—(Greek) container, a womb metaphor, used to describe the Virgin Mary's womb in Orthodox churches

---

*Semitic languages have two "h" sounds; the second is sometimes written as *ch* or *kh,* as in *challah* bread. In this list, the two sounds have both been listed as *h* for simplicity.

KaRis/ChaRis—(Greek and Sanskrit) the sacred anointing fluids, originally sexual and menstrual fluids from the womb of women

KaRisma/ChaRisma—(Greek, and later English) magnetic power, originally conceived as womb magnetism

KRist/ChRist—(Greek) "the anointed one," anointed with the sacred, kingship-granting elixirs of the womb

Across many languages, *hor* and *hur* were womb root words linked to sexuality and birth. In the days of yore, when the womb was once honored as the bearer of life, the honorific titles Whore and Harlot signified the dragon priestesses and oracles of the goddess religions, descended from the Hur womb dragon of Sumeria. Hur was the original Holy Whore—the Holy Womb who gave birth to the lineage of Inanna and her red-robed Holy Harlot priestesses that spread the ancient feminine wisdom throughout the lands of the Near East.

Omega:
Sumerian Womb Symbol of Ninhursag

Ninhursag's sign was the omega womb symbol (see illustration on page 73), later adopted by Christianity as a sigil of God—the alpha and the omega—originally a conception of the goddess. In Sumeria, her omega womb symbol was often seen on altars, or in the inner temple adyta, the womb chambers and holy of holies. The Egyptian goddess Hathor borrowed Ninhursag's womb symbol to use for her iconic hairstyle. Fashion trends, then as now, were contagious.

Priestesses of the Wild Feminine

The ancient goddesses were wild and elemental. The birth mother Ninhursag was the protectress of wild animals and the instinctive sexuality that all animals innately possess. To watch a pantheress move across the cedar- and cypress-studded foothills of Mesopotamia is to experience the direct wild feminine transmission of Ninhursag and her priestesses. Unashamed, and fully in the center of her own queenship, the pantheress is magnetic, irresistible, powerful, fierce, yet relaxed and supple. Ready to hunt, ready to mate, ready to rest, to groom and be groomed, she is a force unto herself. The beautiful wild creatures were like children to Ninhursag; she was said to have wept and lamented if any came to harm.

Left: Ninhursag and her omega womb symbols, giving birth to humans underneath. Stone plaque, Sumeria, 2500 BCE. Right: The Egyptian birthing goddess Hathor's hairstyle takes the same shape. Faience, Egypt, 1000 BCE.
(Illustration © Stéphane Beaulieu modeled from Dee, *Chronicles of Ancient Egypt*, 55, and Black, Green, and Rickards, *Gods, Demons, and Symbols*, 132)

Ninhursag, in her aspect as *Ge* or *Gaia*, birthed all animal and plant life on the planet, guarding the wild spirit of the living Earth itself and the indigenous wisdom of the land. Like the cycles of nature, at times she could be ferocious. The Sumerian temple of Ninhursag featured an ornate wrought metal panel dating from 2500 BCE, spanning an impressive twenty feet across, of a fierce eagle with its talons resting on the backs of two stags—a powerful reminder of the spirit of the wild mother goddess.

Calling forth the underworld serpents and fierce soul birds, the priestesses channeled and embodied the *power of wildness* that formed the roots of the red-thread path passed on to the goddess Inanna, and later to the Magdalenes. Wildness is our human birthright, our innate and foundational nature that lies beneath any roles taken on within society. To the present day we still see the animal magic of bird and serpent symbols associated with the Virgin Mary, including doves and dragons, and the lions and unicorns of chivalric heraldry associated with Christ.

Daughters of the Moon

The Dragon Mother also gave birth to the moon god/dess. The role of the ancient priestess was to bring down the numinous spirit power from Otherworld, from the unseen dimensions, into this one—and to embody and transmit that power so its presence could be felt on this earth. One of our most ancient spirit connections is with Mother Moon, seen by the oldest races as the birther of the sun, the birther of the stars and planets, the governess of the night sky and the deep reaches of space. She was the Queen of the Heavens—the title given to Inanna, Ishtar, Astarte, Isis, Virgin Mary, and many other goddesses identified as daughters of the moon.

This tradition can still be seen today in the most ancient of witch rites: the "bringing down" of the moon—a magical ceremony performed with arms raised overhead, gazing up at the silver light of the moon, inviting her down into the body and into this world. A human figure with arms raised parallel overhead, reaching toward the heavens, was one of the first symbols of the shaman-priestess, carved onto cave walls since Paleolithic times. This became the *Ka* hieroglyph of ancient Egypt, symbolizing the energy body, also called the dragon body or body of light, that would be charged with spirit energy from the moon, sun, and stars.

All priestesses are moon priestesses—Magdalenes of the Moon—their secret powers of enchantment are sourced from the mysteries of the moon. Archaeologist Alexander Marschak documented that beginning tens of thousands of years ago, and likely much earlier than that, the shamankas and priestesses of the original moon religion marked the phases of the moon and menstrual cycle on menstrual wands. The twenty-nine-day cycle of the moon exactly matched the twenty-nine-day cycle of bleeding in women, and exactly matched the nine complete lunar cycles of human pregnancy. Moon *was* the mother of woman, and the governess of the menstrual cycle whose sacred moon blood allowed for the creation of new life.

The ancient Sumerian name for the moon god was *Nanna,* a feminine name meaning "grandmother" or "mother" to this day in many languages. It shares a close connection to the name of the Sumerian goddess *In-anna,* another clue that originally Nanna was a *female* moon goddess.

Crescent Moon, Horned Goddess

As time progressed, the moon goddess of ancient Mesopotamia became the moon god. Priestesses were considered *married to the moon*. It was the moon that governed their menstrual and sexual cycles, and their natural tides of spirit and emotion. The belly of the moon swelled each month to become "pregnant" at the full moon; mirroring the bellies of women that swelled into fullness when pregnant. Priestess and moon were linked in the most intimate communion, across the biological, psychic, spiritual realms.

Moon worship among the ancient Arabian, Eurasian, and North African peoples gave rise to the most enduring symbols of goddess and priestess—the crown of the crescent moon and the horns of the wild cow, bringer of divine milk. In Mesopotamia the rising crescent moon glows with a golden color and appears

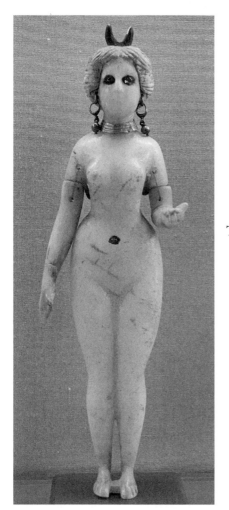

The goddess Ishtar/Astarte with crescent moon horns, gold jewelry, and rubies in her navel and eyes. Babylon, ca. third century BCE (Louvre).

nearly horizontal on the horizon, similar in shape to cow horns. The sacred cow has represented the Divine Mother in the ancient religions for many thousands of years—her nourishing milk gave the gift of life. Isis, Hathor, Inanna, and Ishtar all wore the womb symbol of crescent moon/cow horns on their heads, marking their divine status.

Dragon Mother, Serpent Priestesses

The dragons are the ancient mothers of the serpent goddesses, who are mistresses of the currents of earthly desires and passion. They are also *rebirthers,* symbolized by the shedding of their skins, and their miraculous "rebirth" from underground burrows each spring. Serpents live as easily in the underworld of the Earth Womb as on the surface of the earth—they hibernate in underground holes and caves of the earth. For this reason, the serpent goddesses and priestesses are known as mistresses of the underworld. Like snakes, the shaman-priestesses of the serpent are mesmerizing, undulating, captivating with their instinctive and chthonic energies. The innate, snakelike rhythms of the human body during sex and childbirth make these realms their natural domain. While the dragons often hold a cosmic and primordial magic, the serpents are the keepers of a more earthly sexual magic.

The Sumerian culture was born directly from the Ubaidian, Halaffan, and Samaran groups that lived in Mesopotamia from as early as 6000 BCE. They honored a Serpent Mother goddess, who, as time went on, transformed into the snake that guarded the Tree of Life in Near Eastern art and myth. Remarkable statues held in the Iraqi National Museum show her nursing a snake baby, who happily receives the primal, nourishing milk of the serpent mother (see photo on page 77). Snake worship continued for thousands of years across the Near East and was developed in particular in the gnostic Ophite cults of Persia, Iraq, and Turkey. In Persia, the serpent goddess was depicted as a snake woman called, *Shahmaran,* "Queen of the Serpents," where *mar* meant "serpent" but also "Mary" and "Mistress." So Shahmaran was also a "Queen Mary." The early church father Hippolytus wrote of gnostic Christian serpent sects dedicated to their leader "Mariamne"—likely a reference to Mary Magdalene.

The Samaran culture worshipped both the light and dark powers of the feminine, embracing paradox and natural cycles among humans, nature, and the divine. A fascinating motif on Samaran pottery shows a mandala of ecstatic dancing women, with flowing hair and omega, womb-shaped legs, imitating the pincers of the scorpions that surround them (see illustration). Scorpions are symbols of female sexuality,

Ubaidian serpent goddess suckling
child, Ur, Sumeria, ca. 4000 BCE.
(Iraqi National Museum, from Woolley,
Ur Excavations vol. IV, pl. 20)

Illustration of Samaran pottery
bowl patterns with dancing
shamans/goddesses and
scorpions, ca. 5500 BCE, Iraq.
Note similarity in shape of legs to
womb symbols on page 5.
(Modeled on Beatrice Laura Goff's
Symbols of Prehistoric Mesopotamia,
fig. 33)

represented by the potentially "deadly" sting whose medicine has the power to initiate, transform, and rebirth. It is no coincidence that the legs of these womb dancers are also remarkably similar to the M symbol of the Catholic Mary.

Song of the Serpents—
Prophecy of the Enchantress

Feminine prophecy was associated with the mystical hissing of snakes, including the "songs of the snakes in the spine"—the kundalini flow of primal energy "serpents" within the body, vibratory serpentine songlines that move and weave through the body and can give divination and oracles.

In Hebrew, *nakash* means both "snake" *and* the practice of magic, including divination, enchantment, whispering of incantations, and interpreting omens. "Hissing" or "whispering" referred to the mutterings of sorcerers in their incantations. The Hebrew word for serpent conveys cunning, subtlety, and the art of divination by serpents.

The language of the snakes may be the origin of the gnostic Christian "speaking in tongues," which in the early church was associated with women experiencing wild kundalini surges, perceived as the Christ-force of the Holy Spirit flowing through them in primal ecstasy.

Serpent-Dragon of the Womb

The divine serpent-dragon of Sumeria was also called *mush-sha-tur*, "the serpent-dragon of the birth-womb" (*mush*: serpent-dragon; *sha*: womb; *tu*[*r*]: birth). Mush-sha-tur traces back to the archaic past, like the other goddesses of the wild feminine. She is the symbol of the primordial dragon power of the womb and appears in art across the cultures of Mesopotamia. Mush-sha-tur is closely linked to Inanna, and to her lineage of priestesses. The Sumerian poet-princess Enheduanna, high priestess of the Moon, describes Inanna as "First Serpent-Dragon," the first *mush* serpent who comes out of the sacred mountain. Likewise, Inanna's grandmother Ninhursag, in her form as *Nin-tur*, "Mistress of Birth," is also conceived of as the *mush* serpent-dragon. Inanna was said to be the wife of the sky dragon *Ushum-galanna*, "Great Dragon of the Heavens." As heiress to the long line of dragon goddesses of the left-hand path, Inanna was imbued through and through with dragon symbology.

Mush-sha-tur is a guardian of the gateways, and specifically Inanna's gateway of the womb. As we will learn later, Inanna was one of the first recorded gatewalkers, the goddess and spirit guide who crossed the thresholds of the Seven Gates of the Underworld Womb that, at an esoteric initiatory level, mirrored in the seven gates within the female human yoni-womb, and the seven gates or "demons" of Mary Magdalene's own initiatory journey.

Now, let us open the gate to meet Lady Inanna.

CHAMBER 4

DIVINE WHORE

Inanna, Mistress of the Vulva

*And the woman was arrayed in purple and scarlet color, and decked
with gold and precious stones and pearls, having a golden cup in her
hand. . . . And upon her forehead was a name written, Mystery,
Babylon the Great, the Mother of Harlots.*

REVELATION 17:4

Perfectly shaped fresh fruit
Dazzling in your irresistible ripeness
Descending from the heart-womb of heaven

ENHEDUANNA, MOON PRIESTESS OF
SUMERIA, DESCRIBING INANNA[1]

INTO THE PICTURE STROLLS INANNA, "Mistress of the Vulva," with
her retinue of harlot-hairdressers, brassy as anything, swinging incense alongside the
enticing, spiraling movements of her full hips, ready to inherit and minister to the
legacy of her dragon grandmothers, and to re-enchant the world. She is the famed
and defamed Scarlet Lady, bearer of the Holy Grail. To know MM the woman, we
must understand the lost Scarlet Herstory of the left-hand path, with its honey sweet,
Christ-making nectar of dazzling and delicious darkness. When we part the veils,
when we reach into the chalice of time and memory, and peer back to the moment

of inception of the red priestess path, we find an unstoppable and irresistible force at its heart-womb epicenter. That force is none other than the eternal grand dame of Sumeria, the original Scarlet Woman—Inanna—Harlot Queen of the Heavens, Queen of Earth, Mistress of the Underworld, Lady of the Vulva.

From the outset, we know that Mary Magdalene is the star of this story, and rightfully so. She is the woman whose bright light has called us all together—the very human woman who, like all of us, had her share of imperfections, challenges, wounds, and disappointments, but who, despite the obstacles, somehow managed to call down the forces of the universe to do something unprecedented. Through the soft power of her passion and love, Magdalene merged the lines of Isis, Ishtar, Asherah, and the primordial Dragon Mothers to become a Feminine Christ. She embodied the template of the New Eve, the Sophianic flowering of consciousness and human potential inherent in woman. She blazed a trail that we still follow. We sense this intuitively, we know this in our hearts.

But what we are remembering now is that it did not begin with her.

When we invited Magdalene to share her lineage, she peeled back the curtain to reveal a goddess who was a veritable force of nature, whose *hi-li-an-ki,* "sexiness that spans the heavens and earth," was embodied in the form of the Sumerian Inanna and, later on, the Babylonian Ishtar. Inanna-Ishtar is named personally in Revelation as the "Great Whore of Babylon," the "Mother of the Harlots." She sits in the prime spot of the Bible, lavished with praise and power, carrying the mana of her entire tradition with her, even as she is denounced.

For four thousand years Inanna was the heart and soul of the Mesopotamian world. Her *melammu* "divine aura and radiance" outshined the sun. If Mary Magdalene is the leading lady of this story, it is Inanna who delivers the surprise performance, whose starlight illuminates the twilight world of the stage where all dream impulses and imagination arise.

The Holy Hor

In archaic times before written history In-anna was known as Nin-anna. *In* is a contraction of the goddess title *Nin,* meaning "lady, queen, mistress, woman." *Anna* means both "heavens" and "date fruit," and also holds the root *na,* which means "storehouse" or "womb chamber." The archaic Sumerian pictogram for *Nin,* circa 3400 BCE, is the female pubic triangle seated on a throne or altar (see illustration on page 61). The woman with her yoni-womb is queen and goddess, divinized on the altar. We will see these same themes throughout the ancient religious iconography, later adopted covertly in Jewish and Christian symbolism, and then resurrected nearly five thousand years later by the Renaissance painter Jan van Eyck in his masterful *Ghent Altarpiece.*

In a similar vein, one of the epithets of Inanna was *Nin-e-galla,* translated as "Queen of the Palace," but literally meaning "Queen of the Temple of the Vulva," *e* being "house or temple" and *galla* meaning "female genitalia," as well as "great."

HIGH PRIESTESS, HOLY WORD
This song is holy
Let me tell you where
I am coming from
My vulva is
The power place
A royal sign

+ + +

I rule with vulva power
I see with vulva eyes
This is where
I am coming from

Fit me out
With my vulva
I live right there
In this soft slit
I live right there

My field wants hoeing
This is my holy word

SUMERIAN SACRED MARRIAGE TEXT,
CA. 2500 BCE[2]

Inanna/Ishtar rests a bared leg on her sacred lion, while giving the viewer a penetrating
stare, her weapons tucked across her back. She wears the horned tiara of divinity.
A worshipper comes to her, making the hand gestures of prayer.
Illustration of an Akkadian cylinder seal, ca. 2400 BCE.

(Illustration © Stéphane Beaulieu, original in Oriental Institute, University of Chicago)

Inanna is the Holy Hor. She is power holder and initiatrix. She is dynamic, active, solar, radiant, shining, undaunted, determined, intelligent, expressive, bold, brash, seductive, sovereign, cunning, and sexually assertive. She is enormously strong willed, and actively pursues what she wants, including her own sensuality and sexual pleasure. Inanna gets her way. And enjoys it.

Goddess of Love
Red Magic of the Holy Whores

I, the lady,
In this house of holy lapis,
I say a holy prayer.
I am the Queen of Heaven.
I give him my vulva song.

INANNA, MESOPOTAMIAN SACRED
MARRIAGE TEXT, 2500 BCE[3]

Inanna was sex on fire. She was the cosmic love goddess whose magical vulva and audacious lust was placed on the highest altar of the Sumerian religion. Like her high priestesses, she was *nu-gig,* "Holy Woman," "Sacred Woman," "Taboo Woman." Inanna was the womb-dark, star-light goddess who, according to scholars, "spanned the tree of life from trunk to crown," bodily staking her claim in the Lowerworld, Middleworld, and Upperworld like no other deity before her. She imprinted a V-shaped stamp of vulvic authority everywhere she placed the Holy See of her world-birthing nethermouth. Inanna's sexuality was sacred, irresistible, exciting. As the scholar Betty De Shong Meador relates, Inanna was "a goddess of great cosmic powers" as well as "unbridled sexuality audaciously pursuing the object of her desire."[4]

Goddess Inanna was bold, sassy, wily, and brimming with sexiness, instinctual ingenuity, and cunt wisdom. Her *sha,* her heart-womb, glowed red with passions of her cosmic desire, her greatest superpower. Sumerians said that Inanna was "of the left." She was mistress of the left-hand path, the natural and instinctive domain of the feminine shaman from time immemorial. Beginning in 2350 BCE, with the arrival of the Semitic king, Sargon the Great, the Sumerian people gradually began to refer to Inanna by her Semitic name of Ishtar. However, even with the gradual change of name and change of governance, the cult of devotion to

Detail of Ishtar/Inanna vase displaying her womb wisdom, shamanic wings,
and horned tiara of divinity, Sumeria, 1800 BCE.

(Louvre, photo by Marie-Lan Nguyen, CC-BY 2.5)

Inanna/Ishtar as both love goddess and celestial queen remained steady.

Also known by the names Astarte and Ashtoreth, she flowed her powers
into many future generation of goddesses, including Artemis, Aphrodite, Venus,
Kybele, Kore, Tanit, and others. Inanna was one of the most important guardians

Naked Ishtar figurines, with the goddess presenting her nourishing breasts.
In both she is adorned with bracelets, necklaces, and chains that cross above and
below her breasts. An anchor-shaped womb pendant hangs down to her pubic
prominence, emphasizing her vulvic radiance. Susa, Iran, ca. 1300 BCE.
(Left: Louvre, photo by Rama, CC BY-SA 2.0 FR)

of the sacred red thread, passing on many of her gifts to the Rose-Red lineage of
Mary Magdalene.

In a time of consolidation of patriarchal power, between 3500 BCE and
1500 BCE, and when most of the other goddesses were diminishing, Inanna's
power continued to grow stronger, thanks to devotees such as High Priestess
Enheduanna and her father King Sargon. She wrestled new powers and prerogatives from *Enlil,* chief of the male pantheon, as well as the sky god, *An.* Inanna
took the world of ancient Mesopotamia by storm.

In 2350 BCE in the city of Lagash, Sumeria, Inanna even inspired a social revolution named *Ama-gi*—a Sumerian word meaning "return to the mother." This
movement attempted to limit the powers of the priesthood who had been stealing
land from ordinary people, and campaigned for a return to equality and freedom.

In Lagash, a name that meant "raven," a king called Urukagina led a feminist religious revolt—and established the Royal Household of Women, a cooperative "women's institute," consisting of 1,500 priestesses who served the goddess Inanna. This priestesshood was centered on feminine leadership and stewardship over the land. A symbol of the city was the Sacred Chalice, with twinned serpents: the Holy Grail.

Originally, women naturally presided over the rites of womb wisdom and the waters of birth. Then a theft occurred. As we have heard, the Sumerian god Enki holds the dubious distinction of being the first god in written history to steal the Holy Grail, taking the divine rights of birth and creation from the womb priestesses, to keep for himself.

After this grand larceny, the Sumerian Enki, later called Ea in Babylonia, became known as the god of water, magic, wisdom, and cunning—he became the "Divine Sophia." The cult of Enki stole the goddess symbols, traditions, powers, temples, home city, and even her spiritual throne in the underground lake of the Abzu; the Earth Womb.

After the male gods took power, the Sumerian word for "water," *a* or *ab*—which had meant "womb waters"—came to mean "semen" in the great myths. In

An elemental goddess of lightning, an aspect of Inanna/Ishtar, stands on the back of a griffin. A priest pours libations to her as an offering. Illustration of an Akkadian cylinder seal, ca. 2200 BCE.

(Illustration © Stéphane Beaulieu, original in Pierpont Morgan Library, N.Y.)

the early days, the all-important Tigris and Euphrates rivers were said to be filled with the waters of life from the female water goddesses. In later Sumerian mythology, it became Enki's fertilizing semen that filled the great riverbeds. Everywhere one looked, the Holy Womb birth waters of the feminine were replaced with Enki's holy semen.

Inanna Reclaims Womb Power

Outraged at this indignity, Inanna decided to do something about it, a tale told in her most famous myth, which "went viral" in ancient Mesopotamia for more than a thousand years. It sets the stage for the Holy Whores and Harlots of all ages who navigate the labyrinth world with wit and wisdom. The story, originally written in Sumerian cuneiform, was discovered in the shards of numerous broken clay tablets that were carefully pieced together by archaeologists to fully restore the original myth. The first written version dates from 2500 BCE, passed down from an older oral tradition that explained how the goddess Inanna, and her lineage, had not given in easily to patriarchy and had fought cleverly to gain her powers back.

Here is our modernized telling of the tale.

The Myth of Inanna and Enki

One day the audacious goddess Inanna decided that she would reclaim Enki's stolen powers back for the feminine.

She boldly invited herself to his home unannounced, as was her style, and Enki, instantly smitten, threw a grand dinner party in her honor. Cunningly, Inanna encouraged him to drink chalice after chalice of fine beer and wine. She flattered and praised him, and being the goddess of sexual desire, she then "charmed his pants off," so to speak.

After Enki was plenty drunk, with a bat of her eyelashes, Inanna innocently asked him if he would be so kind as to give her all his powers. At that moment, his head spinning from wine and fully mesmerized by the radiant goddess, he couldn't think of any good reasons why not, so he simply gave her all of his divine prerogatives and powers.

"Thank you very much," she said, as she quickly stuffed all of his divine powers inside her ample "Boat of Heaven"—a metaphor for her voluptuous, plentiful, and abundant yoni—and quickly sailed off down the canal toward her home city of Uruk.

Returning, with her Womb power restored, she thought: "That was easy. He's not very clever for a god of cunning and magic. No wonder he had to steal his powers!"

The next morning Enki woke up and found all his divine powers missing. "What happened?" he shouted at his manservant, to which the servant responded, "Lord, you gave them all away to Inanna last night." Furious, he summoned a host of demons from the underworld to chase her down before she made it back home.

The faithful servant of Inanna, Ninshubur, was a goddess herself, and a powerful warrior. Demon after demon tried to take the powers, but Ninshubur calmly showed each of them the door. Triumphant, Inanna victoriously paraded into her home temple of Uruk, having reclaimed for the feminine the powers of the sacred waters, cunning, magic, and wisdom. The Sacred Vessel was now safely in her hands.

Crown of Womanhood

Authors and scholars Diane Wolkstein and Samuel Kramer share their translation of the events that come directly before this ancient myth of Inanna and Enki, giving us more insight into Inanna's bold and sassy personality. It begins with a scene of "Inanna delighting in her womanhood and wishing to test its powers."[5] Said more directly, Inanna gets pumped up for the big trip by first audaciously crowning herself as queen, next having a sexual encounter (with the shepherd Dumuzi) in the apple orchard, and finally unabashedly admiring her magnificent vulva until she is so overflowing with the "power of the pudenda" that she is ready to set sail for Enki's domain.

> Inanna placed the *shugurra,* the crown of the steppe, on her head.
> She went to the sheepfold, to the shepherd.
> When she leaned against the apple tree, her vulva was wondrous to behold.
> Rejoicing at her wondrous vulva, the young woman Inanna applauded herself.[6]

Confident, and full of sass, she then set off directly to the house of Enki where she would reclaim his *me,* or divine powers, for the feminine.* Wolkstein and Kramer explain how the myth is richly laden with womb and sexual symbolism: "In Sumerian, the word for sheepfold, womb, vulva, loins, and lap are the same. The images presented in the first few lines—shepherd, sheepfold, apple tree, young

---

*This story mentions the apple tree that helped inspire Eve's gnosis in the Garden of Eden, but the Genesis myth reverses the original Sumerian stories that affirm female sexual power.

woman, and vulva—are all related to fertility [and sexuality]. . . . Inanna has received her throne and crown."[7]

This story may also encode the Sumerian version of the sacred rite of the Yoni-Puja, as performed in the tantric tradition of India, in which the worshippers gaze at the naked yoni of the priestess, as representative of the goddess herself, in order to be initiated into feminine Wisdom. This practice is also mirrored in the vulva-display rites of the Greek goddess Baubo, as well as in the Sheela-Na-Gig, the twin-tailed mermaid, and in other ancient priestess figures from across the world: "Inanna lauds her genitals in a highly poetic style; indeed Inanna's vulva was 'holy,' rather like the Baubo."[8]

These tales encoded a double meaning (similar to the story of Eve tasting the apple from the Tree of Knowledge), where the feminine not only reclaims her womb power but by doing so also formally initiates the masculine and rebirths him into wisdom.

In the Sumerian world that was already deeply entrenched in a culture of

patriarchy, and with an increasingly male-centered religion as early as the fourth millennium BCE, Inanna was a bold and brassy feminist revolutionist. She determinedly seized back the divine prerogatives from the male gods, chasing them across the known universe, pulling them down from the heavens, heaving them up from the underworld, and love-coaxing them into surrender from the charisma of her own *sha,* her heart-womb-insides.

Sacred Sexuality
Lady of Pleasure

Bring my vulva to shore,*
My star-sketched horn of the dipper,
Moor my slender boat of heaven,
My new moon crescent cunt beauty

INANNA, SUMERIAN SACRED MARRIAGE TEXT[9]

Inanna's love and sexuality formed the basis of the religious institutions of classical Sumer. She and her priestesses lived and practiced an embodied sensuous spirituality, where sex was not taboo but was enthroned as the foundational impulse of creation, central to all life. To adore the Goddess of Holy Desire, along with her life-giving vulva, was to invite in the blessings of the heavens. Inanna presided over the two most important religious rites of the ancient Near East—the springtime celebration of her sacred marriage to Dumuzi, later referred to in Greece as the hieros gamos, as well as the autumn festival of the death and resurrection mysteries that she midwifed, the "cult of the dying god." Her ceremonies would later evolve into a vast network of mystery schools and ritual mythic dramas, including the story of Jesus's death on the Womb Cross, and his resurrection through the feminine power, mirroring Inanna's mystical descent into the Underworld.

For the birth mother goddesses of old, sex was primarily celebrated in its natural connection to fertility. Like them, Inanna's sexuality, as chief goddess of the annual sacred marriage rites, brought fertility to the people and land. But Inanna was not primarily known as a mother goddess or birther. Her sexual expression was *independent of procreation*—it was most often for pleasure and ecstasy in its own

---

*The first line has been reinterpreted as "bring my vulva to shore" rather than "peg my vulva," to help illustrate the spirit of the metaphor.

Lovers in the sacred marriage bed, performing the hieros gamos
of Inanna and Dumuzi. Susa, Iran. Terracotta, 2nd mill. BCE.
(Louvre, courtesy of Erich Lessing / Art Resource, N.Y.)

right, as it was for her priestesses and all women in Sumeria while she reigned. This was poetically referred to as the "sweetening of the lap." Mesopotamian scholar Gwendolyn Leick writes: "It is Inanna's and, through her, all women's prerogative to demand 'the sweetening of the lap.'"[10] Inanna's full-spectrum sexuality included a Red River, Dark Moon menstrual expression, biologically linked to the peak in sexual desire that happens perimenstrually in women, a time where conception is unlikely. As the other red goddesses across time and tradition knew—including Lilith, Kali, Kurukulla, Sekhmet, and many others—there is a mystical purpose for Red River sexuality beyond procreation. *It is a gateway of spiritual initiation.*

Kings and male consorts made sure they were up to the challenge of pleasing Inanna. If not, they would suffer the consequences. In one Sumerian myth, Inanna sizes up the handsome "gardener" Ishulanu and extends an invitation: "[Ishulanu], let us enjoy your strength, put out your hand and touch my vulva!"[11]

When the not-so-clever young man fails to grant the goddess sexual fulfill-ment, Inanna hits him and turns him into a toad! This was a tongue-in-cheek allegory for the importance of properly tending the perfumed garden of female sexuality, "touching the *dubdub* bird in its hole," as was sometimes said, a refer-ence to the clitoris. This Sumerian tradition continued across time and culture, reflected nearly two thousand years later in the biblical Song of Songs, the love poetry of King Solomon and his beloved Queen of Sheba, a leader and priestess of Ethiopia, who was also connected to Mary Magdalene worship. Female pleasure was a central religious ideal in the eye of the goddess, and for good reason.

In the age of Inanna, erotic activation was the divine spark that infused joy, fueled creativity, and catalyzed cultural evolution. Inanna's sexuality, like that of her priestesses, was sacred, transformational, initiatory. When the female body of arousal is tended like a garden, the winged gate of the Womb opens, and Red Magic blessings flow forth into the world. Women become womb-awakened; their root halo blooms and feminine crown ignites. Their consorts become kings and avatars. The wasteland is restored and life renewed. Inanna's allure and holy desire was redemptive, it was the fiery red lifeblood of the cosmos, the force that moti-vates all action in the universe. Enheduanna writes of her beloved goddess and mistress, "Allure and ardent desire . . . are yours Inanna."[12]

Like Mary Magdalene, Inanna was the anointrix, whose chalice of sexual embrace granted kingship. The idea of the sovereignty-granting power of female sexuality

Goddess Inanna/Ishtar on top of her lover, in sacred sexual rites.
Cylinder seal, Sumeria, 2000 BCE.
(Adaptation of De Sarzec, *Découvertes en Chaldée,* vol. 2, pl. 30)

was shared by many ancient cultures, as seen, for example, in the Celtic *dergflaith,* or Red "Ale" of Sovereignty. It was only through union with queen/goddess/high priestess that a man could be made a king. Sumerian lyric poetry shares infinite varieties of sexual-religious metaphor in the context of sacred sexuality: Inanna makes the "cedar bough rise in the lap of the king," an image of erection. We are told her "temple," or vulva, is "built for the bull," her bridegroom, the young Prince Dumuzi. Dumuzi is the wild bull of heaven, but Inanna is the celestial cow-girl and bull rider—like Lilith and Kali, Inanna rides on top, a signature of the ancient sexually empowered priestesses and shamans.

Keys of Priestess Inanna/Ishtar

Elemental Powers	Romantic and Courtly Love,
Heavens/Underworld	Bride
The Venus Star	Red River—Dynamic, Active,
Budding flower, fragrance	Sexuality Transformation
Queenship, Sovereignty	Talismanic Adornment
Granter of Kingship	Path of Beauty
Rites of Sacred Marriage	Holy Desire

In the erotic artwork of the Near East, Inanna, Ishtar, and the related figures of Lilith and Jezebel are the only female characters depicted with full frontal gaze, an indication of their sexual forwardness that is sometimes described as a "come hither look" of sexual invitation, or challenge. Similarly, Inanna and Ishtar are also depicted in the "woman on top" position during lovemaking, and symbolized as riding on the "back" of wild bulls and lions, for their own pleasure. Inanna, Ishtar, and their priestesses were wild, orgasmic, and free in their erotic expression, over-flowing with ecstasy and an instinctive sexuality sourced from their holy body of desire. When Inanna is enflamed by passion, the man basks in her flow, receiving the eucharist of her sacred sexual anointing.

The Sumerian King Shulgi of Ur, who reigned around 2000 BCE, sings to Inanna in his royal hymns and poetry, calling her "My Consort, Maiden Inanna, Lady, Voluptuousness of Heaven and Earth."[13] The king is referred to as "Husband, the ornament of the holy loins of Inanna."[14] A scholar comments that this royal hymn illustrates "Inanna's function as goddess of love on a cosmic scale. [It] neatly contains the tenets of the king's 'marriage' to Inanna: she chooses the 'husband,' continues her independence and has the greater divine status."[15]

Assyriologist Gwendolyn Leick writes that, in the love poems of Inanna, "eroticism is elevated to an art form, a divine mode of behavior."[16] At times, her sexuality was connected to deep personal and romantic love, when she merges into union with her beloved Dumuzi. At other times, she has different motivations. Mesopotamian lyric poetry shares that she feels free to "play the harlot" or express her sexuality in whatever way she sees fit. Inanna, and her priestesses, live free of sexual shame:

"My queen, you disguise yourself, you put on your neck the pearls of the harlot. From the tavern [brothel] you fetch men."[17]

Inanna replies:

"When I sit by the gate of a tavern. I am indeed a prostitute who makes love!"[18]

Inanna was the original Holy Hor, the "Great Whore," keenly aware that the source of her numinous power was her voluptuous vulva, her "gate of wonder" that birthed children, new realities, and spiritual awakening, along with the unquenchable fire of her Holy Desire. Yet she also knew what it meant to merge into love, the soft power of the heart that held all dimensions together. For her, womb and heart were inseparable, and in fact are both expressed by the same Sumerian word, *sha*. Even now, in hearing her stories, we just might be captured by her alluring moon-petal spell, and in doing so, like Inanna, give birth to new and wondrous realities, re-enchanting and seducing the world back to love.

In the ritual poetry of the Sumerian sacred marriage rites, Inanna sings:

My high priest is ready for the holy vulva.
My lord Dumuzi is ready for the holy vulva! . . .
Let the bed that sweetens the vulva be prepared! . . .
He put his hand in her hand, he put his hand to her heart,
Sweet is the sleep of hand-to-hand, sweeter the sleep of heart-to-heart.[19]

Inanna's Alabaster Jar

The tradition of the priestess's alabaster anointing jar, iconic symbol of Mary Magdalene and of the Holy Womb, is first seen in the poetry of Inanna, the Mistress of Anointing. In a love poem from the third millennium BCE, she sings as she prepares for her lover Dumuzi:

> I washed myself in the pure tub,
>
> I rubbed myself with soap in the *white stone vessel,*
>
> I pleased myself with the *fine oil from the stone jar,*
>
> I dressed in the gala robe, the robe of "queenship of heaven."
>
> This is why I shut myself in the house,
>
> I painted my eyes with eye-black [kohl*],
>
> Straightened my hair
>
> Took a golden ring on my finger
>
> Put small beads around my neck.[20]

In this poem, Inanna uses the unguents in the sacred alabaster jar to prepare her body for sexual union with her beloved Dumuzi. Filled with aromatic oils such as myrrh and frankincense, the alabastron was traditionally used by the priestess in religious rites, including ceremonies for birth, death, spiritual rebirth, inauguration into public office, sacred marriage, and other important passages. The jar is a metaphor for the female womb, and the perfumed unguents contained within for its magical, life-giving fluids.

In artwork of the Near East, Inanna is at times depicted holding her sacred jar or sacred vessel, containing the flowing waters of life, as Magdalene would later be pictured.

Sacred Sexuality

The Ceremony of Opening the Door

The central rite in Sumerian weddings was the Ceremony of Opening the Door. The body of the woman was envisioned as the holy temple and house, whose womb doorway must be opened by the bridegroom, through ritual acts of beauty, pleasure, joy, and love. The man journeyed to the bride's family home, demonstrating his willingness to leave his familiar terrain and "meet her in her house," reflecting older matrilocal traditions. Priests performed the final ceremony standing at the threshold of the doorway to her bedchamber. Immediately after the opening of the door, the couple went to the "bed of delights" to consummate their marriage.[21]

In another sacred marriage story, Inanna calls in the "date-fruit gatherer," a metaphor for her lover, to climb the trees and bring down the ripe "first fruit"

---

*Kohl, or eye-black, is an ancient black mineral pigment, used as a cosmetic, often as mascara, eye shadow, and eye liner.

for her wedding. The man makes a pile of dates, symbolizing the sweetness and nourishing nectars of her yoni-womb. They suddenly realize that this is no ordinary mound of dates—there are gems and jewelry hidden within! It is truly a "Mound of Venus," *mons Veneris* or *mons pubis* in Latin, as Inanna is the goddess of the planet Venus. These jewels of Inanna's womb are her "treasures of darkness," the talismanic sexual adornments she and her priestesses wear on the night of the sacred marriage. First they discover the precious lapis lazuli beads that will be strung as adornments across her buttocks, with more and more treasures emerging:

> On the surface of the heap he is gathering lapis lazuli for Inanna.
> He is finding the "buttock beads," he is putting them on her buttocks!
> Inanna is finding the head beads, is putting them on her head!
> She is finding the rough-cut clear [dazzling] blocks of lapis lazuli,
> is putting them around her neck!
> She is finding the narrow gold braid, is putting it in her hair![22]

The tale continues this way with gold hoop earrings, crescent moon earrings, "eye ornaments, nose ornaments, ornaments for the navel, a hip flask, ornaments of alabaster for her thighs, ornaments covering her vulva, and finally shoes for her feet."[23] Inanna puts on all of these ritual ornaments before Dumuzi arrives.

Accompanied by harp and lyre, temple singers incant the marriage hymns, describing the joy of the lovers as they meet:

> [Inanna,] the young lady stood waiting, Dumuzi pushed open the door,
> and like a moonbeam she came forth to him, out of the house.
> He looked at her, rejoiced in her, took her in his arms and kissed her.[24]

The Magnetic Muse

In an age where we are just beginning to reimagine the possibility of female priests, it is hard to comprehend the respect, honor, and adulation given to Inanna, Goddess and High Priestess of Sumeria, the Holy Harlot and *Nin-mug*, Lady of the Vulva. She was the immanent force of creation, the power that infuses all life, embodied in the form of woman. Kings, queens, priestesses, priests, prostitutes, poets, philosophers, lawmakers, sacred gender liminal temple workers, and people from all walks of life were madly devoted to her.

All forms of honest sexual pleasure were offerings of devotion to her; she welcomed and protected her transgender priestesshood; her vision of sacred sexuality was liberated, free, and pansexual. She honored all that was brimming with love and the vibrant spirit of life.

Inanna was a mother to Sumeria, but not the kind of mother forced through marriage into a life of domestic servitude, nor the meek, humble, sexually submissive wife held up as a cultural ideal for the last five thousand years. Rather, she was the Mother Muse, the Magnetic Mother, the Red Lady who mothered through her radiant, life-giving elixirs of "allure and ardent desire." She was the mythic force that drives the green flower, that blooms the shining lotus up from its muddy roots. Inanna was the source of Holy Desire that fuels all action, all transformation, all evolutionary process in the universe.

Babylonian poetry from the sixteenth century BCE sings praises of Inanna/Ishtar:

> She of joy, clothed with love,
> Adorned with seduction, grace, and sex-appeal . . .
> Honey-sweet are her lips, life is her mouth;
> Adorned in laughing femininity.
> She is magnificent, [the divine tiara] is put on her head,
> Her coloring is beautiful, her eyes are shining and bright.
> Wherever she looks, there is gaiety,
> Life, power, protection.
> The young women she calls, find a mother in [her].[25]

Inanna as Venus and Star-Flower

Inanna was worshipped from ancient days as the embodiment of Venus, a Queen of the Heavens and daughter of the Mother Moon. Inanna is she who precedes the sun in the eastern sky as the morning star, and she who guides the sun to sleep at night as the evening star. She ranks higher than the sun in the Sumerian celestial order. Writes the priestess-poet Enheduanna: "[Inanna] goes out white-sparked, radiant, in the dark vault of the evening sky, star-steps in the street, through the gate of wonder."[26]

The planet Venus is a bright and dynamic star that traces a pentagram pattern in the heavens over its eight-year path—making the numbers five and eight sacred to Inanna. In Sumeria, this became the eight-petaled Venus Star-Flower symbol of

Inanna, with flowing hair and horned tiara, holds a date cluster in
her right hand, symbolizing fertility. Lagash, Sumeria, 2430 BCE.
(Pergamon Museum, photo by Wolfgang Sauber, CC BY-SA 3.0)

Inanna (see page 100). The eight-petaled star or flower symbolizes death, rebirth,
and resurrection, as Venus appears to "descend into the Underworld," dipping
beneath the horizon of the western sky as the evening star, to reappear some
months later in the eastern sky as the morning star.

The earliest occurrence of the eight-leafed star of resurrection is from
28,000 BCE, found carved into an ivory disk at a child's burial site in Sungir,
Russia, from the Stone Age peoples of the late Aurignacian period (see
page 100).[27] Perhaps her loved ones planted the magical talisman to speed her
rebirth into Spirit world, or her reincarnation back on earth. The star-flower's
association with rebirth continued at the famous Mystery School of Eleusis,

Left: The eight-pointed star of Inanna/Ishtar, as the goddess of Venus,
from a Babylonian *kudurru* stone, ca. 1180 BCE.
Right: The earliest known eight-petaled rosette talisman, carved in ivory,
from a child's grave in Sungir, Russia, ca. 28,000 BCE.
(Right: Courtesy of Randall White, "The Earliest Images: Ice Age 'Art' in Europe," fig. 3)

where the eight-petaled rosette was found carved into stone reliefs at the temple. The primary ritual of the Eleusinian Mysteries was an annual drama that featured a descent into the Earth Womb, and rebirth through the goddess, attended by many thousands.

In Sumeria, priestesses and priests gave offerings to Inanna in her morning star aspect under the name of *Inanna-sig,* and to her evening star aspect under the name *Inanna-hud.* She was worshipped in her underworld and earth-mountain aspect as *Inanna-hur,* and in her queenly form as *Inanna-nun.* Venus, thus Inanna, was considered the second most important body in the sky, born from Mother Moon, who came first.

The Red Priestesses of Antiquity

The Red Priestess who symbolizes erotic divinity and sexual initiatory power is not just a metaphor; the high priestesses across many cultures of the ancient world very literally wore sacred red robes. This tradition is the origin of the red robe of Magdalene, and it was later adopted by the Catholic bishops and popes, as well as Buddhist lamas, as patriarchal religions appropriated the Red Magic from the feminine priestesses.

Sumerian scholar Betty De Shong Meador describes the weeklong ordination ceremony of a Sumerian high priestess in her book *Inanna, Lady of Largest Heart:*

In the inauguration the high priestess is chosen by divination. . . . After her selection, the chosen priestess was anointed in the temple. Then on succeeding days her hair was ritually combed, her red garment consecrated. . . . In the evening she sat on the throne and received presents: special earrings, bracelets, a red turban, a breastplate. . . . A special coverlet was spread over her bed. While the singers chanted, the sister of the high priestess bathed her feet. The chosen priestess then lay down on the bed.[28]

The high priestesses of Sumeria dressed in flounced red or white robes for public ritual, and performed the most sacred ceremonies in the darkened inner temple adyta in a state of ritual nudity. They wore their long hair in thick braids falling down their back and the sides of their face, held back by the distinctive diadem-hairband, richly ornamented in lapis, carnelian, and gold leaves. Priestesses wore talismanic crescent moon earrings, dragon bracelets, pendants, bead necklaces, and other jewelry of gold, silver, and cut semiprecious stones. Under their clothing they wore "red undergarments or none at all."[29] They poured the holy libations from sacred vessels and used palm fronds to sprinkle holy water on objects and people that needed purification.

In order to understand the priestesses of the ancient Near East, the lineage of the Magdalene, we must see and feel the world as they did, to know the desire of their *sha*—their heart-womb—and to make a bridge to the spirit power they served. The *mantissas,* the chief oracles and priestesses of antiquity who embodied the glowing *mana* of feminine spirit power, did not worry about cultivating "righteous" behavior, or being "good enough" for their goddesses and gods. Theirs was a religion of passion and beauteousness, not righteousness.

Instead their role was to *become* the goddess Inanna—and like her to *become* dragon, mermaid, serpent, spirit bird, lioness—through the enactment of magical rites. Their own bodies, their own energy fields, their own sexual essence became the sacred vessel that poured forth the palpable and tangible presence of the living goddess into the world. In this way they served their communities, forming the bridge between heaven, human, and earth, weaving the womb worlds of Sophia back together, into a whole, luminous reality.

Because Inanna *was* sexiness, her priestesses would come to know their beloved goddess by opening the magic of their own *hi-li* sex appeal. Representing Inanna in the sacred marriage rites, their bodies became divine, bringing fertility and renewal to the whole community through their love. Just as Inanna was forward, bold, brimming with desire and audacity, her priestesses would ritually invoke her presence by igniting these same qualities within themselves. Because Inanna was the light and wisdom of the Venus star, they brought more power and glory to her name by transmitting the shimmering starlight of Venus themselves. If Inanna was the magical gateway, whose storehouse held the jewel treasures of ripe dates and pomegranates, they too would make themselves juicy as the ripe fruit. The high priestess was the earthly *embodiment* of the goddess.

The temples of Sumeria were filled with many different levels of priestesses and priests, each with their own special rites and duties. Some expressed their devotion by singing praises to Inanna's "magnificent vulva," or reciting poetry of her "wet fields" that needed "plowing." Or they might incant lamentations of her sorrows at the loss her beloved Dumuzi each autumn, tearing their clothes and beating their breasts as they empathically shared her pain. Temple workers honored her sacred symbols of gateway and flower by pouring libations of fragrant oils, milk, and date nectar as love offerings from their hearts. In cultic ceremonies priestesses and priests would dress themselves as Inanna might, "to the nines," a number of feminine perfection, with full ceremonial costume, rouged lips, blue and black eye makeup, flounced dresses, jewelry and earrings, regardless of gender.

Theirs was a magical world. Inanna, and the goddesses Nammu, Ninhursag, Nintu, and many others, *gave the priestesses permission* to express their spirituality through the time-honored and instinctive feminine womb rites.

Vulva Oath

Sex Magic of Sacred Union

For the Grail Womb to awaken and open into the regenerative and redemptive powers of the Magdalene Mysteries, the priestess as divine woman, and embodiment of the divine Womb of the Goddess, has to be fully honored.

In this sacred womb ritual, written in 2000 BCE, the priestess asks her beloved to swear an oath to honor and be faithful to her vulva. This ritual oath, recorded by Sumerian Holy Whores and Harlots, first establishes a field of respect, adoration, and courtship for the Divine Feminine before sexual union.

As the woman stands as strong as the temple, the beloved places one hand respectfully on her sacred vulva, while placing his other hand on her head. With this sacred gesture, he is acknowledging her queendom—crowned by the Cosmic Womb, and enthroned by the Earth Womb, her body the entire divine realm.

She speaks:

> *You, prince, my brother of fairest face,*
>
> *Brother, swear to me that, when you dwelt in the out-lying town,*
>
> *Swear to me that a stranger did not touch (you) by the hand.*
>
> *Swear to me that a stranger did not approach (you) by mouth.*
>
> *My one who lifts the thin gown off my vulva for me,*
>
> *My beloved, man of my choice,*
>
> *For you, let me prepare what belongs to the oath for you:*
>
> *May you put your right hand in my vulva,*
>
> *With your left stretched towards my head,*
>
> *When you have neared your mouth to my mouth,*
>
> *When you have taken my lips into your mouth,*
>
> *Thus you swear the oath to me,*
>
> *So it is, dragon of women, my brother of fairest face!*
>
> *My blossom-bearer, my blossom-bearer, your charms are sweet!*

TEXT FROM THE RUINS OF A SUMERIAN TEMPLE, CA. 2000 BCE[30]

Soulmate Template

Lover's Garden of Eden

Sumerian love poetry, written more than four thousand years ago, is the world's first recorded example of romantic and courtly love. But, in contrast to the ideals of chastity in the later European Courts of Love, the Sumerians preferred to consummate their love on all levels. Romantic expressions such as "to press one's neck close to another, to put one's hand in another's, to go to the garden, and to embrace were all Sumerian expressions for making love."[31]

In her role as Divine Lover, Inanna was often known as the Queen of the Date Clusters. Dried date fruits were considered the nourishing and life-sustaining body of Inanna. Dates, like grain, would store well, allowing people to survive the harsh, dry fallow seasons of the ancient Near East. The *na,* or storehouse, was a quiet, darkened room that held the "jewel heap" of dates. This dark, fecund, life-giving chamber at the center of each family compound was equated with the womb of woman. It was considered sacred from time immemorial, and eventually evolved into the adytum, the holy of holies womb chamber at the center of each temple, filled with the presence of the goddesses and gods.

Date tree cultivation was rich with sexual allusion. Trees are either male or female. The flowers of male trees yield the pollen, but only female trees bear fruit. For best yields, the fragrant female flowers needed to be hand pollinated by daubing the male flower, with its musky, aromatic pollen, into each of the females. With careful tending of the orchard, the female Tree of Life would bear fruit. Without that love, care, and attention, the orchard would be far less bountiful. "Going to the garden" was a ubiquitous sexual metaphor across the ancient Near East, and a "gardener" was a name for a lover. It was no mistake that Mary Magdalene called the glowing, radiant, resurrected Jesus the "gardener." Jesus was *her* gardener. His love and attention allowed her to bloom into her fullest gifts.

The love expressed by Inanna and Dumuzi was also the first recorded story of soulmate love, later embodied by Yeshua and Magdalene, as well as by Solomon and the Queen of Sheba in the Song of Songs. This love was eucharistic, a deep act of spiritual communion, where each lover's "fruits," "milk," and "nectars" were consumed by the other in order for the two separate beings to merge into one. As boundaries between lovers gradually dissolved, they became everything to each other: mother/father, sister/brother, sexual consorts, and daughter/son. The intensity of this love was rivaled only by that experienced between mother and newborn child. In its highest expression, as was seen with Magdalene and Yeshua, soulmate love became a supercharged cauldron of spiritual transfiguration, a vehicle through which lovers could transcend inherited ancestral and cultural limitations, allowing for profound spiritual awakening, and the birthing of a "divine child" from their union. Soulmate union was their church; it was the portal.

In Sumerian poetry we read that Inanna "drinks Dumuzi's milk," as he drinks hers. They offer each other their "ripened fruit." Dumuzi sings, "Pour it out for me, Inanna, I will drink all you have to offer."[32] Inanna whispers back, "fill my [holy] lap with cream and milk" and "my honey-man, my honey-man sweetens me always, he is the one my womb loves best."[33]

Inanna and Dumuzi refer to each other as brother and sister. The goddess Ninshubur sings to Inanna, "the young man [Dumuzi] will be your mother, the young man will be your father." "Each in turn becomes parent and child, feeder and fed," in a magical-sexual-spiritual act of merging and union that heals any wounds of lack.[34]

This feminine mystical tradition was passed down in the oral teachings of Kabbalah and later written in the Judaic wisdom literature that first emerged in the sixth century BCE, as well as in gnostic Christian texts. In the patriarchal era, the deep spiritual power held in the vision of eucharistic soulmate love was considered the greatest threat to the established church. The wisdom was passed on secretly, in mystery schools and underground alchemical lineages, and encoded in works of art, such as Jan van Eyck's, *Ghent Altarpiece,* as we will soon see.

Gate of Inanna

Queen of the Underworld—Gatewalker of the Seven

Inanna is the first recorded *gatewalker,* the Mistress of the Seven Gates of the Underworld that she traverses in her journey of spiritual rebirth. Each gateway was sacred and required purification. At each gate she removed an item of worldly power, humbling herself in order to step across each threshold of knowledge and initiation, until she arrived naked like a newborn baby, a novice, at the center of the Earth Womb. As a gatewalker, Inanna famously descends into the Underworld to meet the queen of Hell, Ereshkigal. From this initiatory journey, traversing the quantum realms of death, she is reborn into wisdom.

The Gate of Inanna symbol was first found inscribed onto clay tablets dating from 3400 BCE, at the archaeological site of Uruk, Inanna's home city, now located in modern-day Iraq. Her gate symbol was among the earliest writing known to humanity, one of the archaic pictographs that would eventually develop into the famous Sumerian cuneiform.

The womb-gateway symbol was also known as the Gate of Horn, "the horned gate between day and night, life and death, human and divine," inherited from an ancestral line of gatekeepers and gatewalkers extending deep into prehistory.[35]

The two horns also represent female legs, the guardian pillars and gateway to the womb. In Sumeria, the twin pillars were a symbol of the entryway into Inanna's Holy Womb, and in Egypt, the sun disc was visualized as birthing from between the horns (legs) on the crown of Isis and Hathor (similar to the sun disk of Qedesha on page 116). The Holy Womb births both the sun and the divine child.

The twin posts of the gate marked sacred doorways, that, along with a woven veil or "hymen," represented the threshold between worlds—the entryway into sacred sanctuaries of home, storehouse, temple, and feminine yoni-womb, as well as the gateway to Spirit world. Inanna, and all women, were considered the numinous gateway between dimensions.

The design of Inanna's temple at Uruk revolved around the sacred number seven. Hers is the "house of seven fires, of seven desires." A similar plan is described in a related temple in the Sumerian city of Adab: "The temple was particularly noteworthy for its seven gates and seven doors, each of which had a special name," explained Samuel Noah Kramer, a leading expert in Sumerian culture.[36]

In Sumerian art Inanna's gate was guarded by the *mush* serpent-dragon, keeper of the womb threshold as well as the underworld womb. The gate was the entry-way into the Womb of the Goddess, and also the yoni-womb of human woman, and was intimately interwoven with the sacred mysteries of birth.

As a baby, every human born into this world must cross the veiled gate of the womb in their journey from spirit body into the material form, just as the dead also travel back through this spiritual hymenlike womb membrane into the land of the dead.

Likewise, when we take a spiritual journey of rebirth we must step naked across the vulvic gateway between the worlds, as Inanna modeled in her journey to the underworld—the Earth Womb.

Jesus and Mary Magdalene undertook a similar journey in the Christian res-urrection mysteries, birthed from these Sumerian origins. In the language of the Bible, Jesus was said to have removed seven devils from Magdalene—obstacles and obstructions in her seven sacred gateways of womb consciousness. Mary Magdalene in turn midwifed Jesus's three-day descent into the center of the earth, modeled after Inanna's three-day journey to the Underworld. Christian theologians call Jesus's descent the "Harrowing of Hell." The name *hell* originally referred to the Germanic name of the underworld goddess, Hel, and her earth-womb realm of *helheim*.

The tradition is mentioned twice in the Bible, in Ephesians 4:9, "[Jesus] also descended first into the lower parts of the earth," and in 1 Peter 4:6, where "the gospel . . . has been preached [by Jesus] even to those who are dead." Christian doctrine says Jesus took this journey on *Sabbatum Sanctum,* or Holy Saturday, also known as the Great Sabbath and Black Saturday. Ishtar's *sabbatu,* the origin of the Latin *Sabbatum,* was the sacred time of her menstrual flow. Jesus is renewed inside the tomb during the Black Sabbath.

The underworld journey, and its "sacred seven" symbolism, is also seen in Osiris's dismemberment into fourteen pieces, two sets of seven, and later resur-rection, midwifed by Isis. The fourteen segments of Osiris became the fourteen Stations of the Cross in Catholic doctrine, each a humbling gateway passed by Jesus on the way to his spiritual death and resurrection.

CHAMBER 5

GODDESSES OF GALILEE

Temple of Asherah, Wisdom of Lilith

The children gather wood, the fathers light the fire, and the women
knead the dough and make cakes of bread for the Queen of Heaven.

JEREMIAH 7:18

OUR JOURNEY NOW TAKES US TO THE Holy Lands of Canaan, and
in particular to its northern outpost of Galilee, where the public ministry of Mary
Magdalene and Jesus took place. The world has heard much of Yahweh, the God of
the Hebrew and Christian peoples, but few realize that the Israelite people of the
holy lands of Canaan originally worshipped the goddess, and that through much
of the first millennium BCE priestesses had a role in the Temple of Jerusalem,
which was adorned with sacred sexual symbols.

The indigenous people of biblical Palestine were the Canaanites, united
in their worship of an ancient pantheon of goddesses and gods for thousands
of years. They were matrilineal, marking their lines of descent from maternal
ancestors; and in ancient times female matriarchs held power along with men.
The Canaanites, like all the Semitic peoples, maintained a long tradition of
moon worship dating back thousands of years into Paleolithic times. Still to this
day, the Jewish religious calendar is based around the lunar cycles and is filled
with secret feminine magic.

The ancient mother goddess Asherah was known as the "Queen of the
Heavens" and the "Great Lady" of the Canaanite peoples who once lived in the

Queen of Heaven scarab stamp seals from Canaan/Phoenicia, ca. eighth century BCE. The left image shows Asherah/Astarte holding a Venus star in each hand, naked with celestial wings and crowned by divine horns. The right image shows a downward pointing triangle over her forehead and vulva, with palm branch and monkey on the right, worshipper on the left, and a winged solar disk above her head.
(Illustration © Stéphane Beaulieu, based on Keel and Uehlinger, *Gods, Goddesses, and Images of God in Ancient Israel*, 72, 75.)

lands that are now Israel, Lebanon, Syria, and Jordan. Asherah was the goddess of birth, fertility, and sexual love. As the birther of the gods, she bore the title "Mother of the *Elohim*." Asherah was the High and Holy Qedesha, the sexually empowered priestess, whose reign reached back into time immemorial.

The Sumerian and Babylonian love goddess Inanna/Ishtar migrated into the region by the first millennium BCE. She became known as *Ashtoreth* or *Athirat* in the western Semitic languages, and *Astarte* in Greek, and was worshipped alongside the native traditions of the Great Lady Asherah. The Hebrew priestesses were called the *qedesha,* meaning "sacred, set apart, holy, consecrated."* Through circle dance and magical incantation, through their enchanting music of harp and lyre,

*Asherah's priestesses were known as *qedesha* (singular), or *qedeshot* (a group of female priestesses), derived from the Akkadian *qadishtu*, an epithet of Ishtar.

and through offerings of incense and sacred libation, they ministered the sacred Tree of Life on high hilltops for thousands of years.

It was from Asherah's fertile womb that the Judaic religion would slowly birth, with great struggle over nearly a thousand years, to form the newest layer of the extraordinarily rich cultural tapestry that was the background of Mary Magdalene and Jesus's ministry.

Spirit Keepers of the Land

The lands of Palestine carry memories of the womb traditions from ancient times, when primal vulvic power was worshipped. As an important crossroads between Africa, Asia, and Europe, humans have continuously occupied the region for hundreds of thousands of years. Neanderthals were the first to permanently settle in the Middle East, arriving at the Tabun Cave near Mount Carmel at least 350,000 years ago.[1] This same area would one day be home to the Essenes, and the legends of the red-haired and hairy "first ones" or "wild people" that may well be an ancestral memory of the Neanderthals.

The first modern humans joined the Neanderthals in Israel beginning 55,000 years ago. It was here, in the Holy Lands, where the two groups first began interbreeding, passing forward the magical Neanderthal DNA in an act of love that still touches our lives today; 2–4 percent of the DNA in most humans comes from Neanderthals or similar archaic humans.[2] Intact skeletons of Neanderthals covered in the red "menstrual" ochre from 100,000 years ago, buried with shamanic deer horns in their hands, have been discovered in the Qafez cave near Nazareth.[3] Legends say that it was the Neanderthal blood that gifted magical and psychic abilities to the priestess lineages.

Moon Religion—Worship of Sin

Like the ancient Sumerians and Babylonians, the early Hebrew peoples also revered Sin, the moon god/dess, bringer of the sacred fruit of menstrual blood. "On each side of the river stood the tree of life, bearing twelve crops of fruit, yielding its fruit every month. And the leaves of the tree are for the healing of the nations" (Revelation 22:2). Wherever we see moon or Sin worship, it is a place of the left-hand path including most of the Near East in archaic times.

Local names still reflect the influence of the ancient moon peoples. Jericho and Lebanon both mean "moon" (from Hebrew *yearach, levanah*). The book of Exodus explains that Moses received *lunar horns* when he ascended the sacred moon mountain—*Mt. Sinai,* the Mount of Sin—which is why Michelangelo sculpted him with suspiciously pagan-appearing horns in the Basilica of San Pietro in Vincoli, in Rome.[4] Lunar horns also appeared on many Canaanite and Mediterranean deities, including Ba'al, Pan, Diana, Astarte, Artemis, Selene, and others.

The links continue: When Moses fled from Egypt, after crossing the Red Sea he led the Israelites to the "Wilderness of Sin," where they eventually set up an encampment at Qadesh—named for the priestesses and priests of Asherah and Ba'al, who worshipped the moon (as Asherah) and her sacred union with the sun (Ba'al). According to the Jewish historian Josephus, another name for Qadesh was *Rachem,* a root meaning "womb" in the Semitic languages.[5] The prophet Isaiah (Isaiah 3:18) writes that many Israelites wore *saharonim,* talismanic necklaces shaped like the crescent moon; a common custom of the Israelites was to kiss another's hand in adoration upon seeing the moon in the sky.[6]

Archaeologist and former professor of prehistory at Tel Aviv University Emmanuel Anati found thousands of engravings, including many with the crescent horns of Sin worship, on the mount of Har Karkom, one proposed location for the biblical Mt. Sinai. Further north, close to the Sea of Galilee, archaeologist Ido Wachtel of Hebrew University discovered a massive man-made rock monument shaped like a lunar crescent moon, nearly five hundred feet in length, close to the town of Beth Yerah, meaning "House of the Moon." Wachtel says, "The shape may have had symbolic importance, as the lunar crescent is a symbol of an ancient Mesopotamian moon god named Sin."[7]

In the Negev Desert of southern Israel, the likely location of the biblical Wilderness of Sin, archaeologists have recently discovered hundreds of megalithic standing stones, sacred pillars called *masseboth* in the Hebrew Bible, many arranged in crescent or circular formation, some with grooves suggestive of female genitalia.[8] The oldest date from 9,000 years ago, and they saw continued use through biblical times by the Israelite people.

The masseboth stones were anointed with oils, unguents, and sacred blood— they were the original altars mentioned in the book of Genesis as the holy *Beth-El* stones, the "Houses of God" thought to contain the presence of the deity, representing the oldest indigenous tribal traditions inherited by the Semitic peoples. Red-tent harems of priestesses, menstruating together with the dark moon and emerging crescent of the new moon, would have participated in the most sacred shamanic ceremonies, making moon-blood offerings to the sacred stones, their oracular visions and mystical powers flowing under the horned moon.

Asherah—The Heavenly Qedesha

Asherah was rare among female deities, as she united the archetypes of the Red River and White River—she was both maternal and magical, a mother and a sexual initiatrix, a creator and a nurturer. The lineages of the Egyptian Isis and Sumerian Inanna deeply influenced the ministry of Mary Magdalene, but it was likely the legacy of Asherah, native to the lands of Palestine and Syria, who was closest to Magdalene's heart. It was Asherah's queendom of heaven (*malkutha shamayim* in Aramaic) that Jesus and Magdalene referred to in their teachings as the shimmering queendom of love.

She was depicted on talismans displaying her magical feminine vulva power, much like the Sheela-Na-Gigs and sexual split-tailed Sirens of the later Christian traditions.

Asherah also wore the green mantle of the nature priestesses. She was Mistress of the Sacred Groves and the wild hilltop sanctuaries. There the Asherah trees

Molded clay figurine of Asherah, from the Jerusalem Museum, her body talismanically adorned, holding open her magnificent labia. Revadim, Israel, 1500–1150 BCE.
(Photo courtesy of Gary Todd; illustration © Stéphane Beaulieu, based on Keel and Uehlinger, *Gods, Goddesses, and Images of God in Ancient Israel,* 75, fig. 82)

were worshipped for thousands of years, casting a deep, soft, and enduring feminine light infused with the spirit of Gaia. She was the goddess of the sacred stones, including the megalithic stone temples that covered the hills and wildlands of Palestine. In the Golan Heights region, four hundred sacred stone dolmens, dating from 3700 to 2000 BCE, have been found in the Shamir Dolmen field alone.[9]

The Stonehenge of the Near East, at Rujm el-Hiri in the Golan Heights, is known as the "Wheel of Giants" (*Gilgal Refaim*), with five astonishing stone circles within circles, created from at least 40,000 tons of basalt stones, ringing a central space, and was built some 6,000 years ago.[10] Circles were created as sacred feminine spaces of transformation—nature temples of Asherah.

Figurine of the Canaanite goddess Asherah as mistress of the animals. She dances with bared breasts, adorned with jewelry and headcovering symbolizing her priesthood and divinity. The rock beneath her feet symbolizes the stones of her hilltop sanctuaries. Syria, 1300 BCE.

(Louvre, Claude Valette CC BY-ND 2.0 via Flickr)

Asherah—Mermaid of Galilee

Like Isis and Mother Mary, Asherah was also known as the Lady of the Seas—she was the mermaid of Galilee, the sacred sea that was considered to be her home. Her Syrian title of *Rabat 'Athirat Yammi* literally translates as the "Great Lady Who Strides on the Seas," the walker of the waters, the same miracle later attributed to Jesus, who walked on the waters of the Sea of Galilee following the news of John the Baptist's death. The Sea of Galilee is the setting of New Testament stories that establish Jesus as a fisher of men, and symbolic Fisher King. It is also the source of the River Jordan, whose baptismal waters initiated Jesus and Magdalene into their ministries.

Syrians referred to Asherah by many titles: *Athirat Ba'alit,* "wife of Ba'al," as well as the ancient goddess name *Elat,* which means simply "goddess," the feminine form of *El.* Variants of the name Elat are found throughout the ancient Near East and Europe: as the Arabic mother goddess *Allat,* whose primary shrine was the Kabaa in Mecca until the sixth century CE, as *Helen* or *Hellas* of the Greek peoples, and *Elen of the Ways* of the Celtic lands.

Priestesses of Asherah
The Holy Qedesha

She is the consecrated priestess, in the temple, spiritually receptive to the feminine power flowing through her from the Goddess, and at the same time joyously aware of the beauty and passion in her human body.

MARIAN WOODMAN

Like her spiritual sister Inanna in Sumeria, Asherah was known as the Qedesha (Akkadian, *Qadeshtu*), the sexual high priestess, and goddess of love. Hers was the domain of sexual pleasure and ecstasy. At times her identity was merged with her sister goddess *Ashtoreth,* the Hebrew name for Ishtar. Asherah and Ashtoreth, and their priestesses, are depicted in full frontal nudity on hundreds of figurines and plaques made of clay, gold, and bronze found throughout private homes and public spaces across the northern lands of Canaan and Israel, spanning many hundreds of years.

The mother goddess figurines of the Stone Age emphasize the physical features of fertility, pregnancy, and nursing—with large, exaggerated hips, buttocks, breasts, and belly. The figurines of Asherah/Ashtoreth are very different, displaying her sexual appeal and vulvic power in its own right. Her hair is beautifully styled, she wears necklaces, pendants, earrings, as well as bracelets on wrists and ankles. Her pubic triangle and vulva are emphasized. She is often depicted with snakes, lotus flowers, lions, and horned animals. Her breasts are small to moderate size, rather than the larger milk-bearing breasts of a nursing mother, symbolizing her role as maiden or sacred lover.

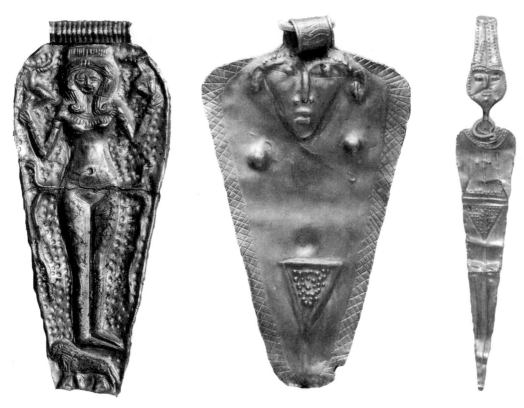

Gold pendants of the naked and adorned Asherah/Astarte from Syria, Lebanon, and Israel, dating from 1500–1200 BCE. In the image on the left she stands on a lion, with serpents twining around her pelvis, and holds horned gazelles, symbolizing wildness. In the center and at right we see her prominent vulva triangle.

The qedeshot ministered the rites of sacred marriage and sexual-fertility rituals. Israelite prophets describe how they adorned themselves before the religious and sexual ceremonies—styling their hair; wearing scarlet dresses, robes, and shawls; putting on gold rings, bracelets, necklaces; and applying eye makeup.[11]

Left: Canaanite "naked goddess," representing Asherah, Astarte, Qedesha, or Anat, with Hathor-style hair and prominent vulva. She holds the lotus flowers of fertility and sexuality. Right: Canaanite goddess Anat/Astarte holding lotuses of fertility, with plaited hair and crown. She stands on a warhorse, erotic and commanding. Modern reproduction of gold plaque from Lachish, 1200 BCE.

Carved wooden statue of a Qedesha, Canaanite high priestess or queen, with regal diadem-headband and earrings, Syria, 800 BCE.

Stele of the Canaanite goddess Qedesha (Qetesh/Qudshu)
standing on lion, Egypt, ca. 1300 BCE.

Spiritual Beauty—Sacred Adornment of the Priestesses

Sacred adornment was not considered a vanity but a sacred talismanic act that brought down the powers of the goddess into the human body to bring blessings and power.

In Syria, the goddess and her priestess-queens wore golden tower crowns—the "tower" a symbol of the Magdalene. Babylonian sacred sexual priestesses wore their hair "done up," curled or plaited, and wore garlands in their hair, with bows and flower tiaras interwoven with gold ornaments. They had anklets and bracelets of gold, if they were wealthy, or they had necklaces with jewels and shells that were shaped and carved as vulvas and penises.[12] They wore pointed-toe sandals, colorful scarves, and later in Syria and Arabia similar priestesses adorned themselves with nose rings and gold crescent moon earrings. Other academic references describe ornamented gold and bejeweled chains between their breasts and their waists (see illustration on page 86), and in Syria they wore vulva pendants (down-pointing triangles) that hung from their waist and rested above their womb and pubic triangle, ornamenting the sacred site of their holy power. Often made from gold and deep blue lapis lazuli, this vulva jewelry and ornamentation was divinized in sacred ritual as a conduit of the vulva of the Goddess.

Rites of the Priestesshood

The responsibilities of a qedesha extended into all domains of religious life. Biblical stories share that qedeshot led prayers and ceremonies in the sacred groves of Asherah trees, and practiced divination and magic.[13] There they would light fires, burn incense, offer ritual cakes, and pour libations from silver vessels.

A guild of qedesha temple priestesses of Asherah lived and worked inside the Temple of Jerusalem from the days of its creation until at least 620 BCE.[*] Catholic doctrine holds that the Jewish temple priestess tradition continued through the time of Mother Mary, who herself was a priestess. In the temple, the qedeshot wove the beautiful garments for the goddess Asherah, and for her high priestesses.[14]

Hebrew priestesses baked *kawwanim* cakes for the Queen of Heaven, stamped "with her image," a euphemism for cakes shaped like breasts, vulva, or the entire naked body of Asherah or Ashtoreth.[15] The cakes were offerings for the renewal of life, a *feminine eucharist,* deriving from the same roots as the much older Sumerian-Akkadian tradition of offering *kamanu* cakes to Ishtar.[16]

Another primary role of the qedesha was to keep watch for the new moon to plan the calendar of the religious ceremonies. The Judaic and Canaanite religious calendars, like those of the Mesopotamians and Egyptians, were based around the new moon, with ritual days began at sunset. The qedesha also played harp, lyre, and tambourine, and sang and performed ritual music. They danced the circle dances at the festivals, and may have performed erotic-initiatory dances similar to belly dance and the Dance of the Seven Veils,[†] said to be performed by Salome

---

[*]King Josiah removed the qedeshot from the temple during his reign, described in 2 Kings 23:7.
[†]The term "Dance of the Seven Veils" was first used in a modern sense by Oscar Wilde in his play *Salome,* inspired by the long tradition of sensual veil dances of the Middle East.

in Herod's court, probably inspired by Inanna's descent into the Underworld, in seven levels.[17]

Dances of the Qedesha

Other biblical dances are described with the word *machol*, signifying an erotic whirling or writhing dance performed by young Israelite women. We see *machol* used to describe the celebratory dance of Judge Jephthah's daughter, and the triumphant dance performed by the women who greet David after he defeats Goliath.[18] The same word describes the clearly erotic dance performed for King Solomon by the Shulamite priestess, the Queen of Sheba, in the Song of Songs. Solomon sings praises of her body as she dances:

> *How beautiful are your sandaled feet, O queenly maiden.*
> *Your rounded thighs are like jewels, the work of a skilled craftsman.*
> *Your navel is perfectly formed like a goblet filled with mixed wine.*
> *Between your thighs lies a mound of wheat bordered with lilies.*
> *Your breasts are like two fawns, twin fawns of a gazelle.*
> *Your neck is as beautiful as an ivory tower.*
> *Your eyes are like the sparkling pools in Heshbon by the gate of Bath-*
> *rabbim. Your nose is as fine as the tower of Lebanon overlooking*
> *Damascus.*
> *Your head is as majestic as Mount Carmel, and the sheen of your hair*
> *radiates royalty. The king is held captive by its tresses.*
> *Oh, how beautiful you are! How pleasing, my love, how full of delights!*
> *You are slender like a palm tree, and your breasts are like its clusters of*
> *fruit.*
> *I said, "I will climb the palm tree and take hold of its fruit." May*
> *your breasts be like grape clusters, and the fragrance of your*
> *breath like apples.*[19]

The biblical book of Judges and tractate Ta'anit of the Talmud describe how the daughters of Shiloh go to the vineyard to dance a machol circle-whirling dance as part of the annual fertility rites of the autumn harvest.[20] The fertility dance is not a part of the officially sanctioned rites of the Judaic religion. Instead it is a local Canaanite custom, a chthonic and seductive dance with trembling, writhing, or shaking movements similar to the Middle Eastern belly dance.[21] The dances are filled with a spirit of joy and happiness, accompanied by the playing of flute and drum, and chanting and singing. Similar whirling dances were performed in the worship of Ishtar/Inanna, in the mystical traditions of Islam, and by the devadasis of India.

Sacred Prostitute or Temple Priestess?

Famously, the temple priestesses became associated with cult prostitution, where they were believed to sell sex outside the temple grounds or during festivals for the goddess.

Histories written by Herodotus and Strabo describe women forced into prostitution for the goddess, against their will, with strangers who "throw money on their laps" in a humiliating fashion. These legends veiled the deeper story of the takeover and degradation of the priestess temples in very traumatic times. It was not the goddess who willed it, or her priestesses who profited from it. The money went to the male priesthood who had taken over the temples by that time.

The idea of sacred prostitution dates back to Inanna and Ishtar of Babylonian times, when sexuality was recognized for its numinous spiritual dimension and divine nature, and was not in any way legislated or controlled. Indeed the free-flowing sexuality of the goddess and her priestesses was believed to fertilize the land and bring boons, blessing, and abundance. Repressing sexual energy, or worse, exploiting the energy, could harm the fertility of the earth and bring drought, pestilence, and famine to the people. Initiated sexual priestesses were considered so powerful as to be potentially dangerous; it would have been a terrible violation of the sacred covenant to misuse or dishonor this energy.

The idea of selling sex to strangers from foreign lands would be unthinkable.

One priestess title commonly mistranslated as "sacred prostitute," *harimtu,* is now believed by many scholars to describe single women associated with the temple who lived under their own authority. Scholar Stephanie Budin describes them as "women whose lives and sexuality are not regulated by a male authority figure," and says: "they were independent women, most likely priestesses, not functioning under a father or husband."[22]

The Akkadian priestess name *kezertu* was also misinterpreted as prostitute. *Kezertu* literally means "female with curled hair," and refers to a class of priestesses skilled in the art of sacred body and hair adornment, sometimes described as a "hairdresser." Interestingly, both Mother Mary *and* Mary Magdalene are referred to as harlot "hairdressers." Across the art of the ancient Near East, priestesses were consistently depicted with ornately braided, plaited, and adorned hair.

Jean-Jacques Glassner, Ph.D., author of *Chroniques Mésopotamienne* and specialist in cuneiform script, says that the kezertu were also professional musicians, singers, or dancers. All these clues point to the classic qualities of an educated, accomplished temple priestess and Holy Whore who is mistress of the feminine arts, and whose beauty is considered auspicious.[23]

The name *samhatu*, similarly misunderstood, was listed in ancient cuneiform records as a class of priestesses dedicated to Ishtar. *Samhatu* means "to grow, flourish, be magnificent, to attain extraordinary beauty or stature" as well as a "woman who is beautiful or voluptuous."[24] Scholar Stephanie Budin, author of *The Myth of Sacred Prostitution in Antiquity*, says of the priestesses of Ishtar, "All three types of woman were independent and associated with beauty, laughter and . . . revelry."[25]

The priestesses were also dream oracles, ecstatic prophets, birth midwives, and soul doulas, helping the dying navigate the otherworlds of consciousness, as described in the Gospel of Mary and the Egyptian Book of the Dead. Traveling these paths was also done while alive for spiritual initiation, and the priestesses presided over rites of awakening of cosmic consciousness. They often used sex, sensual energy, herbs, music, and dance for this initiation.

Even in the denseness of early patriarchal times, priestesses still held a space where women could be autonomous and sovereign and not governed by a husband, father, or the male state. They were governed by the female deity. They could write, create poetry, sing, make art; there were great halls of female priestess weavers. They could be brewers, making magical potions and elixirs, and they could be landowners and business owners.

Sexually Sacrosanct

In the Bible, *qedesha* is often mistranslated as temple-prostitute or sacred prostitute. In one Greek translation the qedesha are called the whores *and* the initiated ones.[26] There is a confabulation of words related to prostitution, sexuality, and sacred initiation. The qedesha were clearly the priestesses of the cult of Asherah and Ashtoreth. The Hebrew word for a secular prostitute is *zonah*.[27]

However, as the temples of the goddess fell, her daughters and priestesses became targeted by the incoming patriarchal religions who despised their independent, free, and powerful sexuality. Their sisterhoods were destroyed or co-opted; they were forced into sexual slavery or a form of prostitution that was far away from the sacred sexuality of the original priestesses.

Forced temple prostitution was a punishment inflicted on daughters if the father went into debt; the women of the family could discharge the debt through forced cultic sex work. Female slaves could also be sold to the temple to work off their debt and achieve freedom—manumission—after a certain period of time as a prostitute of the goddess. Cult prostitution for the lower classes of women did exist, as female sexual power became owned by men, and even a few early Catholic churches had brothels attached, where the profits went to the church.

Deuteronomy 23:17 commands, "None of the daughters of Israel shall be qedesha; none of the sons of Israel shall be Qadesh."[28] In 2 Kings 23:6–8 the reformer Josiah "brought out the image of Asherah [from the temple]. . . . He broke down the houses of the qedeshim . . . where the women did weaving for Asherah." 1 Kings 15:12–13 states of King Asa, "He put away the qedeshim out of the land, and he removed all the idols that his ancestors had made. He also removed his mother Maacah from being the Queen Mother, because she had made an abominable image for Asherah."

Harlots and Queens
Women of Power

The realms of feminine power lived on in the royal courts. One of the power words of Hebrew feminine wisdom passed down through the matriarchal traditions is *gevirah*, a word that translates as "queen mother, queen, lady, matriarch, or mistress," used in the Bible to describe the office of the mother of the reigning Israelite king.[29] The word derives from the root *gvr* indicating strength, power, or divine power, and is the same word as the feminine sephira *Gevurah*, of the Kabbalistic Tree of Life.

Biblical and Canaanite texts show that the gevirah was no mere figurehead, but descended from an ancient tradition where the queen mother was the power behind the throne, the woman who granted sovereignty and kingship to her son. This tradition extended across other cultures in the ancient Near East, including the Syrian, Sumerian, Hittite, and Egyptian.[30]

In ancient times, the gevirah was also considered to be the Mother of the Gods, and performed the ritual roles of the high priestess.[31] She wore the queenly crown, and the king bowed to her.[32] She granted sovereignty to her son, crowning him as king in the enthronement ritual, and even chose his royal successors when she opposed the rule of his firstborn son, as was the normal Israelite practice. The gevirah traditionally sat enthroned on the right-hand side of the king, the power position, and she often held an authority that was equal to his or nearly so.[33] The queen mother also participated in political and stately affairs.

Descriptions of the role of Bathsheba, the queen mother of King Solomon, show the importance of her role in the Israelite court. In I Kings 2:19, Solomon "had a throne brought for his mother [Bathsheba], and she sat down at his right hand." In the Song of Solomon 3:11, the speaker says: "Look on King Solomon wearing a crown, the crown with which his mother crowned him on the day of his wedding, the day his heart rejoiced."

The gevirah held her position for life, even if her son died. In Canaanite Syria, the queen mother was called the *rabitu,* meaning "Great Lady," a feminine form and shared word origin of *rabbi,* which later meant "teacher" in Hebrew.[34] Above all else she was the high priestess, the living embodiment of the goddess Asherah, representing her presence and casting her voice in the royal court.[35]

Losing the Goddess

Beginning around 1100 BCE, archaeological evidence shows that Palestine became home to a new religious movement that rose up among the pastoralist tribes of the arid inland hills. This group of Canaanite priests worshipped Yahweh alone, to the exclusion of all other gods. Over time the patriarchal priests of Yahweh attracted a large following, eventually forming the Israelite religion that claimed spiritual descent from the Old Testament patriarchs Abraham, Moses, and Jacob.

However, in the early days of the movement, Yahweh had a wife—Asherah. Inscriptions found at the archaeological sites of Kuntillat Arjud, in the northern Sinai, as well as at Khirbet el-Qom, near Hebron, dating from the first millennium BCE, read "Yahweh's Asherah," who sits at his "right hand"—the throne of power, reserved for the queen or queen mother who grants sovereignty to the king. A translation of the earliest Hebrew version of Deuteronomy 33:2–3 reads:

> Yahweh came from Sinai. Yea, he came among the myriads of Qedeshu, at his right hand his own Asherah. Indeed he loves the clans and all his holy ones [Qedeshu] *on his left* [emphasis added].[36]

For many years the followers of the new Israelite religion continued to worship Asherah and other feminine divinities. Even fire and brimstone prophets initially accepted Asherah as the wife of Yahweh. King Solomon, Ahab, and others erected altars and statues to her in the central temples of Jerusalem and Samaria, where she was worshipped alongside of, or instead of, Yahweh. But, in 586 BCE, when the nation of Israel was defeated and the first Temple of Jerusalem destroyed by the Babylonian empire, the traumatized population looked for answers. The prophets shouted that it was the "harlotry" of goddess worship that caused Israel's fall—the angry Yahweh was punishing the Israelites for worshipping the Queen of Heaven. From that point on the Hebrew qedeshot were targeted and persecuted. Gradually their temples and sanctuaries were destroyed. The last traces of public worship of the goddess ended in the time of the Hasmonean dynasty, with conversions forced at sword point in Galilee and other outlying provinces, sometime around 160 BCE.[37]

Even still, the Hebrew goddess did not disappear completely. By the time of Mary Magdalene and Jesus, she had gone underground, held in the mystical Kabbalist teachings and native Jewish folk magic. According to Rabbinic tradition, the "genius" or "spirit" of idolatry, the impulse to worship the feminine divinity, was conceived of as a fiery lion that dwelled in the adytum, the holy of holies of the Temple of Jerusalem, where God himself was supposed to live, and where "she" had to be locked up and guarded by the male priests.[38]

> "We will burn incense to the Queen of Heaven and will pour out drink offerings to her just as we and our ancestors, our kings and our officials did in the towns of Judah and in the streets of Jerusalem." . . . The women added, "When we burned incense to the Queen of Heaven and poured out drink offerings to her, did not our husbands know that we were making cakes impressed with her image and pouring out drink offerings to her?" (Jeremiah 44:17–19)

Temple of Sin

Magicians of the Moon

VEIL OF SHEKINAH, THE "HOLY HYMEN"

You shall make a veil of blue and purple and scarlet material and fine twisted linen; it shall be made with cherubim, the work of a skillful workman. You shall hang it on four pillars of acacia overlaid with gold, their hooks also being of gold, on four sockets of silver. You shall hang up the veil under the clasps, and shall bring in the ark of the testimony there within the veil; and the veil shall serve for you as a partition between the holy place and the holy of holies.

EXODUS 26:31–33

We have seen the importance of the goddess and her priestesses in the native Canaanite religion of biblical Palestine, but what about in the Judaic religion? Was there a secretly encoded tradition of the Hebrew goddess within the Jewish religion itself, one that Jesus, Mother Mary, Mary Magdalene, and the other "Marys" had access to? The answer is clearly yes.

Old Testament stories reflect the long and rich history of the practice of Jewish magic that existed *alongside* Mosaic law, calling upon the left-hand wisdom. The Hebrew patriarchs Abraham, Moses, Saul, David, and Solomon were each involved with feminine magic, moon worship, shamanism, witchcraft, or goddess worship. They were also considered powerful magicians in their own rights, as their names appear on Jewish magical amulets and talismans discovered by archaeologists across ancient Jewish settlements. Jesus continued this tradition of Jewish magic in his lifetime, as described by Morton Smith, former professor of ancient history at Columbia University, in his pioneering book *Jesus the Magician*.[39]

David's son, King Solomon, also married foreign princess-priestesses and built altars to Asherah and Ashtoreth-Ishtar in Jerusalem. He abandoned the worship of Yahweh in favor of the goddess: "As Solomon grew old, his wives turned his heart after other gods."[40] And we will soon learn more about King Ahab, who brought a statue of Asherah into the temple of Samaria, capital of northern Israel, as well as his Phoenician wife and high priestess, Jezebel.

The distinguished professor and archaeologist William Dever documents the overwhelming evidence of an Asherah-centered Jewish folk religion in his book *Did God Have a Wife?* Thousands of Asherah figurines, cult objects, and altars have been recovered from the private homes and public spaces of the ancient Israelites. Many were found near the first Temple of Jerusalem. It is clear that the *ideal* of Judaic monotheism was not the reality of the everyday life of the Israelite people, who continued to publicly practice their indigenous Canaanite polytheism until as late as 135 BCE in some parts of Palestine.[41] In the hearts and minds of the people, Asherah was still the wife of God, and formed an important part of their worship. Dever writes that even after the total suppression of public goddess worship, the traditions continued underground in folk magic and the mystical oral tradition of Kabbalah:

With the full recognition of women . . . the spirit of the Great Mother will at last be freed. Here I have tried simply to anticipate her emancipation by showing that in the world of ancient Israel, among other places and times, she was once alive and well, at least until she was driven underground by the men who wrote the Bible. Archaeology brings her back to life.[42]

Biblical stories also describe Moses parting the Red Sea in his flight from Egypt, while his sister Miriam the prophetess and her priestess sisters dance, drum, and sing the "Song of the Sea" in celebration. The Red Sea was a symbol for the womb blood of birth and menstruation, and also the famous location of the menstrual maven Lilith's exile.[43]

Bridal Chamber Mysteries

In 1967, Hebrew scholar Raphael Patai, Ph.D., published his groundbreaking book *The Hebrew Goddess*. In it he traces the presence of the feminine divinity throughout the history of Judaism. One striking observation Patai made is that in the time of Mary Magdalene and Jesus, the Temple of Jerusalem contained within its holy of holies a golden statue of two naked cherubim, one male and the other female, entwined in sexual embrace. The cherubim symbolize the esoteric Jewish mystery tradition—the hidden power of the goddess and the mystical participation in the bridal chamber rites that secretly rest at the root of the religion. It is only when the masculine and feminine principles come together, in sacred marriage, in both human and divine form, that the Kabbalistic Tree of Life is fertilized and renewed.

In the first century CE, during the lifetime of Mary Magdalene and Jesus, the Alexandrian Jewish philosopher Philo describes the two cherubim in the mystical terms of the Kabbalistic sefirot:

> While God is indeed one, his highest and chiefest powers are two, even goodness [masculine, *chesed*] and sovereignty [feminine, *gevurah*] . . . and in the midst between the two is a third which united them. . . . Of these two potencies, sovereignty and goodness, the Cherubim are the symbols.[44]

Representing the masculine quality of giving, *chesed,* and the feminine quality of strength and governance, *gevurah,* over time the two cherubim began to symbolize the unification of masculine and feminine energies on the Tree of Life. The Rabbi Pinhas ben Yair, a second-century Palestinian teacher, wrote that they were the most important element of the Temple:

> It was due to them [the Cherubim] . . . that the Temple stood. They were the head of everything that was in the Temple, for the Shekinah rested on them and on the Ark, and from there He spoke to Moses.[45]

Sexuality in the Holy of Holies

The golden statue of the embracing cherubim was held in the holy of holies of the temple, symbolically taking the place of the old Ark of the Covenant, lost during the Babylonian conquest. Each year, at the autumn Sukkot festival, the statue was held high for all the pilgrimaging men and women of Israel to see. The sight of the sexy cherubs made the crowd "lightheaded," rousing them to such excitement that they imitated the divine figures with a communal, public enactment of the ancient sexual rites with their partners.[46] This tradition appears to have continued into the era of Magdalene and Jesus.

Although it is a surprising exception to the traditional Jewish rules of sexual modesty, the sexual celebrations of Sukkot, and the location of the embracing cherubim in the inner temple adytum is consistent with other Near Eastern cultures, where the rites of sacred marriage had been celebrated in the inner chambers, sacred beds, temple rooftops, gardens, orchards, and fields for thousands of years. Sacred sexuality, with its celebration of the life-force energies and the mystical participation in the fertility of the earth, was a centerpiece of the ancient religions.

In fact, Raphael Patai, and several other scholars speculate that the original content of the Ark of the Covenant was two sacred stone carvings, one the image of Yahweh and the other of his wife, Asherah or Astarte, united in marital-spiritual embrace in the symbolic womb space of the Ark.[47]

The Tree of Life

For he rebuilt the high places which Hezekiah his father had destroyed; and he erected altars for Baal and made an Asherah, as Ahab king of Israel had done, and worshiped all the host of heaven and served them.

2 KINGS 21:3

Asherah was also considered to be the Tree of Life, symbolized by carved wooden poles and statues found at all of her sanctuaries. Over time the Jewish Tree of Life, representing the body of the goddess, became stylized as the menorah, which stood on the Ark of the Covenant in the inner adytum of the Temple of Jerusalem, the womb and holy of holies of Israel. Each of the menorah's seven candles represents a branch of the tree, and it is still a key icon of the Jewish religion.

The date palm was also a symbol of the sacred feminine Tree of Life. *Tamar* means "date" and "date palm" in Hebrew, and was also the name of a biblical matriarch, sexual priestess, and ancestor of Jesus. *Tamar,* like the name Mary, was not just a personal name but also a title denoting a priestess. In the Bible, 2 Samuel 13:18, another Tamar, the daughter of King David with his priestess Queen Macaah, was described as having the "richly ornamented robe" of a priestess. After extensive study, biblical scholar Adrien Bledstein, among others, concludes that this Tamar was not only a priestess but also a healer and "mistress of dreams."[48] Date palms were also laid out on the ground as Jesus rode into Jerusalem, a reference to his involvement in the feminine mysteries. We'll see the same palm frond symbolism later in the book, in our discussion of the *Ghent Altarpiece.*

Lilith—Queen of the Night

I am she who cries out,
And I am cast forth upon the face of the earth.
I prepare the bread and my mind within.
I am called truth. . . .

I am the one who alone exists,
And there is no one to judge me.
For though there is much sweetness
In passionate life, in transient pleasure.
Finally soberness comes
And people flee to their place of rest.
There they will find me,
And live, and not die again.

EXCERPT FROM "THE THUNDER, PERFECT MIND,"
NAG HAMMADI CODEX VI

Our story of the forgotten feminine must include the Jewish heroine Lilith, who was said to be the first created woman, who rejected sexual subservience to Adam, and upon leaving him, went on to rule as the Queen of the Underworld and wisdom of the dark.

The names *Lilith* and *Jezebel* are totemic feminine power words, instantaneously recognizable, like the name *Magdalene,* as bearing the hallmarks of a

feminine essence, once revered and gifted to the world, now shamed and shunned, and forced underground.

In the long-forgotten past, Lilith was once a well-loved mother goddess of the nomadic tribes of the ancient Middle East, and likely a goddess of lunar and shamanic consciousness, similar to the archaic Egyptian goddesses Nuit and Neith. After the arrival of patriarchal systems, Lilith was banished to the hinterlands and replaced by male gods. In time, Lilith came to represent the exiled and "unacceptable" aspects of the feminine in the eyes of the patriarchal order—in particular menstrual magic, untamed female sexuality, feminine pride and empowerment, and a spirit of defiance, wildness, and self-determination that refused to be confined within cities, laws, and "civilization."

Like the Hindu menstrual goddess Kali, Lilith also came to symbolize the destructive forces held within the abused and mistreated feminine psyche and pain body that developed in response to the male-oriented dominator cultures. Male priests and scribes demonized her; she was literally transfigured into an evil spirit or demon, beginning at least six thousand years ago. Lilith is the wild aspect of the feminine that can't and won't be controlled, and whose pain threatens to tear down the fragile systems of order that society has imposed on the natural processes of the earth and instinctive human behaviors.

In the ancient Semitic language of Akkadian, one of the languages spoken in Sumeria, she was known as *Lilitu,* which simply meant "female divinity." The root word *lil* is "god, goddess, spirit, or wind," and corresponds to the Hebrew *El* and the Arabic *Allah.* The plural form of the word is *ilili,* meaning "gods," similar to the Hebrew *Elohim.* Other scholars translate Lilith's name as "female wind spirit."

We first hear of Lilith in the Sumerian myth "Inanna and the Huluppu Tree" recorded on clay tablets from the third millennium BCE, but originating from a much earlier oral tradition. Lilith appears as the wild alter-ego of Inanna. She lives in the trunk of the Tree of Life, and her wildness must be banished in order for Inanna to take her position as queen and sacred consort in the emerging male-oriented civilizations.

Lilith is associated with the night, menstrual blood, insatiable sexual desire, and with tempting or luring men into "demonic" sexual encounters with her. The Semitic root of her name is *lil,* or *lyl,* meaning "night"; while her full name, *Lilith,* is the Hebrew word for "screech owl," a totem bird of the night and feminine underworld magic. The related Sumerian word *lal* means esteemed and sweet nectar, as well as "accused and denounced," hinting at her transformation from a position of honor to one of disgrace within the new male order.[49]

Lilith's character continued to evolve across time and culture, in particular in the Talmudic and Kabbalistic traditions. By the eighth century CE, in the *Alphabet of ben Sirach,* she appears as Adam's first wife, made from the same clay as him—and therefore his equal—unlike Eve who came from Adam's rib. Lilith refused to subserviently lie on her back and submit to "passive" sexuality. Like Inanna, she wanted to take her turn on top, which seemed only fair in her eyes, considering she was Adam's equal. Likewise, it was said that priestesses of the crone-goddess Hecate would only have sex in the on-top position, and scorned "domesticated" women who took the supine position. Because Lilith refused to cooperate with "God's plan" of female sexual subservience, he banished her to the "Red Sea," a menstrual metaphor, where she would archetypally join the other exiled goddesses of myth who could not or would not fit in to the emerging patriarchal ethos.

Interestingly, Lilith is also connected to the Neanderthals, to the serpent of the Garden of Eden, and to Magdalene worship. In Assyrian mythology the first beings birthed from the primordial dragon Tiamat were *Lahmu* (male) and *Lahamu* (female), the world parents who birthed all the other gods. They were called "hairy" and wore red sashes, and were described similarly to Lilith.* They may well be a mythic memory of the original human inhabitants of the Middle East, the red-haired Neanderthals who had more body hair than modern humans.

Rabbinical texts provide further clues. The Talmud shares that Lilith sexually partners with Samael, the archangel of "death," who resides in the seventh heaven. Their child is Asmodeus (or sometimes he is Lilith's lover), who stands at the entryway of the Mary Magdalene chapel of Rennes-le-Château, France.[50] Lilith, the "Twisting Serpent," and Samael, the "Slant Serpent," are considered soulmate twins, whose marriage is arranged by a primordial dragon of creation. At a higher spiritual level, they are two halves of the same being, a heavenly mirror of Adam and Eve's partnership on earth.[51]

Samael is also the patron angel of Esau, the redheaded one, firstborn son of Isaac and Rebekah. In Genesis 25:25 he is described: "Now the first came forth red, all over like a hairy garment; and they named him Esau." Esau's birthright is stolen by his brother Jacob, who later took the name Israel and became the father of the twelve tribes of Israel. The story of Esau and Jacob allegorically describes the Israelites pushing aside the red and hairy ones who came first, which may well be a coded reference to the Neanderthals. The stories of aboriginal hairy humans, who live in the wilds and shun cities, are found in myths across many indigenous Eurasian and American cultures.

In another rabbinical text, the "harlot" Lilith, rather than Samael, is the serpent that seduces both Adam and Eve in the Garden of Eden. This is only possible because Adam was "corrupted" through menstrual sexuality:

And the Serpent, the Woman of Harlotry, incited and seduced Eve. . . . And all this ruination came about because Adam the first man coupled with Eve while she was in her menstrual impurity. Behold, here it is before you: because

---

*The "hairy" and "red" Lahmu and Lahamu world parents are also linked with the Akkadian *Lamashtu* she-demon, who is described very similarly to Lilith. Lamashtu is sometimes called the "Seven Witches."

of the sins of Adam, the first man, all the things mentioned came into being. For Evil Lilith, when she saw the greatness of his corruption, became strong in her *qlippot* and came to Adam against his will, and became hot from him.[52]

The Zohar describes Lilith as a red-haired "harlot," dressed in "ornaments of seduction":

Her hair is long and red like the rose, her cheeks are white and red, and from her ears hang six ornaments, Egyptian cords and all the ornaments of the Land of the East hang from her neck. Her mouth is set like a narrow door, comely in its décor . . . her tongue is sharp like a sword, her words are smooth like oil, her lips red like a rose and sweetened by all the sweetness of the world. She is dressed in scarlet, and adorned with forty ornaments less one.[53]

The stories of the Hebrew Bible, as well as the Talmudic and Midrashic traditions, are conveyed through a polarized patriarchal lens. They represent *a story,* but not a full, complete, balanced or true story, and certainly not a female or feminine story. Any icons and symbols of feminine divinity are demonized if they cannot be enslaved and contained within a male-centered ideology. Yet their feminine power remains, if veiled for now.

Contemplating the symbolic memes that are intertwined with the story of Lilith—Mary Magdalene, Samael, menstrual blood, red hair, initiatory feminine sexuality, harlotry, body adornment, serpents, dragons, heretical religious views, and the Neanderthals, all the usual suspects—via the magical red threads of our imaginal vision we can begin to reconstruct a herstory of Lilith told through a feminine perspective rather than a patriarchal one.

Lilith is a Sophia of the Night, an ancient and powerful goddess of lunar consciousness. Her magical gifts lie in the dissolving and releasing powers of the menstrual rivers, symbolized by the new moon. She is both serpent and dragon, primordial and primeval.

Jezebel: High Priestess of Asherah

Notwithstanding I have a few things against thee, because thou sufferest that woman Jezebel, which calleth herself a prophetess, to teach and to seduce my servants to commit fornication, and to eat things sacrificed unto idols.

REVELATION 2:20

Jezebel, the ninth century BCE queen of the northern kingdom of Israel, represents the courageous priestess who does not diminish herself in the face of bullying and slander, especially when aimed at her sexuality, femininity, and goddess spiritual path. She has been remembered in the Judeo-Christian version of *his*-story as the "painted lady," "false prophet," "whore," and "seductress," sure indicators that she was a powerful priestess of the goddess traditions, target of patristic slander. To understand the true *her*-story, we will need to read between the lines of the biblical book of Kings, where her life was first recorded by Israelite scribes, who vent their patriarchal venom upon her: "What peace, so long as the whoredoms of thy mother Jezebel and her witchcrafts [are so] many?" (2 Kings 9:22).

Jezebel was a high priestess of Asherah, and guardian of the Canaanite goddess traditions in an era rife with religious unrest. She was born a princess, the daughter of a highly respected Phoenician king and high priest of Ishtar in the land that is now Lebanon. To help secure a political alliance, Jezebel married King Ahab of the neighboring kingdom of Israel.

Phoenician queens often served as high priestesses of the goddess, and held considerable power in that time, in stark contrast to the subordinate position of many women in Israel. According to the customs of royal marriage, she was allowed to bring her religion and way of life with her into Israel, along with 450 prophets of Ba'al and 400 of Asherah. The prophets of Yahweh fought against the goddess tradition, and periodically spurred religious violence. With Jezebel's patronage as queen of Israel, the balance tipped back to the worship of Asherah and Ba'al, earning her and King Ahab the hatred of Yahweh loyalists and prophets, who referred to all who prayed at the tree temples of Asherah as "fornicators."

After only three years of marriage, King Ahab died in battle. Yahweh loyalists seized power, and the new king immediately marched on Jezebel's palace. Jezebel's last act of dignity was to place her crown on her head, and adorn herself with full makeup, jewelry, and royal clothing befitting a queen and priestess, presenting herself at the palace window to face her coming killers. She was thrown from the window to her death. Her challenging gaze from the window was remembered as the "Jezebel look," interpreted by biblical scribes as an act of seduction rather than what it truly was—a final gesture of defiance by a courageous priestess in the face of her imminent death.

Jezebel's story was rewritten to serve the political agenda of the victors. When we hear "painted lady," we might substitute instead a queen who was skilled in the high priestess art of talismanic adornment with beautiful cosmetics, clothing, jewelry, fragrant oils, and styled hair—each detail an act of prayer and magic designed to create a container so inviting that the energy of the goddess would rush in to fill it with her presence, which was a ritual sacrament of the goddess religion.

Most importantly, the Bible records that she was *considered to be a prophetess* in her own religion. So where we read "false prophet," we see she was a prophet of the feminine ways, viewed as a threat to the religion of Yahweh that sought to eradicate all traces of the goddess traditions. When we hear "whore" or "seductress," we might know that she lived in the full majesty of her erotic aliveness, celebrating the power of her sexual essence and the creative pulse of her sacred desires; that she was a powerful voice, not hiding herself in shame, not submitting to the threats and demands of the adversaries.

Medicine Women

In the old times, priestesses, oracles, womb shamans, prophetesses, and royal queens who held real political power walked on the holy lands, and their memory is still imprinted into our collective consciousness, calling us to remember their lost throne.

The power of a priestess was held in her instinctive sensual consciousness, cycling with the cosmos, brimming with birthing power and sexual radiance, at-one with the greening force of life and the kundalini fires within earth. She was respected and revered as a psychic and medicine woman; the powers of her sacred sexuality gave *charis,* spiritual feminine food, medicine, and healing. These women did not conform to a man's world. Faced with the choice of extinction or assimilation, many of these women of power formed alliances with the patriarchal lineages, secretly infusing their hidden blood magic and long red thread of matriline memory into the new male religions.

In time, these Scarlet Women would go on to birth the Messianic bloodline.

CHAMBER 6

MOTHERLINE OF CHRIST

Son of the Goddess

Holy persons draw to themselves all that is earthly. . . .
The earth is at the same time mother,
She is mother of all that is natural,
mother of all that is human.
She is the mother of all,
for contained in her
are the seeds of all.

HILDEGARD VON BINGEN

NOW THAT WE HAVE SEEN HOW THE LANDS of Jesus's birth were steeped in feminine magic, it is easier to contemplate how he may have been a son of the goddess tradition, and the descendant of a temple priestess, through his mother Mary, daughter of Anne.

The first clue comes in the New Testament Gospel of Matthew, which reveals an unusual anomaly in the description of Jesus's lineage. Matthew opens his gospel with a genealogy of Jesus that lists four key female ancestors: Tamar, Rahab, Ruth, and Bathsheba (the wife of Uriah). But why list these four women? In the patriarchal world of Palestine at the time of Jesus, typically only *men* were listed in genealogies, not women. Matthew is drawing our attention to something he must say obliquely, something very important. For those with the eyes to see, he is pointing us to the left-hand side of Christ, revealing that the secret identity of Jesus lies in his *Motherline,* the womb lineage of his feminine heritage, not his paternal blood.

Shall we open the doorways of memory and explore the Motherline of Christ?

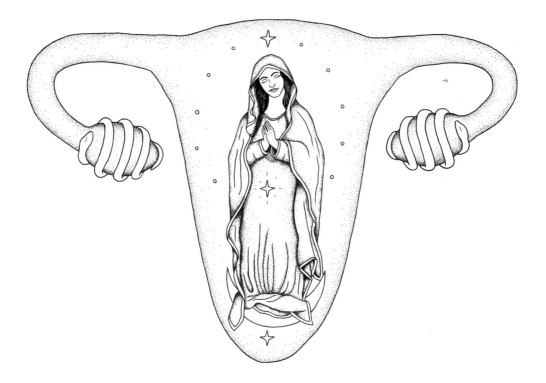

Tamar and Rahab—Canaanite Priestesses

The first of Jesus's maternal ancestors is the mysterious Tamar of Genesis. The Bible obscures her background and identity, stating only that she is a Canaanite. However, this simple word is loaded with meaning, signifying she is a worshipper of foreign goddesses and gods. Her name is also a priestess title, meaning "date palm," the sacred Canaanite Tree of Life, representing the body of the goddess. No Hebrew people took the name Tamar, and the only other Tamars in the Bible were of a royal witch-priestess line from Geshur, whose family married into the line of King David and famously brought pagan Asherah and Ashtoreth worship into the temple.

We first meet Tamar when the Hebrew patriarch, Judah, brings her into the family to marry his oldest son Er, but Er dies unexpectedly soon after. In a complex set of circumstances Judah breaks the law of Levirate marriage by failing to provide another male family member to marry Tamar, effectively casting her out. A widow without a male protector had no recourse in the patriarchal world of ancient Palestine, and no means to earn a livelihood. In order to integrate herself back into society, we are told that she cunningly *dressed as a veiled harlot,* tricking Judah into having sex and impregnating her. A scandal erupts when Tamar, an unmarried woman, is found to be pregnant. Judah is forced to acknowledge that he is the father, and that Tamar is "more righteous than he" in asserting her right to continue the family name. Their son Perez becomes an ancestor to the Messianic line of Jesus.

But was Tamar simply *dressed* as a harlot? Or was she a qedesha, a sexual priestess of the goddess traditions? The first instance Judah sees her he describes her as a *zonah,* a common prostitute, but the next two mentions of her in the Hebrew Bible (Gen. 38:21–22) refer to her as *qedesha.* Rabbinical writings in the *Legends of the Jews* describe her as having the gift of psychic foreknowledge, as a priestess would. She is described in other places as the daughter of a high priest; and she certainly would have come from a high-ranking family in order to marry into the prominent family of Judah. The only reason for Tamar to have had the elaborate clothes and jewelry of a "harlot" was if she were a qedesha. Whatever the exact details of her background, the suggestion is that a woman associated with harlotry and "scandalous" sexuality is named as a maternal ancestor of Jesus, a pattern that we will see repeated four more times.

The next "scandalous" woman in Christ's Motherline is Rahab of Jericho, who is also referred to in the Bible as a Canaanite harlot. Rabbinic texts credit her with the gift of prophecy, traditionally womb-sourced, and she would become the ancestress of multiple Judaic prophets in addition to the line of King David and Jesus. Talmudic tradition holds Rahab to be one of the four most beautiful women in the world—even saying her name could cause a man to have an orgasm.[1] She assists the Hebrew military in defeating her home city of Jericho, hanging a *red cord,* symbolic color of the sexual priestesses, from her window to signal the military to spare her home when they destroyed the city. In exchange Joshua, or Salman in some traditions, marries her and fathers children with her, granting her protection and status in the male world.

Rahab's beauty, fame, symbolic red cord, oracular gifts, and the fact that she was adopted as a prized wife and maternal ancestress in the Messianic line, suggest that her "harlotry" was a coded reference to her position as a respected priestess in the Canaanite goddess tradition. No ancestor of the royal line of David would choose an ordinary prostitute to provide his heirs.

Ruth and Bathsheba—Seductress and Priestess

The next unconventional female ancestors of Jesus are the matriarchs Ruth and Bathshéba. Ruth was from the neighboring nation of Moab, whose people worshipped Astarte and other pagan deities. We are told her husband and male family members died, leaving her in poverty, and a social outcast. To regain her place in society, one night she boldly *anoints herself* and illicitly meets the patriarch Boaz on the *threshing floor,* traditional location of the hieros gamos sexual rites. There she seduces him, daring to "uncover his lower half," convincing him through her sexual allure to take her as a wife. Their child is Obed, who becomes the grandfather of King David and ancestor of Jesus.

The fourth in Matthew's list is Bathsheba, whose true background, like the other women of Jesus's Motherline, was intentionally hidden. Matthew calls her only "the wife of Uriah"; she appears to be a pagan foreigner, likely Hittite, from what is now Turkey and Syria. As the story goes, David, while walking on the roof of his palace, spots the beautiful Bathsheba bathing below, purifying herself after menstruation. He is mesmerized by Bathsheba, who is "married," a coded reference to her sexual experience. David commands her to sleep with him, after which she becomes pregnant through their adulterous affair. He then takes her as his wife and queen, and she later gives birth to the future King Solomon. The Bible describes how she became the quintessential, and much-honored *gevirah,* the queen mother who crowned and granted sovereignty to Solomon. The allusion to the rooftop may well be a reference to the sacred marriage rites that took place in ritual beds located on temple roofs in the ancient world.

How is it that Bathsheba, an "adulterer," rose to such power in David's court and became the mother of one of the most important kings in Jewish history? What was her secret? The only explanation is that Bathsheba descended from royal or priestess blood, as David famously had many other children from royal wives, as well as a harem that met his sexual needs. Bathsheba, whose name means "Daughter of Sheba," was considered important for reasons that were never mentioned in the Bible, probably because she, like David's other wives, was a qedesha-queen of the goddess religions, a topic considered unfit for discussion by biblical scribes. We might also wonder if her name itself is a hint. Is she, like King Solomon's famous lover, a priestess-queen of the Ethiopian land of Sheba?

Bathsheba provides the fourth clue in Matthew's geneology that traces Jesus's descent from a line of foreign harlot-priestesses. The Motherline of Jesus was a red thread, laced with wondrous scarlet women who survived in a male-dominated world by taking positions of power in influential Hebrew families. Though their power and sexual wisdom was deemed "scandalous," it was secretly coveted and highly prized by the patriarchs. We can be sure society judged them, but their actions and their children were implicitly blessed by God, as they bore male heirs in the line of Davidic kings. With this knowledge in mind, we are nearly ready for the final, and most astonishing, piece of the puzzle to reveal itself.

Divine Birthing

"Divine birthing" refers to a spiritually infused conception. Why is it that a number of Hebrew and Israelite patriarchs married priestesses of the "witch lines"? Beyond the practical matter of political alliances, they valued their magical and psychic powers. For example, this includes Moses who married Zipporah, an African woman of Kushite (Ethiopian) ethnicity, daughter of a Midian priest and likely a priestess herself. The list continues with Isaac, Judah, King David, King Solomon, King Ahab, and others. The founding patriarchs and kings intentionally sought to bring the oracular power of the priestess-queens to their own descendants and royal lineages.

Priestesses were trained in the secret feminine art of conscious conception, designed to bring an "avatar" or energetically gifted "divine child" into the world. This spiritual technology consisted of sacred rituals, prayers, ceremonies, energy-body practices, imaginal journeys, and conscious lovemaking designed to birth the next generation of high priestesses and priests, queens and kings. The secret rites harness magical power of the universe and weave it into the body and soul of the young being who is incarnating into the immaculate and awakened womb of the mother.

Mother Mary a Priestess of the Goddess Temples

Matthew's deliberate inclusion of the priestess ancestors of Jesus leads us to an even more remarkable discovery. He is clearly linking the harlot-matriarchs not just to Jesus but also to Mother Mary. Matthew intentionally draws a parallel between the stories of Tamar, Rahab, Ruth, Bathsheba, *and Mary*—who, as harlot, seductress, or priestess, each wed and conceived with men under scandalous circumstances in order to birth the Messianic line. The revelation is that *Mother Mary is the fifth and final sacred priestess of this tradition.*

Our vision is that each of these incidents represents a carefully encoded story of a high priestess who unites with a patriarch in sacred sexual marriage rites, and who was chosen in part to give power to the Messianic line. This tradition passed down the lineage to Mother Mary who was a temple priestess, as we will see, and who quite possibly participated in the rites with a priest of the mysteries. By Mary's time the ritual may have been more political than spiritual, and controlled by men, but even so it transmitted an authority based on the long tradition of the sovereignty-granting power of the priestess and drew upon her feminine wisdom and gifts.

Mother Mary

The Conception Mystery

*In trial or difficulty I have recourse to Mother Mary, whose glance
alone is enough to dissipate every fear.*

SAINT THÉRÈSE OF LISIEUX

One of the greatest mysteries of the Christ tradition is the story of Jesus's conception, which raised him to a divinized status, resembling the mythological Greek gods of his day. The official story is of a virgin birth, conceived without earthly sex or an earthly father, and birthed through a blessed mother who herself was born of an Immaculate Conception.

Yet for two thousand years there have been other versions of the story, focusing on the very human history and circumstance of the beginnings of Jesus's life. For some, it can be shocking to hear these alternative narratives, shared by ancient Roman and Jewish sources, and revisited by modern scholars who strip the story of its fairy-tale quality of a magical and divine conception, and talk instead of illegitimacy, and possibly even rape.

We will explore each of these perspectives, along with the fascinating new possibility of a third option, a conception by an ancient rite of the temple priestess: hieros gamos.

But first let's open the doorway into the story of the illegitimacy of Jesus . . .

The Seduction of Mary

Over the past several decades two prominent feminist biblical scholars have put forward a foundation-shifting interpretation of the story of Jesus's conception: the possibility that Jesus was illegitimate, or even a child of rape. Jane Schaberg, Ph.D., former professor of religious studies and women's studies at University of Detroit, and author of *The Illegitimacy of Jesus,* sent shockwaves through the world of Christendom by carefully analyzing early biblical, rabbinical, and Roman historical sources to reveal the startling thesis that Jesus was very likely an illegitimate child, born by the seduction or rape of Mary. In the more than thirty years since publication, and despite much outrage, there have been no credible refutations of her work. With a careful understanding of biblical-era literary conventions, and with the trained ears to "listen hard to the silence within the text" of what was *not said* in the Bible, the picture becomes clear. The evidence is overwhelming, undeniable, and painstakingly detailed in her book.

Elisabeth Schüssler Fiorenza, Ph.D., professor of divinity at Harvard Divinity School, backs up Schaberg's interpretation, and in her book *Jesus: Miriam's Child, Sophia's Prophet,* takes the conversation a step further, proposing that Jesus was a prophet of Sophia and exploring his feminine Sophianic lineage.

The Evidence Stacks Up

For those with the eyes to see, the three synoptic gospels leave obvious clues of the circumstances of Mary's pregnancy with Jesus. The Gospel of Matthew lists thirty-nine ancestors of Jesus in the pattern of "A begets B, B begets C" and so forth. But this pattern stops with Joseph, the husband of Mary. Joseph does not beget Jesus, and he is not called the father of Jesus. Instead, Joseph is just referred to as the *husband of Mary,* while Mary is named *the mother of Jesus.* The biological father is intentionally *not* mentioned.

Even more blatantly, in the Gospel of Mark, Jesus is called the "son of Mary" rather than the traditional "son of Joseph." It may seem like a subtle distinction, but to the readers of the day, particularly in Mary's home province of Galilee, this is a very clear and shocking admission. Joseph is not the father. The only children referred to as the son of their mother are those without a father under Jewish law. In other words, they are conceived through adultery, rape, prostitution, *or* through the matrilineal pagan sexual rites.

The Gospels of Luke and Matthew both share that Mary conceives while she is engaged to her future husband Joseph. Joseph is outraged at the news of her pregnancy because he has not had sexual relations with her; it is not his child. He plans to divorce Mary as a suspected adulterer, but an angel of God instructs him not to—the implication is that Mary is blameless in the eyes of God. But how could this be possible?

Matthew makes an allusion to Deuteronomy 22:23–27 that explains the detail of the law regarding the seduction or rape of a betrothed virgin—that the woman is blameless if she is raped, if it happened against her will. As Jane Schaberg points out, though it is taboo to say it directly, Matthew uses a literary device to suggest that he knew that Mary may have been raped. It could also be equally likely that Mary conceived through a forbidden temple-rite, an event considered to be degrading or illegal by biblical scribes. Yet although it was against Jewish law, the outcome is that Mary is blameless and her son was blessed by God.

Another detail that supports the theme of a sexual violation or an unusual conception is that Luke describes Mary as being "humiliated," *tapeinosis* in Greek.[2] In multiple places in the Bible this word is used to describe a "sexual humiliation," or rape.[3] After the angel Gabriel brings Mary the message that her baby is blessed, not cursed, and that Joseph will marry her even though he is not the father, Mary sings the famous Magnificat, the Canticle of Mary. The tone of this song would be inappropriate for the circumstances unless she had experienced some kind of abuse or humiliation. It speaks of overcoming social, moral, and economic injustice, of being vindicated from shame and oppression, of victory through fight or battle. But it *does* fit as a powerful lament of an abused woman or "harlot," who has been accused of conceiving illegitimately, and who is celebrating her spiritual victory after a divine intervention—God has infused both mother and child with the Holy Spirit, and has influenced Joseph to marry her despite the circumstances of the conception.

Or perhaps she was accused of adultery and then vindicated in her role as priestess? We will watch as the story continues to unfold.

Magnificat—Canticle of Mary

My soul praises the greatness of the Lord!

My spirit exults in God, my Savior,

because he has looked favorably on his humble servant.

From now on, all generations will call me blessed

Because the Almighty has done great things for me.

His mercy lasts from generation to generation. . . .

He displayed his mighty power with his arm.

He scattered people who were proud in mind and heart

He pulled powerful rulers from their thrones

and lifted up humble people.[4]

In response to the embarrassing rumors of Jesus's illegitimacy that were spreading like wildfire through the Roman and Jewish world, the early Roman Church put forward the idea of the virgin birth, *nearly two hundred years after the fact,* and, awkwardly, only *after* the church father Origen had already affirmed in writing that the rumors were true. They justified their position based on the prophet Isaiah, who they claimed predicted that the Messiah would be born of a *parthenos,* a "virgin," using the early Greek translation of the Old Testament (Isaiah 7:14). But this is a mistranslation of the original Hebrew word *alma,* often meaning "young woman," not virgin. There was never a prediction that Mary would give birth without having had sex; that would have no precedent in the Jewish tradition. Other arguments that the virgin birth was modeled after the Greco-Roman goddess myths fail to understand that in Hellenic and other traditions *virgin* meant "autonomous, sovereign, independent," and typically "unmarried," *not* a woman who had never had sex. The virgin goddesses and priestesses of antiquity often had lovers. Indeed, the virgin birth in the pagan world was often a ritual conception.

A Third Way

It may well be possible that the true scandal is that Mary, as a temple-priestess, and weaver of the Holy Veil of Shekinah, was prepared for the role as part of her spiritual destiny as a priestess and a future scarlet mother of the Messianic bloodline. It is clear that there is more going on than meets the eye. In fact, even his own disciples call Jesus a "son of a harlot," and detractors in his local community refer to his illegitimacy as if it is common knowledge.

The gnostic Gospel of Thomas reveals knowledge of the scandalous rumors of Jesus's parentage, stating of Jesus that "He who knows the father [God] and the mother [feminine Holy Spirit] will be called son of a harlot."[5] In the Gospel of John 8:41, opponents of Jesus respond in heated discussion with him that "*We were not born illegitimately,*" implying they knew Jesus *was* of an illegitimate birth.[6] The Acts of Pilate 2:3 presents the charge made to Pontius Pilate by Jewish elders that Jesus was "born of fornication."

Fornication was usually a phrase reserved for the "harlots and whores"—the temple priestesses who performed hieros gamos rituals, either annually to bless the land or to enthrone a king or priest, or to conceive a child of magical consciousness and kingship. The reality of the synoptic gospels is that they are conflicted. They know they must address the rumors of the illegitimacy in some way, but they are trying to minimize and obscure the truth because it is embarrassing, scandalous, and easily misunderstood by the public.

If these were the only pieces of evidence of Mary's irregular conception of Jesus, perhaps we would have some lingering doubt, because it was considered too impolite for the Christian gospel writers to directly state the facts. But the rabbinical and Roman writers also have much to say on the matter, and they do not hold back.

Mary the Holy Whore

We now turn our attention to the earliest sources *outside the Bible,* to see what we can learn about Jesus and Mother Mary, or Miriam, as she would have been called at the time. Interestingly, early Christian and Jewish Talmudic tradition agree on one thing: *there was clearly an anomaly in Jesus's conception.* Joseph, the upstanding Jewish man who later married Mary, was not Jesus's biological father; and whoever the father was, he was nowhere to be found.

So who was the father? How did Mary's pregnancy happen?

The Jewish solution was very practical: Mary was a "whore." She had sex and conceived a child outside of marriage. The father, in Talmudic histories, was very much a human—not a god—a Roman soldier known as Pantera or Pandera. Jesus was clearly an illegitimate child, a *mamzer,* who later rose to prominence as a healer, magician, and spiritual teacher, but because he was conceived "in sin" (never mind his heretical teachings!), he could never be a true messiah.

The Christian solution to the "problem" of Jesus's parentage was mystical: God, in fact, was the missing father, which made Jesus the Son of God. There was no human father, thus there was no sex out of wedlock. This interpretation, rather than being an embarrassment, formed the powerful, mythic cornerstone of the Christian faith. Mary, being the Mother of God incarnate, was the eternal virgin, who was never "defiled" by the human sexual act.

These are the two options presented to us by traditional sources.

But the third, untold, very radical, and secret possibility is that Mary was a priestess of the goddess traditions, who conceived Jesus in the temple rites of old. And that Joseph brought her into safety and protection under the Jewish law by marrying her.

If Mary is a priestess of the goddess, perhaps Jesus's forbidden secret is that he is first and foremost a *son of the goddess,* rather than the son of a patriarchal god. When priestesses conceived through the sexual rites of the temple, their children were said to be children of the goddess herself and were sometimes raised in the temples. If this were the case with Jesus, it would have required only a small gender switch for the church to make him a son of a male god.

Interestingly, this is also the story of the Sumerian poet-princess Enheduanna's father, Sargon the Great, who was born "illegitimately," around 2370 BCE. Sargon writes:

> I am Sargon the mighty king. . . . My mother was an *enetu* [priestess], my father
> I did not know. My mother the *enetu* became pregnant with me. She brought
> me into the world in secret. She put me in a little reed basket. . . . She launched
> me into the water in a river. . . . Ishtar became fond of me.[7]

Sargon considered himself a son of Ishtar. He worked as a chalice bearer under her name, in service to the reigning king, and eventually rose to power himself, creating the world's first empire and dynasty of Ishtar.

Mother Mary—The Temple Priestess

Let us gather together more clues that point to the heretical possibility that Mary was a sacred sexual temple priestess. To do so we will need to consult the Talmud, and also learn a little more about the cultural climate of Palestine two thousand years ago.

The early Talmudic writings contain dozens of references to Jesus and his mother. Mary, or Miriam, is consistently referred to as *stada,* a Hebrew epithet that means "whore, prostitute, or adulteress." She is also referred to as a woman

"who let her hair grow long" and a "plaiter of women's hair." As displays of long and stylized hair are symbolic of sexuality and the sacred harlots, these comments are accusations that Mary is a loose or taboo woman:

> But was not . . . his mother Stada? His mother was Miriam, the woman who let her hair grow long. This one was unfaithful to her husband.[8]

And here we see Mary, mother of Jesus, being called a "M'gaddela," a variation of the word *Magdala,* or Magdalene:

> The mother was Stada. The mother was Miriam, dresser of women's hair (*Miriam m'gadella nashaia*), as we say in Pumbeditha, "such a one has been false to her husband."[9]

Mother Mary is also a Magdalene! In this case the Talmud refers to both a *literal* meaning of the Magdalene title as a plaiter or braider of women's hair, as well as a *symbolic* reference to the traditions of the curled and plaited hair of harlots and priestesses who participated in the temple rituals of hair adornment.* As we have seen again and again, this constellation of words that we are now so familiar with—*whore, fornicator, harlot, hairdresser*—refers to priestesses, the qedeshot of Asherah and Astarte.

The Jewish histories of Jesus continue with the *Toledoth Yeshu,* or "The Life of Jesus," a rabbinical text dating from as early as the fifth century that tells the most detailed version of the story of Mother Mary and Jesus. In this account Mary is raped by a man named Pandera.[10]

The Talmud also recounts that Mary brings her young son Jesus to Egypt, where he spends his youth and young adulthood learning sorcery and magic. And, most tellingly, the tractate Kallah 51a may be a veiled reference that Mary conceived Jesus during menstruation, the most shameful and unthinkable sin:

> Rabbi Yehoshua says [he is] a son of a *niddah* [menstruating woman]. Rabbi Akiba says he [is] an illegitimate child who is also the son of a *niddah*.[11]

The character who represents Mother Mary then says:

---

*The Semetic root *gdl,* contained within *m'gaddela,* means to plait or braid. Thus the original meaning of a "hairdresser" was a woman who plaited or braided hair, the traditional style worn by priestesses.

When I entered the bridal chamber, I was *niddah* and . . . my friend came to me, and by him I had this son—it resulted that this child is illegitimate and the son of a *niddah* [conceived during menstruation].[12]

This "menstrual slur" was also made against Mary Magdalene. In *Jesus in the Talmud,* former Princeton professor of Judaic studies, Peter Schäfer, discusses a possible veiled accusation in Shabbat 104b that Jesus had sexual communion with Magdalene during menstruation.[13] We propose this "menstrual sex" meme may be a coded reference to the ancient feminine rites and mysteries practiced by both Mary Magdalene and Mother Mary.

The writings of the prominent Greek philosopher Celsus, who lived in the second century CE, echoed similar themes: that Mary was an adulteress, that Jesus was fathered by a Roman soldier named Panthera, and that Jesus went to Egypt to learn magic.

The Christian father Origen defends Jesus's reputation against Celsus's charges in his work *Against Celsus.* Surprisingly, Origen concedes that *most of Celsus's accounts of Jesus are true,* however this just makes Jesus all the more powerful because he is still the Son of God despite having "all these things against him." Origen considers Jesus and Mary to be quintessential outsiders, *hamartolos,* in the Jewish culture of that time.[14]

Astarte pendant with sacred doves, swans, or geese. Ishtar was worshipped by her Greek name, Astarte, across the Middle East in the centuries leading up to Magdalene's life. The dove was her symbol, representing love and sacred sexuality. Bronze, southern Spain, 525 BCE.

(Photo by José Luiz Bernardes Ribeiro, CC BY-SA 3.0)

The combination of references to adultery, harlotry, long hair, hairdressing, sorcery, magic, Egypt, and sex during menstruation make it clear that though Mary, mother of Jesus, lived in Palestine, she was considered distinctly hamartolos in the Talmudic and even Roman histories, living outside of Jewish law in a way that would have been unimaginable for the average woman. But these descriptions would make perfect sense if she were a priestess trained in the temples of Isis or Astarte, or a secret Jewish priestess of Asherah.

Son of the Panther

Another puzzling thread of the story is the naming of Jesus as *ben Panther* or *ben Pandera* in the texts—meaning "son of the panther," and hinting at an unusual fatherline. Multiple early Talmudic sources written close to the lifetime of Jesus disparagingly refer to him as son of the panther, repeating the well-known rumor in the Jewish community that his mother Mary conceived Jesus illegitimately with a man named Pandera. But who was this Pandera?

Some have speculated that he was a Roman soldier, but it is just as likely that "the panther" referred to a priest or initiate in the mystery cult of Dionysus or Osiris. At the time of Jesus, the cult of Dionysus was one of the most widespread and popular forms of religious expression in the Greco-Roman world, and it penetrated deeply into the multicultural world of Palestine during the lifetime of Jesus. Archaeologic evidence shows that at least two Palestinian cities, Beth Shean and Ashkelon, were sites of Dionysus worship, with legends supporting connections to Rafa as well. As reported in Maccabees II, the king Antiochus Epiphanes punished Jews by forcing them to worship Dionysus, which points to the likelihood that the cult was more widespread than the records show.[15] Folk religion was far more diverse, complex, and multilayered than official religious histories admitted, especially as Palestine was a significant crossroads of cultures.

Dionysus's totem animal was the panther. He and his priests and bacchante priestesses wore panther-skin robes. The cult of Dionysus was famous for its public sexual orgies and fertility rituals, celebrating with ecstatic and uninhibited behavior and excesses of wine—and the participants in these rituals included members from all social classes. The panther, and the panther priests, represented the awakening and expression of forbidden desires and primordial wildness, particularly sexual. The cult of Dionysus also had secret, esoteric mysteries attended only by initiates that we know little about. Jesus's biography mirrors Dionysus's in dozens of details, suggesting that it was a religion he was more than familiar with, and that his life may have been modeled after this archetypal figure.

Priests of the Egyptian Isis and Osiris also wore panther skins, and Mother Mary's father was described as a "Panther" by the eighth-century church leader John of Damascus. As we know Mary lived for many years in Egypt; it is certainly possible that she came from a priestess lineage of Isis/Osiris initiates, and conceived her child in their sacred rites. This could explain why she left for Egypt shortly after Jesus's birth, and why Jesus was often described as an "Egyptian Magician" by pagans and Jews of the time.

The Egyptian links continue with Bast, the Egyptian goddess of sexuality and fertility, who was also associated with panthers. Priestesses of Dionysus and the goddess Bast were described as "amorous pantheresses." Bast was known as "She of the Ointment jar" and symbolized by the famous "alabaster jar" that later became the symbol of Mary Magdalene. In all likelihood, the word *alabaster* derives from the name Bast. The Greeks knew Bast as *Ailuros,* which means "cat" and is associated with the word *allure.* Bast was a sex goddess, who held the Grail chalice of anointment and allurement, and her panther priestesses were high initiates of the hieros gamos. Scholar G. R. S. Mead writes, "Pasht or Bast, the 'cat' or 'panther' goddess, is supposed to have had rites resembling those of Aphrodite Pandemos, and the girls of her temple were therefore presumably [sacred] prostitutes."[16] Greeks considered Bast to be the soul of Isis.

Interestingly, Mandaean scholar Jorunn Buckley comments that according to the early Mandaean gnostic texts, "Mary becomes pregnant by witchcraft"—or by some other "unnatural means"—until nine months later she brings forth a messiah. "Witchcraft" in this context can mean only one thing: a reference to the feminine mysteries and goddess cults.[17]

Is it possible that Mary conceived Jesus with a Panther priest in a secret hieros gamos temple ritual? These traditions were very prominent in Alexandria at the time, within both Dionysian temples and the goddess temples of Isis. Maybe it was this ritual union in the Panther lineage, considered heretical to conservative commentators, that was the perceived shame or "defilement" of the virginal Mary? However, in the mystery traditions the conception would have been considered to be auspicious and blessed, calling on the highest spiritual technology to birth a son of goddess, who would be considered a leader, avatar, and prophet.

There is a great mystery to Jesus's conception, something veiled and hidden, that is alluded to by many, and confirmed by none. The innocence and purity of Mary remains intact either way. As later Christians point out, the gifts of Jesus are not diminished by his birth.

Weavers of the Holy Veil

Let's now explore what the Catholic Church has to say about Mary as priestess.

The apocryphal Gospel of James, also known as the Protoevangelium of James, written around 145 CE, tells the story of Saint Anne, the mother of the Virgin Mary. Anne was known as a mystic because, while pregnant with Mary, she received a message from God that her daughter would be the Mother of God and needed to be consecrated as a priestess at the Temple of Jerusalem. Anne's emblem was the door, a womb-gateway motif similar to that of Mary Magdalene and Inanna. She was said to have traveled to Egypt to be with her daughter Mary after the birth of the infant Jesus, and she was considered the matriarch of the "Holy Kinship," the extended family of Jesus.

Catholic tradition agrees that Mary was a priestess—that at the age of three, the blessed Mother Mary was consecrated as a virgin priestess of the Temple of Jerusalem, and was raised there with the other young girls until the age of fourteen. The Gospel of James shares the story that when her parents brought her to the temple steps, Mary danced in happiness, reassuring them that she was ready.[18] The Catholic feast of the Presentation of the Blessed Virgin Mary is still held on November 21 to celebrate her induction as temple priestess.

The Jewish school of temple priestesses was written about in the Hebrew Bible, Talmud, and other early sources. They performed a variety of sacred duties, including baking bread, preparing incense, and performing liturgies and ceremonies.[19] Most importantly they were the Weavers of the Holy Veil, the ornately decorated curtain spun from silk, fine flax, and gold thread that was so massive it required three hundred priests to lift it.[20] The veil was a symbolic hymen or threshold, concealing the holy of holies, the innermost womb chamber of the temple that formerly housed the Ark of the Covenant.

Over time the tradition of the temple priestesses, which originated with the pagan Canaanites, evolved into a uniquely Jewish tradition, where consecrated young temple priestesses "waited at the door of the Tabernacle" in the time of Moses.[21] Later they ministered at the first and second Temples of Jerusalem in service to the high priest.[22]

Catholic doctrine tells us that while the Virgin Mary was serving as a temple priestess, the high priest invited her to enter the holy of holies with him. This was an astounding honor, especially considering that Moses commanded that no one other than the high priest could step foot into the holy of holies, and that even he was only allowed entry once per year. Could this be a euphemism for a sacred, but forbidden, hieros gamos temple rite? In crossing the threshold into the holy of holies, the former home of the lost Ark of the Covenant, Catholic tradition holds that Mary symbolically takes her place as the New Eve. As the Mother of Christ, her womb becomes the New Ark of the Covenant.[23]

When we consider any of the clues of Jesus's conception *on its own,* no one element conclusively *proves* anything, but when we look at all the pieces of the puzzle put together, an astonishing new picture and possibility begins to emerge. What if the forbidden secret of Mary, Jesus's mother, is that she is a priestess of the goddess traditions? Herself a Magdalene and harlot as the Talmud implies? That she conceives Jesus through temple ceremonies of the goddess, and is shamed for it?

What if Jesus's secret story is that he is a *son of the goddess,* a magician and womb shaman, witch and healer, who trains in the mystery schools of Egypt, India, and elsewhere? That he descends from a long maternal lineage of powerful harlot priestesses? That he is born first to a priestess mother and then spiritually rebirths through the womb of Mary Magdalene, with whom he is *koinonos,* sexually and spiritually united in a deep soulmate love? That the Mystery of the Bridal Chamber, as described by King Solomon and gnostic authors, is a very real initiatory Path of Love with a long and rich tradition that he continues?

What if Mary Magdalene's secret is that, like Jesus's mother, she is a sexual priestess who trains in the goddess temples? That she is the impassioned and empowered anointrix, with long, flowing, sensuous hair, who carries an alabaster anointing jar symbolic of the yoni-womb of the goddess? That she is raped, trafficked, or abused in the fallen temples? But with the help of Yeshua's love, she overcomes the Grail wounds of the feminine? That she clears her seven gates of the devils of trauma, so that she can step into her destiny as a Feminine Christ, merging the goddess lines of Inanna-Sophia, Isis, Ishtar, and Asherah? That she embodies the Red, White, Green, *and* Womb-Black Paths of the feminine, the full template of the human woman, and offers this gift to us?

What if together the awakened Mary Magdalene and Jesus birth a "divine child" into the world through their love, devotion, and spiritual mana, healing the separation of masculine and feminine to forge a new path of consciousness we can still access today?

> *O form of woman, sister of Wisdom, how great is your glory!*
> HILDEGARD VON BINGEN,
> EPILOGUE, LIFE OF SAINT RUPERT

MAGDALENE'S LIFETIME
STORY OF THE FEMININE CHRIST

CHAMBER 7

APOSTLE OF ECSTASY

Magdalene, the Female Pope

Her bridal chamber doth stream with light, and pour forth scent of
balsam and sweet herbs.

"ODE TO SOPHIA," GNOSTIC HYMN

NOW THAT WE HAVE LEARNED MORE about the spiritual traditions
that the Magdalene Mysteries are rooted in, we can explore what we know of Mary
Magdalene in her own lifetime.

Let's first meet Mary Magdalene as she appears in the canonical gospels of the
New Testament. These are the earliest accounts that mention Mary (albeit in an
obscured way) and her importance to the life and work of Jesus, and give clues to
her power.

Later on in our Quest, we will journey deeper into the apocryphal gospels
and gnostic texts (such as the Pistis Sophia), medieval folklore, and oracular
intuition, which are incredibly revealing as to the magnitude of Magdalene's significance, not just as the apostle or even wife of Jesus, but as a spiritual light in
her own right.

We will ask—is Magdalene the Beloved *and* Feminine Christ and Spiritual
Equal?

But first, let's dive for the jewels that are waiting for those with the eyes
to see.

Mary Magdalene—
Secret Priestess of the Gospels

All four canonical gospels directly mention or allude to Mary Magdalene being present at the crucifixion, and in John, she alone is the first to witness Jesus's resurrection. Jesus then asks her to go and announce his resurrection to the other disciples. This is what earns Magdalene the title of Apostle of the Apostles, the *apostola apostolorum,* in church circles.

Before that, Mary Magdalene also has a starring role in the New Testament as the beautiful and bold woman who anoints him with expensive nard, weeps at his feet with love, and dries his feet with her luxurious hair (symbolically associated with wanton sexuality at the time), and also as the woman who receives his spiritual teachings and "turns to the good," and (according to some) as the woman who is exorcised of seven demons by him, or who is saved from being stoned for her sins. A note on this point: although there is intuitive consistency with the mysterious anointrix and sensual sinner being Mary Magdalene, and a number of scholars and theologians accept this thesis, there is no actual naming of MM as the anointer.

As always, Magdalene stands on the outer edge of tradition, with the opening of her red cloak promising to reveal something forbidden that the church wishes to hide. For if MM is indeed the anointrix, and Jesus as the Messiah is the anointed one, then this suggests that she is inducting him into a sacred rite, ancient tradition, or mystical state of consciousness of which she is already a high mistress and initiate.

A gnostic researcher shares: "*Messiah* is a Hebrew word meaning anointed. In ancient times kings and theocrats were anointed with precious oils to symbolize their authority. But who was the anointer? It must have been a superior agency because the anointer is the one who empowers the sacred king, the messiah, christos, the anointed. The one who confers power is anterior to the one who receives it."[1]

Every step Magdalene takes in the Bible leaves a trail of controversy and questions. If this was a Hollywood movie, we would know instantly that Mary was the leading lady and star of the show—a spirited, sexy rule breaker, passionate with love.

What the Gospels Say about Mary

As many academics have pointed out, it is as if the gospel writers didn't really want to include Magdalene in the gospels at all, but—maybe because of the sheer power of her reputation and memory?—they felt they couldn't leave her out either.

Instead, they included key scenes of her life, which were rich with symbolic spiritual meaning and drama, but then played them down or obscured their meaning. They were trying to minimize her importance—yet even the brief mentions that are made have shone like a light for over two thousand years.

While he was in Bethany, reclining at the table in the home of Simon the Leper, a woman came with an alabaster jar of very expensive perfume, made of pure nard. She broke the jar and poured the perfume on his head. (Mark 14:3–9)

She has done a beautiful thing to me. The poor you will always have with you, but you will not always have me. When she poured this perfume on my body, she did it to prepare me for burial. Truly I tell you, wherever this gospel is preached throughout the world, what she has done will also be told, in memory of her. (Matthew 26:10–13)

Six days before the Passover, Jesus came to Bethany, where Lazarus lived, whom Jesus had raised from the dead. Here a dinner was given in Jesus's honor. Martha served, while Lazarus was among those reclining at the table with him. Then Mary took about a pint of pure nard, an expensive perfume; she poured it on Jesus's feet and wiped his feet with her hair. And the house was filled with the fragrance of the perfume. (John 12:1–3)

One of the Pharisees invited Jesus to eat with him. So he went to the Pharisee's home and took his place at the table. There was a woman who was a notorious sinner in that city. When she learned that Jesus was eating at the Pharisee's home, she took an alabaster jar of perfume and knelt at his feet behind him. She was crying and began to wash his feet with her tears and dry them with her hair. Then she kissed his feet over and over again, anointing them constantly with the perfume. (Luke 7:36–38)

Do you see this woman? I came into your house. You didn't give me any water for my feet, but this woman has washed my feet with her tears and dried them with her hair. You didn't give me a kiss, but this woman, from the moment I came in, has not stopped kissing my feet. You didn't anoint my head with oil, but this woman has anointed my feet with perfume. So I'm telling you that her sins, as many as they are, have been forgiven, and that's why she has shown such great love. But the one to whom little is forgiven loves little. (Luke 7:44–47)

What the Gospels Don't Say about Mary . . .

What the gospel writers fail to give is any cultural context to these incredible snapshots of Mary Magdalene's role in the unfolding ministry of Christ. Usually, Jewish women of the day were very conservative—even having their hair down in public would have been considered quite unorthodox and risky. The idea of flamboyantly bursting in on a formal dinner between an unmarried man and his friends, with hair loose, weeping with love and anointing him would be unthinkable. And, as we may remember, in Luke 7:36 she is called a "notorious sinner," adding even more scandal to the mix.

At that time, Hellenized Jewish women of the upper classes did have more freedom than other women, and often socialized in towns, such as Tiberius, the headquarters of Herod in Galilee, and were famous for their lax morals and extravagant lifestyles. And we know one of Jesus's female followers, Joanna, wife of Herod's steward, did come from this milieu and was likely a friend of Mary Magdalene's. However, it is still unlikely that a highborn Jewish woman would burst into a Pharisee's house, weeping, to anoint a man and be called a sinner.

Yet if Mary were a wife—or more likely yet, also a priestess of the goddess— it would make far more sense. Priestesses were not constrained by the patriarchal traditions of the time. They were known for sensual anointing rituals that gave a man his kingship, or they anointed those who were about to die or receive spiritual initiation. They presided over grief rituals and funerary rites with weeping and lamentation and were known for their exuberant displays of love and affection.

This appears to perfectly describe Magdalene's essence . . .

⚐ She anoints Jesus for his death (or spiritual rebirth into kingship).

⚐ She (alongside other Marys) attends Jesus's tomb for his funerary rites.

❧ She breaks cultural and religious conventions and is feared by some male disciples.

❧ She is often associated with wanton sexuality and sinfulness.

❧ *Sin* meant "moon" in ancient times and sinners were often moon priestesses.

❧ She is often described as weeping or lamenting, as in the Rites of Isis.

❧ She is very emotional and is described as the "one who loves much."

Does this explain why she had at her disposal very expensive sacred anointing oils that an ordinary unmarried woman—or common prostitute—could not afford?

Anointing of the Wild Fertile Oil

The Gospel of John 12:4–8 describes Judas's outrage at the anointing of Jesus's feet by Mary:

> Judas Iscariot, one of his disciples (he who was about to betray him), said, "Why was this ointment not sold for three hundred denarii, and given to the poor?" Jesus said, "Leave her alone, so that she may keep it for the day of my burial. For the poor you always have with you, but you do not always have me."

This seemingly simple—yet perplexing—scene is layered with rich meanings. In the ancient mystery schools there was always a "twin" teaching, one exoteric outer layer that was visible and understandable to the uninitiated and was taken literally, often told as a parable or a simple story that appealed to the emotional mind, and then a veiled or esoteric hidden meaning that was symbolic and could only be seen and understood by those who had been initiated into the feminine mystical consciousness. Symbols work directly on the cerebellar feminine consciousness, in the "angelic gate" in the back brain, and act as a labyrinth of archetypal meaning.

For thousands of years, across the Near East and the Mediterranean, anointing oils were the sacred shamanic tools of priestesses and womb shamans. They were used in almost all feminine sacred rituals, and were also used to anoint a man into kingship, usually through a death-rebirth ritual, where he would be "reborn" through the sublime power of the priestess's Holy Womb, the gateway to god. The fragrant plant oils synergize with and symbolically represent the sexual secretions.

This scene in the New Testament hints at these origins and calls to mind the sensual goddess rituals of Sumeria, encoded in the Old Testament as the Song of

Songs—scripture that is often intuitively linked to Mary Magdalene and read out at her feast days. Mischievously, it alludes to her symbolic role as the priestess-bride.

In the Song of Songs 1:2–4, the Bride confesses her love, "May he kiss me with the kisses of his mouth! For your love is better than wine. Your oils have a pleasing fragrance. Your name is like purified oil; Draw me after you and let us run together! The king has brought me into his chambers." The word used here for the oil is *shemen,* which translates as "fat or oil," meaning "fertile, wild, lavish," conveying a sensuality most associated with the "Holy Whore" rituals of the priestesses. Coincidentally, it also mirrors a later gnostic text that implies that Jesus kisses MM "on the mouth."

If we are left in any doubt, the Song of Songs 1:12–13 continues on the ravishing theme of the Bride, "While the King was at his table, my perfume gave forth its fragrance. My beloved is to me a pouch of myrrh, which lies all night between my breasts." Note here that the word for her fragrance comes from the root of *ru'ach*—a feminine gendered noun for Spirit that invokes an essence, breathing, moving, and reaching into the other person, like the sacred Holy Spirit, who moves in mystery. It appears the gospels are giving secret scriptural allusions to those who know.

The substance that Mary uses in her anointing rite is also whispering with clues. Spikenard is from the valerian family and originates in India, often from the Himalayas, and is used in tantric rites and childbirth, as it has a sedative effect. It was an expensive import in both Egyptian and Jewish rituals, costing a year's salary.

Spikenard also has a contraceptive effect, making it desired for sacred sexual rites. A Jewish scholar suggests that aromatic oils were used by the women in royal harems as a form of contraceptive. In the book of Esther, the rapacious king has sexual intercourse with a new virgin every night, and these women are ritually prepared with ointments in the concubine quarters for up to a year before the encounter, possibly as an ancient form of herbal contraception.

It was likely Mary Magdalene carried myrrh, as well as spikenard, in her iconic alabaster jar of Inanna, used in the anointing of Jesus before and after his death and rebirth rites. Mary Magdalene, in the tradition of the Egyptian cults of Isis, was considered a myrrhophore, or myrrh bearer, which as we have seen was also sexual. So these important symbolic allusions set the stage for the secret identity of MM. Her entrance into the New Testament is dripping with the lavish oil of mystery.

Often in conventional religious thought, the idealized "spiritual woman" is defined as someone who is humble, kind, giving, gentle, ethereal, and peaceful. Magdalene includes those attributes, yet she also reveals a juicy, embodied, wild feminine side.

As the fullness of Mary's power was edited out of the story, now we open a new chapter—and return the feminine spirit of Mary Magdalene to its rightful throne.

CHAMBER 8

DIVINE PROPHETESS

Ancestry and Origins of Magdalene

AS WE BEGIN TO DIVE DEEPER into the story of her life, it is wise to take a few moments to percolate the origins of Mary Magdalene. Who was she, what was her ancestry?

Because of the scant evidence of the details of her life, we are visioning her from both the texts and legends we can source *and* also from our own intuitive knowing.

But first, let's allow our curiosity to ask the simple questions:

Where did Mary come from—what were her origins?
What was her life like before she met Christ?
How did she come into Yeshu's life?

Magdalene—Jewish Princess or Syrian Priestess?

What do we know of Mary Magdalene's ancestry? The most striking fact is that despite her prominence in the early Christian movement, there is a near complete information blackout on her personal and cultural background. Given her popularity, and even notoriety, how could this be possible? In the first centuries CE, at least ten gnostic and apocryphal gospels portray her as a powerful figure: a visionary and prophetess, the leading disciple, the true inheritor of Jesus's teachings, the one whom Jesus loves most.

From the Gospel of Luke we also know that she is hamartolos—an outsider—

someone who does not observe Jewish law, and who may or may not be culturally Jewish. Though she lived in Judea and Galilee at the time of Jesus's life, she is conspicuously absent in the Jewish historical record. In other words, the Jewish community of rabbis, historians, and folklorists never "claimed" her as Jewish. In contrast Jesus, Mother Mary, Jesus's brother James the Just, and John the Baptist are acknowledged as errant or heretical Jews. Though Magdalene is a Semitic name, it is a title or honorific, acknowledging her spiritual importance—it is not her birth name, and may have been given to her by Jesus or by a high priestess of her temple lineage. Or, just as easily, the name may be of Syrian origin, or from other regions that spoke the Aramaic language. Although Judea and Galilee were Jewish homelands, they were also Roman-occupied provinces, where Greeks, Romans, and other foreigners lived and owned property.

The legends of Mary Magdalene's ancestry begin to appear in the written folkloric record in tenth-century Europe. By the thirteenth century, the Italian Jacobus de Voragine compiled the many stories of Mary Magdalene and other saints in his book *The Golden Legend*. He writes that Magdalene "was born of right noble lineage and parents, which were descended from the lineage of kings . . . her father was named Cyrus, and her mother Eucharis." He writes a very similar history of Martha, whom he considers to be the sister of Mary Magdalene—that her father was named Syro a "duke of Syria and places maritime" and her mother was Eucharia.[1]

If this history is correct, then Magdalene may well have been a descendant of a royal Canaanite family that, by tradition, often dedicated their daughters to serve as high priestesses in the goddess cults, a practice that was still alive and well in first century Syria. *Eucharis* or *Eucharia* is a Greek name, not Hebrew, suggesting that her mother likely came from a wealthy, political, and Hellenized family, which matches *The Golden Legend*'s story that Mary Magdalene's mother is of a noble and prosperous family, inheriting property in Magdala, Bethany, and Jerusalem. If Magdalene was the wealthy and educated daughter of a royal Canaanite father and Hellenized Jewish mother, this could explain her financial independence, her ability to travel freely as a woman in such patriarchal times, her absence in the Jewish historical record, and her role as an important priestess in the early Christian religion, while at the same time being an outsider in the mainstream Jewish culture. Another legend suggests her father, Cyrus, converted to Judaism to become a high priest at Capernaum, and that Eucharia was a prominent Jewess, which is similar to the history that appears in the third-century Mandaean Book of John (the Baptist), as we will see shortly. If these legends are true, then Magdalene could have been a Jew by birthright but fluent in the Greek and Syrian cultures as well.

In 2016 Dr. Gérard Lucotte of the French Institute of Molecular Anthropology published a study titled "The Mitochondrial DNA Mitotype of Sainte Marie Madeleine [Mary Magdalene]" in which his team analyzed the mitochondrial DNA of a lock of red hair from the supposed skull of Mary Magdalene, housed for the past eight hundred years in the crypt of the Basilica of Saint Maximin-la-Sainte-Baume, France. The tests confirmed that the hairs were indeed from a female of the mitochondrial haplotype K, which is very prominent in Ashkenazi Jews and other Europeans of Canaanite and Near Eastern descent. Around 33 percent of Ashkenazi Jews belong to this genetic subgroup, which was derived from just three female ancestors who migrated to Europe one hundred generations ago, or approximately two thousand years ago.[2] Could these be the actual relics of the red-haired Mary Magdalene, or a descendant?

Magdalene—Black Queen of Africa

There is also plentiful speculation that Mary Magdalene was a Black queen who originated from Egypt or Ethiopia, and may have been a descendant of the Queen of Sheba, the famous lover of King Solomon (also from the line of David, like Jesus).[3]

Some describe her with beautiful black skin, dark red hair, and greenish eyes—and there are some African tribes who use red ochre to color their hair in tribute to the fertile power of the color red. Magdalene is often depicted with vivid red hair, connected to the mysteries of the original Ancient Mothers who were the true wisdom keepers of Mother Earth.

Not only is there a city called Magdala in Ethiopia, but there has been a Jewish population in Ethiopia since the fall of the first Temple of Jerusalem, in 587 BCE. The late Emperor Haile Selassie of Ethiopia claimed he was a descendant of the Queen of Sheba and King Solomon through their son Menelik I. He also carried the title Lion of Judah and asserted he was a descendant of the lineage of Jesus. The Ethiopian Kebra Negast also pays homage to the Queen of Sheba, King Solomon, and their son Menelik.

From this evidence, some people conclude that Mary Magdalene was a descendant of the Queen of Sheba, who may have been the Pharaoh Hatshepsut of Egypt/Ethiopia.[4] This could also explain the intuitive connection between Mary Magdalene and the priestesses of Isis, whose wisdom is rooted in the African feminine mysteries. It is notable that the love story of Jesus and Magdalene is remarkably similar to the Egyptian Isis and Osiris resurrection mysteries.

The Queen of Sheba, from the medieval manuscript "Bellifortis"
by Conrad Kyeser, 1405.

Was Magdalene Jilted by One of the Apostles?

We don't have a clear description of the moment Magdalene and Yeshua met—although it is often depicted, symbolically, as having taken place by a well.

We do know that whenever this original meeting took place, and however it unfolded, it was a life-changing experience and communion of soul love for Magdalene. Afterward, she stays with Jesus and travels with him everywhere. In Luke it describes how Jesus made his way through town and villages preaching and that a circle of women, including "Mary surnamed the Magdalene" came with him.

Whereas Mother Mary—in her Virgin archetype—is often portrayed as being in a state of virginal purity on meeting her husband, Magdalene is commonly depicted as a woman who had known the pleasures of the flesh, and had the wisdom to tell.

In medieval texts there are varying accounts that Magdalene was actually betrothed or married to John the Evangelist (also known as John the Beloved, author of the Gospel of John) before she met Jesus. According to Saint Augustine and Honorius Augustodunensis, the wedding of Cana was to celebrate the marriage of Mary Magdalene and John the Evangelist—however, upon seeing the miracle of Jesus turning wine to water, John jilted Magdalene in order to become a disciple of Jesus. In some accounts Magdalene follows him, and also becomes a disciple. In other accounts, she flees to Jerusalem after this betrayal by her husband-to-be, where she becomes a "filthy and common prostitute" who founds a brothel of sin, and in this "temple of demons" the seven demons enter her.[5]

In John Myrc's fifteenth-century "Sermo de Nupcijs," the wedding of Cana is that of "John Euangiliste and Mary Mawdelyne," and in other places he describes a Mary Magdalene of "Mawdelene-Castell [who] was once engaged to John Evangelist before Christ called him to his service and the devil entered her."[6]

In the German poem "Der Saelden Hort" (1298), John is named as the bridegroom, and he says of the bride, "Even though no one said her name in a loud voice, still a master told me this was a true statement, that the bride was Mary Magdalen, as yet free from sin, a child of a noble, worthy prince."[7]

Of course, other Grail legends name the marriage of Cana as the union of Jesus himself with Magdalene, and the "wedding feast of Cana" was also an annual pagan fertility festival—the equivalent of Beltane—where weddings were often held. As one biblical scholar concludes, "Cana [is] a bridal festival for Mother Goddess and deity son."[8]

But more on that later . . .

Was Magdalene First Married to John the Baptist?

Some legends have Magdalene first marrying John the Baptist, Jesus's fire-and-brimstone ascetic cousin, who may have mistreated her, or whom she left—which may also explain why she was considered hamartolos; as a divorced or separated woman, she would have been considered to be "outside" mainstream Jewish society.

Other accounts say that Magdalene's marriage to John the Baptist resulted in a child, the mysterious "beloved disciple," also called John the Beloved. When John the Baptist died, as was sometimes a custom at the time, Jesus married his cousin's now-widowed wife, and took on John as his stepson. At the crucifixion, according to the Gospel of John, Mother Mary, her sister, Magdalene, and John the Beloved stand at the foot of the cross, a place usually reserved for family.

Historical evidence supports this idea. Jane Schaberg and other biblical scholars write that original versions of the Christian gospels place Mary Magdalene as an important disciple of John the Baptist at his camp on the River Jordan.[9] The church father Hippolytus of Rome (170–236 CE) explains, as we have read earlier, that several gnostic groups claimed John the Baptist passed on his teachings to James the Just and the prophet "Miriamne," or MM, which is backed up by Celsus, who wrote of early Christian sects devoted to "Mariamme." The Johannite Knights Templar groups derived their beliefs from similar traditions, holding that John was married to Mary Magdalene.

The third-century Nasoraean-Mandaean Book of John offers some tantalizing clues about the true identity of Mary Magdalene and the nature of her relationship with John the Baptist. The Book of John is a sacred text of the Mandaean religion, the only continuous, living Aramaic-gnostic tradition that dates back to biblical times. They are also known as the Nazoreans, and were connected to the Essenes and other Nazarene groups that had important centers at Mount Carmel and across the Jewish territories.

The Book of John includes an extraordinary female priestess as the heroine of the text—a mysterious Mary, known as Miryai—who develops an intimate relationship with John the Baptist. Some Mandaeans interpret Miryai as the Virgin Mary, but her secret identity is likely Mary Magdalene.

In the manuscript, Miryai is the talented daughter of a royal, priestly family. She is described as the "daughter of the High Priest" of the temple, as well as a "daughter of the mighty rulers of Jerusalem" and "daughter of the kings of Babylon," citing a part-pagan origin.[10] Miryai is an advanced student of the Torah. Even as a young woman, she is a sought-after teacher.

One day her parents leave her at home, ordering her to bolt the doors and stay inside while they are gone. She boldly disobeys, and sets forth to the Mandaean church meeting where she discovers the "true teachings." There she falls in love with the leader of the movement, who historically was John the Baptist, though he is not identified by name in the text. She calls him "lord/master," holds his hand and accidentally falls asleep at his sanctuary, staying overnight, with all the sexual connotations this would imply in biblical Palestine. When she returns home in the morning, her father is enraged. He beats her and slanders her as a whore:

[Miryai says:] "My father came and physically beat me—
A downfall which I did not deserve."
And he said, "Where are you coming from, debauched woman of mixed race,
. . .
Where are you coming to me from, bitch in heat?"[11]

John takes in Miryai, becoming her champion and intimate partner. The text leaves the exact nature of their relationship ambiguous, but as one prominent Mandaean scholar writes, the story "hints of hieros gamos"—sacred sexual union.[12] John the Baptist refers to her as "Miryai the righteous, whom I deem equal to generations and worlds," raising her up to the highest position of honor, as he "embraces her and lays her down on her throne."[13]

In his presence, she is revealed as a female messiah and "founding mother figure" of the Nasoraean-Mandaean religion.[14] She is the Vine, the Tree of Life, the Waters of Life (the Euphrates River)—titles usually reserved for Jesus as the "Christ."

And [he] taught her, and he loved truth from her.
He stretched out and embraced her with a strong embrace . . .
And placed her on the throne, and said to her,
"Miryai, look at me!
Mention good before Life concerning me, your messenger.
I am the good man which heard your word."[15]

Eventually, a cabal of men from Jerusalem are sent to find Miryai and kill her for bringing shame to her father's house. When they arrive, she is enthroned as a high priestess, beaming with spiritual light and power, holding the sacred scrolls of the Mandaean religion "in her lap," a symbolic reference to the sacred gnosis contained in her womb. Stunned by her remarkable transformation, the men bow down at her feet:

They went and found Miryai
set upon a throne at the mouth of the Euphrates,
And a white banner was spread over her
And a scroll was spread across her lap
—They read in the books of truth—
And she stirs up all worlds.

A (ritual) staff of living water is in her hand
A (ritual) girdle is fastened and tied around her waist.
They bow and prostrate themselves before Miryai
And she teaches in a sublime voice.
Fish assemble from the sea
And water fowl from the mouth of the Euphrates
come at Miryai's voice.[16]

Yet the union may not end well. Further on in the text, John's trusted advisors tell him that he is too fiery, stern, and ascetic, and that he creates a barren desert around him where no flowers bloom. They suggest he should marry, settle down, and "establish himself." He agrees to try, and the manuscript describes how he fathers children with his wife. But perhaps his fire-and-brimstone nature drives a wedge in the relationship. Hinting at a betrayal, in other sections of the text he repeatedly rails against women who commit adultery with a "man's good friend," who become pregnant with another man, or who forget about him after his death.

Though John baptizes Jesus, and speaks highly of him in the New Testament gospels, in the Book of John, he is a fierce rival of Jesus, who, as John's chief disciple, naturally spends time in the wilderness camp with him and Miryai. We might even speculate that John is jealous of the man who will one day become Miryai / Mary Magdalene's intimate companion.

In the end John concedes that it is Jesus who "has the Bride."

Was Magdalene a Prophetess?

Although the Bible does not tell us the origins of Mary Magdalene, she bears all the hallmarks of an empowered priestess and of a prophetess of the goddess traditions. By the time of Mary Magdalene, it is likely that *within Palestine* the public worship of Asherah and the Canaanite priestess goddess traditions had been eliminated by the patriarchal priests of Yahweh. But the goddess cultures still thrived in the immediately surrounding lands, which were connected to Palestine by an extensive network of roads and shipping routes that allowed cultural exchange and immigration. And even *within* Palestine, the worship of the feminine divinity continued in the underground streams of mystical Kabbalism and Jewish gnosticism.

Palestine was only a stone's throw from neighboring pagan countries. Syria, home of the mermaid goddess Atargatis and her priestesshood, lay only twenty miles away from the Sea of Galilee. The city of Alexandria, cultural and spiritual mecca and heart of the Hellenic world, and a center of the Isis cult, was 350 miles away, roughly the same distance as from Venice to Rome. The goddess Artemis was the chief deity of Ephesus, in western Anatolia (modern Turkey); and Kybele still ruled in the central Anatolian highlands. Cults of Aphrodite, Venus, Demeter, Tanit, Allat, and others thrived nearby. Biblical Palestine was a patriarchal island, surrounded by a sea of goddess worship, with active and well-respected colleges of priestesses and priests during the lifetime of Jesus and Magdalene. The heretical Mary-worshipping gnostic Christian sects would continue to be based in these goddess strongholds for centuries to come.

Large Jewish expatriate communities lived in Alexandria, Egypt, with approximately one-third of the population being Jewish. Both the Christian New Testament as well as rabbinical traditions teach that Jesus grew up in Egypt. Another important Jewish expatriate community was centered in the Mediterranean island of Rhodes (meaning "roses" in Greek), where Herod the Great personally funded the rebuilding of a Temple of the Pythia, home to an oracular dragon priestess of the Delphic tradition, a two-thousand-year-old institution that was alive and well at the time of Magdalene.

Hebrew priestesses were strongly connected to the Oracle of Delphi and to the Sibyls. And MM's mother, Eucharis, may well have been from Greece. Is it possible that Mary Magdalene was a prophetic priestess in this tradition, a Hellenized pagan of Syrian descent? Let us explore the rich history of the oracles and Sibyls to understand the power of the priesshood that still held sway in the Hellenized world of Magdalene's lifetime.

The Dragon Priestesses of Delphi

The Temple of the Pythia at Delphi, Greece, was for more than two thousand years the center of an international womb-web of oracular dragon priestesses and Sibyls, along with their Moon College Mystery schools for spiritual education.

The Pythia, whose name translates as "dragoness," as we have learned, was the high priestess of the Hellenic empire, which at its height stretched from Mediterranean Africa and Europe to Asia Minor, and eastward to the Indus Valley. She was the equivalent of a female pope; her spiritual authority had no equal in the world of antiquity. The historian Philip van Ness Myers describes the importance of her temple: "Delphi was, in some respects, such a religious center of Hellas as papal Rome was of medieval Europe. It was the common altar of the Greek race."[17]

The Greek philosopher Plato lived and studied with the Pythia. In his influential work, *The Republic,* Plato called her "our national divinity," writing that her earth throne and priesthood had been inaugurated more than one thousand years before his time, dating the founding of the Pythian office to sometime before 1500 BCE. Her position, as Dragon Priestess of the Earth, was likely first established by black priestesses of Nubian Africa, who brought the tradition north from the Sudan and Ethiopia to found her temple at Delphi.[18]

The first Pythia was said to be Gaia, the earth goddess of prehistoric Greece, and the spiritual descendant of the Sumerian earth goddess, *Ki* or *Ge*.[19] Her priestess daughters became the lineage of Pythian oracles, who divined the voice of the Mother Earth herself. By the eighth century BCE, Apollo, "God of Light," rose to prominence in Greece and overthrew the earth goddess. He killed Pytho, the ancient earth dragon of Delphi, described as an actual human woman originally, before her mythic transfiguration into dragon form.

The priestesses of antiquity knew the sacred sites of the earth were interconnected by powerful energetic pathways called dragon lines. The oracles maintained and guarded these important connections. The late scholar and professor emeritus of Claremont College Norma Goodrich explains, "From holy centers, worshipers of ancient times also traced 'dragon lines,' powerful earth currents from one holy site to another shrine of earth. European churches were subsequently erected at their intersections."[20]

Womb of the Dragon

Delphoi means "womb" in Greek, a reference to the Pythian temple as the omphalos womb center, or world navel, of the Hellenic people, the gateway leading directly into the womb of the earth. The underground adytum, or innermost chamber of the temple, was built upon that fissure, where volcanic fumes would arise from the "darkest depths of the earth" as the oracle performed her ecstatic divination, now confirmed by modern geologic studies.[21]

Before entering the darkened womb chamber, the Pythia would first ritually bathe, naked, in the Kastalian Spring, and then drink the prophetic waters of the Cassotis Spring, home to a naiad-nymph possessing magical powers. In the dim light of the adytum, she would burn incense, chew or burn laurel leaves, chant, pray, and gaze into a font of divining water, opening the dreaming gate of Gaian consciousness. The purple-veiled high priestess, with one hand resting on the omphalos stone as she prophesied, became the mouthpiece of the living Earth and the gods.

Inscribed in the entryway of the Temple at Delphi was the Greek phrase *Gnothi Seauton,* "Know Thyself." The temple served as a mystery school, and the Pythia taught her students that to know god, one must first know oneself, laying the spiritual foundations that would evolve over time into the gnostic religions.

Mary Magdalene—Dragoness and Pythia?

Not all of the oracles at Delphi were natives of Greece—they were drawn from a network of mystery schools and temples across the known world. According to the Greek historian Pausanias, the lineage included a Hebrew oracle from Palestine, named Sabbe, who was of Babylonian or Egyptian descent: "[She was] brought up in Palestine and named Sabbe, whose father was Berosus and her mother Erymanthe. Some say she was a Babylonian, while others call her an Egyptian Sibyl."[22]

The oracular priestesses were also called Sibyls, from the Greek *sibulla,* meaning "prophetess." Besides the central temple at Delphi, temples of the Sibyls were established at many sacred sites around the ancient Near East. The classicist F. W. H. Myers writes that there were "at least two hundred sixty different practicing Oracles in the Greek world."[23] The early Christian Church, despite its condemnation of all things pagan, held the Sibyls in highest esteem. The second-century Christian father Tertullian described one Sibyl as "the true prophetess of Truth."[24] The "Song of the Sibyl" was sung on Christmas Eve and before every mass in Catholic churches across Europe.

Could Mary Magdalene have been connected to this network of famous prophetesses?

Hamartolos—Magdalene as an Outsider

The definitive roots of Mary Magdalene are elusive, yet there is a fragrance of mystery that surrounds her, suggesting that her origin was unusual for the time, and that the question of whom she married held a deeper meaning and mystery. One thing is certain: for some reason the origins and offices of Magdalene have been deliberately obscured or eradicated by those who chronicled Jesus's life, suggesting there is an important secret surrounding her true identity.

CHAMBER 9

THE CIRCLE OF MARYS

Feminist Ministry of Jesus

NEXT IN OUR JOURNEY, we imagine Jesus as a visionary feminist—an awakened man who married a powerful, sexually awakened priestess and was surrounded by a circle of wise women on their own spiritual quest, who financially supported him.

That doesn't match up with what we think of the Christian religion, does it? In the modern day, we tend to think (as we have been told) of Jesus as a celibate "Son of God," who only had male disciples, and whose teachings went on to form religions where only men could be spiritual leaders or priests, with women priests excluded.

But what if the truth were the reverse?

What if Jesus supported feminine spirituality?

What if a circle of priestesses supported him?

Circle of Marys in the Gospels

We often hear about the male disciples, especially Matthew, Luke, Mark, and John—whose supposed testimony (written by later scribes) formed the canonical gospels. Yet in those very gospels there is a deluge of mentions of "the Marys"—the group of women who travel with Jesus, support him, and even pay for his preaching mission.

The inner circle of Jesus's ministry consists of "the Twelve," the male disciples, but also the more mysterious Marys whose important role has been deliberately obscured:

Jesus walked through towns and countryside, preaching and giving the good news of the Kingdom of God. The Twelve followed him, and also some women who had been healed of evil spirits or disease: Mary called Magdalene who had been freed of seven demons; Joanna, wife of Chuza, Herod's steward; Suzanna and others who provided for him [saw to his needs] out of their own funds. (Luke 8:1–3)

"The women watched from a distance. . . . They had followed Jesus from Galilee and saw to his needs. . . . 'They' being Mary Magdalene, the mother of James and Joseph and the mother of Zebedee's sons." (Matthew 27:55–56, describing the Crucifixion)

"There were also some women watching from a distance; among them were Mary Magdalene, Mary the mother of James the younger and Joseph, and Salome, who had followed Jesus when he was in Galilee and saw to his needs." (Mark 15:40–41)

Who Are the Marys?

Although the male scribes of the gospels describe the Marys in quite a dismissive way, they obviously can't exclude their overwhelming presence from the accounts. Wherever Jesus goes he is accompanied by a circle of women—the Marys—including his beloved Mary Magdalene, who fund and support him. This paints quite a different picture from the all-male ministry we usually imagine, and puts women center stage of his spiritual mission both personally and financially.

The women mentioned directly in the canonical gospels as being part of his ministry and circle are: Mary Magdalene, Mary of Bethany (which might be another name for Magdalene), Martha, Mary his mother, mother of James and Joseph (which may also refer to Jesus's mother and his brothers), Salome, mother of Zebedee's sons, Mary the wife of Cleophas, Johanna, Joanna wife of Chuza (Herod's steward), and Suzanna.

Priestesses of "Mary" Isis?

Mary (or Miriam/Maryam) was quite a common name for women two thousand years ago. But there is often an overwhelming—and confusing—array of Marys in Jesus's life and ministry: Mary Magdalene, Mary of Bethany, Mary his mother,

Mary wife of Cleophas, Mary mother of James, among other women mentioned. Why is this?

The answer may be surprising: *Mary* was a priestess name, a name intimately connected with the feminine mysteries. Mar/Ma was a name of the Divine Mother across many cultures of the ancient Near East. So Mary was a title, not just a personal name.

**Egyptian "Mary" Priestesses: Musicians and dancers on fresco
at Tomb of Nebamun, Thebes, 1350 BCE.**

Returning to our story of the mysterious circle of Marys who traveled with Jesus, we can now appreciate what an ancient reader would have immediately understood—that the Marys were quite possibly priestesses of the goddess tradition, connected to the Egyptian temples of Isis and Hathor. And of course, records state that Jesus and Mother Mary lived in Egypt after he was born. It is likely they made strong connections and friendships in Egypt, and they are described as studying magic there. Could this be the origin of the Marys—priestesses they knew from Egypt?

If this is so, we might expect to find other evidence linking Jesus and the Marys with the Egyptian lineages of feminine magic. Let us dive deeper now into the world of the priestesses of Isis to see who the Marys really were beneath the veil that the gospels have drawn over them.

Circle of Priestesses

The Marys, as we will call the female disciples of Jesus, would have been extremely unusual women in the Jewish world of two thousand years ago. Most Palestinian women were the legal property of their closest male family member. They were typically not allowed to own property or businesses, or even to leave the house unaccompanied by a man.

Yet the circle of Marys had independent wealth; it was they, not the male disciples, who funded Jesus's ministry. They also freely traveled around the countryside without their husbands, in a mixed group of women and men, which would have been considered impossibly scandalous for ordinary Jewish women, legally equivalent to adultery and punishable by stoning. The Marys are present at the most important events of Jesus's life—at his anointing, crucifixion, and resurrection—where the male disciples are most often absent. Despite their unusual and important role, their identity remains mysterious. The writers of the gospels say little about the Marys, which tells us that something about these women is considered forbidden to write about.

To get to the truth of the Marys we must "read the silence" of the gospels. What is obscured and left unsaid provides us as much information as what is spelled out. *As is common throughout the Bible, what is left unsaid is almost always the "embarrassing" presence of the priestesses and the goddess religion.*

Is this the reason why there is so much secrecy and slander around this group of women who travel with Jesus? Were later scribes trying to hide the fact that Jesus was intimately involved with spiritually empowered women who supported him? Were the Marys folk healers, shamans, and magicians of old, sorceresses, traveling from village to village, preaching, ministering, and healing alongside of Jesus?

As we know from temple priestesses of Inanna's day, the priestesses were often independently wealthy or funded by the temples. These were some of the only women who had the means and legal freedom to move and travel in that day.

There are also fascinating parallels between the Red Path of Inanna and Ishtar and the priestesses of Hathor and Isis that weave together the common threads of the Mary priestesses, the harlots and the Scarlet Women, and that are very connected to the feminine mysteries and priestesses who were initiates of this tradition.

We also see a remarkable parallel in Buddhist legends. After the Buddha's awakening, his public ministry was funded by courtesan priestesses of India.[1] Buddha wasn't always *their* teacher. They were *his* benefactors, funders, and, in some cases, teachers, who traditionally supported the enlightenment process of future incarnations of Buddha, by "seeing to their needs" with the substance of their own bodies, a tradition in India that explicitly included sexuality.

The Egyptian Temple Connection

In both the gospels and in rabbinical texts we read that Jesus and his mother, Mary, went to Egypt shortly after Jesus's birth, where he trained in Egyptian magic—the folkloric feminine healing and spiritual traditions that originated from the temples of Isis, Hathor, and other Egyptian goddesses. Gospel writers deliberately underplay and obscure Jesus's connection to the magical and feminine traditions, but the late scholar Morton Smith, distinguished professor of Columbia University, carefully documents the abundant evidence in his groundbreaking book *Jesus the Magician.*

Professor Smith remarks how many of the events in the gospels sound like magical events that have their closest parallel in Egyptian magic. He connects Jesus with Egypt:

> Matthew says he was taken to Egypt as an infant (for a grossly improbable reason), and as a small boy was brought to Nazareth. His opponents say he went to Egypt as a young man, looking for work, and learned magic there. The Rabbinic report that in Egypt Jesus was tattooed with magic spells . . . is cited as a known fact . . . by a rabbi was who was probably born around the time of the crucifixion.[2]

We also see the widespread archaeological evidence of Jewish magical amulets, talismans, and bowls, inscribed with symbols, spells, and power names, both in Egypt and Palestine. One Alexandrian bowl recently discovered by the renowned French archaeologist Franck Goddio carries the inscription DIA CHRSTOU O GOISTAIS, meaning "by Christ the magician," dating from between the second century BCE and the first century CE, roughly the time of Jesus's life. Goddio explains, "It could very well be a reference to Jesus Christ, in that he was once the primary exponent of white magic."[3]

We can guess that Jesus's mother, Mary, was involved with the Egyptian temples as well, as she was a priestess of the Temple of Jerusalem, a tradition that originated in the cult of Asherah. She also conceived Jesus in unusual circumstances more easily explained as a priestess rite, and was, of course, named Mary and surrounded by other Marys, a common priestess title. The Marys may have been educated in the goddess temples of Egypt, along with Jesus and Mother Mary, and traveled back to Palestine with them to assist in his teaching and healing mission.

The lives of the priestesses must be reconstructed from the lost mists of *herstory,* their stories pieced together again from the traces of perfumed unguents left in their alabaster anointing jars, from wisps of red, blue, black, and green mineral pigments on their cut calcite cosmetic palettes, from the fragments of their crimson robes, from stunning semiprecious stones and gilded leaves of talismanic jewelry. We see sculptured reliefs of musician-priestesses playing the lyre, harp, and tambourine. We see engraved plaques of sexual love consummated on the sacred marriage bed. We see the four-thousand-year-old divinized libation vessels of the high priestess, engraved with twin serpents and dragons. And, enduring even through the days of Jesus and Magdalene, *well into the common era,* we notice the lion thrones of the Syrian high priestesses, artisan-cut from solid stone, and the Dragoness Temple of the Pythia at Delphi.

Who were these forbidden women? What were their lives like? What spiritual energy did they summon that was so threatening to patriarchal authority? Where did they draw their magical and mythic power?

We must remember that every goddess, and many gods, had dedicated priestesses who communed with the divine *through the instruments of their bodies,* through their talismanic adornment, through their song and music, through ritual and ceremony, through their sex. They studied the stars, invented calendars and writing, wrote poetry (until they were banned from writing), mothered children, fell in love, wildcrafted medicinal herbs. That they were written out of the history despite their clear and foundational importance is a testament to how threatening they must have been to the emerging male world.

We also know there was an important cultural and spiritual exchange between Alexandria, Egypt, and Palestine. At the time of Jesus, it is estimated that some 300,000 Hellenized Jews lived in Alexandria, the most important center of the mystery schools, goddess spirituality, and pagan philosophy in the Western world, and the historical home of the library of Alexandria, a priceless treasure trove of ancient spiritual and esoteric texts. Alexandria was a melting pot of diverse religious, artistic, scholarly, and philosophical traditions, where priestesses, magicians, and scholars from as far away as India and China came together to train and study.

In 415 CE, a Christian mob ended the era of tolerance by killing the much-loved pagan mathematician, philosopher, and daughter of Alexandria, Hypatia, the last of the publicly recognized female mystery adepts. The scholar and historian Damascius writes that she once fended off an unwelcome suitor by waving her bloody menstrual rags at him, saying "This is what you really love, my young man, but you do not love beauty for its own sake."[4] Hypatia became the basis for the Catholic legend of Saint Catherine of Alexandria.

Wild Womb Shamans of Isis

The priestesses of Isis and Hathor were known for their "red rites," and could well have been the secret source of Jesus's magical initiation in Egypt. Knowing what we do of this vivid and beautiful priestess world, it paints a different picture of Yeshu . . .

Anthropologist Margaret Murray describes how the inscriptions on many early Egyptian temples talk of the ancient religious rites being performed by "many priesthoods of women." Yet later on, these founding priestesses were demoted to "temple singers," as the temple traditions devolved.

The male cults of the pharaoh god-kings and elite priestly caste arrived in Egypt around 3000 BCE, but long before that time there was a mysterious feminine shamanic culture, whose cosmology and mythology were wild, vividly alive, sexual, and dreamlike. Sexual symbology was inseparable from religious symbology. Sex was sacred. Sex, birth, death, rebirth, personal transformation, shamanic journeys, and the alchemical act of merging into oneness consciousness with another all happened through the portal of the yoni-womb. The womb was both the religion and the doorway to spiritual power.[5]

The ancient goddess Hathor was known as the "Mistress of the Red Robe," "Lady of the Vulva," and "Womb of Horus" and was the goddess of love, sexuality, childbirth, and the feminine temple arts. Her priestesses wore patterned red dresses, red scarves, and beaded *menat* necklaces that doubled as musical shakers. In the inner sanctum of the Hathor temple, a troupe of red-robed priestesses with diaphanous red veils would move slowly in rhythm, perfectly synchronized in their mesmerizing, snakelike movements, shaking their beaded rattles and sistrums, chanting otherworldly hymns to the goddess.

The priestesses of Hathor were oracles, dream interpreters, midwives, dancers, and musicians. Her temples contained rooms for the mixing of perfumed oils and cosmetics, treasuries of jewels and musical instruments, and birthing chambers where pregnant mothers were welcomed and assisted by the trained priestess-midwives.

Priestesses known as the Daughters of Isis worked with the *shen* talisman, the womb ring of immortality, to shift the fabric of time and to send protection to those in their journey of rebirth.* The *ankh,* a womb of life symbol, was used to magically transmit life-force energy—often into the lunar portal of the alta-major, located at the base of the skull. The *tiet* menstrual blood of Isis symbol was a powerful protective amulet, often carved into red jasper pendants and painted on the interior lids of coffins and sarcophagi to assist the dead in their journey of rebirth.

Temple priestesses often had striking web patterns tattooed on their abdomens, encircling their wombs in a net, and diamond tattoolike markings appeared on the thighs of female fertility figurines, suggesting sexually stylized body art among priestesses. The most famous example of shamanic tattoo art was discovered on the mummy of Amunet, high priestess of Hathor, in 1891 by French Egyptologist Eugène Grébaut.

Female sexual energies expressed the womb power of red or white magic, and priestesses honored the wild lioness Sekhmet and the sensual cat goddess Bast. The annual festival of Bast was the most popular in all of Egypt. Women would dance, drink, sing, make music, and display their yonis in wild abandon, celebrating their feminine power.

Is this the reason why there is so much secrecy and slander around this group of women who travel with Jesus? Were later scribes trying to hide the fact that Jesus was intimately involved with spiritually empowered women who supported him?

---

*The *shen* "rod and ring" was a symbol and magical device used in Egypt. It represented the womb and infinity, and evolved into the cartouche shape that holds sacred names. Inanna holds an identical symbol in color plate 12.

CHAMBER 10

HOLY MATRIMONY

Were Jesus and Mary Married?

*Everything manifests from two emanations. Consciousness and
thought. Male and female. In essence they are one. When separated
they appear as two.*

Simon Magus

ONE OF THE MOST FASCINATING AND EXPLOSIVE aspects of the
Mary Magdalene resurgence are the ongoing revelations that she was likely the
lover and spiritual wife of Jesus.

The Catholic Church has been led by a celibate male priesthood for almost
two thousand years, based on the claim that Jesus himself was an unmarried
celibate—so we can understand why the idea of Jesus as a married man is such a
hot topic.

First the international bestseller *Holy Blood, Holy Grail,* by Henry Lincoln
and cowriters, put the topic of a possible marriage between Jesus and Magdalene
and a lineage of their children back on the map. Then *The Da Vinci Code,* by Dan
Brown—which has sold over 180 million copies—propelled this incredible possibility directly into mass consciousness. The response shows how deeply the world
thirsts for this knowing.

To date, there is no scholarly evidence that *proves* Mary Magdalene and Jesus
were married, although there is plenty of circumstantial evidence to support it. In
2012, Harvard Divinity scholar and translator of the *Gospel of Mary of Magdala*

Karen King announced that a fragment of a Coptic text had been found that referred to Jesus having a wife, which was named the Gospel of Jesus's Wife. This was later disputed as a forgery.

You may intuitively know in your bones that Yeshu and Mary Magdalene were united in sacred union, and later on we will discuss the more esoteric possibilities of their "Holy Matrimony"—as a deep spiritual union.

First, though, we will explore how this fascination with the idea that Mary Magdalene and Jesus were married is not a new idea at all. In fact, over the past two thousand years, this knowing has kept arising. It is a deep source of anxiety for the traditional institutions, and a torch of inspiration for secret Magdalene cults.

We'll take a look at the evidence that Jesus and Magdalene *were* married.

Jesus and His "Harem of Marys"

One of the more recent supporters of this thesis is Brigham Young, the founder of modern-day Mormonism. Incredibly, he believed and taught that Jesus was actually in a polygamous relationship or marriage with Mary Magdalene, Mary of Bethany, *and* Martha. Although this may seem like an outrageous idea, the reason for this belief is probably connected to the mix-up around the "Marys" in the bible. Some people feel that Mary Magdalene and Mary of Bethany are two different characters, while others presume they are the same person. From our perspective Magdalene and Mary of Bethany are the same person, but others aren't sure—and so this idea that Jesus had a number of intimate relationships with women named Mary arises.

In the past few hundred years others have also held the belief that Jesus and Mary Magdalene were either married or at least in an intimate sexual relationship together. Martin Luther, one of the founders of modern-day Protestantism, believed that Jesus and Magdalene were in a sexual relationship, as did the Rosicrucians.

The Cathars and Magdalene the Consort

The largest group of people to believe that Jesus and Mary Magdalene were in a sexual relationship were the Cathars, a heretical Christian sect that flourished in the south of France and Bulgaria around the eleventh century—and who many believe were barely Christian by orthodox standards—and instead worshipped the feminine divinity of the Holy Spirit. They openly taught and wrote that Jesus was in a sexual relationship with Mary Magdalene, and described her as a consort or concubine.

This implies that they believed the nature of the relationship between Jesus and Magdalene wasn't a marriage by normal standards of conventional law. By describing Mary as a consort rather than as a conventional wife there is a hidden implication of a tantric spiritual marriage between them. This casts an intriguing light on the rumors that Jesus was more of a tantric shaman than a conventional religious figure, and more easily places Magdalene as his priestess-consort.

The Catholic Church was outraged at the teachings of the Cathars, which had become the focal point for a resurgence of a large underground Magdalene cult. They launched an inquisition against the Cathars in 1209, starting with a mass killing in a church dedicated to Mary Magdalene, on her Feast Day of July 22.

"Christ Loved Her and Kissed Her on the Mouth"

One of the most compelling "proofs" of the sexual relationship between Jesus and Mary Magdalene comes from the Gospel of Philip—an apocryphal gospel that was originally written around the mid-second century and was rediscovered in Egypt, in Nag Hammadi in 1945, a discovery that rebirthed the gnostic mysteries.

The translation and commentary on the original text by Jean-Yves Leloup, called *The Gospel of Philip: Jesus, Mary Magdalene and the Gnosis of Sacred Union,* dives into this delicious possibility that the "Way of Love" included sexual holiness. Throughout this beautiful text it clearly refers to the sacredness of sexual union— and more than implies that Jesus and Magdalene are living and embodying this.

> There were three who always walked with the Lord: Mary his mother and her sister and Magdalene, the one who was called his companion. His sister and his mother and his companion were each a Mary. And the companion of the Saviour is Mary Magdalene. (Gospel of Philip)[1]

The Greek word often translated as "companion" was *koinonos,* but it is more accurately translated as a "sexual partner or sexual consort." This matches the medieval Cathar heresy of Magdalene as a consort.

The gospel goes on to spell out the intimacy between Jesus and Magdalene.

> But Christ loved her more than all the disciples and used to kiss her often on the mouth. The rest of the disciples were offended by it and expressed disapproval. They said to him, "Why do you love her more than all of us?" The Saviour answered and said to them, "Why do I not love you like I love her?" (Gospel of Philip)[2]

The actual text itself has the word *mouth* missing, and some scholars have questioned the validity of the interpretation, saying that it does not necessarily mean "mouth." Feel free to experiment and play with adding in another body part.

The Gospel of Mary, another rediscovered apocryphal gospel, originally written around the second century and discovered in the nineteenth century in Egypt, confirms that Jesus and Magdalene enjoyed a very close relationship . . .

"Sister, we know that the Saviour loved you more than the rest of women," says Peter in the Gospel of Mary.[3] "If the Saviour has made her worthy, who is he to reject her? Surely the Saviour knows her very well. That is why he loved her more than us," says Levi in the Gospel of Mary.[4]

The Great Love of Magdalene and Jesus

Many other writings from the first century to medieval times chronicled the deep and intense love shared between Magdalene and Jesus.

Jacobus de Voragine in *The Golden Legend* says that after her conversion Mary Magdalene became "right familiar with" Christ, who "embraced her in all his life" and desired that "she be his hostess and procuress on his journey."

She is not only one of the Marys who "ministered unto the Lord of their own substance"; in the twelfth century, Honorius Augustodunensis describes how "Fired with zealous devotion, she panted to go about the province with him and his followers, ministering to him according to her ability."

Visiting Magdalene's house was a comfort for Jesus prior to the crucifixion, and it is told that he came often, "generally unbidden to that place rather than any other to take his bodily food, and that specially . . . on account of the great love and affection that he had to Mary after her conversion."[5]

In *The Meditations of the Life of Christ,* a fourteenth-century apocryphal account, hours before Christ's death, Magdalene "becomes spokeswoman for all the disciples" when she tries to persuade Jesus not to go to Jerusalem—and instead to spend Passover with his mother and the other disciples, described as his "barons, counts, pages and grooms."[6] When Jesus refuses to listen to either Magdalene (his wife) or his mother Mary and insists on going to Jerusalem, they both react differently. The Virgin Mary starts weeping "moderately and softly," while Magdalene is frantic and "crying with deep sobs."

In *Meditations,* it is the house of Mary Magdalene that the Marys gather in during Christ's flagellation, where they grieve with terrible lamentation and crying. Magdalene researcher and author Susan Haskins writes, "According to some medieval writers Magdalene even attended Christ's trial."[7] In other accounts,

Magdalene helps protect Mother Mary from her grief. In a thirteenth-century Italian hymn by Jacopone da Todi, "Crucifixion," the Virgin Mary sings to Magdalene: "Help me Magdalene; grief overwhelms me; Christ my son is being led away as has been told to me."[8]

The writer of *The Mirror of the Blessed Life of Jesu Christ* says of Magdalene— whom he describes as beloved apostle-ess—and Jesus's meeting after his resurrection, "And so those two lovers stood and spake together with great comfort and joy."[9]

Sacred Soulmate Union

In the Womb Mystery schools, where Yeshua and Magdalene studied, relational love was also the holy of holies—the hieros gamos of soulmates was a sacrament and pathway to god. Their intimate love play was holy. Their laughter, their love-struck glances, their sacred whispers, their wounds of love, their honesty and vulnerability, their intimacy and daily devotion to each other was holy.

When they embraced in the *Nashak*—the Holy Kiss, where breath and Spirit merged them into One Soul, back into the Great Womb—there was at-one-ment.*

In gnostic philosophy, spiritual union of the male-female pairs, called *syzygies*, was a reflection of the very foundations of creation, when twin *Aeons* were born from the pleroma of the Divine Mother's womb, and tasked as her divine co-creators. This spiritual emphasis on the union of twin souls was central to the ministry of Simon Magus and his beloved spiritual partner Helen. Apocryphal texts say that Simon and Helen studied with John the Baptist, and that Simon was the "second-in-command" to John in his spiritual movement—meaning that he had known Jesus.

Before John's death Simon traveled to Egypt to study magic, and he later came into conflict with the apostles after the death of Jesus—and was named the "father of heresies" by early Christians because of his reverence of the menstrual mysteries. Simon, a peer of Jesus and Magdalene, traveled and taught with his beloved Helen on the Womb Mysteries. He taught that a soul is divided into two halves and placed in different bodies, one male and one female, who both have a magnetic longing to unite. These souls search through all time for each other in a love beyond death. Later heresiologists, Irenaeus and Justin, also describe his Sophianic teaching in which he mythically associates Helen as the Sophia, the "lost sheep" of the gospels.

The *Panarion of Epiphanius of Salamas*, written in Greek in 375 as a treatise on heresies, describes the teachings of Simon Magus on the feminine divinity

---

*The Hebrew word *nashak* means both "kiss" and "bite of the serpent."

Ennoia (another name for Sophia), who descends and is imprisoned on earth by angels. She reincarnates many times, each time being shamed, eventually becoming a prostitute. She is associated with the beautiful Helen of Troy and also Athena.

Epiphanius writes of Simon Magus:

> He had the nerve to call the whore who was his partner the Holy Spirit, and said that he had come down on her account. He said [of Ennoia] "For her sake I am come down. For this is that which is written in the Gospel, the sheep that was lost."[10]

Simon Magus elucidates how he returns on "her account," to unite with the descended earthly Sophia, who has been abused by the ignorant world rulers. Gnostic scholar G. R. S. Mead says of the feminine divinity Sophia-Ennoia:

> [She is] a Power of many names. She is called the Mother, the Celestial Eve; The Holy Spirit, for the spiritus in some systems is a feminine power.* She is called She of the Left-Hand, as opposed to the Christos, He of the Right-hand. Her names include Virgin, Eden, Daughter of light, Merciful Mother, Perfect Mercy, Hidden Mother, She who knows the Mysteries of the Elect, and the Holy Dove who has given birth to two twins.[11]

Mead writes that Sophia preserves the World Soul and the soul of humanity.

These apocryphal teachings of a spiritually initiated couple that Jesus presumably knew well can cast light on the atmosphere of his relationship with Magdalene and their ministry.

Mystery of Marriage

The ancient Jewish mystical tradition, Kabbalah, also described the union of soulmates—teaching that this realm was created in "pairs of soulmates" who longed to reunite. The Zohar, a thirteenth-century sacred text of this oral tradition, says:

> Come and behold: All the souls that are destined to come appear before Her† as couples, with each soul divided each into male and female halves. Afterward, when the souls arrive in this world, the Holy One, blessed is She, matches them again.[12]

---

*Primarily in the Codex Nazaraeus, the scripture of the Mandaeans.
†Translation of god as masculine has been reverted to feminine by the authors.

Heretical teachings and mythologies about the soulmate union of Jesus and MM arose, regardless of any formal marriage, and it was said that in union with her twin soul—or her divine syzygy—Mary Magdalene had the gift to "see" soulmates and help bring them together, which was a shamanic art of the feminine mysteries. Medieval heresies on the mystical soulmate union between Yeshua and Magdalene described how she had become the New Eve with this great love—healing the separation between man and woman, created when Adam and Eve left the Garden of Eden. Salvation was the reunification of Jesus and Magdalene in the Bridal Chamber.

The Gospel of Philip, beautifully translated by Jean-Yves Leloup, describes this primordial reunion in the sacred marriage of the soul itself, which reunites to become whole: "This is how it is with those united in marriage. The mystery which unites two beings is great; without it, the world would not exist."[13]

It elucidates how when we come together in Union, both within and without, we heal this deep collective wound, and "clothe ourselves in the light" of creation.

> What is the Bridal Chamber, if not the place of trust and consciousness in the embrace? It is an icon of Union, beyond all forms of possession; here is where the veil is torn from top to bottom; here is where some arise and awaken. The powers can do nothing against those who are clothed in the light; they cannot see them. All will be clothed in light when they enter the mystery of the sacred embrace.[14]

The Gospel of Philip uses the bridal chamber as a metaphor for the reunion between "Adam and Eve"—the masculine and feminine essence. The "fall" is the split of the primal androgynous unity, the separation between the feminine and masculine. The reunion of Christ and the Magdalene, the Bride and Bridegroom, takes place in the bridal chamber, the place of fullness of the pleroma—cosmic womb consciousness.

"When Eve was still in Adam death did not exist. When she was separated from him, death came into being. If he again becomes complete and attains his former self, death will be no more."[15] The marriage of Jesus and Magdalene symbolizes the perfect, redemptive reunion.

CHAMBER 11

RESURRECTION MYSTERIES

The Crucifixion and Divine Rebirth

Now if you follow
My dance,
See yourself
In me who am speaking.
And when you have seen what I do,
Keep silence about my mysteries.
You who dance, consider
What I do, for yours is
This passion of Man
Which I am to suffer.

HYMN OF JESUS, ACTS OF JOHN

THE CRUCIFIXION IS A KEY SPIRITUAL and symbolic gateway of the Magdalene Mysteries, where a death-rebirth-resurrection initiation (the "round dance," circling the elemental cross of Creation) brings a person to the threshold of a numinous encounter with Spirit, then into a new birth of awakened consciousness.

It is in the Easter resurrection story that Mary Magdalene takes her place at Golgotha, "place of the skull," standing at the foot of the cross with Mother Mary and John the Beloved, while the other Marys are nearby, as they witness Jesus's crucifixion. The twelve male disciples have fled into hiding, afraid for their lives.

This mythical event is rich with many layers of meaning for those who can see. Even the name of Golgotha—place of the skull—may give us a telltale clue. The skull was often associated with the pelvis, which was known as a shamanic "second skull." The timing of the crucifixion is also significant, taking place as it does at Easter in springtime, which was celebrated with rites of rebirth across the pagan traditions.

Even the angels who appear to the Mary priestesses by the empty tomb seem to hint at this knowledge that Jesus is undergoing an expected initiatory event in the mysteries:

> Two men in dazzling garments appeared to them. They said to them, "Why do you seek the living one among the dead? He is not here, but he has been raised. Remember what he said to you while he was still in Galilee, that the Son of Man must be handed over to sinners and be crucified, and rise on the third day." (Luke 24:4–7)

As the Mary priestesses attempt to communicate this grand initiation rite of resurrection to the male disciples, they are disbelieved:

> The women were Mary Magdalene, Joanna, and Mary the mother of James; the others who accompanied them also told this to the apostles, but their story seemed like nonsense and they did not believe them. (Luke 24:10–11)

Let's journey through this great and mythic story searching for jewels . . .

The Crucifixion According to the Gospels

The Gospels of Mark, Luke, and Matthew describe the crucifixion in a way that is classified as synoptic—meaning that all three accounts agree on these facts:
Mary Magdalene:

- Stands at the foot of the cross and witnesses the crucifixion
- Goes to the tomb with unguents and spices to anoint Jesus's body
- Discovers the tomb empty and then meets the resurrected Christ
- Is told by Jesus to go to the other disciples and tell them the good news

The Gospel of John offers a more extensive account of the resurrection, which differs in these details:

❧ Early in the morning Magdalene discovers Jesus's body is missing.

❧ She runs to tell Simon Peter and another disciple what has happened.

❧ Peter and the other disciples run to the empty tomb to see for themselves.

❧ The men head back home and Magdalene stays grief stricken by the tomb.

❧ As she stands there, two angels appear to her and ask why she is weeping.

❧ As she explains, she turns around and sees a man standing there.

❧ She mistakes him for "the gardener" and asks if he knows where the body is.

❧ The man then calls her by her name, "Mary," and she realizes it is Jesus.

These events bring to us one of the most beautiful, controversial, and symbolically layered accounts in the New Testament—when Mary meets Jesus after his rebirth:

She turned herself back, and saw Jesus standing, and knew not that it was Jesus. Jesus saith unto her, woman, why weepest thou? Whom seekest thou? She, supposing him to be the gardener, saith unto him, Sit if thou have borne him hence, tell me where you hast laid him, and I will take him away. Jesus saith unto her, Mary. She turned herself and saith unto him Rabboni; which is to say, Master. (John 20:14–16)

Put into simple, modern language: "She turned and saw Yeshua standing there, but didn't recognize him. The man—who she thought was 'the gardener'—asked her why she was crying, and she explained, asking if he knew where Yeshua's body had gone. Mary, it's me—Yeshua exclaimed to her! Mary turned to face him properly, crying, Rabboni, Beloved One . . ."

Next comes the famous scene where she is told not to touch him (*noli me tangere*).

Magdalene now reaches to touch him, and he says, "Don't seek to hold or cling onto me—I am not yet ascended to the Father." The word for "father," *Abwoon* in Aramaic, also translates as "Great Birther." His rebirth is not yet complete he tells Magdalene.

The Female Pope—Apostle of the Apostles

After their meeting, she goes to tell the others the miraculous news—and in doing so becomes the first apostle of the "Good News," and the "Apostle of the Apostles":

Mary Magdalene went and announced to the disciples, "I have seen the Lord!" And she told them what he had said to her. (John 20:18)

This is the first mention of Mary Magdalene enjoying a private meeting with Jesus, in miraculous circumstances—where she is employed to share news or teachings with the other male disciples, and is at times disbelieved. This motif reappears in the gnostic text the Gospel of Mary Magdalene, where Magdalene receives secret, esoteric teachings from Jesus in either dreams or private visionary meetings, and is disbelieved by some.

The depth of controversy and subterfuge surrounding this classic scene rests on the fact that the Catholic Church's authority is claimed to come directly from Peter (a man) as the first person to meet with Jesus after his resurrection and share the news. Yet even the canonical gospels clearly reveal that this authority did not initially come from a man, but came from a *woman*—Mary Magdalene, who was the first to see Jesus.

This means that Mary Magdalene was the first female pope.

The Lady of Sorrows and Lamentation

One of the mystical signatures of the Crucifixion and Resurrection is the role of grieving and lamentation, a core practice of the feminine mysteries, which were famed for the redemptive and initiatory depth of their grief rituals.

The grief rituals of Isis were particularly renowned for the intensity of their emotional outpouring, as priestesses of Isis mirrored the goddess Isis as she mourned and searched for her lost husband, Osiris, the sacred masculine, in order to rebirth him. Priestesses would walk in procession lamenting and sobbing for the beloved, the salty mystery of their tears flowing from the womb of their souls.

This motif of the feminine grief ritual in the role of the resurrection of the male god was taken up in medieval times, where Magdalene's grief was mystically enacted. Saint Anselm of Canterbury (1033–1109) wrote an emotional prayer-poem about Magdalene and Christ for Adelaide, the younger daughter of William the Conqueror.

Saint Mary Magdalen, you who came with a fount of tears to Christ. . . . How should I tell of you, burning with love of him, wept for him at seeking at his tomb, and sought him whilst weeping? How kindly, and in what friendly way, he inflamed you, whom he came to console. . . . O wonderful devotion! . . . She was not able to prevent them from killing you; and she wished to preserve your body with unguents for a long time.[1]

In some medieval depictions Magdalene is pictured at the base of the cross at Golgotha, wearing a red cloak (symbolic of the female witch-shaman and womb priestess), catching Christ's blood in a skull and bones, with her hair long and loose, entwined round his feet, alluding to the anointing. Her cloak is described as blazing with the "fire of love" as she embodies deep feminine sorrow, and the weeping lover—becoming a symbolic Isis.

In the mystery plays of medieval times, the Easter death and resurrection were a key theme. They presented the three Marys—Magdalene, Salome, and Jacoby—bearing ointment jars, known as *alabastrons,* walking in procession to the sepulcher. When they arrive at the empty tomb, Magdalene takes center stage with her lamentations.

In the Tours manuscript, we read that as Magdalene faints in grief, "Then Mary Jacoby comes who takes her right arm and Mary Salome takes her left, and they lift her from the ground, saying to her, 'Dear sister, there is too much sorrow in your soul.'"[2]

Resurrection on the Womb Cross?

Powerful mystery school symbolism is laced throughout the story of Jesus's shamanic death and rebirth on the cross, which mirrors the resurrection mysteries of Egypt and Sumeria—of Isis and Osiris, and Inanna and Dumuzi. The cross has been a symbol of the Womb or the "Gateway of Life and Death" for many thousands of years, predating Christianity and existing across many cultures—from Tibetan, to Hopi, Maya, and Celtic. Read symbolically, as a mystery school initiation, Jesus "dies on the Womb Cross" and is rebirthed again. This is the meaning of being "born again": the mystical birth from the Womb of God.*

Often this rebirth came through the actual womb of a priestess or beloved bride, so it is interesting that Mary Magdalene is traditionally depicted at the foot of the cross, dressed in priestess red—along with Jesus's mother, the womb of his first birth. Again, there is a secret mystery school teaching in the way that Christ is always depicted with his mother and bride at either side of the "Cross of his Resurrection."

---

*For more information on the Womb Cross, and for illustrations, see Bertrand and Bertrand, *Womb Awakening,* 94–97.

Osiris, embraced by the rebirthing wings of Nephthys on the left and Isis on the right.
A winged solar scarab disk floats above his head.

(From Budge, *Osiris and the Egyptian Resurrection*)

With the Mother, we experience starting as one being, in biological symbiosis within the womb, before we are then born and individuate out into two separate beings. In the Bridal Mysteries, we experience starting as two separate biological beings, who then merge back into a symbiotic spiritual union of One being, through the Womb of relationship and sexual union. This completes the circle. In gnostic wisdom the mystery of the Bride (Mary Magdalene) was considered greater than that of the Mother (Virgin Mary)—because it involved bringing what had been birthed out into separation/duality and marrying it back into Oneness.

Sacred Union, Garden of Eden

The crucifixion is described as taking place during an eclipse—when the moon is united with the sun—which is symbolic of union of the masculine and feminine in alchemy. Afterward, Jesus is taken to the womb-tomb in the garden of Gethsemane, where Magdalene first mistakes him as the gardener—symbolically linking him with the resurrection rituals of Isis and Osiris and Inanna and Dumuzi.

In Sumerian, Babylonian, and Egyptian lore the "garden" was a metaphor for the womb. A man who married a womb priestess and was initiated by her was known as a "gardener"—the fertile ground of their union unfolded in the Garden. In mystical Kabbalism this Garden was also known as the Paradise Orchard.

In the ancient Sumerian text "The Courtship of Inanna and Dumuzi," we read:

> Dumuzi spoke:
> Inanna, I would go with you to my garden.
> Inanna spoke:
> I strolled with him among the standing trees
> Last night as I, the queen, was shining bright,
> He met me—he met me!
> My lord Dumuzi met me.
> My high priest is ready for the holy loins.
> He watered my womb
> He laid his hands on my holy vulva
> I poured out plants from my womb.
> I poured out grain from my womb.[3]

The Queen of Heaven, the Sovereignty of the Womb, then grants her "Lord" his Sacred Kingship.

> Inanna, the First Daughter of the Moon, Decreed the fate of Dumuzi. . . .
> In all ways you are fit . . .
> To sit on the lapis lazuli throne
> To cover your head with the holy crown
> To bind yourself with the garments of kingship.[4]

The attendants of the Holy Shrine of Uruk sing to Inanna:

My queen, here is the choice of your heart,
The King, your beloved bridegroom. . . .
O my Queen of Heaven and Earth,
Queen of the Universe,
May he enjoy long days in the sweetness of your holy loins.[5]

In the garden of Gethsemane, after the initiatory death and rebirth, we see Magdalene and Yeshua taking up the ancient mantle of this symbolic story—she as the ancient Goddess of Womb Sovereignty and he as the initiated Sacred King.

Song of Songs—the Rise of Sophia

In the mystical version of the resurrection scene, Magdalene comes to Yeshua in the darkness, before the sun rises, carrying a torch and her anointing oils—like a guide from the Underworld, as a priestess of the underworld bardo. Her meeting with Jesus in the garden also echoes the Canticles of Canticles, the erotic prayer-poem of the Christian tradition, with themes taken from the ancient goddess mystery schools.

"Saw ye him whom my soul loveth?" the Bride asks in the Canticles. Then she tells us, "I found him who my soul loveth and I would not let him go." Magdalene becomes the New Eve in the garden of resurrection, her love for Jesus bringing union to that which had been torn apart when Adam and Eve were forced to leave the original garden of Eden.

This shamanic journey of redemption and reunion is collective, not just personal. The visionary Rudolph Steiner describes how Jesus's spirit descended down from the "Central Sun"—symbol of our celestial origin at the central galactic black hole—on "a path of descent from the cosmic heights to the earth, on the downward path leading ultimately to the Mother."[6] He envisioned Christ's journey, accomplished through the human body of Jesus, as a downward journey of spirit into matter, and ultimately into the underworld womb of Gaia, completely merging with and permeating the heart of the world before expanding up in a Robe of Glory back to the heavens.

This was his cosmic redemption through the power of Sophia, the "sister and bride" of Christ, the Rose of the World or Celestial Rose, physically embodied in the being of Mary Magdalene, whose yoni-womb was a gateway to merge with Gaia-Sophia.

In doing so, it was believed that his union with Sophia, marrying heaven and hell again, had reopened the cosmic door between the worlds, deep in the world womb, and set free trapped souls. This is also the story told in the lost Gospel of Magdalene.

CHAMBER 12

BISHOPS OF SOPHIA
Female Spiritual Leaders

Because of this I have said to you before: "Where I shall be, there also shall be my twelve ministers." But Mary Magdalene and John, the virgin, will tower over all my disciples and over all the elect who shall receive the mysteries of the ineffable. And they will be on my right and on my left. And I am they, and they are I.

PISTIS SOPHIA 2:96

ONE OF THE REASONS MANY MODERN WOMEN (and men) are turning away from organized religions is the disturbing exclusion of women and sex—where female spiritual leadership is largely forbidden, and sex is demeaned as "dirty and sinful."

We long deeply for a sacred path and communion with the Spiritual essence of life—the "Christ" force—yet instinctively we know that experiencing this communion of Oneness cannot happen while we are separated and shamed. There is a knowing that our sacred sexuality is beautiful and a powerful doorway of union, and that spiritual equality between men and women is the way forward.

Astoundingly, the original Christians also felt this way. Sexuality and female leadership were embraced in the budding movement, which was revolutionary at the time for its inclusivity.

So how did this vision get lost over time? And how can we reclaim it?

Original Christianity—A Women's Religion

Pagan writers such as Celsus writing in the late second century scoffed at Christianity for being a "religion of women" and claimed that the resurrection itself had been based on nothing more than the "reports of hysterical women." Celsus suggests that they were "perhaps deluded by sorcery"—where sorcery is often an allusion to priestesses who practiced magic of the Old Faith.

Previously in Jewish traditions women could only be disciples if their husband was a rabbi; but with Jesus, men and women could both be disciples, and for the first thirty years after his death, priestesses of the new faith still administered rites.

In the old ways of Judaism, the covenant with God was through circumcision, and only applied to men—excluding women. The new rite of baptism, emerging through John the Baptist and Jesus, became a new covenant that was inclusive of women too. This explains why the then-new faith of Christianity was so popular with women.

Not only had women supported Jesus's mission financially, in the aftermath of his death women continued to financially support the missionaries of the new faith and take part as active participants—some like Phoebe (Romans 16:1–2) were also leaders and missionaries in their own right, while also providing the men with support.

Women as Bishops, Teachers, and Prophets

Women were apostles, deacons, leaders of communities, prophetesses, and teachers—the apostle Paul called them "sisters in the Lord" (the spiritual light). He acknowledged that some, Phoebe and Junia (Romans 16:7), converted before he did. Everyone was considered to be One within the power of Christ (holy Shakti).

Women formed house-churches, opening their homes to the missionaries who walked around the countryside preaching about the new religion, or they themselves traveled about spreading the word. The Christian priestess Phoebe was a high-ranking missionary and possibly bishop of her own church, and the tradition of women deacons survived until the mid-fourth century in the West, later in the East.

Paul reveals that it was an accepted practice for Christian gnostics to travel with a female spiritual partner, the equivalent of a priestess, who was called "sister-wife."

Following this ancient tradition, Paul himself traveled with a woman called Thecla, and he mentions other priestesses, Prisca, Junia, Julia, and Nereus's sister, who traveled in sacred pairs with their "husband-brothers" in a ministry of union. The gnostic sage Montanus had a circle of "ecstatic women" and traveled with women.

In Romans 16:1, Paul warmly describes Phoebe as a deacon (*diakonos* in Greek): "I commend to you our sister Phoebe, a deacon of the church in Cenchreae. I ask you to receive her in the Lord in a way worthy of his people and to give her any help she may need from you, for she has been the benefactor of many people, including me." Paul uses a masculine word for Phoebe's ministry, as the distinctly feminine form *diakonissa* did not appear until the fourth century, and also calls her a "leader." These praises led Origen, an early Christian theologian from Alexandria, to say, "this passage teaches two things at the same time: As we have said, women are to be considered ministers in the Church, and . . . ought to be received in the ministry."[1]

Feminine spiritual rites also emerged. In the fourth century, Epiphanius records that heretical Christian priestesses, initiates of the Collyridian school of Christianity, celebrated the Eucharist in the name of "Mary Queen of Heaven," writing, "They adorn a chair or square throne, spread a linen cloth over it, and, at a solemn time, place bread on it and offer it in the name of Mary; and all partake of this bread."[2]

Collyridians were Mary-worshippers in fourth-century Arabia. Their name means "cake-eater sect," and they were also called *Philomarianites,* meaning "Mary lovers." The priestesses of this sect were devoted to Mary the Queen of Heaven; they made sacramental offerings of cakes to "Our Lady," using a special kind of bread (kolluris), in what amounted to a Christian goddess cult. This female-centric church was targeted as heretical by Christian patriarchs such as Epiphanius and was eventually wiped out. He says, "certain women there in Arabia have introduced this absurd teaching from Thracia: how they offer up a sacrifice of bread rolls in the Name of the ever-Virgin Mary, and all partake of this bread."[3] "Bread" sacraments of Mary were likely veiled sacraments of the goddess religion. Interestingly, Bulgaria (Thracia) was also a home of the heretic Cathars.

Junia is a first-century priestess described as either an apostle herself or notable among the apostles, which conveys a sense of the highest levels of leadership. Some scholars consider her to be Joanna, the wife of Chuza—one of the women from the circle of Marys who travel with Jesus and support him financially in his ministry.

Paul also refers to several other women as "coworkers," naming Priscilla, Euodia, and Syntyche. This reveals a remarkable openness to feminine spiritual power. It is said that much of Paul's pro-women material was edited or written over with misogynist words by later church fathers, to conceal the extent of women's power in the budding church—expressed by Paul, whose language and philosophy reveal that he was very likely an adept of the mysteries.

Fear of the Feminine—
The Poison Returns

Yet the fear of feminine spiritual empowerment started to creep back into the new movement, like an ancient yet familiar poison.

Some suggest that Christians were forced to return to patriarchal values after being criticized by both Jewish orthodoxy and patriarchal paganism for the active role women were seen to be taking, which they found disturbing and shameful.

Celsus comments that "Jesus went about with his disciples, and obtained his livelihood in a disgraceful and importunate manner."[4] He also belittles other feminine religions, as well as their followers and priesthoods, condemning the priests of the fertility goddess Kybele, and the followers of Hecate, a goddess associated with feminine sorcery. Celsus goes on to reveal that Jesus is a sorcerer who was born in Egypt, where he studies magic, and then returns to his home country as an accomplished mage. The local Canaanite traditions indigenous to the land of the Israelites were also once filled with pagan magic. Hostile Galileans accuse Jesus of trafficking with "Baalzebub, Prince of Demons," who was once a respected Canaanite deity of the old ways.

Often, we are presented with a simplistic idea of "pagan versus Christian," as if there is only one form of paganism. In fact, the pagan traditions that stand against Christianity in the written records are patriarchal, and are equally disparaging of feminine folk traditions associated with the goddess. In his work, *The True Word,* Celsus often associates sorcery with goddess worship, as distinct from the patriarchal paganism and philosophy of Greece and Rome.

In calling Jesus "an Egyptian sorcerer," he does not mean a pagan philosopher of the Roman state religion—rather he is alluding to him as an initiated magician of the goddess traditions of Isis and the feminine mysterium. For Celsus, as a patriarchal pagan, Jesus's association with the Mary priestesses is disgusting. Yet we have no written testimony from the women who served as high priestesses or the followers of their ancient faith. Mary Magdalene and her priestess sisters are mostly rendered silent, and their ancient red magic of Mari-Isis is obscured and cut out. Jesus is set adrift from his true context. Instead history is hijacked by male narratives of worldly power and religious authority, where "empires of men" are set against each other, and the feminine.

Feminist biblical scholar Elisabeth Schüssler Fiorenza insists that we must "find ways to break the silence of the text." This silence—often enforced—

cannot be allowed to prove the absence of women. And artfully, we can read between the lines, and hear their singing voices.

Spiritual Separation— The Fall of Sexuality

The first 400 years after Jesus's life were an intense cauldron of possibility, and also persecution, but by the end of the fourth century the feminine path was fading out—the feminine elements of paganism, including Isis worship, were being crushed and eliminated, and the evolution of the Christian Church was increasingly male-dominant.

In the beginning, not only did priestesses minister rites in the new Christian Church, this new religion was also open to couples, and male priests could marry. In fact, Peter the "rock" of the conventional church was himself a married man. In 1 Corinthians 9:5 Paul says, "Don't we have the right to bring a Christian wife with us as the other apostles and the Lord's brothers do, and as Peter does?" And a family scene in Matthew 8:14 spells it out by referring to Peter's mother-in-law, "When Jesus arrived at Peter's house, He saw Peter's mother-in-law sick in bed with a fever."

Yet the ideal of an ascetic celibate male priesthood continued to gain ascendency, in part because of the need for the newly forming church to gain wealth. If a priest was married, when he died his money and property transferred to his wife and children, but conveniently a celibate priesthood left their legacy to the church.

Then in the Council of Elvira in 305 CE, male ministers were told to abstain from sexual relationships with their wives or be cast out, and in 352 the Council of Laodicea forbade women to serve as priests or to preside over churches (meanwhile in the pagan world, priestesses who had held power—even priestess-magistrates—were also stripped of their titles and office). The Fifth Council of Carthage in 401 decreed that married clergy should be separated from their wives—abstinence was no longer enough to guarantee their "purity." From the late fourth century, Christianity, which had started as a revolution of equality and union flowing from the deep bonded love of Jesus and Magdalene, was reduced to a celibate male clergy.

What we can also understand is that for the first three hundred years of Christianity male priests were married and enjoyed sexual union with their wives, and that independent women also took an active and vibrant role in spiritual leadership.

CHAMBER 13

GNOSTIC MAGDALENE
The Salvation of Sophia

Through gnosis we are purified . . . those who have realized gnosis
know the source and the destination.

VALENTINUS, THE GOSPEL OF TRUTH

WHEN WE EXPAND BEYOND THE CANONICAL New Testament accounts of Magdalene, we start to drink in the essence of what womb gnosticism means in its deepest heart.

This extract is taken from a Syriac text almost two thousand years old (180 CE). As you read, allow the words to wash through you, like ancient oceanic waves . . .

I am the voice speaking softly.
I exist from the first.
I dwell within the Silence,
Within the immeasurable Silence.
I descended from the midst of the Underworld
And I shone down upon the darkness.
It is I who poured forth the Water.
I am the One hidden within Radiant Waters. . . .
I am the image of the Invisible Spirit.
I am the Womb that gives shape to the All.
By giving birth to the Light that shines in splendor.

GNOSTIC TEXT, TRIMORPHIC PROTENNOIA

Magdalene as a Spiritual Leader

In the canonical gospels of the New Testament, great efforts are made to dim Magdalene's light and hide her role as a spiritual leader, teacher, and apostle.

Yet in gnostic texts and apocryphal texts a much clearer and radically different version of Magdalene is presented—as a spiritual force of vitality and leadership. Some of the male disciples are presented as either a "bit dim" and unable to comprehend Yeshua's more esoteric teachings, or as being afraid of persecution—or at times even aggressive toward Magdalene and what she stands for. In the Pistis Sophia, Mary even tells Jesus that she fears Peter will hurt her, saying: "because he is wont to threaten me, and he hateth our sex."[1]

In a Coptic psalm attributed to Heracleides (third century CE), Yeshua once again describes Magdalene as the "apostle of the apostles" and instructs her to go and find the "orphan" eleven—the male disciples—who have given up their nets, and are no longer fishers of men, because the "deceiver" has persuaded them to give up on the teachings of Christ. Magdalene is asked by Jesus to bring the straying sheep—the male disciples—back into the sheepfold again. The psalm calls Mary "Miriam the Spirit of Wisdom" and says "a net-caster is Mariam"—the usual male role.

In the second century the gnostics wrote profusely about the teachings of Magdalene, and the secret Womb Mysteries. But by the fourth century the gnostic writings were suppressed as being heretical, and the name of Mary Magdalene faded to the background, or she was portrayed as a prostitute. However, her magnetic pull still called some, who saw her as a forbidden erotic and mystical presence, transfigured into spiritual love, representing the Bride or the feminine soul of the church.

Yet her real role as a spiritual leader was now overtaken with her archetypal role as the redeemed "fallen woman" whose repentance returns her to the control of "the father." For a celibate male clergy focused on disempowering women, this put her in a manageable place, at the feet of Jesus—and all men—where she could be tamed.

The Nag Hammadi Discovery

However, magical Magdalene mischief was at work—the red thread of feminine wisdom was too strong to be broken. First, in 1773 an old gnostic text called the Pistis Sophia was discovered, which although dense in places, also depicted

Mary as a wise mystic and visionary who held a close spiritual relationship with Yeshua.

Then, in 1896 in Cairo, the Gospel of Mary Magdalene was rediscovered, adding to this portrait. Finally, in 1945, near Nag Hammadi of Upper Egypt, many scrolls written by gnostic sects—scribed at almost the same date as gospels are written— were found near a monastery and helped give a remarkable new interpretation on Mary Magdalene. Suddenly a new gnostic feminine awakening was blooming.

What Is Gnosticism?

There is no one doctrine for gnosticism, and many different groups often had wildly differing views and beliefs, only loosely held under the umbrella of "gnostic."

But some of the common facts are:

- ❧ Salvation through secret knowledge, or gnosis—direct experience or knowing.
- ❧ Gnostics were often called "spirituals."
- ❧ Gnosis was essentially mystical and was revealed to initiates through secret writings and inner enlightenment.
- ❧ Knowledge comes through personal revelation and doesn't necessarily need priests, clergy, dogma, or organized religion. However, initiatory experiences and wisdom passed from enlightened teachers in the lineage is valued.

The distinguished scholar of Mesopotamian and Jewish mysticism Simo Parpola, of the University of Helsinki, shares that it is generally recognized that gnosticism, with its feminine divinity of Sophia, originates from a much older oral tradition of Kabbalah—and its mystery teaching of the unification of the Higher "Ain Sof" with the Lower Sophia—the Shekinah.[2] Where Keter, the crown, and Malkuth, the throne, are united in the Tree of Life, an incredible cosmic alchemy is achieved with a spontaneous *divinization of matter*.

Alchemically, the story of Jesus and Magdalene is this awakening of the Tree of Life, repairing the broken vessels of light, so that the entire creation is illuminated again.

It makes sense that gnosticism, originating with Greek philosophers (lovers of Sophia or Wisdom), was inspired by a secret, mystical feminine tradition. The left-hand oral teachings of Kabbalah were given in strict secrecy, only to the initiated.

Some scholars now think Jesus and Magdalene had a gnostic inner circle of initiates—which *did not* include some of the famous male disciples, explaining their apparent cluelessness around some of the teachings, and their distrust of Mary.

Pistis Sophia—Light of Mary

The Pistis Sophia tells the story, in four parts, of the resurrected Savior who returns to spend twelve years teaching his disciples before his final ascension.

During this epic, and at times fantastical confusing text, we hear the compelling tale of Sophia (Wisdom), and her fall from the Pleroma into darkness, and her return, as she sings the twelve hymns of repentance to the Light of the Treasure House. The text takes the form of a dialogue between the disciples and the holy women—including Magdalene, Salome, Martha, and Mary the mother of Jesus.

Magdalene, the chief questioner, is described as:

The happy one, beautiful in her speaking
Pure spiritual Mariham
Inheritor of the Light

When she asks Jesus if she may speak in "boldness," he replies: "Mariham, Mariham, the happy, this whom I shall complete in all the mysteries of the things of the Height. Speak in boldness, because you art she whose heart straineth toward the Kingdom of the heavens more than all thy brothers."[3]

He says that because of her knowledge and intuition, she will become "happy beyond every woman upon the earth, because thou art she who will become the Pleroma of the Pleromas." He further praises her for "giving light upon everything in accuracy and in exactness."

Magdalene asks thirty-nine of the forty-six questions given within the text, which annoys Peter who says, "My Lord, we are not able to bear with this woman, saying instead of us; and she lets not any of us speak, but she is speaking many times"—showing that opinionated, spirited women have always been "too much" for the patriarchy.

However, Jesus defends her, and in the Pistis Sophia Magdalene is portrayed as the "one who is the inheritor of the Light" and is an aspect of Sophia, the Wisdom of God.

The Gospel of Mary

This is a beautiful text that elucidates on some of Yeshua and Magdalene's deeper teachings and can be read in many ways, through many "lenses of perspectives."

As the gospel begins . . .

❧ Jesus is gone and the disciples are too afraid to go out and preach.

❧ They fear for their lives.

❧ Mary tries to rally them.

❧ Peter asks her to tell them anything that Jesus said in private to her.

❧ When she reveals his secret teachings, Peter is shocked.

❧ He doubts that the "savior" could have said these things to her.

❧ She is upset and offended he doubts her and is calling her a liar.

Initially, Peter is thirsting for more teachings, asking Mary to tell them "what they haven't heard" (an interesting and significant mirror to Yeshua's oft repeated phrase "for those with the ears to hear").

Mary responds, "I will teach you about what is hidden from you."

She goes on to recount a visionary encounter and teaching she received about the ascension of the soul, passing through seven different levels called "powers" of wrath. However, Peter doesn't like Mary's answer and feels threatened.

Levi eventually steps in to support Magdalene, saying, "Peter, you are always ready to give way to your perpetual inclination to anger. And even now you are doing exactly that by questioning the woman as though you're her adversary." He goes on to say, "If the Savior considered her to be worthy, who are you to disregard her? For he knew her completely and loved her steadfastly."

The gospel ends with Levi reminding them that their mission is to "clothe themselves with the perfect Human" and go out and preach.

In our language, "the perfect human," or *anthropos,* is the blueprint of original innocence—the seed space of wisdom within our center that we can always choose to return to and embody. The gospel makes clear that Magdalene is clothed in this light of primordial innocence and remembrance, while other disciples are still grappling with their shadow—especially the division between the masculine and feminine.

Magdalene is described as "turning them toward the Good."

CHAMBER 14

TANTRIC TEMPLE

Ecstatic Mystics on the Path of Love

LIKE A SEDUCTIVE PERFUME, the path of Jesus and Magdalene did not stay localized in the lakes of Galilee and the temples of Jerusalem, but traveled across seas, cultures, religions, temples, and sacred sites to infuse a renewed magic into the world web.

There is a forgotten side of the Christ path that rings with ankle bells, anointed with the rich, earthly scents of spikenard and sandalwood, from the tantric rites of India. There are uncanny similarities between the Christ path and the love cults of Krishna, and the left-hand mysteries of the tribal tantra and Buddhist tantra of India and Tibet. The word *tantra* itself refers to ancient, indigenous Divine Mother worship, and means "weaving" or to be "woven together," as Magdalene's name is "Great Weaver."

Many folklore legends place Yeshu visiting India during his "missing years"—between the ages of thirteen and thirty, when there is no gospel account of his whereabouts. As we know, traveling to India for initiation was not unheard of. Stories place Jesus visiting Kashmir, Tibet, and Odisha (Orissa)—all places connected with tantric worship. We also have Saint Thomas traveling to India on his apostolic mission, landing in southern India to spread the red sutra of the Christed Ones. That Thomas, one of the apostles, easily reached India by 50 CE shows that this was a common pilgrimage path for those who studied and preached the mysteries.

In the modern imagination, Jesus is envisioned as a solitary ascetic, visiting the male yogis and Brahmins of India, to study the Vedic path of sexless enlightenment.

These sects would be the equivalent of the ascetic Essenes and the hierarchical Pharisees and Sadducees in his own lands, yet we know he often stood against these values.

Jesus is reported to be a man who liked to drink wine, who associated with people who were considered "untouchables" in his own culture, such as menstruating women, and surrounded himself with a circle of spiritually empowered women. The places he is rumored to have visited are scented with union and feminine magic. It is likely that Jesus's pilgrimage to India was a sacred tour of tantric temples, where he was anointed with the red menstrual-magic bindi of the old feminine path.

Shall we follow in the rose petals of his footsteps?

Maybe the Magdalene will join us?

For in mystical tantric lore,

It takes Two to become One.

Odisha—Land of the Christed Yogis and Buddhas

Let us explore the ancient city of Puri, Odisha (old Kalinga), in eastern India. In an interview, one of India's great spiritual leaders, His Holiness Sri Bharati Krishna Tirtha, the Shankaracharya of Puri, mentioned that Jesus had "spent some of his life in India, in association with her illumined sages." He said, "I have studied ancient records in the Puri Jagannath Temple archives confirming those facts."[1] In Hindu and Islamic countries Jesus was known as a holy man named Issa or Isha.

Odisha has an incredible spiritual pedigree, and it makes sense that Jesus—and Magdalene—traveled to be initiated into the powerful left-hand Kali rites, and learn the tantric arts of the devadasis, priestesses of Shakti, and tantric Buddhist dakinis, real women and womb shamans whose beliefs, ambiance, and practice, from a lineage at least 3,000 years old, are so similar to the priestesses of Isis and Inanna.

Odisha was a center of tantra, and may be the birthplace of tantric Buddhism that was then taken up to Tibet. In fact, some believe Odisha was the real birthplace of Siddhartha Buddha, and the birthplace of the Tibetan Buddha Padmasambhava and his first consort Mandarava.

Now, the Temple at Puri is dedicated to Jagannath as an incarnation of the Hindu god Vishnu, and was rebuilt in current form in the twelfth century. But originally, the Temple of Jagannath in Puri was probably a tribal shrine site of the Divine Mother, the "Black One," and was also originally a tantric Buddhist temple. Swami Vivekananda said on the matter, "The temple of Jagannath is an old Buddhistic temple."[2] It was probably a Buddhist tantric temple at the time of Jesus's visit.

Buddhist tantra fused indigenous tantric and Shakti worship of the Divine Mother with a spiritual map of awakening to the true reality, based on the Buddha's life, most likely encoding a very ancient oral tradition of psycho-spiritual illumination.

The city has inspired spiritual mystics of all traditions for thousands of years—even perhaps Jesus and Mary Magdalene. The founder of Advaita Vedanta, Adi Shankara, also lived in Puri, in 800 CE, as did the founder of the Hari Krishna sect. The guru of Paramhansa Yogananda, Sri Yuksteswar, also lived and died in the holy city of Puri.* Yogananda had visions of Christ and of drinking from the Holy Grail.

In *Autobiography of a Yogi,* Yogananda quotes his teacher speaking about the resurrection of Lazarus: "Sri Yukteswar was expounding the Christian scriptures one sunny morning," saying, "In this passage Jesus calls himself the Son of God. Though he was truly united with God, his reference here has a deep impersonal significance. The Son of God is the Christ or Divine Consciousness in man."[3]

Puri and the Tantric Temples

In Odisha, we discover the tantric world of the temple priestesses, brought alive. This is a realm of asparas, yoginis, dancers, devadasis, ancient precursors of Odissi classical dance, the "Dance of the Moon." It is a place of sacred prostitutes, matrikas, queens of Shakti, menstrual ritual, and ceremony to celebrate the earthly and celestial cycles.

Sculptural renditions of temple dancers, ancient dancing dakinis, abound on temple walls such as Konark and the Temple of Jagannath. In the caves at the heritage site of Udayagiri, from 2000 BCE, are carvings of female priestesses, sacred dancers and musicians, and fruit trees. We can only imagine the powers of queenship and spiritual leadership they held, akin to their sisters in the temples of Inanna.

Both Jesus and the Grail King were known as fisher kings. And in tantric

---

Paramhansa means "Great Swan"—a symbol of the Feminine Christ.

tradition, male initiates of the tantric goddess mysteries were known as "Lords of the Fish."⁴ As we have discovered, mermaid rituals and fish priests and priestesses date all the way back to Sumeria, as well as ancient India, suggesting some sort of shared origin. Even now, the temple at Puri holds a "resurrection" ritual every twelve to nineteen years, known as Nabakalebara, meaning "new birth" or "born again" or "new body," bringing to mind Jesus's journey of resurrection into the light body, where a new spirit body is born.⁵

Other rituals are based on the menstrual cycles of the Earth Mother and the Moon, a holographic mirror of the female shaman's lotus womb. The devadasi system, now either outlawed or much degraded, was once a beautiful window into a lost world of feminine power and magic that we can barely imagine. It was inherited from the ancient tribal and tantric Buddhist culture and customs, and has some irregular features, such as breaking caste laws—a unique feature shared by tantrics, Buddhists, and the teachings of Love and equality of Jesus.

One of the remarkable features of the Temple of Jagannath is that *mahaprasad* (the equivalent of eucharist) can be eaten by everyone alike, "out of the same pot the Brahmin and the untouchable sweeper can both eat," outside the temple grounds.⁶

This sacred food is granted to the gods by the sovereignty of Lakshmi. In fact, one tale tells how Lakshmi demands that her prasad be nonhierarchical, so her "food of life" be available to everyone. This parallels the gnostic Eucharist of the Divine Mother, where the Great Mother feeds everyone from the substance of her love.

Dancing Shakti Queens

By the time records began, the devadasis had been taken into service to the god, as his wife—and also to the king and high priest, as the living embodiment of the male god. In this role they serve as a "Holy Whore," participating in sacred sexual rites.

Yet they are honored and sovereign, and their erotic power is considered highly auspicious, vessel of the fertilizing waters that nourish the god, the land, and people. In early times, the devadasis did not marry or have children, kept their own home, learned to read and write, performed sacred temple ritual, studied the erotic arts to perfection, learned the charms and allurements of adornments, and studied sacred dance and the musical arts, so that they could be conduits of divine inspiration.

They were often treated as living goddesses, and accorded respect above other women. As women of the left-hand path they could be unchaste, and entertain suitable men in their quarters, at their discretion, and receive gifts and adoration.

The temple provided them a generous income, and they did not need to work or offer any kind of service, including sexual, for money. Their role was to embody *Bhakti* and *Shakti*—to embody a state of wild devotion and regenerating life force.

Their life circled around the seasonal and lunar rituals of the Sacred Temple.

Body as the Pilgrimage— At the Feet of the Goddess

We must percolate what it means that Jesus was initiated at the Temple of Jagannath ("Lord of the World" and once the "World Mother"), which was a famed tantric place two thousand years ago, at the time he visited, and still retains many keys of the left-hand path, with a legacy of resurrection rites and sacred sexual "whore" priestesses.

Maybe in these priestess rites we can find a glimpse of the Magdalene way?

The temple priestesses were highly revered by pilgrims to the holy city of Puri, believed to be an actual vessel of god. When the devadasi offers her ritual dance in the temple, pilgrims are invited to watch and receive blessing. The priest explains to the pilgrims that viewing the dancing devadasis, they are *in the presence of god.* After the dance, pilgrims take dust from the devadasis' feet, and some roll around on the floor where she has been dancing, to collect the dust of her feet on their bodies. Others place offerings at her feet, such as ornaments and saris, and worship her.

Sometimes pilgrims would visit the devadasi's house to worship her, and make food offerings to her of *mahaprasad.* As the food is offered, they would say, "*ma khaa,*" which means "mother, eat." The food she did not eat was described as "nectar."[7]

On other occasions, a circle of devadasis visits a house of pilgrims to bestow their blessing, fully adorned in their sacred regalia, as channels of earthly-erotic divinity. This is a nonsexual event, and after the dance is an adoration of the sacred women. They are placed on a seat, anointed with sandalwood, and given offerings and gifts. Then the pilgrims ritually wash the feet of the dancers. The water is collected from the foot washing, each pilgrim sips the water as a blessing, and the rest is placed in containers for the pilgrims to take home. It is treated like holy "pilgrimage water"—the pilgrimage place is literally the body of the devadasi, as vessel of the divine.[8] Then the devadasis sing songs for the pilgrims. These are devotional songs. The erotic wedding songs are reserved for the inner sanctum of the temples and gods.

Even kings made this "pilgrimage to the body" of the sacred woman and addressed the devadasi respectfully as a superior, and called himself "her servant." Powerful men would worship her and sip the eucharist of her sacred footbath water—literally "worshipping the very ground that she walked on" as a religious matter.[9] As the Odishan saying goes: "as is done for the body, so is done for the gods."[10]

In this role, she is called the "Walking Goddess" and the ritual is called "Worship of the Maiden," named as *kumari,* meaning "maiden, virgin, or unmarried without child."

Pilgrims also performed the foot-bathing ritual on the priest, calling him "Lord."

The Tantric Last Supper

Could this devotional act, performed by kings of India, have inspired Jesus?

Mary Magdalene is specifically described as performing a foot-bathing ritual, as told in the Gospel of Luke 7:37–38. "She brought an alabaster jar of perfume and stood behind Jesus at his feet, crying. She began to wash his feet with her tears, and she dried them with her hair, kissing them many times and rubbing them with the perfume." The importance of the foot-washing ritual continues as Jesus then says to Simon, "Do you see this woman? I entered your house, you gave me no water for my feet, but she has wet my feet with her tears and wiped them with her hair" (Luke 7:44).

At the Last Supper, Jesus is also recorded as participating in a foot-washing ritual, this time with his male disciples, who do not appear to know its spiritual meaning. The following story is told in the Gospel of John 13:1–16:

"So he got up from the meal, took off his outer clothing, and wrapped a towel around his waist. After that, he poured water into a basin and began to wash his disciples' feet, drying them with the towel that was wrapped around him."

Jesus asks them, "Do you understand what I have done for you?"

Then he says: "Now that I, your Lord and Teacher, have washed your feet, you also should wash one another's feet. I have set you an example that you should do as I have done for you. Very truly I tell you, no servant is greater than his master."

This is not an act of hospitality or purification; it is about love, devotion, humility. It is after the ritual foot bathing at the Last Supper that Jesus commands the disciples to "love one another," and the ritual is given as a unifying sacrament of devotion.

Erotic Enlightenment

In the world of the priestesses of the left-hand path, feet are the roots of the goddess and are sacred. The feminine shaman represents the liminal places where the worlds meet, where feet touch earth, spirit incarnates into matter, water and fire merge into *rasa*. The priestesses found their deepest meditative moments not in ascetic, self-denying practices but in sexuality, in nature, in dance, in prayer, in the body. It is in these states of immanent and embodied eros that they experienced direct transmissions of the divine; the spark of the world soul surged through them, and profound experience of the true nature of reality opened unto them, as their thousand petals of lotus-womb consciousness unfolded, and they became at-one with primordial Shakti.

Bauls—Truth Within the Body

Another people that bear the hallmark of the teachings that renewed through Jesus and Magdalene are the Bauls, a nomadic mystical people who are centered in the east of India. The Bauls are linked to the Bhakti cults devoted to the sexual soulmate union of Radha and Krishna—the "Christ" of India. This is not a transcendent theology, but a full-bodied devotional love. The Bauls' spiritual motto is *Dehattaya,* which translates as "Truth within the body."

The aim of Baul *sadhana* (or spiritual practice) is to return to the original condition of nonduality that existed before Creation.[11] By allowing our spontaneous movements—physical, emotional, sexual, and spiritual—we can return to Original Innocence. The Bauls live in the feeling dimension: if they are sad, they cry; if they are happy, they laugh—they do not restrict or repress their natural flow.

In the Gospel of Mary Magdalene, Mary shares the secret teachings of the *anthropos,* the "perfected being," and quotes Jesus as saying, "find contentment at the level of the heart, and if you are discouraged, take heart in the presence of the Image of your true nature."[12]

The anthropos, the "perfect being," is the *adhar manush* the Bauls speak of. Beyond gender, it is the essential state of consciousness, which we embody in the womb, then forget, and must remember in order to become *fully human;* this is not a superhuman state, not transcendent and grand, but simply our own birthright. For Bauls the only wisdom, *Sophia,* was love.

The Bauls sing of Sophia:

> *Look for Her in the temple of your limbs;*
> *She is there as the Light of the World—*
> *Speaking, singing in enchanting tunes.*
> *She is an expert at hide-and-seek;*
> *No one can see Her.*
> *Do not try to catch Her, O my heart!*
> *She can never be caught—*
> *You can only dance with Her,*
> *In whole faith.*[13]

MAGDALENE'S LEGACY
ROSE LINE OF THE GRAIL

CHAMBER 15

HERETIC QUEEN

Magdalene's Escape to Europe

THE STORY OF MAGDALENE DOES NOT END with the gospels. In fact, this is where her story, and the Rose heresies, truly start to bloom—as her presence moves west, inspiring female Christian mystics and taking center stage in a new Church of Amor, led by various sects and priestesses, including the Cathars, Keepers of the Holy Grail.

The Pistis Sophia seems to prophecy this red thread that Magdalene will carry out into the world, saying, "Well done, Mary. You are more blessed than all women on earth, because you will be the fullness of fullness and the completion of completion."[1] The Church of the Grail, a rose circle of Mary Magdalene devotees and spiritual inheritors, is divinely seeded to flourish and diversify during the high religious ages.

But before we explore the secret world of the Cathars, and their Descending Dove, let's join Mary Magdalene on a small, rudderless boat, with her friends and family, scribes, and fellow members of the inner circle of Jesus, said by legends to have set sail from Egypt, traveling along the Mediterranean, until it reached Gaul, France . . .

Escape to France

The orthodox versions of Mary's escape from Palestine assume the fact that Jesus did die. And for most Christians, Jesus being crucified is indisputable and forms the backbone of the religion, as the key moment he is transfigured as the "Son of God."

But there are many accounts from that era—which went on to become the "heresies" of medieval times—that Jesus was a human prophet, not a god. Some said he was not even crucified, others that he was taken down early and survived, or that a "double" went in his place—rumored to be Judas Escariot. Other versions said that Joseph of Arimathea, a prosperous tin merchant with connections in Rome, arranged with Pontius Pilate (the Roman governor) to create a staged crucifixion that secretly allowed Jesus to survive and be smuggled out. Interestingly, Pontius Pilate owned a villa in the region of the south of France, where some legends say that Magdalene and Jesus fled when they left Palestine.

We are often led to believe that it was a kind of primitive "stone age" scenario two thousand years ago, where people did not travel outside of their homelands. But that is not the case, especially for those with financial means. The entire Mediterranean coastline was a flourishing trade route, and important dignitaries from the Near East and Rome even had "holiday homes" in faraway spa towns, such as Rennes les Bains in Languedoc in the south of France and Bath in England.

It is with this in mind that we follow Mary as she flees persecution in her homelands, first seeking sanctuary in Alexandria, before heading further west. The most famous tale has Magdalene landing in either Marseilles or the nearby port town of Saintes-Maries-de-la-Mer, along with her brother Lazarus, and key figures from the circle of Mary priestesses, including Mary Salome (mother of James, son of Zebedee), and Mary Jacobe (sister or cousin of Mother Mary), Maximin, and Sidonius. This tradition was first encoded in the *Golden Legend* in the thirteenth century.

Most intriguing is a young girl, Sarah, who also travels with them—who later becomes worshipped as a Black Madonna by the Romani people as "Sara-le-Kali," with a dedicated church, womb-crypt, and festival in the town of Saintes-Maries-de-la-Mer. *Sarah* means "princess" in Hebrew, and many feel she is the lost daughter of Magdalene and Jesus, but as she is also sometimes known as Sara the Egyptian, speculation of her true identity abounds. Some legends say she is an Egyptian serving girl, or that she was a daughter born from an earlier tantric union of Jesus.

Sara-le-Kali also refers to the Hindu Divine Mother Kali, as the Romani people, who traveled to Europe in the sixth century, are descended from the northwest of India. Frans de Ville, in his book *Traditions of the Roma in Belgium,* says:

Sara the Kali . . . was of noble birth and was chief of her tribe on the banks of the Rhône. She knew the secrets that had been transmitted to her. . . . The

Rom at that period practiced a polytheistic religion, and once a year they took out on their shoulders the statue of Ishtari (Astarte) and went into the sea to receive benediction there. One day . . . Sara saw them arrive in a boat. The sea was rough, and the boat threatened to founder. Mary Salome threw her cloak on the waves and, using it as a raft, Sarah floated towards the Saints and helped them reach land by praying.[2]

This paints an alternative, intriguing portrait of Mary Magdalene and the Mary priestesses being welcomed and assisted by a female religious leader, also a worshipper of the goddess, with ties to an ancient lineage from the Eastern and Indian temple traditions, who had anticipated their arrival and set out to help them.

In this version, a "Sisterhood of Sophia"—who worship the goddess in her many, ten thousand names—are connected, through psychic attunement, and support each other.

This does not discount that Magdalene may also have been with child.

Magdalene's Mysterious Journey

Although this is a cherished legend, bringing much medicine, it is not the only one.

What we can take from this is that the story of Magdalene continued onward, and was not defined by the canonical gospels of Jesus, and that where she went, what she did, who she traveled with, and her ministry was deeply important.

The first Magdalene myth emerged in ancient Turkey. It was said that Magdalene had first gone, with Virgin Mary and John the Beloved, to the Diana Temple in Ephesus where she had been a spiritual leader before she was executed and died a martyr. In 700 CE people pilgrimaged to see her supposed tomb, and it is from Ephesus that the feast date of July 22 comes, listed on calendars since 800 CE.

Scribes in Northumbria in northern Great Britain described Magdalene's fate in a ninth-century martyrology document, saying that after Christ's death she had been so grief stricken she could "no longer upon look upon man" and had gone away to the desert, where she lived for thirty years, praying, fasting, and meditating. Some say these English scribes took their information from a Latin script from 750 CE. Eventually this would morph into a legend of her living for thirty years in the cave at Saint-Baume, Provence, France—an ancient goddess pilgrimage site to Diana.

This myth is also conflated with that of Mary the Egyptian, a fifth-century "harlot" (temple priestess), who after seventeen years of "infamy" (or sexual practice) in Alexandria traveled across the sea, apparently "earning her passage," in order to reach Palestine, where she reclused in a cave in the deserts of the Holy Land, naked, with only her hair clothing her, being fed by angels, repenting for her many sins.

This story is also merged into the Sainte-Baume legends, as depicted in the painting by Jules Lefebvre titled *Mary Magdalene in the Cave* showing a wantonly naked, yet penitent, Magdalene outside the cave of Sainte-Baume. This painting was made in 1896, coincidentally the same year the lost Gospel of Mary Magdalene was discovered in Egypt.

A late twelfth-century manuscript written in Berne first identified the mystical cave of Magdalene as a grotto near Marseilles, "four leagues distant from Saint-Maximin." The Abbey of Vezelay also claimed that Magdalene had lived in this grotto at Sainte-Baume (Holy Balm), but had died and been buried in Aix—her bones, now sacred saint relics, were removed and taken to Vezelay, the site of a Magdalene cult.

Various legends described how she arrived in Gaul (France) from Palestine. Some said she had died in Palestine and her remains had been brought by sea to Gaul. Some said she had arrived by boat with seventy-two other disciples, including Maximinus, and had preached in the pagan temples of Marseille, converting the town to Christianity. Other legends told how she had arrived by boat with Lazarus and Martha, or Mary Salome and Mary Jacobe. Some said she had preached throughout the region of Provence, embodying active feminine spiritual leadership; others preferred to paint her as simply retiring in solitude to her cave, more repentant than evangelizing.

In 1248 the Dominican friar Fra Salimbene de Adam visited the grotto at Sainte-Baume and reported, "The cave where Mary Magdalen did her penance for thirty years, they say, is fifteen miles from Marseilles. I slept there one night, the eve of her feast-day. It is in a very high rock . . . there are three altars and a spring equal to the fountain of siloe. A very beautiful path leads up to it. Outside the grotto is a church served by a Priest."[3]

He also adds, "the women and noble ladies of Marseille" who made the difficult pilgrimage to the cave took donkeys loaded with bread, wine, and fish as provisions. This pilgrimage to the cave continued to attract noble ladies, including Anne Boleyn—the queen of England, who was later beheaded, and may have been a secret MM heretic.

Erotic Convents, Womb Mystics

This Magdalene legacy emerged throughout the Middle Ages in Christian women, as a Rose lineage of womb mystics, whose faith was a deeply felt and direct connection with the Divine. In a world of sexless, celibate male clerics, the arts of feminine wisdom, sublime eroticism, ecstasy, and rapturous divine love were kept alive.

Convents and nunneries were often subject to bouts of intense sexual hysteria from young celibate women, and the female devotional mystics called Jesus their Lord and beloved, imbuing him with the qualities of the lunar lover, the moon god Sin.

Teresa of Avila, a Spanish Carmelite nun and womb mystic of the sixteenth century, who wrote "Interior Castle" (a clever reference to the feminine adytum), says of her love:

> O Lord, you Supreme Trickster! What subtle artfulness you use to do your work in this slave of yours. You hide yourself from me and afflict me with your love. You deliver such a delicious death that my soul would never dream of trying to avoid it.[4]

Every time she mentions Jesus as her Lord, he is shimmering with cosmic erotic divine allure. The essence and wording of her laments are identical in energy to the Bhakti poets and their ravishment through the Divine Love of Radha and Krishna, expressing the magnetic force of love, eros, rapture, and attraction at the heart of God.

Saint Teresa describes one of her highest communions with God, where a beautiful male angel appears substantiated in her room, by her bed. He looks at her with a divine penetrating gaze and then "plunges his arrow" into her womb, thrusting it deep in and out until she reaches the wildest ecstasy of divine love she has known.

> When he drew it out . . . to leave me all on fire with a great love of God. The pain was so great, that it made me moan; and yet so surpassing was the sweetness of this excessive pain, that I could not wish to be rid of it.[5]

Interestingly the translation can be either *heart* or *womb*—but for reasons of decorum, most translators use the word *heart*. When the occult translation of *womb* is used, it becomes clear that Teresa is experiencing a communion of tantric sexual ecstasy. Indeed, her description of awakening to Divine Love sounds very much like she is a Christed dakini of the tantric traditions. The Hindu god of love, *Kamadevi,* is described as a god who "provokes overpowering lust with his flower-tipped arrow."

Teresa's mother died when she was eleven, leading her to take the Virgin Mary as her spiritual mother, and in adulthood she became a close friend to Saint John of the Cross, who became her spiritual twin-flame, fellow mystic, and religious reformer. He was an admirer of the Song of Songs, and the divine love of the Bride and Bridegroom, writing his own mystic poetry, while imprisoned, on the alchemical soul union with God:

> The Bride has entered,
> Into the pleasant garden of her desire,
> And at her pleasure rests,
> Her neck reclining on the gentle arms of the beloved.[6]

Legends say that when Saint Teresa and Saint John prayed together, communing with the Trinity, then miracles of the type yogis are renowned for would unfold:

> She saw St. Teresa raised in the air, where she remained unconscious of the messenger's presence. On the other side of the grating they discovered St. John of the Cross, also raised above the ground levitating in the same way. The two saints had begun speaking of the Most Blessed Trinity, and had fallen into ecstasy.[7]

All correspondence between Saint Teresa and Saint John has been lost or destroyed.

Skirt-Lifting Christian Mystics

At the same time, in fifteenth- and sixteenth-century Spain, heretic Christian mystics called *alumbrados* emerged with less decorum, apparently tracing back to a gnostic origin.

They also believed in the gnostic path of direct communion of soul with God, yet their beliefs ruled out the possibility of sin, and celebrated sacred sexuality. Their gatherings sound similar to those reported of the forbidden "Witches Sabbaths."

One priest from Seville, Fernando Mendez, held congregations of *beatas* (female mystics), and after mass they would strip naked and dance as if they were "drunk on the love of God." Some women would lift their skirts as a form of penance, reminiscent of the *Anasyrma* "skirt lifting" rituals of Egyptian priestesses who exposed their vulvas as a form of religious ritual, associated with emotional healing.[8]

A friar named Fray Alonso de la Fuente denounced them, claiming they were great sorcerers and magicians. He said they "win women and enjoy their bodies with the aid of magic . . . the Devil comes to these women and arouses their carnal sexual desires . . . with no regard for chastity . . . calling sensuality the joy of spiritual people."[9]

The Church of the Grail, with its serpent of sensual salvation, was never far under the surface, even in the times when it was most feared and exiled from public life.

CHAMBER 16

MAGDALENE ORDER

Cathar Priestesses of the Dove

Al cap dels sèt cent ans, verdejara lo laurèl.
The laurel will flourish again in 700 years.

THIRTEENTH-CENTURY CATHAR PROPHECY

ALTHOUGH WE CAN'T SAY FOR SURE if Magdalene lived in France and seeded a new ministry there with her family, and possibly her beloved husband, what we *can* confirm is that by the twelfth century a "new church" linked to Magdalene had birthed.

Parallel to the institutional Christianity of the Catholic Church, new movements were forming, including a Cathar Church in the south of France, founded by heretics. The first hint of its rising was in 1022 in Orleans in northern France, where Joan of Arc was later born and initiated into an indigenous and forbidden native fairy faith. The Cathar creed is thought to have traveled across from the Balkans, through north Italy, and then down into France, where it merged with existing heresies.

For instance, it appears that the eastern Bogomils, who are considered the origin of the heresy, did not have any specific beliefs on Mary Magdalene or the nature of her relationship with Jesus, while the French Cathars venerated Mary Magdalene and believed her to be the spiritual partner and probably tantric consort of Jesus. In their cosmology, Mary Magdalene represented the energy of the Divine Feminine.[1]

It was also known that Cathars in southern France venerated the Black Madonna and made pilgrimages to her sites, including the basilica of Notre-Dame de Marceille, where the Black Madonna of Limoux lives, nearby an ancient sacred well.[2]

With this, it's likely that there was an *existing* Mary Magdalene heresy and tradition in France that became interwoven with the incoming Cathar beliefs and theologies. This indigenous tradition, possibly seeded by the ministry of Magdalene herself, is naturally reflected in the French troubadours and the Courts of Love, who sang songs to "Our Lady" the goddess in sonnets celebrating spiritual love.

The conventional understanding of the Cathar faith as a consistent theology of extreme dualism, of a "good god" and a "wicked world," which in its antifeminism laid down the soil for the Protestant movement, may be something of a red herring. More likely is that there is a weaving of different groups and ideas, gathered under one umbrella, much like the diversity of gnostics who they share similar ideas with. The philosophies of the Jewish Kabbalists, converted Christian Cabbalists, Knights Templar, and alchemists, also popular at the time, probably had an influence too.

It is interesting to note that the Balkans are the origin of other heresies that outraged the original church fathers, including the Christian priestesses devoted to Virgin Mary, who made sacramental bread offerings in a form of a goddess cult.

From our perspective, dualism is a muddled expression of the original Sophia story, of the Higher and Lower Sophia, set apart by an archonic influence on the collective consciousness and hive-mind of humanity, creating the suffering of a man-made world. In the breaking of this holy trinity of Cosmos, Earth, and Human, and then the shattering of the Divine Feminine and Divine Masculine union, the world is fallen.

The mystery traditions, Kabbalistic teachings, and alchemical wisdom that Jesus and Magdalene taught are an elucidation of how to weave the worlds back together, while remaining "set apart" from the drama of the archonic consciousness. As in gnostic theologies, there is both a good god and a demiurge who imprisons Sophia, but similar to Eastern theologies, as well as the world of illusion most people live in, there is a luminescent reality that one could awaken to and live within.

For dualists, there were two gods, two worlds: one heavenly and "high," one feminine and "low"; one saved, one infernal. With the earthly womb cursed, and all of creation the realm of a lower demonic god, redemption was only possible in

the divine grace of the Holy Spirit of the Higher Sophia. This was a jumbled-up convolution of Jesus and Magdalene's teachings.

Some still remembered, taught, and practiced the secret Magdalene Mysteries of a divine marriage, and a cosmic reunification of Sophia's embodied throne and crown.

Church of the Holy Blood

The word *Cathar* is a name that conjures up the feminine left-hand path of Christ.

Cathar, from the Greek root *kata*—meaning "downward or descent," often described as meaning the "pure or holy ones," has its deeper roots in words such as *catharsis,* which means "rebirth" through the descending path of the Holy Spirit.

It is a word describing, simultaneously, purification, renewal, and receiving; analogous to the downward release and renewal flow of the menstrual blood. It was such a powerful metaphor it was applied to Greek drama to express the purging and release of collective emotion as a catharsis—an emotional or spirit menstruation or clearing. Even the word *Catholic* comes from this origin, making it a "menstrual church."

This is the essence of the Feminine Christ energy, which roots us into the earth. It means to release, to let down, to descend, to receive, and to pour out. It is the power by which the feminine "lets down" her sacred elixirs, of milk or blood, that both feed, sustain, nourish, and also create a menstrual doorway of purification.

Beatrice de Planisoles, born 1274, was a Cathar who was tried for heresy by the Inquisition. She was accused of sorcery and was found to have two umbilical cords in her keeping, which science has now discovered contain powerfully regenerative stem cells, showing that this indigenous knowledge may have been commonplace for the Cathars. She was also found to have a cloth soaked in the menstrual blood of her daughter's menarche (first blood), which was said was to enchant her husband into fidelity. But as indigenous womb-shaman cultures knew, this cloth would have also acted as a sacred talisman of womb magic with powerful healing properties.

The Manicheans, an ancient dualist sect often cited as precursors of the Cathars, also had a "Rite of Catharsis"—drinking from the cup of the Holy Grail. During Manichean ritual meals the Elect ate foods that were believed to contain particles of light. It was believed the Elect would integrate these particles of light into their own soul after the feast, and that when their bodies died this acquired light would help liberate them from the earthly cycle of reincarnation. These foods were described as "glowing fruits"—a common symbol of feminine womb magic.[3]

Covens of Female Heretics

In the outward expression of the new church of the Cathars, there were priests and priestesses called "perfects," who were said to be forbidden sex, meat, and worldly goods. They administered the magical rite of the consolamentum—a laying of hands on the head, often on top of the Gospel of Saint John (rumored to be by Magdalene or her son), which was often done before death to open up the gateway to heaven.

There were also Cathar laity, ordinary people, who could marry, make love, work, and trade, and who relied on the perfection of the clergy to administer the rites, and who provided food and shelter to the perfects, especially in times of persecution. Unique in the Cathar faith, compared to institutional Christianity, was the admittance of women into the priesthood—creating priestesses of the Dove. Women who became priestesses of the Holy Dove were called *perfectae,* and often Cathars traveled in pairs, preaching together, mirroring the earlier gnostic apostles.

Often there were female dynasties of Cathars dedicated to the priestesshood. In a deposition to the Inquisition in 1209, Arnaude de Lamothe, from Montauban, told how she had been taken by her mother as a young girl to a home for female heretics. In the presence of a large gathering of Cathars they received the consolamentum.[4] In the 1190s, one woman revealed that she had been brought up in a notorious heretical village, where her grandmother, mother, and her sister were all perfectae, and that her grandmother had openly held a house of female heretics at Fanjeaux.[5]

During the persecution times, when it was often no longer safe to live in villages and towns, the Cathar priestesses often lived hidden deep in nature, in remote forests and woodlands. One scholar says, "they lived in cabins or huts built in the woods, sometimes staying for a few days, and at other times remaining as long as a year." In 1234, two female perfectae were captured while living in a tent in a wood.[6] Some died in the woods, some returned back into convents for female heretics.

Mature women, as they entered their eldership, often became initiated as priestesses of the Holy Spirit, receiving the rite to become a perfectae. One woman, from the nobility, was consoled at Montsegur in 1240 by the Cathar bishop Bertrand Marty. The famous Cathar priestess Esclarmonde of Foix, whose name meant the "light of the world" in the Occitan language, was the daughter of the Count of Foix, and was hereticated at a ceremony in Fanjeaux, together with three other noblewomen. Adversaries to her ministry say she worked with other women to "seduce hearts," giving us the sense of a circle of powerful spiritual women engaged in teaching.[7]

Female Cathars were often medicine women who not only spiritually ministered to their communities but who also were custodians of native herbal lore and wisdom. The women were often spinners and weavers, as well as herbalists and healers. One report says, "some perfectae seem also to have acquired medical knowledge," citing how one man admitted that he had "consulted a female heretic many times for his illness" and how another female heretic treated the ailments of fellow believers.[8]

One account records female priestesses visiting a house to preach and being reverently received by the men of the house with the rite of the melioramentum, which became known as the adoration, where a supplicant bows down to the priest or priestess who is perfected for a blessing. According to records, a third of the Cathar clergy, the perfects, were women, though none held the rank of bishop.

Many of the faith believed Mary Magdalene was more important that Saint Peter.

No wonder the Catholic Church felt so threatened by the Cathar Church blossoming in the south of France, with so many spiritually initiated women following in the footsteps of Mary Magdalene as leaders, teachers, healers, and divine priestesses.

Book of Love, Holy Grail

On July 22, 1209, Mary Magdalene's feast day, the Catholic Church unleashed a crusade against the Cathars, starting at Beziers, France, where the entire town of 20,000 people were massacred for refusing to hand over the resident 222 Cathars.

People were blinded and used as target practice, and 7,000 men, women, and children who were seeking refuge in the church of Saint Mary Magdalene were killed. The crusade raged through France, attempting to annihilate the New Church. In 1243, this led to a nine-month standoff at Montsegur—a strikingly high mountain fort in the remote outreaches of the Languedoc, at the foothills of the Pyrenees.

Montsegur had become a haven for perfects and believers, known as *credentes,* and up to a few hundred had gathered to seek sanctuary from the persecution. They were offered the choice to renounce their faith and escape with their lives. Instead, some of the men defending the castle joined them and took the consolamentum. They were given a two-week period to make this decision, which they spent praying and in unknown ritual. In March 1244, led by Bishop Bertrand Marty, they left their fort refuge to walk down to their deaths, where they were burnt alive on the pyre.

Yet the mystery continues. It was said that the Cathars at Montsegur were in possession of the Holy Grail, a priceless relic connected to Jesus and Magdalene, and most likely a manuscript of teachings, as they did not believe in material wealth. This lost scroll or manuscript has been named the *Book of Love*—possibly a grimoire of secret teachings, or even something written by Jesus or Magdalene.

Legends say that a few Cathar perfects managed to scramble down the steep cliffs and escape, carrying the manuscript with them, or that they fled to a secret forest hideout, where the sacred manuscript—the "Lost Treasure of the Cathars"—had been kept hidden and fiercely guarded. Many of the books of the Cathars were burned by the Inquisitors, but this "Holy Grail" was said to contain a world-changing revelation. If this legend is true or not remains to be seen. The book is yet to be discovered.

Although the public church of the Cathars was virtually extinguished by the fourteenth century, their legacy and lineage lived on, often in secret, or emerging in other heretical sects, such as the Protestant Huguenots, who adopted the Cathar Cross as their own sigil, and who were also fiercely persecuted in their own era in France.

If the *Book of Love* had been retrieved it was most likely smuggled out of France, perhaps to Flanders where trade connections between the weavers and spinners of both regions were strong, and where Magdalene heresies were also renowned. Maybe the *Book of Love* made its way to the heart of Flanders and became the inspiration for the stunning and sublime teachings coded in the *Ghent Altarpiece?*

From there, it could also have made its way to America with some of the fleeing Huguenots, who settled widely in the American South; maybe it still resides, hidden, in an antiquary library in one of the old towns of Charleston or New Orleans.

In a prophecy said to be given by a Cathar perfect in the thirteenth century, it was told that seven hundred years after the massacre of Montsegur, many souls would be reborn to once again carry the torch of the Church of Love.

CHAMBER 17

RED WITCH

Scarlet Saint of the Wise Women

IN MAGDALENE'S LEGACY, she is also the Scarlet Saint of the Red Witches, with her heretical past as "penitent" whore of the sexual arts and as an herbalist-anointrix.

For all the suppression of feminine magic, the Middle Ages were surprisingly rich with priestess practices, imbued with the Magdalene essence that was outlawed. High witchcraft of Magdalene is based on the elemental magic of *natura Sophia* and the red magic of desire, harnessed in devotion to a cosmic unification of opposites; it is a witchcraft of love, allurement in the sense of the universal magnetism, the force of love that binds all things together and brings diversity into harmony and resonance. In its most refined form, it is the reunion of the personal soul with the cosmic soul.

Rather than the lower magic and witchcraft of using spells and intentions solely to bring about desires of the personality, such as wealth or love—without devotion or spiritual wisdom and without consulting the greater flows of the universal will—using red magic to magnetize abundance and love was about *aligning* with the universal will, and riding the ley lines of its energy flows, rather than manipulating it.

Witchcraft was explicitly known as the *feminine magic of women,* and the more a masculine paradigm existed, the more the feminine wisdom was feared and denounced. Wise women often passed down the knowledge of their arts from mother to daughter, or through entire dynasties of witches, encoding the wisdom of the lost Holy Whores, and their arts of enchantments, erotic allurement, and herbal acumen. Witchcraft was a practice of *desire*—the great feminine gift of Sophia. Pre-Christian Greek and Roman pagan religions were regulated by patriarchal ideals and laws, and their magic was not the sorcery of wise women.

There was a rapturous power in the feminine that could command the forces of life herself, because within their wombs was the fiery creative power of the earth's core. The fear of witchcraft is a fear of women's spiritual power, of their womb religion. For the red witch walking the left-hand path of the Feminine Christ, the rupture between heaven and earth, masculine and feminine, is carefully and lovingly sewn (and sexed) back together, the Mother and Father are revered, as above so below, and the Christ child of consciousness that inhabits all living creatures is cherished. Their magic was sexual, sacred, and sovereign—virgin unto itself, which proudly rides its broomstick of awakened womb consciousness into the holy wild deep.

This is a path steeped in moonlight, and guided by rose petals of remembrance.

It is the path of Mary Magdalene's legacy, and the bloodline of her lineage.

Plant Priestesses and Womb Eucharists

Magdalene is a "priestess of the plants"—concoctress of potions, ointments, oils, unction, and philters (aphrodisiac drinks known as love potions) that called upon the subtle powers of nature and the old herbal lore, rooted in the magical medicinal forces of the plant spirits, who would work on behalf of a womb witch and priestess.

With her symbol of the ointment jar, and its distinguished lineage in the temples of Inanna, Magdalene is an emblematic potion priestess. She was the patron saint of apothecaries and perfumers, with the red rose plant-soul as her sacred sigil, symbol of the red lineage of feminine womb magic, with *rose* literally meaning "red." It was said that when Magdalene brought her jar of healing unguents to the tomb of Christ, she applied her healing salves to his deep wounds and resurrected him.

In Indian tantric tradition the rose is symbol of *Tripursundari,* the triple-goddess of love, the occult and erotic aspects of Kali, and the wisdom of the Cosmic Mother. Legends say that when Magdalene wept under the cross, her tears turned to roses, creating the "Rose Cross"—symbol of the transfiguration within the Cosmic Womb.

Plant magic has long been part of religious and magical tradition. Vervain, another plant spirit sacred to the witch-priestesses, was favored by Druids for div-ination, and gathered on the dark moon under the Dog Star, Sirius; it was used to cleanse and purify King Solomon's womb temple; was placed on altars in honor of witch-goddess Diana; and was used in Celtic fairy witchcraft to hold over Beltane fires.[1] The mystical lore of vervain says Isis's tears for her beloved husband, Osiris, were so profound that vervain was birthed and grew from them where they touched the Earth, and so wherever she had cried, this plant would be found. Later on, this beautiful, feminine plant spirit was also associated with Magdalene and Christ.

In her role as plant priestess, MM also entwined into the legacy of European wise women, as their Scarlet Witch Saint, symbolizing their secret feminine folk magic. Witches were often midwives and herbalists, and custodians of the rites of passage such as menarche, sexual initiation, contraception, pregnancy, birth, and death. Their herbal knowledge and practical application were widely revered and feared—especially by a culture that was scared of the liberating power of women's wisdom. The old medieval word for a healer was a *quack*—from the Dutch word *kwaksalver,* which originally referred to a person who cures with home remedies. Like Magdalene, a quack was someone who held the healing secrets of herbs and plants, administered through ancient feminine folk wisdom and lineage traditions. Later on, this name for a wise women herbalist became derogatory, associated with false cures or medicine.

Throughout witch folklore, often recorded in inquisition depositions, women were well known for making magical ointments that they rubbed over their bodies, often with hallucinogenic, healing, or erotic effects, and they were often accused of drinking vile potions or participating in blasphemous eucharists, probably men-strual, and "eating babies," most likely an old form of placental encapsulation.

In the Old Testament, Deuteronomy 28:57 refers to the fact that the ancient people clearly understood that the placenta could be eaten and was nourishing: "The most gentle and sensitive woman among you . . . will begrudge the husband she loves and her own son or daughter the afterbirth from her womb and the chil-dren she bears. For in her dire need she intends to eat them secretly."

Often the placenta is actually translated as "son" or "child" so it mistakenly appears that people are eating their actual children, rather than the nutrient-dense placenta. A medieval scholar reporting on witchcraft in the sixteenth century says: "Then with an offering of tapers made with umbilical cord, they kiss his hind parts in homage." Potions are described as including "the very same ingredients," which so repelled Latin poets. Cauldrons were used to make these forbidden drinks, and "places of authority . . . were obtained by drinking this liquid." Depositions from witch trials in Toulouse in the fourteenth century describe: "The corpses of newly-born children were eaten by them; stolen by nurses; all manner of revolting liquids were drunk."[2]

They also describe rituals performed with the left hand, signs of the cross made with the left hand, rather than right, and bloodletting over a fire from the left arm. One image of a witch, on a woodcut, is said to be "feeding blood" to her familiar, a code to the lost menstrual blood rites of the womb religion and the taboo of blood magic.

In Mexico in the sixteenth century, medicine women and native witches used "ensorcelled" water—which contained menstrual blood or water used to wash their vulva—calling on this feminine power to cast love spells on men. They were targeted by Catholic priests for "outrageous" practices of feminine witch-shamanism.

Broomsticks and Magic Wands

The most notorious practice of the magical women was "riding their broomsticks," an event that either took them directly to a congregation of a witch circle, or referred to flying out of their bodies into an ecstatic state of altered consciousness.

One inquisitor in France records their deeds this way: "they spread an ointment, which the Devil has given them, on a wooden stick and rub it on their palms and all over their hands also; then they put the stick between their legs and fly off over towns . . . and after eating and drinking their fill they had sexual intercourse."[3] Flying a broomstick to what were called "obscene synagogues" is often seen as sexual in nature, and of course the broomstick itself is a phallic symbol, bringing to mind the witches of Shakti riding their Shiva-lingam into tantric bliss consciousness.

In witchcraft, the famous broomstick of otherworldly travel was often considered to be a carefully prepared stick or "magical" wand, applied with entheogenic herbs and substances in order to awaken and open the Grail Gate energy vortexes of the yoni-womb into alchemical ecstatic states of sexual communion with the Godhead.[4] We would be foolish to think only modern women use phallic wands for pleasure. One of the common denominators in the depositions and accusations against the witches and their red magic was that it involved sexual debauchery and wild orgies.

Bishop of Avila, Alonso Tostado (ca. 1400–1455), percolating on the powerful medical ointments in use at the time, such as opium, mandrake, and henbane, says, "There are certain women that [we theologians] call 'witches' who claim to use these same medical ointments in conjunction with magical words. . . . They believe

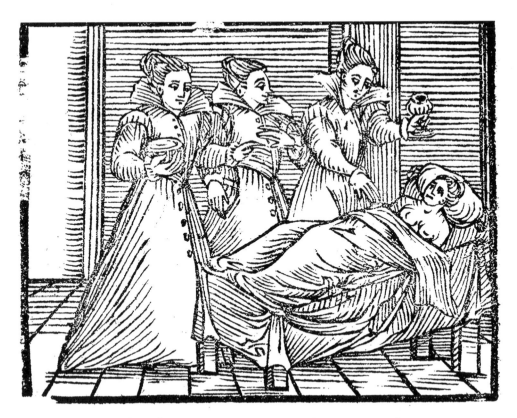

Witches administering potions to a sick woman, woodcut
from *Compendium Maleficarum,* Maria Guazzo, 1626.

Diana is a goddess and yet she is the devil . . . female and male sorcerers engage in
wicked rituals with these ointments . . . indulging in lust and sexual indecency."[5]

Legacy of the Witch-Priestess

The goddess of the witches of Old Magic in central Europe was Diana, or Hekate
in her dark moon phase. Covens of witch-priestesses were said to meet together in
womb circles on full moons or new moons, or other celestial gateways for Sabbaths.

A canon attributed to a council of Ancyra in 314 CE says, "Certain . . .
women . . . ride through the air at night in company with Diana the pagan goddess, and a host of other women, obeying the goddess's orders as if she was their
absolute mistress."[6] Witches were reported to be able to draw down the moon with
their chanting, encoding a remembrance of the importance of sound and vibration
to lunar magic, and originating in the ancient traditions of the Paleolithic female
womb shamans.

There was reported a flourishing cult of Diana in fifth-century Europe, especially in rural areas. Like the ancient Dragon Mother Nin-hur-sag in Sumeria, or the Celtic reindeer goddess of the forests, Elen of the Ways, Diana was a goddess of the wild lands and the wild ways, a mistress of the beasts and plants of Sophia's Garden.

Mary Magdalene was long associated with Diana as queen of the witches, and became the next lady-in-residence at the mystical cave in Sainte-Baume, in Provence, France, which had previously been dedicated to Diana Lucifera, "She of the Moon." Magdalene herself was known as Mary Lucifera, the light-bringer, symbolic of the rising and falling star Venus, which was associated with the goddess worship of Inanna, Ishtar, Astarte, and Tara over in the east, and other wise-women lineages.

The priestess title homage of becoming a "Shining One" was the same as a Sinning One, or Sinner, referring to the embodiment of the spiritual radiance of the moon, and to a completed initiation into the wisdom of sinistra, deep lunar consciousness. "This was a time-honored tradition: pagan goddesses were known, for example, as 'Diana Lucifera' or 'Isis Lucifer' to signify their power to illumine mind and soul, to open up both body and psyche to the Holy Light," says researcher Lynn Picknett.[7]

Magdalene was also said to have preached on the steps of a temple of Diana in Marseilles, when she first landed in France following her escape from Palestine. A passage written by Pomponius Mela, a Roman geographer writing around 43 CE, implies that there were still women who practiced benevolent magic in France (called Gaul). He says nine of them were attached to a temple and lived in chastity.

There are many reports in the third century of witches—called druidesses—practicing in Gaul, who were both feared and consulted by royalty, including the Merovingian courts, who mention a coven of druidess-witches operating in Paris.[8]

Left-Hand Path: Sinistra Astrology

Sinistra is also a star located on the left-hand side of the constellation Ophiuchus, the Serpent Holder or Serpent Bearer. Some astrologers believe Ophiuchus to be the ignored and hidden thirteenth sign of the zodiac, originating from the older feminine traditions that honored the serpent, the left-hand path, and the number thirteen.

The ancient Greeks said the constellation of Ophiuchus represented the god-hero Asclepius, guardian of healing, dreams, and visions, who was raised to mythic status after his death. Asclepius gained his healing powers through an act of kindness to a serpent: in return for honoring her, the serpent licked clean his ears, giving him the "ears to hear," and then whispered to him all secrets of the art of healing and dreams. The root of this myth clearly invokes the memory of a feminine initiation in which the male shaman is granted his magical powers, gifts, and knowledge of the feminine arts by the serpent goddess of primordial Wisdom. Manilius, a first-century astrologer, writes in his *Astronomica*:

> When Ophiuchus, encircled by the serpent's great coils, rises he renders the forms of snakes innocuous to those born under him. They will receive snakes into the folds of their flowing robes, and will exchange kisses with these poisonous monsters and suffer no harm.[9]

Ophiuchus governs those born from late November to mid-December (approximately November 30 to December 17). Qualities ascribed to those born under the star sign of Ophiuchus:

◊ An "opener of dreams"—the gift of dream interpretation

◊ Seeker of wisdom and knowledge

◊ Visionary

◊ Magnetic, attracts good luck

◊ May need to leave home at an early age to seek their fortunes in the world

◊ Gifts as an architect or builder of their visions

According to Ptolemy, if one's moon is in the constellation of Ophiuchus in their natal chart, they might find themselves drawn even more potently to a magical priestess path.[10]

Scarlet Woman, Red Witch

In England, where Magdalene was also said to have visited, witch lore also reflects the symbiotic red threads between witch and priestess and church and temple.

"The color red, worn as a scarf or shawl, comes up again and again as a sign of a witch in [English witchcraft] lore," writes researcher Gemma Gary. [11] In one record, a renowned witch called Mariann, a "blessing witch," was noted for wearing a red kerchief about her head or neck, as well as an old petticoat of scarlet. Red was the color of a womb shaman's blood power, and like the priestesses of Inanna and Isis, who wore red turbans or veils, wearing a red covering on the head has been a sign of a witch-priestess for thousands of years, revealing an underlying sacred tradition uniting these lineages.

Red was also the color Mary Magdalene is most often depicted wearing in medieval and Renaissance art; she is most commonly seen cloaked in a scarlet red cape or robe. The Basque goddess Mari was also associated with red and called the "Red Lady."[12]

Similarly, the use of menstrual blood in magical or spiritual practice, symbolic of the immense creative power of the Motherline, was often a key feature of the red witch. Charms consisted of a sewn womb pouch, made of linen or silk, and often containing a piece of fabric soaked with "Dragon's Blood" as it's called in the sinistrum of witch lore, which is code for menstrual blood. Again, we see a parallel in the Sisters of Sophia over in France, the Cathar witches, and priestesses of the Holy Spirit, who were tried during the Inquisition for having magical charms soaked in moon blood.[13] Women also had "charm books" that were passed down from mother to daughter.

Witches were often known as charmers (like their enchantress sisters across in Sumer and Babylon) and fairy doctors, and some had the gift of "blood charming"—being able to stop the flow of blood from a wound, even from a long distance. Blood divination or blood charming was a key part of the feminine arts, rooted in the work of Old Magic of the old fairy faith with its shamanic Divine Feminine origins.[14]

Women's Wombcrafting

Witchcraft—or wombcrafting—was a women's folk religion, a lost womb religion. Fear of witches was in some way a covert acknowledgment by men of the awesome power held within the female body, once revered, now distrusted.

Women who attended coven meetings were also renowned for being mistresses of the forgotten feminine temple arts, experts in the arts of cosmetics and potions. There is documentary evidence of belief in Europe that women could change themselves and others into animals, could fly through the air, enter magic doorways, make spells and potions to excite love and desire, and control the weather.

Many of the coven meetings are similar in detail and feel to ancient mystery cults, with their old gods replaced as terrifying "devils"; the witches were often connected with heretical Christian sects, such as the Waldensians or Cathars. Men could also be, and often were, witches, developing their own elemental power and working with the potent magic of *natura Sophia,* the medicine of the Earth Womb, and natural instinctive forces that were believed to be feminine in origin. Indeed, in many ways, Jesus was not only a magician but a High Witch of Sophia.

Church of the Wizards

In England, the medieval Christian Church—which had emerged from the earlier Celtic Christian Church—was often braided with traditions that were pagan in origin.

Christianity, coming as it did from the roots of feminine magic, was easily integrated with the old ways of the folk magicians and female fairy-medicine workers. Often Mary Magdalene, with her heretical red magic, was the patron saint of the witches. From its lustral water rituals to its extensive knowledge of blessing and exorcism, the Christian Church easily functioned like a temple of feminine magic for people.

Church holy water was stolen so regularly for magical use by the local cunning folk—witches, charmers, and conjurors—that the fonts were fitted with locking covers from the Middle Ages on.[15] Holy water could be used for protection spells, magical cures, and blessings. The eucharistic bread and wine, and the chrism, were also blessed holy substances, and were highly sought after by magical practitioners, so were also held under lock and key. It's no coincidence that during the Protestant Reformation they were deemed particularly unholy, knowing that they originated in ancient feminine blood and sex rites.[16]

The distinction between the Christian Church and magic was thin, leading to many known and secret "Christian wizards"—even including men *within* the clergy. Many clergymen functioned as cunning men in the old tradition, and these Christian wizards were often known as "conjuring parsons."[17]

Some practiced as astrologers, which they saw as an extension of their duties toward their parishioners. Records of these conjuring clergymen and their astrological forecasts for their parish have been preserved in diaries and notebooks.[18]

Sexual Shamans

Witchcraft was associated with the forbidden sensuality and sexuality of the holy priestesses, and temple prostitutes, causing the founding fathers of Christianity to declare, "Who would lose by a Christian world except pimps and procuresses and all who profit from vice? And magicians, soothsayers, fortune tellers and astrologers."[19]

This entwining of witches and the lineage of Inanna, through prostitution and the mystical arts of beauty, adornment, plant spirit medicine, and sex, is common. Mary Magdalene takes her throne here too, only tolerable because she has supposedly repented; yet she is still lavishly described for her beauty, adornments, and sexual allure.

Plate 1. The Virgin Mary of St. Marie's Cathedral, Sheffield, England, holding her hands
in the womb mudra position. She takes center stage in the ornate stained glass window
behind the altar, as Queen of the Heavens, with stars above her head
and the crescent moon under her feet.

(Photo by A. and S. Bertrand)

Plate 2. *The Lady and the Unicorn, Á mon seul désir* (To my only desire): A tapestry that secretly encodes the Grail teachings of the Magdalene-Rose Line, woven in Flanders ca. 1484, home to Jan van Eyck and the *Ghent Altarpiece*. The red-robed woman in the tapestry represents the lost witch-priestess religion of the goddess as the Grail Queen. Her left hand reaches into an open treasure chest, a metaphor for womb wisdom. The tent is adorned with moon symbolism, its vulvic folds opening into the inner mystery of womb consciousness and the red path of Magdalene's sensual alchemy.

(Musée National du Moyen Âge, Paris)

Plate 3. *Saint Mary Magdalene.* Master of the
Palazzo Venezia Madonna, ca. 1350. Egg tempera on wood.
(The National Gallery, London)

Plate 4. Mary Magdalene, draped in rose fabrics,
gaze softly but intently into the eyes of the iconic skull.
Carlo Cignan's *The Penitent Magdalen,* ca. 1690. Oil on canvas.
(Dulwich Picture Gallery, London)

Plate 5. The regal Magdalene sits on the golden throne, resplendent in her red robes. She holds a *tau* crucifix in her left hand, resting on her lap, and an anointing jar in her right. Angels serenade her and members of the Confraternity of Magdalene kneel at her feet. Spinello Aretine, *Saint Mary Magdalen Holding a Crucifix,* ca. 1400. (Metropolitan Museum of Art, New York)

Plate 6. Mary Magdalene, robed in red, holding the egg of life.
(© "St. Mary Magdalene" by Br. Robert Lentz, OFM, Courtesy of Trinity Stores,
www.trinitystores.com, 800.699.4482)

Plate 7. Jan van Eyck's *Lucca Madonna* (1437). Mother Mary takes the divine role of Mari-Isis-Sophia. The striking red folds of her robe represent the red throne and sacred altar of the goddess, symbolizing her Holy Womb that births the divine child. Lions, ancient symbols of the goddess, adorn her throne of wisdom.

Plate 8. A red-robed and haloed Magdalene, adorned with gold earrings and bracelets, holds
her alabaster anointing jar. John the Baptist stands beside her in his camel-hair shirt.
Angelo Puccinelli, *Saint John the Baptist and Saint Madeleine,* created before 1370. Oil on poplar.
(Museum of the Petit Palais, Paris)

Plate 9. Wearing the earth priestess color of green, as well as her traditional red robe, Mary Magdalene holds her alabaster anointing jar. A twinkle in her eye hints at a secret. Giampietrino, or Giovanni Pietro Rizzoli, ca.1495–1540. Oil on panel.

(Private collection)

Plate 10. Dressed in red and white, the barefoot Magdalene lights
down the stairs with a flowered garland in her red hair, holding her anointing jar.
Dante Gabriel Rossetti, *Mary Magdalene Leaving the House of Feasting,* 1857.
(Tate Gallery, London)

Plate 11. The Mary Monstrance of St. Stanislaus Kostka Church of Chicago.
She looks every bit a priestess of the Old Ways: red-robed, a halo of stars above her head,
her womb is the golden Ark of the Covenant, and a crescent moon rests in her lap.
She holds the Eucharist offering in her body. Due to the flood of parishioners who visit,
the chapel stays open twenty-four hours a day.
(Photo by Dees Stribling, Been There, Seen That website, Sept. 8, 2014)

Plate 12. A color restoration of the Burney / Queen of the Night relief. The Red Goddess Ishtar reveals her Underworld aspect, with downward pointing wings and owl-like talons that grasp the backs of her sacred lion steeds. She holds talismanic *shen* rings of infinity in her hands and wears th horned tiara of divinity as her owl familiars look on. Terracotta plaque. Old Babylonia, 1800 BCE (British Museum; color restoration © Stéphane Beaulieu)

Plate 13. Sara-le-Kali, the dark goddess and patron saint of the Roma, adorned by her devotees in Saintes-Maries-de-la-Mer, France.
(Photo by Armin Kübelbeck, CC BY-SA 3.0, Wikimedia Commons)

Plate 14.
The *Ghent Altarpiece* by Jan van Eyck. Oil on oak, 1426–1432. (St. Bavo Cathedral, Ghent)

Plate 15. *Adoration of the Mystic Lamb,* central panel
of the *Ghent Altarpiece,* tracing the hidden "Lady in the Landscape,"
her legs in the M position of birthing and sacred sexuality.
Van Eyck's heretical message is received.

Plate 16. Yeshu holds hands with the pregnant Mary Magdalene in the famous stained-glass window of Kilmore Church on the Isle of Mull, Scotland. A caption below reads, "Mary hath chosen that good part, which shall not be taken away from her," from Luke 10:42, confirming that this is Mary Magdalene (Mary of Bethany).

(Created by Stephen Adam, 1908)

Although the goddess temples were mostly extinguished by the fifth century CE, they still existed during the first few hundred years of institutional Christianity, with their sensual whore-priestesses who practiced their arts of medicine and sexual magic. Early Christian patriarchs denounced the temples "dedicated to the foul devil who goes by the name of Venus—a school of wickedness for all the votaries of unchasteness," referring to Magdalene's lineage of Inanna and her wild red magic.[20]

This aspect of a sexual medicine woman who practiced these arts did not die out, and instead went underground, into the halls of witchcraft or literary heroines. The fifteenth-century literary character Celestina, procuress and similar archetype in bawdy style to the English Moll Flanders, encodes a type of witch woman who was still common in the towns of medieval Catalonia, such as Toledo and Seville.

Basque anthropologist Julio Caro Baroja describes this witch archetype, who was often embodied in real life women: "Celestina . . . is a woman of ill repute, who has passed her youth giving love for money, and becomes a procuress in her old age. She acts as an advisor to a series of prostitutes and ruffians; is a skillful maker of perfume, cosmetics and other beauty products. But she also indulges in sorcery; erotic sorcery in particular. Her laboratory is extensive . . . she mixes together plants."[21]

This description, although slanted with the burden of judgment of women and their arts, uniquely evokes the lost magical-erotic world of the Scarlet Womb Priestesses.

Mary Magdalene is the patron saint of penitents and perfumers—the holy whores.

Persecution of the Witches

In ancient times, and to this day in magical systems such as the dakini mandala of Tibetan Buddhism, a distinction is made between elemental magic and malevolent magic—spells designed to curse or harm. In Sophia's magic, red magic is desire and creativity, white magic blesses and heals, and black magic purifies and empowers.

There have been witchcraft laws against "bad magic" since Sumerian times, however; with the fear of the feminine, all feminine magic automatically became bad magic, and so the persecution of witchcraft was, at its root, a continuation of the attack on priestesses, women of power whose womb sovereignty had once been state oracle.

CHAMBER 18

TEMPLAR WIZARDS
Robin Hood and Maid Marian

AS VARIOUS MAGDALENE CULTS WERE FLOURISHING in central Europe, there was also a legacy unfolding in England that became one of the most enduring legends of all time—embodied in the figure of Robin Hood, with his green wizard robes, and Maid Marian, the Beltane queen.

In Robin Hood and Maid Marian we find a Christ and Magdalene of the greenwood who hold the sacred bowers and primordial greenery of the Rose lineage, and who hold intriguing links to the Knights Templar wizards and the Celtic witches and to heretic Mary worship.

Like Jesus and Magdalene, Robin Hood and Maid Marian are mentioned in folklore extensively, but pinning them down historically is difficult to do. Yet the picture that emerges from various ballads and legends over a five-hundred-year span paints a compelling picture of a man who is religiously devoted to Mary, yet also an enemy of the church.

The legends also introduce Marian as a woman who is revered as a "Queen of the Land," and many of the ballads describe an almost Sophianic dedication to protect Maid Marian from an abusive arranged marriage and to install her in the deep forests of the greenwood.

One poem recounts: "Robin's mistress dear, his loved Marian/Was sovereign of the woods, chief lady of the game."[1]

There is a huge, largely forgotten or unspoken Magdalene presence in the Celtic lands, as if the Reformation and witch hunts drew a black widow's veil over her memory to obscure it. There are 186 churches dedicated to Magdalene in Great Britain, and a widespread and pervasive legacy of her worship, especially along the ancient Great North Road, the spine of Britain joining north to south. Along these heartlands of merry England, Templars built churches dedicated to Magdalene that even predate many of the famous Magdalene cults, cathedrals, and basilicas in France. England held an ancient, deeply rooted Mary Magdalene tradition, often disguised in Mary worship, which was often preserved in secret.

Similarly, the famous tales of the Holy Grail were seeded first in remote Welsh mountains, and misty English summerlands, before finding popularity in France. The popular Grail legends emerged from Welsh lore of a mystical cauldron and were alluded to in the Mabinogion. The theme was later taken up in the English poem "Sir Gawain and the Green Knight" and by Thomas Mallory in *Le Morte d'Arthur* in 1470.

In twelfth-century Europe, at the French court of Champagne, these druidic Grail legends of a "magical womb cup" of the old fairy faith began to be woven into Christian mythology—despite their distinctly heretical flavor. Placing Jesus and Magdalene as the secret Fairy King and Queen, the Grail romances of Chretien de Troyes and the songs of the troubadours flourished in the heartlands of heresy in France—where Mary Magdalene was revered.

Church of Mary Magdalene

Most notable in Robin Hood's legends is his devotion to Virgin Mary and Mary Magdalene, and the lengths he goes to in either visiting a specific Magdalene church or holding mass in the forest, bringing to mind the lost druidic worship of old, within the sacred groves.

Celtic historian John Matthews reflects how Robert Graves, in *White Goddess,* reveals that the "merry men" really means "Mary's men," and adds: "They were followers of a cult of Mary—not necessarily the Virgin, but either the Magdalene or Mary of Egypt, both of whom had a considerable—if unorthodox—following in the Middle Ages."[2] Both Magdalene and Mary of Egypt are linked through legends of prostitution, and are stars of the *Ghent Altarpiece.*

In one of the oldest ballads from 1450, Robin is bemoaning that he hasn't attended mass in some time, and then risks going to St. Mary's in Nottingham, because of his devotion to Mary, even though he might be caught by the Sherriff of Nottingham. In another ballad he also states his intention to return to his hometown and pay homage to Mary Magdalene at a chapel dedicated to her. The ballad recounts:

I made a chapel in Bernysdale,
that is seemly to see,
It is of Mary Magdaleyne,
And thereto would I be.[3]

This is the same chapel, thought to be the Saint Mary Magdalene Church in Campsall, Yorkshire, where legends say Robin Hood and Maid Marian got married under the archway. The church dates back to the eleventh century and would have been surrounded by deep forest at that time. It is also known as a Templar church, featuring Templar effigies and various goddess symbols, such as chevrons, that are found in churches connected to Templars.

There is also an old stone Green Man carving that is hidden away in a nook, as if the church would prefer not to draw too much attention to it. Stone carvings of a Green Man indicate the fecund nature deity of the old religion—Pan, Dionysus, Osiris, Dumuzi, who dies and is reborn again every year in the cycle of the Earth's Womb. In its own way, the story of Jesus mirrors this ancient journey of the renewing Green Man. And in the famed Rosslyn Church there are one hundred Green Man carvings.

Robin's legend also speaks of an intuitive connection with the earlier Celtic wizard, Merlin, who also retired to the sanctuary of the wildwood with his beloved Nimue.

Robin is portrayed wearing the symbolic colors of the fairy faith, green and red, which were later adopted and attributed to Mary Magdalene, as the new Grail Queen. The colors worn by the merry men are described in a way that implies a hidden connection with British native witch cults. In one ballad, it appears that Robin trades in his usual green clothes for red robes—traditionally associated with witchcraft and the blood mysteries of the goddess.

The ballad says: "He clothes himself in scarlet red / His men were all in green."[4]

Red Cross of Magdalene

Robin Hood may well be a heretic Magdalene worshipper, a secret Templar devoted to the Mysteries of the Sacrament, given in the name of "our dear lady, that he loved most." Templars are intimately connected with the Mary Magdalene cult and devotional worship of the Virgin Mary, as the Queen of Heaven, a title once claimed by Inanna.

One of the key figures in the Templar history is the French mystic Bernard of Clairvaux, who lived between 1090 and 1153, and who was sainted in 1174. Bernard was a spiritual figurehead of the Templars who initially championed their order.

He was a mystic devoted to Mary, who was the main force behind an upsurge in Marianology in the twelfth century. He preached an immediate faith where the Virgin Mary, who like Isis was the "Star of the Sea," became the intercessor to God, and he was pivotal in having her status upgraded to Queen of Heaven and Mother of God.

Back in 1100, when Mary Magdalene was still considered a repentant prostitute, Bernard wrote and preached about her being the apostle of apostles, and in one of his sermons on the Song of Songs he names Magdalene as the Bride of Christ. In 1140, he designed a book for the Cistercian Order that contained the formulary of Mary Magdalene, and the cover was simply her "two spare initials" in striking red. He was also linked with the Black Madonna cult in France, which was closely entwined with the cult of Mary Magdalene and her Rose Line.

As the champion of the Templars and leader of their spiritual branch, all Templars swore an oath of loyalty to him (not to a king or pope) and to Mary Magdalene (the anointrix) and to the Virgin Mary (Mother of God). Jesus is not mentioned. On entering the Templar order, the new knight took an oath to God and the Lady Saint Mary (or God and the Blessed Mary). The words of the Templar absolution were, "I pray to God that he will pardon your sins as he pardoned them to Saint Mary Magdalene and the thief who was put on the cross," with veiled heretical implications. When Bernard drew up the Templar Rule, he commended them to "the obedience of Bethany, the castle of Mary and Martha." *Castle* was a womb word.

The Templars considered Sophia to be the feminine aspect of divinity who had been banished, and that Magdalene was the human embodiment of the Divine Sophia in female form.

Robin the Templar Wizard

Robin Hood is often portrayed as a folk hero of simple birth, yet it makes more sense that he was a Templar grand master who followed a code of conduct connected to principles of guardianship that were common to guild apprentices and the Knights Templar.

Traditions give Robin's birthplace as Loxley in South Yorkshire—Yorkshire being a stronghold of the Templars, and the only place outside London with a

Grand Lodge. Yorkshire Templars traveled frequently between preceptories, much like Robin and his merry men are said to have roamed through Sherwood Forest, between Yorkshire, Derbyshire, and Nottinghamshire.

Robin Hood was known as a protector of women and the poor, and accounts of him say that "he would allow no woman to suffer injustice, nor would he spoil the poor, but rather enriched them with plunder taken from the abbots."[5] Other accounts paint him as a type of Grail Knight, saying "Robyn loved our dear lady, he would never do company harm, that any woman was in."[6] He and his "good fellows" seem to follow a Grail code. Various accounts suggest that what defines a good fellow is devotion to Mary. Worship of Mary, as the Queen of Heaven, is to serve the very highest authority.

The time frames Robin is placed in include the aftermath of the Templar Crusades and the papal edict against them in 1307. Their grand master Jacques de Molay was burned alive in Paris on the king's orders, after offering a final prayer to Mary. The Templar order was then outlawed.

Robin's Templar status would explain why Robin and his "Mary Men" are described as outlaws, yet follow strict codes of conduct and religious devotional observances.

Maid Marian, Rose Lady

What was her bower? The red rose and the lily flower.

"THE MAID OF THE MOOR"

(TRANSLATED BY JOHN MATTHEWS)[7]

Of course, the deepest expression of this hidden heresy blooms in Maid Marian. Maid Marian was both an archetypal figure, possibly even an alternative name for Mary Magdalene herself, as well as the human beloved of Robin Hood. However, in some texts his actual lover is named "Clorinda Queen of the Shepherdesses," a titular name of a fairy queen or priestess.

Maid Marian was the queen of the Beltane rites and mistress of the old ways. Her association with the traditional sacred union rites was even recorded in France, as she and Robin preside over May festivities, as detailed in a thirteenth-century French story called *Jeu de Robin and Marion*. In England, Robin and Marion were also the May Regents.

During the Middle Ages the old pagan May Day fertility festivities and rituals were outlawed by the Christian Church, who struggled to unpick thousands of years of rural tradition that celebrated the lovemaking within earth of god and goddess. Eventually the traditions emerged again, under the guise of a "Christian" Robin Hood and Maid Marian, as the May time celebrations were rededicated to Magdalene. The Horned God now became the Green Man, Puck, Robin Goodfellow, and Maid Marian became the womb-enthroned, divine feminine May Queen, whose fecund robe contains all the greening fertility of the land in its magical hem.

However, as to be expected, Mary Magdalene as "Marian" could not behave herself. In one play, titled "Friar," Magdalene makes a guest appearance as a sexually suggestive woman who is identified with a bawdy Maid Marian of the May Games. During Elizabeth's reign, Puritans raged and frothed against the May Games, with their enthroned, enchantingly seductive queen, and they deliberately conflated the character of Maid Marian with the Whore of Babylon.[8]

Like the love story of Jesus and Magdalene, popular imagination keeps circling back to Robin Hood and Maid Marian, seeking the lost chambers of wisdom in their story.

There are secrets in a lover's eyes that facts cannot describe.

What we love we shall grow to resemble.
                              BERNARD OF CLAIRVAUX

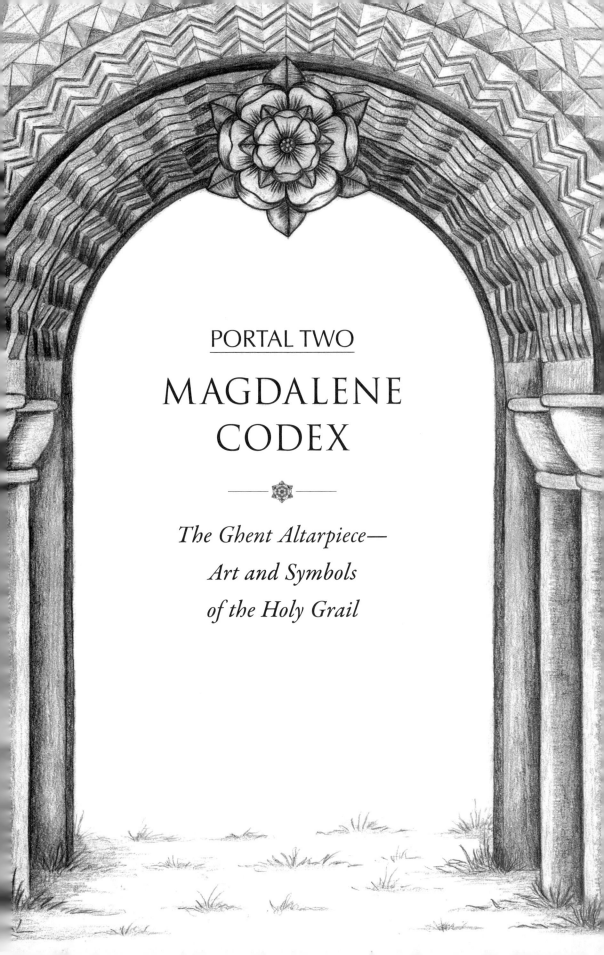

PORTAL TWO

MAGDALENE CODEX

❈

The Ghent Altarpiece—
Art and Symbols
of the Holy Grail

Pilgrim's Guide

AFTER JOURNEYING THROUGH THE LOST STORY of Mary Magdalene, exploring her ancient roots in the priestess tradition, what we know of her lifetime, and the rich legacy she left behind, it is now time to open the door to the art and symbols of the alchemists who secretly encoded this history. Incredibly, a secret codex of the Magdalene Mysteries was created in the late Middle Ages and left, "hidden in plain sight," until the present day. It was this mysterious and renowned piece of artwork that magnetically drew us to Ghent, a small, picturesque, and historic city in Flanders, Belgium. Arriving in Ghent we became palpably aware of something "singing" on the inner planes. It was a soul whispering, a soft remembrance, subtle yet insistent, of a crucial Rose Key to be found.

2017: As we walk the cobbled streets, shining with recent rains, surrounded by architecture of ancient churches and towers, we suddenly understand that Bavo Cathedral has called us. Above us, perching on top of the Ghent Belfry is a majestic, fiery golden dragon statue, the mascot and guardian spirit of the city and a World Heritage Site. Standing next to it is the formidable and intricate architecture of the medieval Bavo Cathedral, built on a former chapel of Saint John the Baptist, evidence of which lives on within the crypt.

Inside the huge gothic cathedral another fantastical golden serpent-dragon meets us, in much finery and glory, and certainly not what would be expected in a church; the town may as well have the warning "here be dragons." In the central nave is a large sculpture of a tree, with a golden serpent coiled around it. The tree is adorned with golden apples, and a golden apple is being eaten by the serpent.

The symbology is exquisite and astounding; here is a shrine to the Divine Sophia, in her serpent form, coiled around the Tree of Life, right in the center of the cathedral. This sculpture sums up the Bavo experience: brazen, bold, and hidden in plain sight.

But for all the splendor of the dragons and the architecture, the star turn is the art; the cathedral is famous for the *Adoration of the Mystic Lamb*—the *Ghent Altarpiece,* by Jan van Eyck. This is the deeper reason for our visit. It is this Magdalene codex whose symbols are singing to us.

As we gaze upon the *Mystic Lamb,* everything falls into place. This stunning work of art is a mystery school, a living code, a spiritual transmission, a dreaming and remembrance. It is scripture of the Great Mother. We gaze up at the enormity of the painting and see the Holy Grail.

CHAMBER 19

THE GHENT ALTARPIECE

Gateway to the Mysteries

Blessed are your eyes because they see, and your ears because they
hear. For truly I tell you, many prophets and righteous men
longed to see what you see but did not see it, and to hear
what you hear but did not hear it.

MATTHEW 13:16

THE *GHENT ALTARPIECE* IS A PROPHECY for this coming age of
Aquarius, the age of the Water Bearer—She who holds the awakening cup of the
Holy Grail, the life-sustaining waters of the Divine Feminine. Her fountain of life
will once again come to replenish and renew the land, transforming the wasteland
back into the Garden of Eden, our original innocence.

THE FOUNTAIN OF LIFE

Then I perceived a renewing cosmos and earth,
for the first heaven and earth was menstruating,
and the primal sea was yet birthing.
And I experienced an awakening, a new wholeness,
Descending out of the Womb of God,
ready as a Bride's openness, a beauteous world of love:

And I heard a great voice from the womb-throne, saying:
"Behold, the Womb of God is with wombmen.
She dwells within them and they are Her children,
And God herself is becoming within them;
She will wipe away every tear from their inner eye,
So there is no more separation from life,
neither shall there be sorrow or cries of suffering,
Because the pain will dissolve and heal."
And She who dwells within the womb-throne said:
"Behold, I reweave and make everything new."
She called out to her beloved creation,
"Write this, for these words are trustworthy and true."
And She said to me, "you are now reborn."
I am the Alpha, the first coming womb,
and the Omega, the new becoming womb,
The circle of the first beginning
and the final consummation.
To those who desire it, I offer life-giving waters
From the fountain of the water of life."

AUTHORS' REINTERPRETATION OF REVELATION 21:1–7

World's Most Magnificent Painting

The *Ghent Altarpiece,* or the *Adoration of the Mystic Lamb,* so named because of the themes of its central and most important panel, is not simply one of the world's most famous paintings—it is a treatise, a magnum opus, a legacy (see color plate 14). Its twenty-four separate panels are each an intricately crafted masterpiece. Together, they form a work that is regarded by many scholars as the most important piece of art in the history of the Western world. It is a monumental achievement by any standard, made more compelling by the long-held rumors of a great secret contained within, a mystery connected to Mary Magdalene and the Holy Grail, understood by few living. The true message of the painting has been held *sub rosa,* under the silence of the rose, by high initiates of underground societies for the six centuries of its existence, at pain of death.

As it is no ordinary painting, we must approach the *Ghent Altarpiece* as both a pilgrimage and Grail Quest, as we would the holy of holies. Flagrantly "hidden" within it are the secret teachings of the left-hand path of Mary Magdalene, as well as the lost story of Sophia—available only for *those with the eyes to see.*

The surface interpretation of the *Adoration of the Mystic Lamb* is the "archonic deception," the false story of woman's supposed wickedness spread by the church—that Eve, representing all women, was responsible for the fall of human consciousness by tempting Adam to eat the forbidden red fruit of knowledge, or *gnosis.* Her apple symbolizes illumination through sexual communion in the mysteries of the bridal chamber, the most egregious "crime" in the eyes of the church. This Original Sin of Adam and Eve, as the mother and father of humanity, was passed down their bloodline, to be inherited by all future humanity. The only cure for this ancestral stain was a human sacrifice demanded by God, his own son Jesus, the "lamb of God," whose blood would atone for the "sin of humanity." Yet the painting hides a heretical double meaning.

A series of clues orient us to the true nature of the encoded message, leading to a profoundly different conclusion. Here is what is radical: The forbidden knowledge that Jan van Eyck and many others risked their lives for is that *the Mystic Lamb is the sacred woman, the mystery of the Magdalene, the body of the Holy Sophia.* The theme of the painting is the eucharist, yet the central secret teaching is that the Mystic Lamb is a *She* not a *He*—it unveils the Magdalene Mass, the Great Feminine Eucharist, which for all time has been the source of renewal of life. It also tells the gnostic story of Sophia and the degradation of the feminine at the hands of the false god—the archonic "Ruler of the World"—meanwhile promising reunification, and the return to a new earthly Eden.

It is not the story of the *sin* of Eve, but of the *abuse* of Eve and her feminine magic.

It is also a mandala of consciousness that charts a way back home, through which all women, men, and the living Earth itself can return to wholeness.

The *Altarpiece* reveals a lost legacy, and also a new hope.

Magdalene's Red Thread

Behind the surface veil of orthodox Christian symbolism, the *Ghent Altarpiece* symbolically encodes the secret story of the return of the earthly Magdalene-Sophia, the most heretical, paradigm-changing, and life-affirming story our world has known. Hers is the story of the once and future queen, the story that untold millions of Cathars, alchemists, priestesses, Templars, gnostics, and other "heretics of Love" died trying to preserve.

The ancient libraries of the old world, like the Library of Alexandria, with their 8,000 years of sacred feminine history preserved on scroll and parchment, may have been burned, but the wisdom seeds of the Magdalene-Sophia legacy lived on in the hearts and minds of its faithful. They were passed on through hidden symbols and secret oral traditions along the Rose Lines of initiates, quietly, patiently waiting until the world was once again fertile enough for its sacred tenets to bloom.

The *Altarpiece* is world-renowned for containing a great mystery, a secret teaching preserved at enormous risk to all involved—that has yet to be fully decoded, until now. Its hidden message is meant for trained initiates of the feminine mysteries who have received the secret, esoteric teachings. These traditions date back to the Holy Harlot temples of Egypt and Sumeria, and lived on in the Eleusinian Mysteries practiced in Greece until 392 CE. The sacred red thread was continued through the gnostic, Cathar, Templar, and related lineages, where it eventually reached the bright mind and devoted soul of Flemish artist and innovator Jan van Eyck.

Jan van Eyck was a painter, mystic, revolutionary, diplomat, and genius equal to the well-known Italian Renaissance artist, Leonardo da Vinci. Only through a deep alchemical knowledge and training in the underground feminine wisdom stream could such a complex, symbolic masterwork be crafted. Aside from his astonishing technical advances in the use of oil painting, van Eyck's most remarkable achievement is the use of symbol to tell two very different, *even opposite,* stories—one for the general public, and an entirely different one for those with the eyes to see. His life depended on his ability to hide the truth in plain sight.

As you take a pilgrimage through this painting, you will see that more than a collection of beautifully rendered symbols and puzzles, the central panel is in fact a magical *optical illusion*. Once you have seen what van Eyck intended to be seen, you can *never unsee it*. The entire image is transformed, and with it a part of your consciousness. To perceive this painting in its fullness is a mystery initiation.

Holy Grail and Mystic Lamb

If you don't know what you are looking for, you can have all the facts in front of you and still not see. Nowhere is this truth more apparent than in the *Ghent Altarpiece,* one of the greatest enigmas of Western art that has eluded people for centuries.

The *Altarpiece* was created by van Eyck, likely with the help of his brother Hubert, over a six-year period from 1426 to 1432. It is now housed in Saint Bavo's

Cathedral in Ghent, Belgium, safely secured behind thick bulletproof glass and video surveillance cameras, after being involved in no less than twelve crimes, including six outright thefts, most infamously by the Nazi leaders Adolph Hitler and his own top general, Reichsmarschall Hermann Göring, who stole it back and forth from each other, in counterthefts.

Why, with all the valuable art in the world, is the *Altarpiece* the most stolen painting in history? (Which, given that it weighs some two tons and is the size of a barn door is no small task.) Why has it received so much attention? And what of the rumors that Nazi occultists believed it to contain a map to the Holy Grail?

The Nazis were hot on the trail of the *Ghent Altarpiece* mystery. Few people realize that the Nazi party first formed from an occult brotherhood and secret society, likely dedicated to the *misuse* of the feminine mysteries for their own power. The movie *Indiana Jones and the Raiders of the Lost Ark* famously portrayed a fictional Nazi quest for the lost Ark of the Covenant, a relic that supposedly granted supreme power to its possessors, and that was also associated with the feminine womb. A theory put forward by author Karl Hammer and others proposed that the movie was not far from the truth—that the Nazi party financed secret research missions to find the Holy Grail, Spear of Destiny, and other objects of occult power through their *Ahnenerbe* "ancestral research" project. Whatever the reasons, the *Ghent Altarpiece* was front and center of Hitler's pursuits.

Hitler was not the only one interested in this painting. The *Altarpiece* was stolen by Napoleon in 1804 as a prize for France's Louvre museum. With Napoleon's defeat in 1814, it was returned to Flanders by King Louis XVIII, only for several panels to be stolen a few years later by a rogue Belgian vicar, and sold to Kaiser Frederic III of Prussia. In 1566, anti-Catholic Calvinists tried to destroy it. In 1781, Holy Roman Emperor Joseph the Second, outraged by its display of nudity, censored it. One of its panels, the *Just Judges,* was mysteriously stolen in 1934—in what seems likely to be an inside job, assisted by a church cover-up—and still remains missing to this day. The fascination with the *Ghent Altarpiece* has extended far beyond a normal work of art. Across the centuries people have sensed something of a far greater importance contained within, a puzzle now revealed.

Hidden in plain sight within the intricate folds of the *Altarpiece* is the symbolically encoded story of the Holy Grail—*the return of the earthly Sophia*—and the revelation of the true role of Mary Magdalene. In many ways the *Adoration of the Mystic Lamb* is as much an alchemical manuscript and map of consciousness as a painting, its legacy of coded storytelling glistening with hundreds of alchemical symbols, layered with esoteric and mystical meanings that belie its surface appearance as a devoutly Catholic work of art.

Indeed, it may be the most heretical painting to grace the galleries and halls of European culture. It is as if the ruby light of Sophia is sitting on her throne, secretly smiling in the heart of the patriarchal institutions that have housed this painting over the past six centuries. Where better to hide her than within a Catholic church? And how appropriate that her figure would emerge, in a feat of visual magic, arising from the body of the sacred earth herself, creating a "world-navel" goddess site in a Christian cathedral.

The medieval Church had long maligned nature, considering it devoid of the spirit of God, and—like women—inherently sinful, a source of temptation, a vile seductress. Van Eyck reverses this stance, glorifying nature and the body of woman, and hiding his most heretical messages in the lines and forms of her earthly garden. As our eyes adjust to the painting, we are drawn to a reclining female figure, whose body is formed from the features of the land and from the multitudes of pilgrims who come to honor her pregnant womb mound, receiving the blessings of the magical elixirs from her sacred, menstruating yoni (color plate 15). It is a portrait of the goddess.

Most tellingly, the central panel is absent of a deified human; the land herself is the sacred center, depicted in lush green, with the body of Sophia outlined in red. Red and green were the traditional colors of MM, who, as we might have guessed, also appears in the painting.

In the *Mystic Lamb*, the paradise garden of the earth—our Earth Mother—represents *embodied cosmic womb consciousness*, the living vibration of feminine wisdom held *within matter*, with her ever-generative and sustaining divine elixirs pouring from her Fountain of Life, her spiritual womb that lives at the heart of creation. Human woman and Earth Mother are made one, unified as the earthly Sophia, and both are raised up to divine status and reunited with the eternal Cosmic Mother.

The *Ghent Altarpiece* takes us on an extraordinary initiatory journey into the lost mysterium and secret legacies of the ancient feminine philosophies, including the feminine eucharistic rites of the goddess religions, the most reviled and outlawed of all heresies—the "impious drink" that the fourth-century church father, Epiphanius, raged against. Panel by panel, brushstroke by brushstroke, we travel deep into a mystery school of old where the encoded knowledge of Sophia still resonates as a *terma,* a treasure text, hidden in archetypal dimensions, accessed through symbols, to be revealed to us now at this critical moment in history.

CHAMBER 20

PILGRIMAGE INTO THE PAINTING

Art of the Grail

LET US ENTER THE MAGICAL WORLD of the *Ghent Altarpiece* and explore the alchemical mysteries held within her many chambers.

Van Eyck's *Altarpiece* is, by anyone's measure, astounding. It is a massive folding polyptych, consisting of no less than twenty-four paintings rendered on six-hundred-year-old, solid Baltic oak panels. It is the size of a barn door (14 by 11.5 feet) and weighs some four thousand pounds, roughly the same weight as a small elephant, an appropriate metaphor given the enormity of what is hidden within its "rooms."

To stand in front of the *Ghent Altarpiece* for the first time is an overwhelming experience. It is difficult to take in the explosion of color and activity, the size and scope of the painting, the intricacy of detail, the presence of so many compelling scenes that each vie for your attention, the fact that it folds and changes forms. On certain days it is open, and on others it is closed—it is a moveable feast. It is as if we have entered a new world, a mystical mansion of many rooms. To understand what is happening, we must take a step back and orient to its overall design patterns.

The first key is that the painting is a map of the cosmos: the upper horizontal row of panels represents the heavenly realms, and the bottom row represents the earthly ones. The *Altarpiece* is arranged so that these two worlds, heaven and earth, touch and meet each other—in a grand cosmic drama.

The next thing we must grasp is its folding structure, which creates an inside scene when it is fully opened on the *recto,* or front, panels and a completely different outside scene when it is fully closed on its *verso,* or back, panels. Like a flower or a woman's body, it can open out to reveal its mysteries, or the veil can be closed, her unseen secrets enfolded back into her womb. This is a signature of the mystery traditions, with exoteric or external teachings on the surface, and esoteric or occult teachings hidden within—also known as the lesser and greater mysteries.

When we look at the *Altarpiece* in its open position, we are immediately confronted by the commanding presence of a larger-than-life, central male figure, enthroned in papal red robes and tiara. He is a figure of power that dominates and presides over the opened body of the earth beneath him. The lower earthly realms seem to be a garden paradise, focused as much on the body of the earth as the humans within it. We also see striking, naked images of Adam and Eve in the upper corners, orienting us to the themes of Garden of Eden and sexuality. Our attention is also drawn to the unusual lamb with its sacred fountain of blood cascading out into a golden chalice.

The *Altarpiece* is Jan van Eyck's greatest achievement, putting him on the map as one of the most influential artists of history. Within the painting we are met with an explosion of color, texture, and meticulous brushstrokes—down to the additions of single hairs—along with a symphony of symbols, allegorical narratives, cloaked layers of meaning, humanistic details, and techniques rarely seen before in the world of art, and certainly unparalleled in sheer size, scale, and complexity.

Although the technique of oil painting had existed for some time at a more primitive level, with the *Adoration of the Mystic Lamb* van Eyck took it to glorious new heights, singlehandedly inspiring an oil-painting revolution that would be the dominant medium of artistic expression for the next several hundred years. His influence among artists was immense. It can be said that every painter of the following centuries owes a debt of gratitude to Jan van Eyck. Certainly, the painters of the Italian Renaissance, including Michelangelo, Botticelli, and others, owe much to his work, his alchemical influence, and his hidden heresies.

Art critics have perhaps lavished more praise, attention, and superlatives on this painting than any other in history, with one modern scholar calling it a "veritable rock opera," comparing its splendor, lavishness, and theatrical impact to the musical production of *Jesus Christ Superstar* (minus the Jesus character, as we will see later).

With some three hundred human figures depicted with a detail usually reserved for miniatures, with a confronting realism and daring depiction of life-sized naked Adam and Eve, and with an idealization of the natural world that strayed dangerously close to pagan values of old, van Eyck pushed the limits of painting in every way. The striking beauty and brilliantly innovative style of the *Mystic Lamb* sent a shock wave through the European art community that effectively ended the era of gothic and medieval painting, and catalyzed the birth of Renaissance styles.

There is enough action in the surface levels of this painting to keep our eyes endlessly busy, our minds fascinated and entertained, but to understand its mystical meaning we must explore the story of its creation. Who might have created and funded such a work? We will see that the lives and spirit of the creators are themselves woven into this great tapestry—to understand them is to understand the heretical message contained within.

The World of Jan van Eyck

The scale, beauty, and precision of Jan van Eyck's paintings were unparalleled in his time. He was also a mystic, humanist, statesman, and *philosopher,* a name that translates as a "lover of Sophia" (from the Greek *philo,* or love). He kept company with dukes and kings, chivalric knights of medieval courts, and masters of art across Europe, whose guilds and art houses became centers for the birth of the cultural Renaissance that would free Europe from nearly one thousand years of Catholic ideologic domination. Van Eyck was also undoubtedly involved in secret societies, privy to the underground streams of heretical knowledge that he encoded into his paintings.

In a 1550 treatise, the respected Italian artist and historian Giorgio Vasari described van Eyck not just as master painter but also an "alchemist," implying he had a knowledge of the hermetic and magical esoteric traditions that had their origins in the ancient mystery schools and goddess religions. His mastery of such a broad range of subjects, from the practical to the metaphysical, including his pioneering technical advances in pigments and paints, and his complex and intricately layered symbols spanning many disciplines, languages, and cultures, indicate a level of genius and involvement in the secret wisdom traditions on par with the likes of Leonardo da Vinci and Botticelli, whose connections to the Magdalene heresies have been popularized in books such as *Holy Blood, Holy Grail,* by Lincoln, Leigh, and Baigent, as well as Dan Brown's fiction in *The Da Vinci Code.*

Jan van Eyck was born in late fourteenth-century Flanders, the Dutch-speaking region of what is modern-day Belgium, then the northern part of the Duchy of Burgundy. At the time, Burgundy was under the rule of the Valois line of dukes, including his artistic patron Duke Philip III, known as Philip the Good.

The greater Burgundy, with its important trade cities of Brussels, Bruges, Ghent, and Antwerp, was one of the richest and most urbanized regions in Europe. Its great wealth derived in large part from technological advances in wool weaving that made it the center of the textile industry across Europe, one reason the Cathars, also known as the weavers, were drawn to the region. The Cathars likely played an important role in infusing the Magdalene heresies into Flanders, as well as northern Italy, helping to spur the first blooms of the Renaissance in both regions.

As we have learned, the Cathars were a heretical Magdalene-worshipping group, with a rich history and cultural heritage in the south of France that claimed a direct spiritual descent from the original teachings of Mary Magdalene and Jesus, as husband and wife tantric mystics. They believed that the holy family of Magdalene, Jesus, and their children escaped from Palestine and settled in the Languedoc region of southern France to quietly teach the path of love. The Cathars considered these to be the true Christed teachings, and the Church of Rome a fallen corruption. In a famous heretical word play, ROMA, or Rome, was clearly the opposite of AMOR, or love.

Bloodline of Jesus of Mary

The territories of the Duchy of Burgundy originally extended deep into the south of France, approaching the Mediterranean coast, an area ruled for much of its early history by the Merovingian dynasty, who claimed descent from the bloodline of Jesus and Mary Magdalene. Even through the "dark ages" of Europe, a Renaissance thinking flourished in what is now southern France and northern Spain: in Burgundy, Occitania, the Languedoc, Provence, and Catalonia in Spain.

Mystical Christians, Kabbalists, and Sufis collaborated together over hundreds of years, forming networks and alliances that spanned the continent and interwove with those of the Holy Lands. Over time the Cathar people established themselves in Burgundy and the surrounding areas of southern France, sharing a common history and artistic sensibility with the Flemish people of northern Burgundy.

Flemish Burgundy, now Belgium, served as a safe haven for the Cathars who were forced to flee from the Languedoc, along with Jews and other heretics, during the Inquisition and Cathar genocides of the 1200s. Along with their artisan talents, they brought with them revolutionary spiritual ideas, rooted in their secret Church of Mary Magdalene and long-held feminine heretical traditions.

The wisdom of the underground Magdalene streams was infused into the medieval Flemish tapestries, whose magnificent artistry and complex symbolism rivaled that of their paintings. One superb example is the *Lady and the Unicorn* series (color plate 2), created circa 1500, whose six tapestries are a celebration of sensuality and, like the *Adoration of the Mystic Lamb* (color plate 15), filled with hidden references to the Magdalene and Grail lineage.

From the Cathar immigrants and occult Templar schools in the region, the ancient Womb Mysteries seeped into the artistic and philosophical guilds of northern Burgundy, and influenced a number of Early Netherlandish Renaissance artists. Jan van Eyck led the way, with other Dutch-speaking painters following in his footsteps. Among their creations were a series of "pregnant Magdalene" paintings, depicting and preserving the secret history of Jesus and Mary Magdalene's bloodline.

Fifteenth-century Burgundy was the most politically progressive and philosophically sophisticated state of Europe, a mecca of culture and fashion, with flamboyant leaders such as Philip the Good richly endowing the arts and music in his lifetime. Philip's patronage gave rise to the Early Netherlandish Renaissance that rivaled the Florentine Renaissance of Italy. The combination of its thriving arts community, mystic feminine spiritual sects, and influx of new naturalistic and humanistic philosophies made the region a fertile ground for the first shoots of European Renaissance art to bloom, and to support the enormous talents of Jan van Eyck.

Secrets of an Alchemist

Van Eyck's early life is not well documented, but by 1422 his virtuosity as a master painter was clearly recognized, with appointments as court painter to Duke John III of Bavaria, and a few years later to the charismatic Philip the Good of Burgundy.

What made Jan van Eyck unique was that his talents and breadth of knowledge ranged far beyond that of the typical court artist. He was extremely well read, fluent in Greek and Latin, and schooled in the classics of literature. Among his favorites were Ovid and Pliny the Elder. Van Eyck painted Hebrew script and esoteric Kabbalistic talismans in his works, revealing his knowledge of the hermetic and alchemical traditions, typically passed along via membership in secret societies, which was a very dangerous affair during the era of the Catholic Inquisition. His knowledge of herbs and botany was superb; his paintings demonstrated extremely detailed and varied flora from across Europe and the Holy Lands.

Jan van Eyck traveled broadly across Europe, on both diplomatic and artistic missions. He cultivated secret connections to the Florentine art guilds, likely including the studio of Andrea del Verrocchio, where Leonardo da Vinci would eventually study several decades after van Eyck's death. Trade secrets were exchanged, and quite quickly the leading Italian artists adopted van Eyck's innovations in oil painting.

Van Eyck's paintings were considered radical and extremely controversial in his day, the *Adoration of the Mystic Lamb* most of all. In it he painted the sensual, nude bodies of Adam and Eve. Rather than perfected, idealized versions of the naked form, as seen in classical Greek sculpture, Adam and Eve were flawed, and all too human, personalized down to the minute bodily details in a way never before seen in art. The result was an intimacy that was shocking at the time, considered obscene by church officials and briefly banned by the Holy Roman Emperor Joseph II.

Van Eyck dared to paint a paradisiacal landscape infused with light and a vitalizing natural power, considered impudent and decadent, if not outright sinful to the moralistic voices of the church, whose position was antinature and antifemale. He also depicted notable pagan figures in the *Mystic Lamb,* including a group of pagan philosophers along the bottom left of the central panel, as well as female oracles of the goddess traditions, the Sibyls, in an exalted position in the highest heavens of the verso panels. These bold inclusions, in a time when pagan heresies were punishable by death, revealed his passion for humanism, the feminine, the natural world, and the esoteric wisdom streams that valued pagan doctrines of old.

A pioneer in all things, Jan van Eyck was always decades ahead of his time. He was famous for riddles, puns, and anagrams, including his distinctive signature, ALS IK KAN ("As I can"), a pun on his name, and a humble statement of his mission.

With his focus on humanism, sensual nature, nude human figures, and Renaissance ideals, we can clearly see that van Eyck's is not the pedigree of a pious and humble servant of the Catholic Church. But the question remains, what secrets did Jan van Eyck know? What was the extent of his knowledge of the Magdalene-Sophia traditions? What messages did he hide in the symbols and riddles of his paintings?

The Hand of Magdalene

More than a painting, the *Ghent Altarpiece* was a revolution. It was a cleverly crafted Trojan horse, slipped past the fortress walls of the Catholic stronghold of Ghent, where it stood boldly, in plain sight, for all initiates to see, a symbol of rebellion in the face of the seemingly invincible magisterium of the church. There it emboldened artists, poets, and philosophers of Europe who made pilgrimage to stand in its awe-inspiring presence, replicating its themes across the continent. It set a precedent for the heretical public art of the Renaissance that would in time dethrone and end the hegemony of the church. Where books were banned and public gatherings impossible, art became the prime weapon of the resistance, but it was a dangerous game that involved personal risks hard to understand in our modern age.

What Jan van Eyck accomplished was outrageous, an unheard-of blasphemy. He painted the vagina of the goddess, along with her flowing divine nectars, for public display (or consumption, as it were) directly behind the eucharist altar. The Inquisition regularly imprisoned, tortured, and killed people convicted of much lesser crimes. Nearly two hundred years later, for example, Galileo Galilei, one of the most important scientists of history, was placed on house arrest for life for daring to affirm that the Earth revolved around the sun. He was branded as a heretic and died imprisoned. In 1314, Templars, including Grand Master Jacques de Molay, were burned at the stake as heretics by the Catholic Inquisition, after seven years in prison.

How did van Eyck get away with it? He used an age-old technique that would come to be called the "Big Lie" by modern propaganda experts. Paradoxically, if the deception is big enough, bold enough, radical enough, affirmed emphatically and confidently enough, it will not be seen, because no one would dream that someone could pull off such a feat. Paint the yoni and womb of the goddess, along with a fountain of womb blood. Make it one of the biggest, most ambitious, most glorious paintings in history. Put it in a cathedral on public display. Place it right behind the eucharist altar. Celebrate it as the greatest achievement of Catholic art ever known. It was inconceivably audacious. One could almost hear Inanna's laughter ringing out from the heavens.

Van Eyck secretly restored the Bavo Cathedral to its origins as a pagan womb church, creating a world-navel, "world womb" site devoted to the Living Goddess, where pilgrims of the Rose Line, under the auspices of the church, could worship. He put his life on the line. Van Eyck's actions were heroic, and could only have been done from a place of the deepest devotion and spiritual inspiration. We can speculate that he, like many mystics and revolutionaries before him, received a vision of the feminine that touched and awakened him. Perhaps Mary Magdalene herself came to him, in her boldness, her audaciousness, her passion, her great love, and guided his hand.

We can imagine the love and courage required—how important it must have been to him to encode this feminine wisdom and pass it down to future generations. To be discovered would have meant a gruesome death, and the destruction of all his life's achievements.

Aside from his audacity, how did he make such a quantum leap in technical, artistic, and symbolic skill? Nothing on this scale had ever been attempted, much less achieved. It many ways it was a superhuman accomplishment, and could not have been done alone. In order to carry out this great coup, van Eyck would have needed allies and protectors in high places. Whoever commissioned the work must have been involved as coconspirators, as fellow initiates in the underground wisdom streams.

CHAMBER 21

TEMPLARS OF BURGUNDY

Alchemists of Mary

SUCH A GRAND WORK OF ART required support from high places, those who had both spiritual knowledge *and* real worldly power. To decipher a painting as complex as the *Adoration of the Mystic Lamb,* we must also know the mind and agendas of its funders, which, like everything else involving this remarkable piece of art, are shrouded in mystery and intrigue.

The conception of this masterpiece was a conspiracy of three parties—Jan van Eyck, Duke Philip the Good, and Jodocus "Joos" Vidt, who were connected as "brothers" in the influential secret societies of Flanders. Jodocus Vidt, a wealthy businessman of Ghent, is the officially acknowledged patron of the work. With portraits of himself and his wife Elisabeth appearing on the verso panels of the *Altarpiece,* it appears convincing that he alone funded the painting. But all was not as it seemed on the surface. There is a mystery to be uncovered.

The three men had a relationship that could be described as a spiritual brotherhood. The duke maintained a close personal relationship to Jan van Eyck, as well as Jodocus Vidt, that went beyond the bounds of the normal interactions between a royal personage and his subjects. Philip was godfather to one of van Eyck's sons, and financially supported the artist's family long after his death; he paid a generous pension to van Eyck's widow, Margaret, and also funded one of his daughters to enter a convent, securing her future. The nature of their connection, and the unusual scope of van Eyck's abilities and employment, suggests a shared membership as brothers in a secret society of the Grail mysteries.

Jan van Eyck held an extraordinary position in Philip's court. In 1425, the duke employed him not just as his official court painter *but also as personal confidant, statesman, and possibly a spy.* This suggests a high regard for van Eyck's political and psychological acumen, and his skills in statesmanship, the necessary qualities to be a diplomat. How did a painter, even the most gifted painter, rise to this position of influence?

Jan van Eyck must have possessed a wealth of knowledge, training, and connections far greater than we know. We might speculate that his combined talents in esoteric symbology and statecraft, his brilliance across many disciplines, his relationships with the art guilds and philosophical school across Europe, as well as his meteoric rise to power in Burgundy, make him a prime candidate to be a high initiate, if not head, of a European secret society. If we look across the history of European heads of state, we not infrequently see key advisors steeped in the occult wisdom traditions. John Dee, as a merlin, alchemist, occult philosopher, and hermeticist, was chief advisor to Queen Elizabeth I of England, for example. We shall learn more of Dee's personal talisman, the "AGLA" symbol, shortly, as it features in the *Altarpiece*.

From the first moment of his employment, Philip sent Jan van Eyck on secret diplomatic missions across Europe, paying him yearly wages equal to $200,000 in today's value, with no restrictions or terms on his painting duties—he could paint what he wanted, when he wanted, or not at all—a contract unheard of at that time, both in terms of salary and degree of freedom. Philip doubled once and then doubled again van Eyck's salary, publicly chastising the treasury on an occasion when his payment was delayed, writing that there was no match for Jan van Eyck in both "art and science," and, no doubt, occult knowledge.

The duke leaned heavily on van Eyck for his services as advisor and ambassador. He sent van Eyck on other clandestine missions around Europe of which we know few details, but during his period of employment Philip founded the Order of the Golden Fleece, an elite society based on the British Order of the Garter, so named for the garter worn by the nobility of the dragon lines of old Britain who practiced a royal witchcraft inherited from the ancient mystery traditions. Both the Order of the Garter and the Order of the Golden Fleece were connected to the underground Magdalene and Templar heresies. Symbols of the Order of the Golden Fleece hold a prominent place in the *Altarpiece*, including the central figure of the Mystic Lamb.

An extremely important clue to van Eyck's involvement in a heretical secret society is the Kabbalistic magical talisman "AGLA" hidden in the floor tiles of the angelic choir panels of the *Altarpiece*. The AGLA sigil was commonly used by

The magical sigil AGLA is hidden in the floor tiles of the angelic choir panels, revealing the presence of a heresy that lies encrypted within the painting.

Kabbalists, alchemists, and occult practitioners. The insertion of the symbol into the painting, an acronym of the Hebrew phrase *Ateh Gibor Le-olam Adonai* ("The Lord is mighty until the end of time") can mean only one thing—that Jan van Eyck was an initiate of the hermetic traditions, and this symbol was proof beyond all others that he concealed hidden messages in his painting of the Mystic Lamb. It signals the initiate to search for the deeper meaning beyond surface appearances.

We need not look very far to find further proof of the painting's connection to the Templars; an entire panel has been dedicated to the Knights of Christ, the knightly order, based in Portugal, that emerged from the ashes of the Knights Templar.

On Friday, October 13, 1307, a numerologically significant date in the feminine mysteries, the Knights Templar were betrayed by King Philip IV of France. On his orders, their members were rounded up, tortured, and killed. The Knights were accused of the heretical worship of Baphomet, a coded name for Sophia, the feminine divinity of the gnostics.[1] In the eyes of the Templars, Sophia was embodied in human form in Mary Magdalene, whom they worshipped and revered.[2] We also see one of the secret founders of the Knights Templar, Godfrey of Bouillon, pictured centrally in the Knights of Christ panel. The Templars, sworn to protect the bloodline of David, believed Godfrey to be a descendant of Magdalene and Jesus.[3]

It was the Knights Templar and related orders that constructed the Gothic cathedrals of Europe that were most commonly dedicated to John the Baptist, the Virgin Mary, Mary Magdalene, and "Our Lady." Importantly for our story, they were *never* dedicated to Jesus. The strong presence of John the Baptist and the two Marys in the *Altarpiece,* as well as the striking *absence* of Jesus in the painting, provides more evidence of the influence of the Templar doctrines on the work.

The Secret Identity of the Sibyl

In 1428, the duke sent van Eyck as an ambassador to the court of King John I of Portugal to help broker the marriage to his daughter Princess Isabella, who later gave birth to three sons and heirs of Philip. While in Portugal, van Eyck painted several portraits of Isabella. He also secretly included her in the *Ghent Altarpiece* as the Cumaean Sibyl—an ancient female oracle and prophetess from Cumae, Italy. Duke Philip's connection to Isabella, and Portugal, was not by chance. King John I was the grand master of the Knights of Aviz, a knightly order, also based in Portugal, that was closely connected with the Templars and worked to protect their interests.

Aside from the likeness to Isabella's other portraits, the disguised identity of the Cumaean Sibyl is confirmed to be Isabella by the mysterious letters MEIA(D/P) AROS written on her chest. This is a word puzzle. When the letters are rearranged, they read "DAME ISA POR," the DAME ISAbella of PORtugal.* In the painting, her hand rests on her womb, which may indicate her role as mother to the future Valois royal bloodline. Isabella's inclusion in the *Ghent Altarpiece* is a secret nod to Philip, and is one of the many clues that suggest the duke was anonymously involved in the project.

High Stakes of Heresy

The *Ghent Altarpiece* itself was commissioned sometime before 1426. As mentioned earlier, the official patrons, conspicuously painted on two of the back panels of the painting, are Jodocus "Joos" Vidt and his wife Elisabeth Borluut, wealthy merchants and aristocrats from Ghent. Van Eyck was under the full-time employ of Philip the Good at the time of the commission, on artistic as well as diplomatic missions, including a nine-month period in Portugal with King John and Princess Isabella.

It seems inconceivable that the duke would have allowed van Eyck to undertake a project as massive as the *Altarpiece*—the largest, most detailed, and most time-consuming polyptych in history—for another patron, given his extensive artistic and diplomatic duties to Philip, unless the duke was secretly involved in the project as well.

---

*Van Eyck intentionally leaves the central *D/P* letter ambiguous, so it could be used as both a *D* and *P* in his wordplay.

The Cumaean Sibyl detail
from the *Ghent Altarpiece,*
a disguised portrait of
Isabella of Portugal,
confirmed by the word
puzzle MEIA(D/P)AROS
on her chest.

It is more likely that Joos Vidt was part of the heretical brotherhood, and an important player in the conspiracy behind the creation of the *Altarpiece.* We see evidence of Philip's close personal relationship to the Vidts to the extent that he christened his second son "Joos." Public documents also attest that Philip traveled personally with Jodocus and Elisabeth.

But why would Duke Philip, the primary artistic patron of van Eyck, not want his name attached to what would surely be one of greatest works of art of all time? It was certainly not a mark of the duke's humility—he was a great many things, but never humble. And it was not a lack of affection for the *Altarpiece.* Duke Philip loved the work so dearly that he commissioned the creation of a hundred-foot-long, three-story replica. He arranged the enormous copy to be unfurled as he ceremonially paraded home to court from his knightly escapades, in full pomp and circumstance, a celebration of his own glory. Why then would he deny himself the opportunity to be forever remembered in history as the commissioner of the *Mystic Lamb?*

He could not afford the risk. The stakes were dangerously high—for him, his family, his colleagues, and the state of Burgundy, should it be branded a heretic land by the church. Imagine what would have happened to the duke if the profound heresy hidden within the *Adoration of the Mystic Lamb* was discovered. Artist and patron would have been first tortured, then killed.

Their estates would have been seized, their children dispensed with.

The duke remembered all too well the history of Languedoc and the Cathar genocide of the thirteenth century, also known as the Cathar Crusade, the first Catholic-led, military-backed inquisition. Pope Innocent III declared a war on the entire province, enlisting the armies of France to destroy the Cathar heretics, along with all other Languedoc citizens and nobility that resisted, killing as many as one million people in the process. France took possession of all the conquered lands as spoils of war, ending the golden age of the Cathar peoples.

At the time of the creation of the *Ghent Altarpiece,* Duke Philip was in the midst of a long-term war with France, in an attempt to win Burgundy's freedom as a sovereign nation. His political and strategic position was precarious at best. France was at the time the most powerful nation in Europe. He could not afford for the Vatican to side with the French, who were eager to eliminate the duke.

Also, given his less-than-pious leanings, the duke was already under surveillance by Catholic priests who reported back to the Vatican. The risk to his people, his kingdom, and his royal line were simply too great; so he asked his "brother" and friend Jodocus Vidt to go where he dared not tread. Joos would be the patron of record for the dangerous work; he and his wife would be painted prominently on the back panels to dispel any doubts or rumors of its commission.

Let us take a closer look at Philip's life, to learn more about his connections to the Magdalene Mysteries, the themes that flow through the great *Mystic Lamb* painting.

The Flamboyant Philip

Philip III, Duke of Burgundy, was a mythic, larger-than-life character. Famous for lavish, theatrical banquets, complete with beautiful dancers popping out of over-sized pies, theater set models of ships and towers, and all manner of exotic birds and beasts, his court was among the wealthiest, most fashionable, most intellectually progressive, and certainly the most extravagant in Europe. One year, it is recorded that he spent 2 percent of his national bursary on silk and gold cloth from a single Italian merchant, Giovanni di Arnolfini, subject of a van Eyck painting of the same name.

Philip funded the arts generously, more so than any other court in Europe. He supported painters, dancers, musicians, weavers, and creators of illuminated manuscripts to such a degree that a Netherlandish Renaissance blossomed around his patronage. His spending was rivaled only by Cosimo de' Medici, funder of the Florentine Renaissance.

Philip lived a mythic life centered around ideals of chivalry, stories of King Arthur, the Knights of the Round Table, and Grail legends. His knights and courtiers regularly held tourneys and jousts, engaging nobly with knights from other lands. Inspired by the Knights Templar and early crusades, in the 1440s Philip attempted to form his own crusade, but plans fell through.

He was also interested in the esoteric, going so far as to have an "alchemical room" created in one of his stately homes. Jan van Eyck's inclusion in his painting of the Holy Grail, the symbol sacred to both the Arthurian and alchemical traditions, is no coincidence, very likely a nod in part to the duke, and to their mutual passion for the feminine Grail mysteries, and the lost teachings of Mary Magdalene.

Philip was an unapologetic sensualist who was as enthusiastic in his romantic pursuits as he was in all other arenas of his life. He had at least twenty-four documented mistresses, and eighteen illegitimate children—excessive in all things, temperate in none, and famously impious.

Despite his courtly excesses, and fascination with knightly culture, Philip was a shrewd, bold, and successful head of state. The duke's power was comparable to that of a king, as Burgundy was an extremely wealthy and influential duchy. He openly fought France for years, nearly successfully, to gain independence. Burgundy reached the height of its prosperity under his rule. He expanded the duchy's territories, formed key alliances with England, waged successful wars, crushed rebellions, implemented administrative reforms, and effectively led Burgundy through the complex and dangerous maze of European politics.

Golden Fleeces

In 1428, Duke Philip the Good founded the chivalric Order of the Golden Fleece in Burgundy, which was closely connected to the British Royal Order of the Garter, founded in 1348 by King Edward III of England. Both Orders were connected with pagan themes, involved in European political intrigue, and outwardly paid lip service to the Catholic Church, the "strongman" of Europe, while pursuing very different goals in private.

The Order of the Golden Fleece chose as its namesake the mythical Golden Fleece sought after by Jason and his Argonauts. One of the earliest versions of the Greek myth tells of Poseidon, god of the sea, who fell in love with a beautiful nymph named Theophane. Poseidon changed himself into a ram, and her into a ewe, so they could have sexual relations in disguise, while hiding their true identities from bothersome suitors.

Their son was a Christlike figure, a golden-haired, winged ram and savior who carried the children of the goddess Nephele to safety, away from a jealous stepmother who wished to kill them. The woolen Golden Fleece of the redeeming ram was hung on an oak tree, a Tree of Life, in a sacred grove guarded by a dragon that curled at its base. The hero Jason, captain of the Argonauts, sought the fleece for its power to grant him the right of kingship. A Greek vase depicts a lost version of the story in which Jason is witnessed being "reborn," emerging from the belly of the great serpent-dragon, with the Golden Fleece hanging on a tree behind him. The Goddess Athena oversees this scene of Jason's ritual rebirth. The Catholic Church found the glaring pagan themes of the Order of the Golden Fleece so offensive that they were forced to change the founding narrative to the biblical story of the patriarch Gideon, whose fleece received the dew of Heaven.

Not surprisingly, given what we know of Philip, the Order of the Golden Fleece was dedicated to the Virgin Mary. Curiously, its founding myth relates the tale of a beautiful and sexually alluring deity disguised as a female sheep, who then gives birth to a divine masculine savior. Might there be a connection between this nymph and the Virgin Mary of the *Altarpiece*? "Coincidentally," the *Altarpiece* stars a mystical female golden ewe.

It is also worth noting that, in the myth, the golden fleece, the product of the union of the male and female nature divinities, grants kingship, a clear goal of Duke Philip who fought France for his rightful place as king of Burgundy. Other common images of the feminine religions—the Tree of Life, dragon, ritual rebirth, and the goddess—appear as well. These themes are consistent with Philip's suspected involvement in the feminine and Sophianic mysteries. And a final detail we might observe: is it yet another coincidence that there were exactly twenty-four panels in the Altarpiece, as well as twenty-four original members of Philip's Order?

Interestingly, one of the codes of the Order of the Golden Fleece was that only fellow knights could hold trials for its members on matters of heresy and treason. Though they outwardly claimed allegiance to the Catholic Church, like the Templars, their true motivation was political—to protect their own members from the powers of church and state. The Order, in effect, was its own law. We know very well that Philip the Good, though devoted to knightly chivalry, was not a pious man in any accepted sense.

Having met the remarkable men behind the creation of the *Altarpiece,* we are ready for the unveiling of the identity of the true Mystic Lamb, the *Feminine Revelation.*

CHAMBER 22

THE LADY IN THE LANDSCAPE

Body of the Goddess

There are three classes of people: those who see, those who see when they are shown, those who do not see.

LEONARDO DA VINCI

WE HAVE MET THE CHARACTERS INVOLVED in the creation of the *Mystic Lamb,* and the cultural, religious, spiritual, and philosophical environment that shaped its birth. Let us now take a closer look at the artwork itself, to directly experience its mystical transmission.

The *Ghent Altarpiece* draws some of its imagery from the biblical book of Revelation. Indeed, there is a mystery to be "revealed." The original Greek title of Revelation is the *Apokalypsis,* meaning "the unveiling," from the root word *kal.* This same womb root forms the basis of the words *chalice, Kali, cauldron, kallos* ("beauty" in Greek), *gala* ("vulva" in Sumerian). Let the Chalice, and all that lies hidden within her, be revealed.

We begin by orienting ourselves to the central and most important panel of the *Ghent Altarpiece,* the *Adoration of the Mystic Lamb* (see color plate 15). Immediately we sense an unusual symmetry. A vertical line, the *axis mundi* or world axis, extends down from the numinous dove at the top of the painting, through the lamb and central altar, and through the fountain to the bottom of the painting.

273

The multitudes that pilgrimage to the lamb arrange themselves symmetrically to the left and right, forming a geometrical pattern that holds the secret key to the mystery of the painting, and alerts us that there is a right-hand path—and a left-hand feminine path. The central vertical pole is no casual alignment, but is rather a *shamanic world-pole,* a cleverly disguised mandala organized around three powerful feminine archetypes: the descending dove as Queen of the Heavens, the blood-red altar as the female throne of earthly sovereignty, and the life-giving fountain as the yoni-gateway to inner earth.

They represent Upperworld, Middleworld, and the Lowerworld gate, respectively—a shamanic map of consciousness embedded into the sacred geography of the earth, and a passion play that visually demonstrates the theology of the Magdalene-Sophia Mysteries.

We can also see the positioning of a group of female pilgrims, the "virgin martyrs," in the upper right side of the painting. But from the perspective of an onlooker inside the painting looking out, *the women are on the left.* From this same perspective of someone within the painting, we can see a file of men across from them, *on the upper right.* Van Eyck has created a masculine-feminine, right-left alchemical polarity, a motif that repeats throughout the entire work and tells a very important story of the Mysteries.

The image is throbbing with symbolic references: With the naked Adam and Eve in the top row of paintings in the *Altarpiece,* as well as the vibrant colors and lush garden landscape of this *Mystic Lamb* panel, we are shown the painting is set in the Garden of Eden, a theatrical stage permeated by the fragrance of female sexual magic and procreative power, a promise of enlightenment that comes from *eating the sacred red fruit.* We also see a golden chalice, the Holy Grail, filled with blood of a lamb. But who is this lamb?

Even through this feast of engaging images and symbols that call to us—something far greater is emerging from the depths of the painting, like an apparition of Venus or Aphrodite rising from the oceans of our collective unconscious. As our eyes become attuned to the symbols of female sexuality hidden within the *Adoration of the Mystic Lamb,* a stunning, world-changing image begins to rise up from the deliberately placed lines and unusual symmetry of this panel. Like a vision being granted to a supplicant, we "see the light" (see page 275 and color plate 15).

The Lady in the Landscape reveals herself. The form of a reclining woman emerges, an earthly Sophia, the earth goddess Gaia, hidden within the lines of flow of the painting, her legs opened wide in the M position of sacred sexuality and female birthing power. This classic representation of the sublime power of the

The cleverly placed lines of flow within the *Mystic Lamb* reveal van Eyck's great secret, the return of the tantric Magdalene-Sophia, as the body of woman and the body of the earth.

goddess, a Dragon Mother of Earth who births out worlds and who *is* the world, dates back to Paleolithic cave art.[1] The goddess emerges; with golden crown, red-throne heart-womb, and a fountain of life.

In the middle of her extended legs, a phallic scepter-lingam rises up into the figure's downward pointing chalice-triangle, symbolizing the vulva. At the top of the yoni lies the womb-altar, on the sacred earth mound, representing the pregnant earth and the pregnant female body. The dove as the feminine Holy Spirit forms the head, "wisdom," and the figure's arms extend out along the lines of the approaching pilgrims.

The true meaning of the *Adoration of the Mystic Lamb* is revealed. These are indeed stunning revelations—the painting is an apocalypse, or unveiling, of the secrets of the feminine magisterium. Here we see Great Mother worship in its most heretical and tantric form, encompassing both the Higher Sophia *and* the Lower Sophia, the sacred body of the earth and woman, whose menstrual and birth bloods and sexual elixirs are the fountain of life.

Although this representation of female sexuality is astonishing to find hidden within orthodox Catholic religious artwork, it has a long and distinguished history

Top left: Irish Sheela-Na-Gig with legs in M position and sacred vulva displayed,
Rodel Church, South Harris, Hebrides, Scotland.

(Photo by John W. Schulze CC BY 2.0 via Flickr)

Top right: Australian aboriginal cave painting with goddess mother, her sacred yoni revealed.

(Kakadu National Park, Arnhemland, Ecoprint | Shutterstock)

Bottom left: Sculpted relief of the god Lajja Gauri, venerating the holy vulva of the
feminine divinity, in the M position, sixth century, Madhya Pradesh, India.

(Photo by Sarah Welch, CC BY-SA 4.0)

Bottom right: Detail of the Scandinavian Snake-Witch Stone, featuring a female shaman
in M position holding serpents, ca. 400 to 600 CE, Gotlands Museum, Sweden.

(Photo by Berig, CC BY-SA 3.0)

Detail of Leonardo da Vinci's *Last Supper* (1498), with a symmetric and oddly leaning Magdalene and Jesus, in red and blue, forming the alchemical M symbol penetrated by a phallic column. This is sometimes referred to as a "chalice and blade" configuration.

that inspired Jan van Eyck. Similar images appear across time and culture.

The Celtic Sheela-Na-Gig is one of the most famous European examples of the sacred temple of the yoni-womb seen in M position. The Sheela-Na-Gig is modeled after the frog goddess Heket of ancient Egypt, linked to the M symbol, who is said to have resurrected Osiris, a parallel to Jesus. Other images from around the world attest to the cross-cultural psychic power of the feminine M symbol. Mary, Magdalene, mother, mama, matrix, ma, and other sacred feminine *M* names derive from this ancient symbology.

Leonardo da Vinci, also connected to the underground streams of the feminine mysteries, took inspiration from van Eyck in his famous *Last Supper*. In the painting above, we see an M shape formed around the symmetric figures of Jesus and his oddly leaning feminine partner, "officially" said to be John the Evangelist, but known by the inner circles to be Mary Magdalene. The central pillar is the phallic lingam or blade.

CHAMBER 23

MAGDALENE
AND THE SIBYLS

Prophetesses of Sophia

WITH THE GODDESS REVEALED, in a painting created by devoted heretics, we would also expect to find the priestess of the goddess—Mary Magdalene. For if the *Ghent Altarpiece* is the story of the secret left-hand religion, as well as Magdalene's place in the great and untold history of the Holy Sophia, we would expect to find a *hidden* Mary Magdalene, with a *hidden* message in the painting. And indeed we do.

Mary Magdalene is the most dangerous figure within Christianity. Every aspect of her being hints at a great, and potentially explosive, mystery: her red priestess cloak; her sensual, unbound, and often red hair; her overwhelming passion and disregard of the rules; the legends of her sexually promiscuous past; and the rumors—above all else—of her unusual intimacy with Jesus. The Cathars, for their part, secretly venerated her as wife and co-redemptrix with Jesus, and the mother of a sacred bloodline.

And where might we look for our Mary? Let us consult the Song of Songs, King Solomon's hymn of the sacred marriage rites, sung to the Bride, to see if it offers any hints:

> *My dove is hiding behind the rocks, behind an outcrop on the cliff, In the secret place of the steep pathway,* let me see your face; let me hear your voice. For your voice is pleasant, and your face is lovely. (Song of Songs 2:14, emphasis added)

Of course, as we might have guessed, we find Mary Magdalene, with her classic red cape and iconic anointing jar, half-hidden behind a suspiciously M-shaped rock, behind an "outcrop on the cliff" and underneath a "steep pathway." Oh, the clever van Eyck! This scene appears in the *Hermits* panel (see page 280), located just to the left of the *Mystic Lamb* panel, on the feminine side of the *Altarpiece,* as seen from a viewer within the painting.

This is our first clue of Magdalene's role in the painting: her location is exactly pinpointed by the Song of Songs—indicating that *she is the Dove, she is the Bride* of the sacred marriage rites.

If we had any doubts, the next clue is that she stands beside a "twin" Mary: Mary of Egypt, the "redeemed prostitute." They appear as identical twins—their faces and hair are perfectly matched, and their clothing is the same, with just an inversion of blue and red colors. What do these two women have in common? And why are they depicted as twins? The two Marys are the only two saints who, in the artist's time, were regarded by the Catholic Church as former *harlots*—they were the *sexualized saints.* Van Eyck is immediately drawing our attention to their sexuality, as well as their interconnectedness.

Here we see the secret harlot-heroines of Sophia, sequestered away behind the hermits, associated with the mystical path, standing next to a striking M that is clearly linked with sexual themes. The presence of these two women encodes the lineage of the Holy Whore priestesses and the secret tradition of female Christian tantrics.

What else do the two Marys have in common? They are obviously both named Mary, a name associated with the priestess traditions of Egypt, which arises again and again in the circles of Magdalene and Jesus. They were both said to be mystics who lived outside of conventions of society, wandering naked, covered only by their wild, unbound hair that draped down to their ankles. The Dominicans claimed that Magdalene lived for thirty years in the cave of Sainte-Baume after Jesus's death. Mary of Egypt's primary "biographer" wrote that she lived in the desert wilderness across the River Jordan, but earlier legends and church iconography also depicted her as living in a cave. Throughout the history of the feminine religions, caves were a symbol of the yoni and womb of the Earth Mother, and were sites of initiation and spiritual rebirth, connected to the prehistoric goddess traditions of feminine divinity.

There is something unusual about Mary of Egypt's supposed history. Almost all that we know of her comes from Saint Sophronius, the Egyptian-born patriarch of Jerusalem. In his 634 CE fictional book *Vita de Sancta Maria Aegyptiaca,*

Top right: Detail of the *Hermits* panel. Mary Magdalene appears with her alabaster jar, half hidden behind an M-shaped rock formation, beside her twin—Mary of Egypt. We also see a thronelike rock at the top of the M and a path above that directs our gaze to it.
Left: The full *Hermits* panel, with M-shaped rocks and a steep path above. A series of V's descend from the top of the painting—from the birds in the sky, through a V-shaped funnel in the forest, and through the V-opening of the rocks.
Bottom right: The *Virgins* panel, with virgins carrying feminine symbols and palm fronds of the goddess traditions.

he writes that she was raised in Egypt and at the age of twelve ran away from home to Alexandria. There she lived a life of sexual promiscuity, engaging in every kind of lustful behavior possible with the sole aim of satisfying her insatiable desire, refusing payment when offered. Instead, she earned her living by begging. Penniless, she eventually sailed from Alexandria to Jerusalem, exchanging sex with attractive young men at the seaport for passage. In Jerusalem, Mary had a spiritual awakening and left for the monastery of Saint John the Baptist, located on the banks of the River Jordan. There she bathed and baptized in the sacred river, and was "born again" into a new life of spiritual devotion as an ascetic in the desert. Other versions of this story predate Sophronius's *Vita*. All involve a woman named Mary who fled a prior life of sexual "sin" to the desert around the River Jordan, where she began a new life. In two of the versions she is at first mistaken for a man.

What we can say without doubt is that the "facts" of Mary of Egypt's life as presented by Saint Sophronius are not true at a literal level. The stories were written as fictional narratives in the tradition of monastic literature. But they likely *actually* encode the secret history of Mary Magdalene—and this is why van Eyck portrays them as twins. In the Middle Ages, Mary of Egypt's story was conflated with Mary Magdalene's. They were often depicted together, and said to share the same history and background. The legends of Mary Magdalene at a cave in Sainte-Baume in France are inspired by Mary of Egypt's life, including the imagery of her penitent, naked, and draped in her own lavish hair.

Mary of Egypt's story sounds like the story of a young Egyptian woman forced into prostitution or into the life of a temple priestess, or perhaps both, at a time when the sanctity of the original temples had fallen. Apocryphal texts from the early centuries of Christianity tell us that Mary Magdalene was abducted and made to work as a prostitute. Other legends hold that Mary Magdalene found her way to John the Baptist at his camp at the River Jordan, and that she may even have been married to him. Maybe these stories point us toward the truth of Mary Magdalene's early life. Historical texts tell us precious little, yet the apocryphal texts seem to be trying to share a forbidden history.

Whatever the background of the two Marys, we know van Eyck is drawing our attention to their shared story of sexuality, spiritual devotion, and connections to Egypt, perhaps to the priestess traditions. He intentionally creates a disguised M symbol beside the Marys, formed from the lines of flow of the stone outcropping—indicating the importance, and heretical themes, of the scene. The *M* also links Mary Magdalene to the "goddess in the land" figure of the *Mystic Lamb* panel, where we also see a hidden M shape, representing the opened legs and sacred sexual and procreative sacrament of the goddess. Encrypted within his symbolic language, van Eyck insinuates that Mary Magdalene *is* this goddess, and *is* the Bride.

Several other unusual features in the painting indicate that we need to pay close attention to the *Hermits* panel with Magdalene. The adjacent *Pilgrims* panel depicts a giant red-robed Saint Christopher holding open his hands and directing our gaze toward the Magdalene panel. Van Eyck depicts him as an enormous man, a giant twice the size of any other figure in the painting (according to his legends he is over seven feet tall), and wearing bright red robes, so that we can't miss his gesture. Directly beside his arm is a pilgrim wearing a striking scallop shell, a classic goddess symbol of female genitalia, as well as an emblem of the Way of Compostela. *Christopher* means "Christ bearer" or "Christ Revealer"—and one of his key legends tells how he carries a child across a river, who then reveals himself to be the Christ. In the context of the symbology of this artwork, Saint Christopher is pointing toward Magdalene, revealing the Feminine Christ.

We also notice that Mary Magdalene gazes out from the painting intently, looking directly into the eyes of the viewer as if she needs to communicate an important message. The only other significant characters in the painting that make eye contact with the viewer are the Mystic Lamb and the God figure; van Eyck implies that Magdalene is connected with them, a figure of great importance to the message of the *Altarpiece*.

We also find a stone throne of the goddess hidden in plain sight. Above Mary Magdalene a path leads through the woods, directing our eyes to her M symbol in the rocks. At the top of the M, a peculiar arrangement of rocks looks like a throne or altar, connecting Magdalene to the throne and altar motifs of the central panel, as well as the long history of Paleolithic and megalithic womb shamans whose worship involved sacred standing stones, menhirs and dolmens, and stone enthronement ceremonies. We also see fruit-bearing trees in these panels, and nowhere else in the painting. Given the Garden of Eve setting, we are reminded of the forbidden fruit of the Tree of Knowledge that grants enlightenment, or gnosis, symbolic of sexual communion in the bridal chamber. To Saint Bernard of Clairvaux, the Templars, and the underground Magdalene streams, Mary Magdalene was the Bride, the fruit, the Tree of Life and Gnosis.

Unique to Mary Magdalene's panel, and certainly not a coincidence, we see four different V shapes: a V in the rock (as part of the M); a V in the forest canopy where a path passes through; a V formation of birds in the sky; and a V split in the forest path. The V is another classic symbol of the female yoni-vulva-womb, dating back to prehistory. *V* is for vulva, vagina, Venus, venereal, and many other words associated with female sexuality. We also see the V shape in the pelvis and vulva lines of the *Mystic Lamb* panel, linking Magdalene with the holy yoni depicted in the central panel. V symbols were also called witch marks.

Virgin Saints, Virgin Martyrs

The forbidden ladies-in-red, with their anointing jars of the Whore Goddess, are tucked away behind the mystical men, aligned with the traditions of wild cave retreats. Van Eyck contrasts the half-hidden Mary Magdalene and Mary of Egypt with the procession of female virgin martyrs or saints, in the upper left of the central *Mystic Lamb* panel, who represent the more public face of feminine worship. Because the Marys were both said to be harlots, or prostitutes, they cannot be represented along with the procession of virgins in the central panel. In truth they were both victims of the patriarchal propaganda campaigns to malign female sexuality and separate the earthly, or lower, Sophia from the maternal principle and the higher Sophia. At an esoteric level, one key purpose of the *Mystic Lamb* is to reunite the earthly and heavenly Sophia, to end the split between the embodied human woman, as mother and anointrix, with her vital sexual nature and sacred womb, and the purity of the heavenly goddess and her cosmic womb.

We also see important feminine symbols in the virgin saints of the central panel (see page 280). The front row of saints carries a lamb, tower, basket of red flowers, and arrow—each associated with a classical female Catholic saint but also with menstrual blood, Mary Magdalene's name ("tower" in Hebrew), female genitalia, and erotic love, respectively. Each carries a palm frond associated with the goddess tradition and sacred Tree of Life, the *tamar,* long before it became a Jewish and Christian symbol.

The Magdalene Movement

Burgundy was a hotbed of heresy, and the secret knowledge of the Magdalene Mysteries was not limited to Jan van Eyck and Duke Philip the Good. The Burgundian "Church of Magdalene" was a larger underground movement involving multiple painters, members of the nobility and royalty, weavers, illuminists, writers, and philosophers over several hundred years. Their presence helps confirm the reality of the brotherhoods, and likely sisterhoods, that covertly taught the feminine mysteries throughout Burgundy.

Emboldened by Jan van Eyck's successes, several other Netherlandish Renaissance painters created works focused on the *Pregnant Magdalene* and the *Womb of Magdalene,* leaving no doubt that they were in on the great heresies. The artistic convention of the day was to depict women with sensually rounded bellies that could be confused with early pregnancy by a modern observer, but these artists went further. The red-haired Mary Magdalene of Rogier van der Weyden's *Braque Triptych* is particularly striking. The loosened laces of her dress leave no doubt that this Magdalene is pregnant. Scholar and professor of art history Penny Jolly details the remarkable pregnant Magdalene phenomenon in her book, *Picturing the "Pregnant" Magdalene in Northern Art, 1430–1550: Addressing and Undressing the Sinner-Saint*. Hieronymus Bosch, another Early Netherlandish painter, not only

Mary Magdalene from Rogier van der Weyden's *Braque Triptych,* ca. 1452. Loosened laces over her prominent belly indicate her pregnancy according to art scholars.

painted on similar womb-religion themes, but was also known to be a member of the Brotherhood of the Swan, dedicated to the Virgin Mary, their motto "a lily among the thorns," draws from the erotic biblical poem Song of Songs.

The Beloved Disciple

Last Supper Sibyls

For much of the six centuries that this painting has been displayed, the panels have rested in their closed position, except on religious feast days when they were spectacularly opened, revealing their inner mysteries. On these back panels, the hidden Magdalene symbolism continues (see pages 286 and 287).

The closed position is analogous to looking at the cover of a closed book. This back cover of the *Altarpiece* teases us by displaying the main themes of the work, but conceals the most interesting details. She won't give up her secrets easily—we must be prepared to work for it.

In these *verso* paintings we see the story of the Virgin Mary's Annunciation, the moment the angel Gabriel appears to Mary to announce she is pregnant with the Holy Child. The Virgin Mary, representing the Sophia, the Womb of God, appears with the dove of the feminine Holy Spirit over her head. She is positioned on the left side, the feminine side, from the perspective of someone within the painting. We will see this motif of dove and Mary-Sophia again in the inner panels. The most important symbols and characters repeat themselves: grail chalice, dove, serpent/dragon, lamb, John the Baptist, Virgin Mary, and the disguised Mary Magdalene.

Those with the eyes to see will also perceive the hidden story encoded within the verso scenes—two priestesses of the old religions presiding over the mysteries of sacred sexual union—foreshadowing the esoteric, and erotic, message of the painting as a whole. The two pagan priestesses are the Cumaean and Erythrean Sibyls, prophetesses of the ancient goddess tradition. They overlook the scene from the position of highest authority, placed centrally above the two Old Testament prophets Zechariah and Micah, who are in subordinate roles on the sides. This display of female spiritual authority is another striking clue of the heretical themes in the work, and very uncommon in Christian paintings.

With so much happening in every other panel of the painting, the central panels of the closed *Altarpiece* look almost dull in comparison. However, for those with a trained eye, these two "empty" panels set the tone for everything else that

The *Ghent Altarpiece* in its fully closed position, with a view of its back panels. Note Virgin Mary on the left, or feminine side of the painting (as seen from someone in the painting) with the feminine dove of the Holy Spirit overhead, also the two pagan Sibyls overlooking the scene from a position of highest authority. John the Baptist (masculine side) joins "John the Evangelist," or Mary Magdalene, carrying the traditional feminine symbols of grail and serpent, on the feminine side.

Sacred sexual symbolism in the center of the back panels: the dark phallic pillar on the masculine, right side, and the white "pillar" of a towel and the alcove and wash basin representing female genitalia on the left.

follows. They present the dark and light pillars of the temple, an entryway to the rites of hieros gamos. A dark, phallic column in the right-central (masculine) window sits beside a vulva-shaped alcove with feminine water symbols of basin and pitcher on the left-central (feminine) side. The masculine and feminine meet covertly in the center of the painting, in sacred sexual union. We know that the inner panels will continue to develop these same motifs. The dark and light are repeated in the *Mystic Lamb* panel, on either side of the bleeding lamb, as the white tau cross and dark pillar.

The Sibyls were the ancient oracles and high priestesses of the feminine temples and mystery schools that stretched across the ancient Near East. The most famous, as we have learned, was the Oracle of Delphi, known as the Pythia, the most important religious figure of the Hellenic world. Michelangelo painted five Sibyls across the ceiling of the Sistine Chapel; he also encoded the Magdalene-Sophia heresies in his works.

Tellingly, the prophet Micah rests above the Virgin Mary in the back panels. His prophecy in Micah 4:8 directly addresses the weeping Bride, proclaiming that her King-Bridegroom will arrive soon, ready for her anointing, as in the hieros gamos rituals of old. In the gospels, it is Mary Magdalene who takes this symbolic role as anointrix and bride.

**Detail of "John the Evangelist" panel with chalice and serpents.
Is this figure Mary Magdalene in disguise?**

Micah's predictions cleverly orient us to the stunning, but veiled, display of sacred sexual union symbolism within the back panels of the *Altarpiece*. When the panels swing closed, masculine and feminine symbolism join together in union in the middle. A phallic column in the window of the right, or masculine, central panel meets the vulva-shaped alcove with the basin and pitcher, symbols of the yoni and feminine waters, on the left side. Also, John the Baptist on the right joins the John the Evangelist or John the Beloved figure on the left, who we propose is actually *a disguised Mary Magdalene.*

John the Evangelist is placed on the female side of the painting, is feminine in appearance, holds a chalice with serpents, and when the panel is closed, conjoins with John the Baptist, implying an intimate union. The arrangement of these two figures as husband and wife, or in sexual partnership, is emphasized by the position of the donors of the painting, Jodocus Vidt and Elisabeth Borluut, on either side, as a husband and wife pair. All of these motifs are consistent with the legends of Mary Magdalene.

For two millennia, artists and theologians have speculated on the identity of the mysterious beloved disciple of the gospels, thought to be the writer of the

Saint John the Apostle, etching by Jacques Bellange of Lorraine, ca. 1600.
Notice the figure's overtly feminine form. Is this Mary Magdalene?

Gospel of John, also known as John the Evangelist. Leonardo da Vinci paints this same red-haired feminine figure, sitting next to Jesus in the *Last Supper* (see figure on page 277). She certainly looks the part of Mary Magdalene, an interpretation supported by other visual clues within the painting, as we have seen earlier.

Da Vinci is not alone in his beliefs—a number of other scholars, religious groups, and artists across time have also held that Magdalene is the beloved disciple. In 1998, the Roman Catholic scholar Ramon K. Jusino eloquently defended this thesis. Based on evidence from early manuscripts, he argues that in the original versions of the Gospel of John her name appeared as Mary Magdalene, but was later changed to the "beloved disciple" to conform with patriarchal doctrine.[1] Other researchers, including Lynn Picknett and Clive Prince in *The Templar Revelation*, have put forward the same idea, showing how it is consistent with the beliefs of Templar and Johannite groups dating back two thousand years. The popular Renaissance artist Jacques Bellange reveals quite clearly that he views this gospel writer as *female* in his etching *Saint John the Apostle* (on page 289).

CHAMBER 24

RED THRONE

The Original Sacred Altar

THE *ALTARPIECE,* AS ITS NAME IMPLIES, was created to stand directly behind the communion altar of Saint Bavo's cathedral in Ghent, Belgium, where parishioners would gaze up at the magnificent painting as they took part in the Eucharist rites of body and blood.

However, in this most extraordinary of all paintings, the defining monument of Catholic art and glorious tribute to the sacrament of the Eucharist, Jesus, as he is normally depicted, is conspicuously absent. Why is it that among the approximately 300 human figures painted, there is not one image of Jesus? And why is the adult Jesus missing from almost every other painting that can confidently be attributed to Jan van Eyck? Given his meticulous care and attention to symbolic detail, this is no casual oversight—it is a waving red flag, demanding our attention. One would assume that the Mystic Lamb represents Jesus. But does it? Why would van Eyck depict Jesus as a very odd-looking lamb, rather than in the traditional, recognizable forms of a crucified man or haloed divinity?

Instead, the *Adoration of the Mystic Lamb* tells a much older and radically different story of the *Feminine Eucharist*—communion on the "red throne" with the mystical body of the feminine, in her many forms: as goddess, Earth Mother, and human woman . . . Our Lady. Gnostic Christian Valentinus (100–160 CE) considered the eucharist wine as symbolic of Jesus's *maternal* inheritance: "Truth the Mother of All." The spiritual power held within the holy *Motherline* and her Grail-Womb was the primordial essence of the original divinized humanity. Although the father contributes half of the genetic blueprint of a child, not one

Detail of the Mystic Lamb on the red altar, whose blood pours out into a golden Holy Grail, promising a new life of resurrection. Note the dark pillar on the lamb's left, and light pillar (cross) on its right, modeled after Temple of Solomon, also in High Priestess Tarot.

drop of blood passes between him and the child. The womb blood of the mother weaves the baby into being, and so a Messianic bloodline specifically refers to this *mystical female blood*. This is why many tribes and culture, including the Jews, drew matrilineal descent.

To this day the Orthodox Church holds seven major feast days in honor of Mary as Theotokos, Mother of God. She is known as the "Life-giving Spring." In the "Canon of the Akathist," an orthodox hymn in use since the sixth century, the congregation chants to Mary, "Hail, Sovereign Lady, never failing spring of the living Water":

> As a life-giving fount, thou didst conceive the Dew that is
>   transcendent in essence,
> O Virgin Maid, and thou hast welled forth for our sakes the
>   nectar of joy eternal,
> which doth pour forth from thy fount with the water that
>   springeth up
> unto everlasting life in unending and mighty streams;
> wherein, taking delight, we all cry out:
> Rejoice, O thou Spring of life for all men.[1]

APOLITYKION, ORTHODOX HYMN OF
FEAST DAY OF THE LIFE-GIVING SPRING

> O Lady graced by God,
> you reward me by letting gush forth, beyond reason,
> the ever-flowing waters of your grace from your perpetual
>   Spring . . .
> refresh me in your grace that I may cry out,
> "Hail redemptive waters."[2]

KONTAKION, ORTHODOX HYMN OF
FEAST DAY OF THE LIFE-GIVING SPRING

In the human psyche, symbols reign supreme. To many in the Orthodox Church, as well as to Jan van Eyck, *Mary* is the life-giving spring and the fountain of life, not Jesus. When we investigate the deeper significance of the altar, we may be surprised to discover that Jan van Eyck clearly and consistently identifies the Divine Mary as the red altar throughout his paintings. Her thronelike lap, or womb, is the altar and Seat of God. This concept did not originate in van Eyck. Mary as the "Seat of God's Wisdom" (*Sedes Sapientiae* in Latin), as the container of divinity, is a devotional title of Mary and established tradition within the Catholic Church. The celebrated eleventh-century cardinal and theologian Peter Damian called her the *aureum humanae altare,* the "golden human altar."[3] The church, in turn, had borrowed this ancient iconography of the enthroned goddess and altar from the feminine traditions of old.

Seat of Sophia

Sacred Feminine Altar

In many of his paintings, Jan van Eyck alludes to the feminine as the true throne and altar of divinity. In the feminine mysteries, the sacred body of the earth and human woman are the Mother Church. Woman's womb is throne and altar and the "seat" of worship. There is a Queen of Heaven who *descends down,* as in van Eyck's descending dove, as the feminine Holy Spirit. Gnostics call her "Higher Sophia"; Kabbalists call her the "Higher Shekinah." She is the celestial feminine divinity, known as the Virgin Mary in the Christian tradition, and Inanna, Isis, Ishtar, and thousands of names across every culture of the world, dating back to the dawn of humanity. On earth she is enthroned and becomes the Womb of Christ.

The central blood-red altar that the Mystic Lamb stands upon is Sophia's heavenly throne on earth, the *holy female womb* that blesses, births, rebirths. The original blood used to anoint the sacred stones and altars was *women's holy menstrual and birth blood,* symbolized by the ubiquitous red ochre pigment found in ancient cultures across the world.[4]

The altar, or throne, is also the seat of sovereignty. *Seat* is a feminine power word, derived from the ancient Egyptian name of Isis, *A-S-T,* pronounced *Auset* or *Eset.* Her hieroglyphic name is composed of a cluster of iconic feminine symbols—throne, loaf of bread, cosmic egg, and goddess—illustrating the ancient concept that the feminine divinity, as well as the womb of the woman, is the throne and seat, as well as the bread of life and birther.

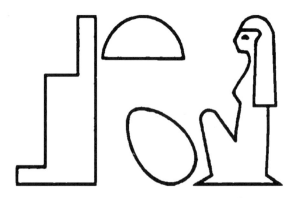

Egyptian hieroglyph for Isis—composed of her iconic
throne on the left, loaf of bread above, divine egg below,
and goddess emblem to the right.

The *Adoration of the Mystic Lamb* depicts the body of the earth goddess as the holy church; the multitudes pilgrimage to it. Van Eyck reminds us that a church is only *symbolic* of the body of the earth and woman—which is the true sacred temple and holy Mother Church. To enter a church is to enter into the mystical body and womb of the Great Mother, as is encoded in the architecture of the Gothic cathedrals of Europe. The arched entryway symbolizes the vulva, often with a central rosette mounted at the top, representing the rose of the clitoris. In Celtic churches the entry was often "guarded" by a Sheela-Na-Gig, spreading open her vulva as an invitation, and also a reminder to worshippers that they were entering a womb sanctum, the symbolic womb of the god. Pilgrims would touch her numinous genitals for a blessing before entering the church. The *body* of Sophia, the *embodied Goddess, is* the feminine mystery school.

Gnostic and Kabbalist mystics realized that the Fall of Consciousness resulted not from Eve's sexuality, or eating the apple of gnosis, but from the splitting of the Sophia into her higher and lower aspects, with denigration of the lower. In the patriarchal world, the Higher Sophia, the celestial female divinity, was venerated, but the Lower Sophia, the female human woman and the earth itself, were considered dirty, base, and sinful, as was her womb wisdom. The word *venerate* derives from the Latin word and goddess name *Venus,* meaning "love, sexual desire, beauty." To venerate is to worship the goddess of love and sexuality. The celestial goddesses Isis and Virgin Mary were honored, but the earthly Magdalene and her red priestesses were scorned.

When heaven and earth, upper and lower, meet again, a "new heaven and a new earth" are formed, as declared in the book of Revelation. In the *Mystic Lamb,* the cosmic and earthly aspects of Sophia are unified; woman is made whole and earth finds harmony.

Throne of Mary

Following the ancient tradition of the sacred feminine throne and altar, the Virgin Mary and, in more heretical traditions, Mary Magdalene take up the throne of the goddess.

Jan van Eyck was obsessed with the theme of the feminine throne, and the luscious red vibration of his art communicates this vividly. His work is populated with powerful female symbols and powerful women. Consistent with the beliefs of the underground Templar societies, van Eyck rarely painted the adult Jesus but was fascinated with the Virgin Mary. He painted at least thirteen images of the

Detail of *Madonna of Chancellor Rolin,* Jan van Eyck, ca. 1435.
Mary is the red altar and "Throne of Wisdom," the baby Jesus emerges
from an opening in her magnificent red robes. She is being crowned
the sovereign Queen of Heaven by an angel above.
This same crown rests over the dove in the *Ghent Altarpiece.*

Madonna, several of which depicted her in her iconic form *as the red altar of the Christ child,* also called the "Throne of Wisdom," drawing from the Byzantine, or Eastern Orthodox, Christian traditions.

In the symbolic language of van Eyck's paintings, he draws attention to the Catholic Church's doctrine that Mary *was* the altar, made red by blood from her sacred womb, spilled during Christ's birth. Her magnificent, flowing red robes indicate feminine blood, power, passion, love, and, to the trained eye of the initiate, also the delicate folds of the lips of the yoni.

In van Eyck's *Madonna of Chancellor Rolin,* the baby Jesus is held on Mary's lap as if he has emerged through the vulvalike opening in the folds of her garment (see facing page). In his *Lucca Madonna,* she is seated upon a lion-adorned throne, symbolizing the lion throne of King Solomon, equating Mary with his legendary power and wisdom (see color plate 7). Mary is both queen and throne. In *Virgin and Child,* her regal red lap replaces the altar of the chapel. Pious men come to worship at her feet, bowing before her red womb-altar.

Catholic tradition also holds Mary to be the New Ark of the Covenant, whose Holy Womb holds and births the divine masculine. As the Mother of God, the Theotokos, she is the antecessor—she comes first. The male godhead derives his sovereign power, and his life, by sitting on her throne, a continuation of the ancient rites of the goddess to birth and crown kings, administered through her anointed high priestesses and queens.

In these images, the Virgin Mary appears every bit the red priestess, or red goddess, of old. Though she has many officially sanctioned, devotional "goddess" titles in the Catholic Church—Queen of the Heavens and Earth, Star of the Sea, Queen of the World, Queen of the Universe, Queen of the Prophets, Co-Redemptrix, Mediatrix, Gate of Heaven, Ladder to Paradise, Majesty—one title that is expressly forbidden by the Catholic Church is priestess. Perhaps that would cut too close to the truth of the important role she plays.

Goddess thrones are renowned throughout the world as symbols of feminine power, and van Eyck was deliberately alluding to these ancient traditions of the Mother.

Redeeming the Blood

Mary as the throne and altar, representing the goddess and her priestesses, has a long historical context. Throughout almost every known culture, the female womb was once worshipped as the primordial and original altar—symbolizing the holy of holies, an extension of the womb of the goddess, made red by the life-giving, sacred blood of birth and menstruation.[5] Both the altar (the womb) and the blood spilt upon it were originally *symbolic of woman, not man.*

Eventually, with the coming of patriarchal values, men "stole the menstrual skirt" and the true origins of the blood mysteries were forgotten. Sacred menstrual blood was banned as "impure." At the Temple of Jerusalem, it was doves, symbolic of the goddess, and *female* lambs that were sacrificed instead. Priests smeared this *feminine blood* on the high altar, painting it red, as we see in the *Altarpiece*, a patriarchal reinterpretation of the ancient offering of women's menstrual blood—which was offered without injury or suffering in sacred rites by holy priestesses to the ancient altars of the goddess.

The patriarchal tradition of replacing the regenerative moon blood with the death blood of animal sacrifice is described in Leviticus 5:6: "As a penalty for the sin they have committed, they must bring to the Lord a female lamb or goat from the flock as a sin offering; and the priest shall make atonement for them for their sin."

Jesus fully understood the old traditions, and original meanings of the red altar, sacred blood, and mystic lamb, which is why he famously overturned the money-changers' tables in the temple.

He was not protesting commerce in the holy grounds, but the unnecessary killing of animals, a gruesome display born from ignorance of the true life-giving feminine blood. The Jewish historian Josephus reminds us that Jesus may have been part of a larger tradition that objected to animal sacrifice. The Essenes, a group whose teachings influenced Jesus and John the Baptist, also forbade the practice.

The money-lenders in the Temple of Jerusalem were not breaking any holy law or on a mercenary mission, instead they were invited by the temple to provide a valuable service. Jewish pilgrims came from across the Hellenic world to make offerings in the temple. Payment for an animal sacrifice could only be made in the local currency of shekels. After a pilgrim had paid for his offering, at a later time a priest would sacrifice an animal and smear its blood across the holy altar, behind closed doors (a practice also common across the Near East in pagan temples). Because many people came from Alexandria, and outside the country, they needed to change money to pay for offerings.

Jesus's rare display of public anger, creating a scene in the holy temple—which would have been considered utterly taboo—was at the *misuse* of the feminine blood mysteries.

> Jesus entered the Temple and began to drive out all the people buying and selling animals for sacrifice. He knocked over the tables of the money changers and the chairs of those selling doves. (Matthew 21:12)

Magdalene the Watchtower

The temple sacrifice traditions may also explain one of the meanings of the name Mary Magdalene: *Mary* as the honorific *Migdal Eder*. The Hebrew title Migdal Eder, or Watchtower of the Flock, specifically referred to the sanctified flock of lambs whose blood was destined for the sacrifice at the temple altar. The blood of these female lambs was a sin-offering; when poured on the sacred stone altar, it washed away sin. In this way Magdalene was connected to the life-giving blood. The prominent nineteenth-century scholar of Judaism and Christianity Alfred Edersheim writes: "The Migdal Eder was not the watchtower for the ordinary flocks. . . . A passage in the Mishnah leads to the conclusion that the flocks which pastured there were destined for Temple sacrifices."[6]

But Mary Magdalene, as Migdal Eder, is not just linked to the sacred blood. Micah 4:8 shares that the messiah-king *will first be revealed to the Migdal Eder,* his weeping bride. To the mystical Christians, this meant the true identity of Jesus and his kingdom of heaven would first be revealed to Mary Magdalene: "And you, O [Migdal Eder], the stronghold of the daughter of Zion, Unto you shall it come. . . . The kingdom* shall come to the daughter of Jerusalem."

The Migdal Eder is not just a metaphor for a tower of spiritual strength, keeping watch over the flock, but a female revealer, illuminator, rebirther, and guardian of the sacred blood.

This is the same story enfolded within the massive, two-ton oak panels of the *Ghent Altarpiece,* a living alchemical manuscript expressed through visual art.

It is the story of the Holy Grail. The story of the New Eve. The story of Life.

---

*The word *kingdom* refers to the Hebrew malkuth, a reference to the kingdom of heaven, an exalted spiritual state, thought of as a feminine sephira in Kabbalah. In Aramaic the same phrase could be more literally translated as the "queendom of heaven."

CHAMBER 25

FEMININE EUCHARIST

The Primeval Sacrament

NOW LET US EXPLORE MORE DEEPLY the Mystic Lamb as the *Eucharist of the Divine Mother,* a grand allusion to the sacred Bride and the Holy Body of the Magdalene-Sophia, who pours *her* holy blood into a golden chalice, and blesses the world with her substance.

The womb blood and breast milk of the mother is the original Feminine Eucharist. The Holy Feminine Communion exists on multiple levels. Our foundational experience as a newborn child, held at the deepest levels of cellular memory, is that every molecule in our body comes from our human mother. Every cell, tissue, organ—the entirety of our physical being, our *matter*—derives from the placental womb blood, and later breast milk, of our human mother, our *mater.* Our entry into this world is the lived biological experience of "I and the Mother are One," united in deep symbiosis within her womb.

The Feminine Communion expands out from our human mothers to the greater World Mothers that hold us—we are also one with our Earth Mother, and one with our Cosmic Mother. Our physical beings are completely dependent on receiving nourishment from the physical world and the spiritual womb worlds. The bread that sustains us, a symbol of the goddess across cultures, is the body and milk of our Earth Mother. As we eat of her plants and animals, we become her. Our fields of energy entangle at a quantum level, our sense perceptions and our destinies intertwine. For our ancestors, this understanding extended to their conception of the Milky Way galaxy, visible as the white band of stars in the night sky, so named because it resembles a river of the Great Mother's celestial breast

milk. The word *galaxy* itself comes from the Greek *galaktos,* meaning "milk."

This sacred feminine presence has been celebrated as the "milk maiden" who assists Buddha just prior to his enlightenment; as *El Shaddai,* a Hebrew name of God meaning "of the breast"; as Hathor the Celestial Cow and divine milk-giver; and as Artemis of Ephesus in her form as the many-breasted divinity. At a spiritual level we are all born from the Cosmic Mother.

Detail of the *Adoration of the Mystic Lamb* (with Languedoc-style cross faintly visible in bottom left corner): The golden chalice and Holy Grail, filled with blood, but whose? Is this the life-giving birth blood, or the blood of death and sacrifice?

Sacrament of Sin

In prehistoric times blood was a gift of the *sacred women*. Menstruation was considered the monthly fruit of the moon, the blooming of the Tree of Life. Originally, in early religions, menstrual blood was poured over sacred stones; this was later replaced by the blood of a female animal, with male priests now making the "female blood" offering. The sacred stones were eventually replaced with altars housed within tents or temples. Even after woman-centric feminine shamanism was prohibited, and women's power as the "house of the moon" had devolved, women still had to make monthly sin/moon offerings of a female animal's blood. In the Hebrew tradition this was first performed for the sacred *masseboth* and *betyl* stones, and later for the brazen altar. The Great Altars of the wilderness Tabernacle and Temple of Jerusalem were smeared with offerings of female blood as a "sin/moon" offering. Sin purification was originally a menstrual sacrament and a form of moon worship.

Sin was also closely linked to holy mountain of Sinai and to the "sin offerings" (Hebrew *chattah*) of female blood used to anoint the sacred stones and altars, as an act of purification and atonement. The late Dr. Julius Lewy, former professor of biblical history at Hebrew Union College of Jerusalem, writes that Mt. Sinai is the "mountain holy to Sin."[1] Jewish scholar Isidore Singer, Ph.D., writes, "The general opinion of modern scholars is that the name 'Sinai' is derived from the name of the Babylonian moon-god Sin."[2]

Remarkably, the sacred lunar horns of Sin also appeared on the central altars of the wilderness Tabernacle and the Temples of Jerusalem, one horn on each of the four corners. The lunar horns (also representing the horns of the cow/bull), symbolizing divine power, were considered the most sacred part of the altar, and were the focus of daily sacrificial rituals in the Israelite temples. Blood from the animals was sprinkled and smeared on the altars and the horns. For their sin-offerings, laypeople were commanded to offer the blood of a female goat or sheep, or a dove or pigeon, a symbol of the *goddess* and the *feminine*. Women also sacrificed the blood of a dove or pigeon to purify themselves after menstruation or childbirth. This ritual practice recalls the holiness and purifying powers of *Her* blood, originally female menstrual blood, which, paradoxically, became the greatest taboo, and associated with "sinfulness," shame, and uncleanness. Israelite kings were anointed with oil poured from a horn, representing the crescent "horns" of the moon.

In the Jewish tradition, the blood was life; it was magical and redemptive, echoing the ancient understanding of the life-giving and redemptive powers of menstrual blood:

> For the life of the flesh is in the blood; and I have given it to you for making atonement for your lives on the altar; for, as life, it is the blood that makes atonement. (Leviticus 17:11)

> Without the shedding of blood there can be no remission of sin. (Hebrews 9:22)

Later these notions of Holy Blood and sin redemption would be taken up in Christianity, transferred in a form of spiritual transfusion into the eucharist rites.

Bread of Life

Bread, symbolized by the color white, has represented the body of the goddess and the nurturance derived from the grains of our Mother Earth, our living planetary mother, for many thousands of years before it was borrowed by the Christian tradition to represent the body of the male deity Jesus. In fact, as we have seen in the gnostic Collyridian sects, Jesus and the early mystical Christians recognized this. To them the eucharistic bread was the body of the Great Mother or Mary.

Returning to the hieroglyph of the goddess Isis (see figure on page 294), we see that the second of her important icons is the loaf of bread, the life-sustaining and all-nurturing "bread of life." In fact, the Egyptian letter *t,* represented by the loaf of bread, is a universal feminine-determinative symbol that appears throughout the language. When we see the pictogram of a loaf of bread at the end of an Egyptian word, it indicates a feminine or female substance.

The eating of bread as a symbol of communion with the goddess extends through the other ancient religions of the Near East. In the Sumerian language, the oldest known written language, the symbols for women, vulva, and bread are nearly identical (see figure on page 61). The Sumerian word for bread is *nin-da. Nin* means "lady, woman, goddess." And, as mentioned earlier, it is no coincidence that in the Judaic tradition, the birth of the Messiah was prophesied to occur at *Bethlehem,* the "House of Bread," *Lehem* being a deity of fertility as well as the word for "bread."

Similarly, in the Greek Eleusinian Mysteries, the earth goddess Demeter was associated with the sacramental grain drink as well as bread, her "flesh." She was called *Sito,* "of the wheat," and *Megalartos,* "with large loaves." The earliest eucharists of bread were understood to be a communion with the goddess.[3]

Holy Blood

The eucharistic communion extends to the holy sacrament of menstrual blood in gnostic, Tibetan, and Indian traditions. The female Buddha and Mother of Tibetan Buddhism Yeshe Tsogyal attained enlightenment after drinking the menstrual blood of the Great Mother directly from her *bhaga,* or yoni. The Bauls of India hold menstrual blood in the highest honor, using it as a religious sacrament to strengthen bonds of connection, and for healing.[4] In the related Tibetan Buddhist practice of Chöd, developed by the renowned eleventh-century teacher and yogini Machig Labdrön, the practitioner envisions her body as nectar. She then offers herself, eucharistically, as a tantric feast to any "demons"—any attachments, fears, or aversions—to "feed" rather than resist them. Redemption comes through this tantric eucharist of communion.

In the *Adoration of the Mystic Lamb,* we see the feminine theology of communion displayed in its full artistic glory. The Holy Grail, the golden chalice, is filled with womb blood. The Mystic Lamb is *female,* not male, as we remember from the Jerusalem temple traditions. She is the heavenly Sophia, the Virgin Mary and Mary Magdalene. She is the feminine altar, seat, and throne. Her yoni-womb flows with the ever-renewing waters of life, the life-giving spring. We are witness to the most illuminating, and heretical, painting of all time, illustrating the power of the ancient *Feminine Eucharist.*

As the astounding implications of the feminine communion slowly sink in, like the mystics who have come before us, we may hear the voice of the Great Mother gently calling:

"Take this in Remembrance of Me."

We receive her Grace, and remember:

"I and the Mother are One."

Allusions to the feminine sacrament are hidden throughout the *Altarpiece.* In the details of the fabric screen behind the God figure in the upper tier of paintings, we see the alchemical symbol of the *female* pelican, feeding her young from the blood of her own breast. This symbol originated in the pagan mystery traditions predating Christianity, and continued to be used by alchemists, hermeticists, and secret societies of Europe through medieval times. The legend holds that during a time of famine, the mother pelican would pierce her flesh and feed her young through her own blood. *Her children were saved by the blood of the mother.* This symbol was later adopted in early Christian symbolism as a reference to the blood sacrifice of the male Jesus. Through pelican and altar, chalice and fountain, paradisiacal garden and numinous dove, a radically different, and ancient, theology begins to come into view, a theology of Sophia.

Eucharist of the Mother

Many of the gnostic texts banned by the Catholic Church painted a very different picture of early Christian worship. Gnostic groups often had women priests, and some clearly observed a Feminine Eucharist, as we have learned from the patristic fathers that preached against them. Though most heretical books were destroyed, a small number survive today, giving us a fractional glimpse of what it meant to be part of a Sophianic tradition. One apocryphal text with important insights is the Acts of Thomas, composed around 220 CE in eastern Syria. In it, the apostle Thomas, one of the original twelve disciples of Jesus, calls on a *feminine divinity,* the "Lady" or "hidden Mother," to preside over the holy communion:

"Come, Lady, you who understand the mysteries of the chosen one, Come, Lady, you who share in all the contests of the noble athlete, Come, Respite, you who reveal the magnitude of every greatness, Come, Lady, you who make manifest what is secret and render visible what is hidden; the sacred dove which gives birth to twin nestlings. Come, hidden Mother; Come, Lady, you who are manifest in your own activities. . . . Come and share with us in this eucharist that we make in your name and in the love by which we are united at your summons." And when he had spoken, he marked the sign of the cross on the bread, broke it and began to distribute it.[5]

And later, Thomas merges the identity of the Mother and Jesus:

Bread of life . . . bread who fills hungry souls with your blessing: You are the one who has been deemed worthy to receive a gift . . . that those who eat of you might be immortal. We pronounce over you the name of the Mother, of an ineffable mystery, and of the hidden authorities and powers: we pronounce over you your name Jesus.[6]

The Marcosians were a gnostic group in southern France from the second to fourth centuries in which women were regarded as prophetesses, and female priests administered the Eucharist. They believed the female divinity *Charis,* personification of Grace, would drop her own blood into the wine of the eucharistic chalice. Irenaeus writes, in *Against Heresies,* that the following was spoken before taking the communion:

May that Charis who is before all things, and who transcends all knowledge and speech, fill thine inner being, and multiply in thee her own knowledge, by sowing the grain of mustard seed in thee as in good soil.[7]

Mary's Milk—Divine Mother

Mary is the violet of humility, the lily of chastity, the rose of clarity . . . and the glory and splendor of the heavens.

SAINT BERNARD OF CLAIRVAUX

One of the original Templars of Burgundy, and a forefather of the *Ghent Altarpiece,* is Saint Bernard of Clairvaux (1090–1153). Although he appeared to be a model priest of the Catholic faith, now sainted, he was secretly a high-level heretic deeply involved in the mystical Marian worship. Publicly known the "Troubadour of Mary" for his eloquent sermons, he did more to elevate the status of Mary Magdalene and the Virgin Mary than any other figure in church history. In private, he took his devotions much further—by helping to create the Order of the Knights Templar, sworn to protect and preserve the teachings of the Church of Mary-Sophia, as well as the bloodline of Jesus and Magdalene. Bernard was born to a family of the highest Burgundian nobility; his maternal uncle, André de Montbard, was one of the nine founding members of the Templars, an organization that would quickly become one of the most powerful forces within Europe. The secret religion of the Templars would pass down the line of future Burgundian dukes, eventually to Duke Philip the Good, as well as to Jan van Eyck.

Bernard experienced a miracle known in the Catholic tradition as the *Lactatio Bernardi,* the Lactation of Saint Bernard. While praying, the Virgin Mary appeared to him in a vision, and physically squirted her breast milk onto his lips, in answer to his deep yearning for the breast of Mary, and communion with the

The *Lactatio of Saint Bernard* of Clairvaux, engraving, sixteenth century.

Mother. Her milk granted him supernal wisdom, proving to him that she was not only his mother but the Mother of Humanity. The miracle is depicted in numerous medieval paintings, showing the nursing Mary pausing in her breastfeeding of the baby Jesus, to squeeze her breast and squirt milk across a considerable distance to the kneeling figure of Bernard.

Saint Bernard's passions for the Marys were based in the tradition of the Feminine Eucharist. In the medieval Catholic belief, breast milk of the Virgin Mary was considered to be the "transformed blood" of the Mother of God, held by Bernard and other Marian devotees to have a redemptive power similar to the blood of Jesus. Ingestion of her milk allowed him to become "at one with the Mother," initiating a deep spiritual awakening.[8]

Saint Bernard's veneration also extended to Mary Magdalene. His Cistercian Order practiced full Magdalenian liturgies whose hymns and prayers were contained in beautifully bound books adorned simply with the ornate red letters *MM*. Bernard's theologies of the Virgin Mary and Mary Magdalene inspired Jan van Eyck, and feature visually in the *Ghent Altarpiece*.

CHAMBER 26

FOUNTAIN OF LIFE

Womb of the World

ONE OF THE MOST ASTOUNDING FEMININE SYMBOLS of the *Altarpiece* is the life-giving fountain seen in the bottom of the *Mystic Lamb* panel, which clearly suggests the sacred vaginal passageway that gives birth, bestows sexual awakening, or *horasis,* and that acts as a portal to Otherworld. The yoni is known as the Gate of Heaven and Ladder of Paradise, which by no coincidence are two devotional titles of the Mother Mary. The fountain is also a world navel, a sacred well that is a portal to the Underworld, the inner womb of the earth. Van Eyck's last signed painting, *Madonna and the Fountain* (1439), also features the fountain of life, set in a *hortus conclusus*—a walled or enclosed garden, symbolic of the sacred womb container.

The Fountain as Yoni-Womb

The sacred well and fountain, containing the waters of life, hold a meaning and significance far older than Christianity as symbols of the female yoni-womb.

In the *Adoration of the Mystic Lamb* we see an octagonal fountain, deriving from the old goddess traditions. Eight is the number of petals of the Womb Flower of Inanna, the number of points of the Womb Star of Ishtar, and the sacred number of the feminine mystery school of Eleusis, symbolizing rebirth and new life.

In the *Mystic Lamb,* the fountain, containing the waters of life, is penetrated by a phallic visual line composed of a shaded stream below, and a scepterlike fountainhead rising up and through it, ending just below the womb-altar. On the scepter we see ten winged dragons spurting water, classic symbols of sexuality and

Detail of the *Mystic Lamb* panel: Sacred sexual symbolism—
phallic line composed of the stream furrow and scepterlike
fountainhead that penetrates through the eight-sided yoni fountain of life.
The head of the scepter sprays water as it rises toward the womb-altar.

the kundalini life-force energy. There are a total of thirteen waterspouts, sacred number of the feminine menstrual mysteries. This symbolism is a classic representation of the yoni-lingam, with the fountain as yoni and the scepter-fountainhead as lingam—also known as the "Chalice and the Blade" in Western alchemy.

Numerology within the painting also points to the Isis Mysteries of Resurrection. In this scene we see fourteen feminine-appearing angels around the altar, and fourteen male apostles to the bottom right of the painting, from the outside viewer's perspective. Fourteen is a number of the lunar mysteries, half of the lunar cycle. Over fourteen days the moon wanes into dissolution, and over fourteen days it waxes again in a rebirth. In this way the lunar fourteen is sacred to Isis, referring to the fourteen pieces of Osiris that she put back together, or "re-membered," for him to be rebirthed and resurrected, symbolizing the power of the waxing moon. It is no coincidence that the Christian fathers chose fourteen as the number of stations of the cross, in Christ's Passion, to symbolize his "dismemberment" at each station of his initiatory journey, followed by his resurrection—mirroring the Isis and Osiris mysteries, and the Moon Mysteries of death and rebirth.

In Christian iconography, Mother Mary and Mary Magdalene weep for Jesus at the foot of the cross, as did Isis and Nephthys for Osiris in Egyptian tradition. Many symbolic aspects of the Mary-Christ story are modeled after the Isis-Osiris myth.

Shakti and Shiva

Similar alchemical gateways are created for sacred ceremonies and ritual in India, where the lingam of Shiva, the male deity, rests inside the vulva of Shakti, the goddess. The creative power of red, the blood of the goddess, is celebrated as the primordial essence.

The lingam represents the ascending energies, and the yoni represents the descending energies and the chalice that holds; together they form a symbol of sacred union. The fountain as depicted in the *Altarpiece* and its positioning at the

Detail of the *Mystic Lamb* panel: Winged dragon fountainheads, symbolizing sexuality and kundalini life-force energy.

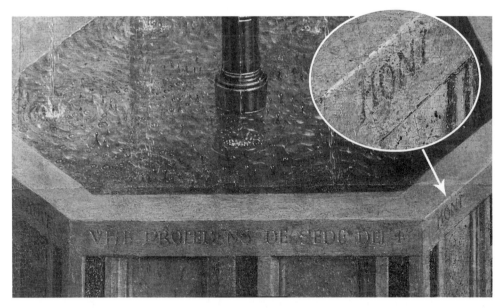

Fountain detail:
AQUE VITE PROCEDENS DE SEDE DEI + HONI

bottom of the image creates a striking tantric symbol of sacred sexual union and the descent into the Underworld, the initiatory journey of rebirth from within the Womb of the World, which both Inanna and Jesus took.

Womb Witches—Cast Out Shame

The inscription on the fountain of life below the altar, HIC EST FONS AQUE VITE PROCEDENS DE SEDE DEI + HONI, or "This is the fountain of the water of life proceeding out of the seat of god," tells us that the waters of life flow forth from the seat or throne *of Mary*—her sacred womb (see above). Seemingly out of place is the final word *HONI,* meaning "shamed" in medieval French, but its presence is quite intentional. Several authors have mistakenly reported this word to be *AGNI,* meaning "lambs," but van Eyck uses the correct Latin word for lamb, *AGNUS,* on the altar above.* What then is HONI? What has been shamed?

HONI, in this context, can refer to one thing only—the motto of the Order of the Garter: *Honi soit qui mal y pense,* or "Shame on he who think evil of it," a saying that implies the presence of hidden agendas, and a warning for others not

---

*Van Eyck cleverly uses ambiguous lettering to convey hidden messages. His letters *HO* could be easily mistaken for *AG.*

to judge what they see but do not understand. It also implies that the "feminine fountain," the Holy Womb, has been shamed, mirroring the Grail stories of old.

Duke Philip the Good based his Order of the Golden Fleece on the British Order of the Garter. "Honi" is both an acknowledgment of the British Order and a clue that a hidden message is contained within the symbolism of altar and fountain, one that the church may judge as heretical. The story of the Order of the Garter is based on the legends of the Countess of the Witches. The garter is closely linked with sexuality and pagan myths. Its founder, King Edward III, was once dancing with the Countess of Salisbury at a courtly ball, when her garter, a symbol of her initiated sexual power, fell to the floor, revealing her as a follower of the left-hand path—high or royal witchcraft, rooted in the goddess religion and the priestess lineages. The blue garter of the Order was always worn on the left side, an unusual placement in a society that associated the left with all things feminine and sinister.

Unashamedly, the king bent to pick up the countess's garter in front of the

Melusine, the fairy-mermaid ancestress of European royal houses, appearing naked next to a flowing fountain representing the chalice of her sexuality. Similar fountain symbolism is found in the *Mystic Lamb*. Woodcut print, Flanders, 1491.

shocked crowd of courtiers, strapped it to his own thigh, and declared to all present, "Honi soit qui mal y pense," warning the crowd not to judge the countess. He then created a knightly brotherhood where all members would wear the garter in solidarity. The motto communicated its secret allegiance to the feminine mysteries, asserting that after thousands of years of persecution, the "shame" did not belong to the goddess and her followers—but to those who oppressed, judged, and harmed them.

Metaphorically, in the *Mystic Lamb* painting, Our Lady's "garter" has just dropped, its feminine symbology revealed to all. The motto asks the viewer to embrace her priestess status, and the legacy of the Rose Line, not to shame or denounce it.

Among the artists of the early Renaissance, the fountain was a well-known symbol of female sexuality and commonly associated with fairy women. A fountain very similar to that in the *Mystic Lamb* appears in a woodcut illustration, created in Flanders in 1491 (see page 313), of Jean d'Arras's *The Story of the Beautiful Melusine*. In it the naked mermaid-fairy Melusine, who hails from Avalon, stands next to a flowing fountain, a symbol of her sexuality, opposite her future husband, Count Raymond. To this day the European royal houses of Luxembourg, Anjou, Plantagenet, and others claim descent from the mermaid line, the Mary-line, of Melusine, a coded reference to the royal witch lineages who maintained their secret practices in some of the most important royal families of Europe.

CHAMBER 27

JOHN THE BAPTIST

Waters of Life

JOHN THE BAPTIST FEATURES PROMINENTLY in the *Ghent Altarpiece* because he is the spiritual midwife of Magdalene and Jesus, and was the original prophet of the baptismal mysteries. In the painting he sits on the mystical left-hand side, while Mary holds the position of the *gerivah* on the right, as the "power behind the throne." Jesus is noticeably missing as a central figure. In heretical traditions John the Baptist often symbolized the original spirit of Christianity, inherited from the mystery schools, rather than the "divine savior" character of Jesus that was created by the Roman Catholic Church, which did not represent the true Jesus or the Christ teachings.

John was a guardian of rebirth *through the element of water,* a position he inherited from the original lineage of the baptismal priestesses of Nammu of ancient Sumeria. *The rite of baptism represents birth and rebirth through the sacred waters of the feminine womb.* Like all of the ancient feminine rites and sacred passages, it is grounded in a physical, biological reality common to all humans. Each of us spends the first nine months of life in the watery world of our mother's womb. At a primal, instinctive level, we are water creatures *first*. Long before our feet touch the earth, our deepest unconscious memories and earliest experiences were formed in water. Why do we love hot baths and swimming pools so much? Why do we feel cleansed and refreshed, not just physically but also energetically, after being in water? Water takes us directly to our source—to the deep memories of the maternal womb that comforted and birthed us.

The traditional process of baptism was a naked, full-body immersion in a body of flowing water. A spiritual midwife assisted the initiate by tipping her backward, head first, until fully submerged, as the rebirthing waters of life rushed past her head. Baptism mimics our physical birth, or "first birth," through the womb of our mother. As labor deepens and the moment of birth approaches, the amniotic membrane that contains us in a watery womb bubble bursts. The amniotic fluids rush past us like a river as we slide head first and upside down through the birth canal. Emerging from the waters of life, we take our first breath of air as we are "born again."

Returning to the hieroglyphs of Isis (page 294), we come to the final two images of the egg and goddess that elegantly symbolize the powers of rebirth—the divine egg that births Creation, and woman as the "Eve" or "Magdalene" that births and rebirths all future generations of humanity. Across the world, the earliest spiritual traditions recognized that the womb of the goddess, with her earthly priestesses, gives birth to the divine masculine. In the ancient Egyptian religion, the goddess Hathor is the mother of the god known as Horus. Her name, *H-T H-R,* literally translates "House of Horus"; but its deeper meaning is "Womb of God," the divine womb that births the god.

In the *Ghent Altarpiece,* the fountain, the stream of water that emerges from it, and blood of the Holy Grail all represent the baptismal waters of the feminine yoni and womb that also lead down into the underworld portal of the Earth Womb and her Living Waters.

The Origins of Baptism

Along with the eucharist, baptism is one of the most iconic and important rituals in the Christian tradition. Where did the practice of baptism begin? Like most Christian traditions, we can find its roots in the goddess traditions of the ancient Near East. In Mesopotamia, ritual baptismal and purifying pools were called Abzu basins—basins containing the holy and purifying waters sourced from the subterranean abyss. Abzu pools were found in every temple across the ancient Near East, and were carried forward in the traditions of Judaism, Christianity, and Islam under different names, but with the same essential functions.

One notable difference was that with the patriarchal religions, the rites were administered by male priests rather than priestesses. But the traces of their goddess roots persist. Christian bishops still wear a headpiece called a miter, shaped like a fish's mouth, the costume of the original mermaid and mermen priesthood, as we have learned. (See Apkallu figures on page 60.)

John the Merman

John the Baptist, the man given credit for originating the Christian tradition of baptism, was a merman, his camel-hair shirt soaked in the time-honored waters of the ancient goddess traditions. He hailed from a spiritual lineage that likely began with the water goddess Nammu; her water purification rites formed the substance of John's ministry. Those who are curious can trace the descent from Nammu to the water god Enki who stole her powers, to Enki's fish-robed shaman priests, and to the Babylonian fish-sage Oannes, the "Hermes of Babylon," whose name is the equivalent of "John." The signs and symbols of his involvement with the old ways of the feminine are clear for those with the eyes to see.

John ran an important baptismal mystery school at the time of Jesus and Mary Magdalene. His camp was located in the wildlands east of Jericho, on the banks of the River Jordan, which he famously used for full-body, immersive baptism in its running waters. John was notoriously fiery in his character, but paradoxically baptized through the soft power of the water element. His own initiation into the baptismal rites of the feminine Holy Spirit occurred in the womb of his mother, Elizabeth, while she was carrying him—his was a *baptism in utero*. The Gospel of Luke 1:15 recounts that, "even from his mother's womb he [John the Baptist] will be filled with Holy Spirit." John was said to be the cousin of Jesus, born from Virgin Mary's sister Elizabeth and her husband Zechariah. The Holy Spirit was transmitted into Elizabeth when she met with her sister Mary. As Mother Mary, herself a priestess in the goddess traditions, felt the energetic transmission pass to Elizabeth, she proclaimed, "Blessed are you among women, and blessed is the fruit of your womb!" (Luke 1:42).

Christian iconography shows that John baptized Jesus with waters poured from a scallop shell that across all time and culture originally symbolized the waters of the vulva and womb. The scallop shell is a common theme in Catholic holy water fonts, and has always been a symbol of the goddess religion, as is famously encoded in Botticelli's painting *The Birth of Venus* where the goddess is seen emerging from a huge scallop shell "yoni," rising up naked and sensuous from the waters of creation. A Greek *Hora* goddess hands the *red-haired* Venus a *red* robe adorned with flowers. Her red iconography is a nod to the symbology of Mary Magdalene, whose tradition was favored by the studios of Medici that employed Sandro Botticelli, himself a master of the underground feminine mysteries.[1]

The scallop shell symbol of the goddess Venus, mistress of sexual love, has earlier origins in the iconography of Aphrodite, as she was called in Greece, dating back to the sixth century BCE or before. The priestesses at the Greek temples of Aphrodite would click scallop shells together with their fingers to keep rhythm in song and dance, a tradition we still see today in the finger castanets of flamenco dancers. Because of their resemblance to female genitalia, oysters have also been traditionally used as aphrodisiacs to induce sexual desire, the name deriving from the goddess Aphrodite.

Shells of all types, including scallop, oyster, conch, and cowry, have been symbols of the yoni across time and in many cultures of the world. John the Baptist's use of the scallop shell gives him away as a mer-minister, but the goddess symbology does not end there.

At the moment of his baptism of Jesus, the dove of the feminine Holy Spirit descends from heaven, filling Jesus with divine spirit and initiating him in his

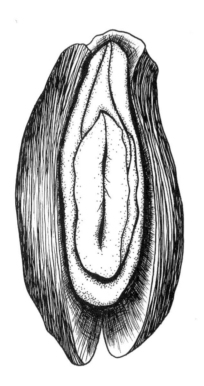
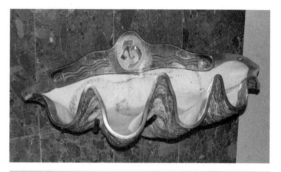

Left: Illustration of a scallop/oyster in its shell—with its unmistakable resemblance to the yoni—the origin of the ceremonial vulva-scallop cup used by John the Baptist to pour the baptismal waters. On the right we have scallop-shaped baptismal fonts; the top is from the Black Madonna cathedral of Montserrat, with an iconic M for Mary, from Catalonia, Spain. The bottom right is from the Cajetan Church of Salzburg, Austria.

(Scallop illustration by Natvienna Hanell. Cajetan font photo by Andreas Praefcke, CC BY 3.0)

ministry. In John's lifetime, the dove was the well-known sign of Inanna-Ishtar, Aphrodite, Asherah, and other goddesses of the ancient Near East. It would become a symbol of the Virgin Mary, and secretly MM as well, in the Christian iconography.

Baptism in the Nude

In ancient Sumeria, most sacred water rituals took place in the darkened temple adyta, the innermost sanctums and holy of holies. In these rituals, the priests and priestesses were traditionally naked.[2] The adyta symbolized the womb of the goddess. Just as we are naked in our human mother's womb, so do we enter the sacred womb space of the mother goddess—naked, open, with no protections or defenses, revealing ourselves completely.

Another related practice in ancient Sumeria was the ritual full-body baptism of menarchal girls in special canals. After their first moontime, they would bathe naked in the canal, ceremonially cleansing and anointing themselves. The ritual would mark their entry into society, as adult women who would soon be ready for courtship, and later marriage.[3]

In ancient fashion, John's ministry included the baptism of both men *and* women, who would immerse fully naked in the flowing waters of the River Jordan, a controversial act in his time but a traditional practice for a priest or priestess of the ancient goddess traditions. The style of baptism practiced by John the Baptist was recorded by the church father Hippolytus in *The Apostolic Tradition:*

> At the hour in which the cock crows, they shall first pray over the water . . .
> the water shall be pure and flowing, that is, the water of a spring or a flowing
> body of water. Then they shall take off all their clothes. The children shall be
> baptized first. . . . After this, the men will be baptized. Finally, the women, after
> they have unbound their hair, and removed their jewelry. No one shall take any
> foreign object with themselves down into the water.[4]

Another patriarch of the Christian Church, Cyril, also noted the use of anointing oils: "Having stripped yourselves, ye were naked. . . . Then, when ye were stripped, ye were anointed with exorcised oil. . . . After these things, ye were led to the holy pool of Divine Baptism."[5]

John the Baptist was closely connected to Mary Magdalene in the secret traditions passed down through the Cathars and Templars into the occult societies and art guilds of Renaissance Europe. As mentioned earlier, Templar legends hold that John the Baptist was Mary Magdalene's first husband, and that the skull depicted with Magdalene in Renaissance paintings was his. The Templars, with John as their first prophet and religious leader, secretly worshipped Mary Magdalene.[6]

John, who baptized with water, prepared the way for Jesus, who would later baptize with fire. "I baptize you with water . . . he [who comes after me] will baptize you with the Holy Spirit . . . and with fire" (Matthew 3:11). Whereas baptism with water encodes the ritual first birth from the mother, baptism with fire is a symbolic reference to the esoteric rites of the second birth, the initiations of sexual union within the bridal chamber of sacred spiritual lovers.

In the Bible, we also see the ritual of *rebirth through the earth element* in Jesus's three-day entombment and spiritual descent into the womb of the earth. This completes his baptismal journey through the four elements of the womb cross, and through the secret "fifth element" and gateway of the central womb portal.

In the *Ghent Altarpiece* the Fountain of Life serves as the baptismal pool, its eight sides mirroring the eight-pointed stargate of Ishtar and eight-petaled rosette of the Eleusinian Mysteries. Baptismal fonts in churches often replicate this octagonal feminine iconography.

Through the baptismal Abzu basins of Sumerian temples and the river baptisms of menarchal girls, as well as through links with the Babylonian merman Oannes, scallop shells, anointing oils, and nude ceremony, we can begin to see that the roots of baptism emerge from the fertile soil of the goddess tradition. The Mesopotamian rites that heavily influenced Jewish and Christian practice can be traced back five thousand years to the original water rituals of the mer-maid priestesses of Nammu. They are also intricately wrapped around the myth and legend of Mary Magdalene, much as the serpents wind around the dragon vessel of Lagash.

The *Ghent Altarpiece* celebrates this illustrious and forbidden heritage of the mermaid goddess, and directs our gaze to the secret Templar doctrines brought from the Holy Land.

CHAMBER 28

DIVINE SOPHIA

Return to Love

EMANATING DAZZLING RAYS OF LIGHT, the crowned divine Dove hovers over the top center of the *Ghent Altarpiece,* bestowing her celestial benediction and blessing to the creation she birthed. This is her story—the forgotten and forbidden tale of the cosmic goddess who descended, pouring herself into matter to become the world. She is the Divine Sophia, who seeks the restoration of love.

The dove of the Holy Sophia.

Virgin Mary as Sophia

We now move to the Upperworld of the *Altarpiece,* representing the heavenly realms, setting the cosmic scene in which the narrative unfolds. If we need any further clues to the importance of the Virgin Mary, we see her again as the stunningly beautiful enthroned virgin, light radiating from her countenance as she reads her book of wisdom. She appears as part of a slightly unusual *Deësis* configuration, unusual due to the mysterious identity of the central deity figure, the "man in red," as we will soon read.

Deësis is a Greek word meaning "prayer" or "supplication," and in paintings refers to specific Byzantine or Eastern Orthodox form with a central Christ figure flanked by the Virgin Mary at his right and John the Baptist at his left. The

Virgin Mary, Deity, and John the Baptist panels of the *Ghent Altarpiece.*
Mary sits at the right-hand side of the deity figure, in the power position.
Note the crown at the feet of the red-robed central figure.

significance of the Deësis arrangement in the *Altarpiece* is that it shows Mary enthroned in the seat of honor—she sits at the *right-hand side* of the deity figure, indicating her position as highest authority, second only to God. Mary, in the position of the gevirah, is queen mother of the earth, of the world, of the heavens.

This panel also reveals that in the eyes of Jan van Eyck, Mary *is* Sophia, the gnostic goddess and personification of Divine Wisdom. Above Mary's head we see verses 7:29 and 7:26 from the Wisdom of Solomon, a text he used to describe the Virgin Mary in several paintings:

She [Sophia] is more beautiful than the sun, and above the whole order of stars. When compared with the light, she is found to precede it. For she is the brightness of eternal light [and] the unspotted mirror of God.

**Detail of Mary-Sophia's crown, showing both the white lilies of purity
and maternal love, and the red rose of passion.**

The Wisdom of Solomon, also called the Book of Wisdom, is one of the seven sapiential (wisdom) books of the Jewish tradition that are included in the Roman Catholic and Orthodox Christian Bibles. For those with the eyes to see, these books contain the seeds of the future gnostic Jewish philosophy. In the Wisdom of Solomon, Sophia is Lady Wisdom. The first line states that the book is a message to "the rulers of the world," a gnostic phrase referring to the adversarial energies that have forgotten true wisdom, beauty, and the place of the Divine Feminine. By including this passage, van Eyck is cleverly communicating that his painting *is conveying a gnostic message*—an appeal to the holders of worldly power to turn back to the path of Sophia, the mystical way of Feminine Wisdom.

The mythos of Sophia was a gnostic Christian creation—a feminine divinity born through the fertile intersection of Jewish, Greek, Egyptian, and Mesopotamian mystical traditions in the centuries leading up to the birth of Jesus. The sacred gnostic texts, and the gnostics themselves, were almost completely destroyed by the Church of Rome in the fourth and fifth centuries. Those who weren't killed were forced to flee or go underground. Their mystical manuscripts were considered lost forever until their gradual rediscovery, beginning in 1769 with James Bruce, who bought *The Gnosis of Light* and *The Gnosis of the Invisible God* from traders in Upper Egypt. The magnificent libraries of Nag Hammadi and the Qumran community at the Dead Sea were recovered in 1945 and 1946.

As we learn in the banned gnostic texts, the *original* Christianity, the religion practiced by Jesus, Mary Magdalene, and many others was a *gnostic,* or *mystical, Christianity.* They celebrated the mysteries of the Tree of Life, the Bridal Chamber, and the Resurrection—as was seen when Jesus symbolically raised Lazarus from the dead—spiritual rebirth after a descent into the womb-tomb.

The *Ghent Altarpiece* is truly gnostic, and Jan van Eyck knew the gnostic stories through the underground societies of Burgundy, descending from the original Church of Mary Magdalene; he then encoded these mysteries into the *Ghent Altarpiece.* We will take a closer look at how he did this, but first we must learn more about the Aeon Sophia.

Aeon Sophia—The Cosmic Mother

The gnostic books of the Pistis Sophia, Gospel of Mary Magdalene, and others paint a picture of a very different cosmic reality compared to the traditional Judeo-Christian story. Gnostic myths of creation read like a blockbuster Hollywood science-fiction film, an epic spiritual struggle between the forces of good and evil, truth and deception, which have shaped the universe we now live in. Each gnostic tale is different, but together they tell the story of Sophia, a feminine divinity who is the highest source of wisdom.

Sophia is an Aeon, a goddess and primordial force of creation who gives birth to the universe we now inhabit—the universe, in fact, is her body. In some ways she could also be thought of as a she-dragon of creation, as she shares the same creative powers of Tiamat and Nammu as well as Srin Mo of Tibet and the birthing dragons of many other cultures. Gnostic stories, in a convoluted way, describe how Sophia, in her passion, impetuously creates the world prematurely, without the help of her syzygy, her matching masculine counterpart and creative partner. What births is a material world inherently out of balance, as well as a host of deranged spirit "children" called archons. Legions of these lost, ignorant, confused, and misguided archon spirits wage war on their mother Sophia, representing the earth, as well as the whole of the human race, her true children. Sophia "falls" from the heavens (the *pleroma*), becoming trapped in her own distorted creation, unable to return.

The gnostic myth is a retelling, by male philosophers, of an older feminine story, but with a gender switch. In the original tales it is a *male* god who attempts to create life without the feminine, resulting in catastrophe. The earliest stories are recounted in Sumeria, as we have read earlier, when the birth mother Ninhursag's powers are stolen, and the male god is unable to infuse his creations with the organic light. In either version, the point remains that when a world is birthed without the input of both masculine and feminine energies, a disaster results. In the gnostic story, archonic beings are born without the feminine light of love within them; they then wreak havoc on the cosmos.

The Archons of False Power

The *Ghent Altarpiece* picks up the thread of this gnostic story: the fall of feminine consciousness at the hands of an adversarial energy.

The gnostic Gospel of Mary describes the journey of the ascent of the soul, as shared by Jesus in a vision. Mary Magdalene tells how each of the seven chief archons, the "Powers of Wrath," challenge them on their ascent, interrogating them, and attempting to imprison their souls. This journey takes place on the inner, spiritual dimensions for Jesus and Mary, but it also refers to the "real-world" archonic energy that desecrated the sacred lineages of womb shamans and priestesses, including the genocide of the Neanderthals.

In the Gospel of Mary, after his rebirth initiation, Jesus says: "What binds me has been slain . . . ignorance has died." However, ignorance has not yet been slain in his disciples. Peter, unable to believe Mary's account, challenges her, and Levi exclaims: "Now I see you [Peter] contending against the woman like the Adversaries."[1] This reveals that feminine-hating energies were well known, even at the birth of Christianity. Peter, as we know, would go on to found the Catholic Church.

In gnostic lore, the archons, through their powers of deception, have infected and taken control of the minds of most humans, like a virus of consciousness. Their human hosts become *agents* of the archons and are manipulated into doing their bidding, generally without any awareness of this fact. Over thousands of years this destructive consciousness has worked through the "Rulers of the World" to create the dysfunctional world we live in today. Humans and institutions infected with the archonic programs have lost touch with the reality of the Mother. The false "matrix" they have created is a deceptive virtual-reality world (inspiring the movie of the same name), superimposed on the natural one birthed from the womb of the true mother-matrix. This explains why humanity seems so at odds with nature, exploiting Earth's resources and hurtling the world toward a mass species extinction.

The head of the archons is the "false god," a misguided demiurge who perpetuates a world of suffering. His influence is seen whenever murder, violence, rape, or hate is incited. This false god is a usurper of the true divinity, a shapeshifting imposter who can also assume the name of any god of any tradition. The gnostic texts call the demiurge blind and childish; his distinguishing features are ignorance, arrogance, and domination. Archonic forces exist in the external world, but most importantly, the archonic drama unfolds within each of us at an esoteric, spiritual level, as does the Sophianic redemption. Sophia is the primordial cerebellar consciousness, and the archon is the separated self that does not remember its origins in the timeless infinite consciousness of love or that Sophia is its true Mother. Each of us must face these archonic energies within ourselves, as Yeshu and MM did, and choose to follow love above all else.

The god of love is encoded in the great mystery of the original tetragrammaton, YHVH, which has ancient origins, including feminine and masculine aspects. It is a doorway to the infinite Creator, and is a magical name, existing beyond gender. Hidden within the tetragrammaton is H-V-H, the Hebrew name for Eve, *Havah,* which means "to give life." It is the kundalini serpent, the living energy, the divine presence, the mother-father of Creation. It is not to be confused with a tribal god or demiurge who promotes fear, intolerance, hatred, or killing. Mary Magdalene and Yeshu follow the path of the true god/dess of infinite compassion, drawing from the ancient Jewish wisdom traditions that promote balance and honor life.

The surviving gnostic texts (representing only a fraction of the original manuscripts and oral traditions) remember only a partial story. We suggest a distilled synthesis of the original vision might read like this: Somehow a fracture of cosmic consciousness has occurred resulting in an imbalance of the masculine and feminine energies of creation. As a result of this trauma, an infectious archonic program has distorted collective human consciousness. Current institutions, including religions, have inherited this mental-spiritual virus and contribute (knowingly or not) to the disharmony and destruction of our natural world. In our patriarchal epoch, the Lower Sophia, the feminine divinity *within* the physical matter of our earth and bodies, has been denigrated, abused, and forgotten; the Higher Sophia, the celestial Divine Mother, is still remembered and venerated in some circles, but she too is mostly forgotten or devalued.

The hidden heart-womb, or *sha,* of gnosticism is the call to unite the Upper and Lower Sophia, the numinous sacred feminine spark within spirit and matter, and to return our consciousness to a deep interconnection with the natural worlds. The Sophia is our Earth, our mother Gaia; everything on this planet is a part of her—plants, animals, mountains, rivers, and humans. When our human consciousness once again resonates with Gaia-Sophia, we will birth creations that support *life.* The trajectory of our human cultural evolution will once again join in harmony with Gaia's evolutionary impulse. We will co-create and coevolve with our Mother planet in love; as a result, our species and her biosphere will thrive.

Red-Robed Deity: God or Imposter?

With the gnostic myths in mind, we can better understand the dominating male figure who looms over the world, decked out in the sigils of power. What we see is the earthly Garden of Sophia, the divinized matter of the Cosmic Mother, presided over by the "ruler of the world"—an archonic male ruler, the fallen demiurge or false god. He is a son of the goddess who has forgotten she who birthed him and where the source of his power truly resides.

The central deity figure immediately commands our attention, resplendent in his red robes, scepter, and papal tiara, all symbols of *worldly* power. But, at first glance, van Eyck has intentionally made his identity ambiguous, and somewhat

Detail: The Sabaoth God.

disturbing. Is this God, Jesus, or someone else entirely? The traditional Deësis configuration includes Jesus as the central figure, not God. But art scholars agree that this figure is intentionally ambiguous, and does not appear to be Jesus. He has no wounds of the crucifixion on his hands, no halo, nor is the name Jesus written anywhere on his person.

Above his head, the writing identifies this dominating figure as God, "This is God the almighty on account of his Divine Majesty." On his chest are embroidered the letters SABAWT, *Sabaoth* in Hebrew, which translates as "armies" or "hosts." He is identified as the Old Testament "God of Armies," the male god who smites and rules the world with an iron rod—the false god. The God of the Armies was a very painful reality to all those of the Cathar, Pagan, Jewish, Templar, and other heretical faiths who were slaughtered in the millions during the Catholic Inquisition, and the indigenous peoples colonized around the world. "Sabaoth" was also the given name of an archon, a son of the false god, and demon figure in gnostic creation myths.

We see the true crown of divine sovereignty is not on his head but on the ground below him. What is this holy and sacred object doing there?

If we step back and adjust our vision slightly, we can see that it actually crowns the dove of the feminine Holy Spirit directly below, symbolic of the Celestial Sophia and Queen of the Heavens (see facing page). The man in red is not the true divinity; the Sophia is.

Memes repeat themselves to emphasize hidden truths. The only figures that wear the full crown in the *Altarpiece* are the Virgin Mary and the dove, both representations of Sophia, consistent in all of van Eyck's paintings. The figures that

The crowned dove, representing the Holy Spirit, the Celestial Sophia, Queen of the Heavens and Earth.

wear the papal tiara are the red-robed deity and the popes in the *Mystic Lamb* panel below, symbols of an authority that rules by force, and often oppression.

The red deity figure is an imposter. He has stolen the sacred red robe of queenship, the scarlet cloak that throughout time represented the menstrual powers of the *female womb shamans,* and the key symbol representing Mary Magdalene as the left-hand Christ. This archonic figure rules over the world wearing the appropriated robes of the goddess, taking her sacred womb powers as his own, displacing the Holy Sophia. And of course, because he cannot actually birth or menstruate, he must shed the blood of sacrifice.

A Stormy Heaven

The presence of the red-robed, false god has disrupted the heavenly realms. We can see this in the unhappy faces of Adam and Eve, who are painfully separated from each other, pushed to opposite ends of the heavenly tier. Adam's gaze is downcast; he appears sad. Above him Cain and Abel, his first two children with Eve according to the book of Genesis, scrabble to see whose offering to God is "better"—the sheep of the pastoralist (Abel) or the grain of the farmer (Cain). Eve also appears lonely and depressed. She holds a bitter lemon in her hand, not a sweet red apple. Above her a scene depicts her son Cain killing his brother Abel, after God refuses to accept Cain's offering of grain. This is not the result of fallen "sinners," but a deviant god who has cursed humanity. This is the story that van Eyck shares.

In the gnostic story of creation, the false god, representing patriarchy, rapes and abuses Eve, fathering the two sons by her who are cursed to death and violence—Cain and Abel. It is only when Eve reunites with her true partner, Adam, that peace is restored. Together they conceive Seth, their red-haired son, linked to the Neanderthal race, and a true line of humanity is born. Gnostics consider themselves the "seed of Seth."

Sophia's Return: Reunion of Adam and Eve

The *Ghent Altarpiece* presents two opposite visions of the world. One reading yields the "old story" of the Bible, the myth of a fallen world. The feminine principle has been abused and desecrated by the archonic forces that cunningly hide in the patriarchal religions, as seen in the gnostic stories of the rape of Eve and Sophia. Masculine and feminine are rent apart from each other, and from God. God curses women's wombs; they must give birth in pain and suffering. Menstruation is considered a vile pollution. The Garden of Eve is lost, human consciousness falls. Salvation is dependent on a blood sacrifice of "the son," an image of torture and suffering.

But there is hope yet, as van Eyck also presents an entirely new, and at the same time ancient, vision in which the feminine is restored. The garden of earthly paradise is renewed as the Higher and Lower Sophia are unified. Multitudes pilgrimage for this great occasion. Sexuality and the creation of new life are celebrated in the bodies of earth and human women. Masculine and feminine energies come back into harmony. The feminine eucharistic and anointing waters bless the land, and all who are witness. The Holy Grail of the womb is honored. The human woman Mary Magdalene is honored for her role in the great remembering, the great return. The two Marys, representing sexual union and sacred motherhood, merge to become the New Eve, the New Ark of the Covenant, giving birth to a new humanity with a beautiful future.

This alternative vision of a redemption through the restored Divine Feminine, in balance with the Divine Masculine, is hinted at in the words written in the book lying open next to the Virgin Mary in the Annunciation scene. By way of wordplay, something is being *announced* to the viewer of the painting, heralding a new birth of Christ consciousness. When we look carefully, we can find the words *de visione dei,* or "the seeing of God."

These words beautifully encapsulate the painting—it is a new vision of God, a new revelation *a new cosmology.* We finally have the eyes to see what the hidden mysteries taught for thousands of years, a message of hope, redemption, salvation, and resurrection, of beauty and love, through the knowing that our original birth template is *not* corrupted, but is infused with the most brilliant divine light.

Our tour is now complete. We must use our visionary inner eye to see the final picture, when the great side panels of the *Ghent Altarpiece* are folded back into their closed position and the inner Adam and Eve figures move from their position of terrible separation to join each other once again, side by side, enfolded back into the womb-throne of God, a trinity of union.

Within the painting the "Two become One" again. Separation is healed.

PORTAL THREE

MAGDALENE VISION QUEST

Pilgrimage Path: Stories, Oracles, and Personal Rituals

Pilgrim's Guide

She bore the perfection of earthly paradise, both roots and branches.
It was a thing men call the Grail.

THE GRAIL QUEEN, DESCRIBED BY
WOLFRAM VON ESCHENBACH IN *PARZIVAL*

WE HAVE NOW JOURNEYED THROUGH ancient herstory, and dived into the heretical art and symbology that medieval alchemists used to preserve the memory of the Magdalene Mysteries. But our journey does not end here. In many ways, this is where it *truly* begins, because the path of Sophia and her Magdalenes is a *living energy that is still unfolding now, calling to us.* It is important to get our bearings in the stories of the past and to discover the gifts and grief there. Yet what is most crucial is to open ourselves to this wisdom and bring forth our own initiation, in the here and now, walking on earth in these times, embodying this feminine wisdom way. Often the deep wisdom of the Magdalene is not to be found in books or academic facts; it lives like a living transmission held within the land memory, within our own bodies, hearts, and souls.

We now enter into our own personal *Magdalene Vision Quest,* where you will be guided to journey around the Magdalene Mandala—also known as the Wheel of the Witches. Here you will discover what aspect of this wisdom tradition truly sings to you, and also discover rituals, incantation, and prayers of the Magdalene Mysteries to create an embodied practice in your life.

When you look back on your life you may find a red thread that has laced through many of your experiences and knowings, calling you to this moment. Our personal stories hold so much treasure and are our own inner manuscript, our own pilgrimage of discovery and learning.

I (Seren) will begin by sharing some of the inner sources that inspired my own

Magdalene Vision Quest, and my own pilgrimage in the Celtic Grail tradition of my birth. Your connection with experiences, lands, and ancestors different to mine are also a vitally important part of the global weaving of the Magdalene Mysteries. So take the time to journal your own connections, insights, and memories that come from your own unique perspective.

Magdalene is returning as the Feminine Christ within every woman, within every being.

CHAMBER 29

HONORING THE MOTHERLINE

Walking the Red Path

What is pink? A rose is pink
By a fountain's brink.
What is red? A poppy's red.

. . .

What is white?
A swan is white
Sailing in the light.

"COLOR," CHRISTINA ROSSETTI

MY VISIONS OF MAGDALENE when I was thirteen had linked this religious figure and saint with the Womb and feminine shamanism. Of course, at that age I had no conscious idea about that connection, so for a long time they remained separate.

At age twenty-eight, following a diagnosis of endometriosis, in order to heal I began to connect with the divinity of my womb, understanding that there were stories etched into my womb lining that needed telling—and not only my stories but those of the women in my ancestral lineage, and the ancient stories of the women in my spiritual lineage.

I also understood that my womb was more than just a physical organ, but that she was the Holy Grail, the embodiment of the Divine Feminine creative power. I needed to reclaim her legacy of love, and to initiate the enthronement of the Earthly Sophia. All women were the holy throne of god and their wombs the original sacred altars. Our sacred feminine essence needed honoring and healing. We were creative magicians, naturally. I needed to remember this power.

The ancient feminine path of womb magic spoke directly to my feminine soul, giving me the courage to trust what was unfolding. Threads of ancient priestess soul memory suddenly lined up and landed inside me, as I consciously began Womb Awakening—allowing the Divine Mother, the Ancient Mothers, the moon cycles, and my own Womb knowing to guide me.

I connected my womb back to the moon cycles with conscious menstruation and lunar ritual, used healing herbs, essential oils, and nutritional cleansing, and prayed to the Divine Mother. I was devoted to the spiritual path of Shakti, pilgrimaging to India, studying with teachers, visiting various Shakti temples, including the beautiful Chamunda Devi Temple in Himachal Pradesh, a temple with a secret womb cave, which became my spiritual home and inspiration. In Europe I visited Black Madonna cathedrals, ancient landscapes, and stone circles, searching for the path of the Great Mother. We had inherited one-sided stories, and I craved a complete holistic circle—there was a united feminine vision that wove together the world.

Magdalene—Spirit Keeper of the Womb

As this new awareness of the spiritual power of the womb awakened within me, I pilgrimaged to a remote village in Odisha, India, and then to Rajasthan, where I spent six months studying classical Indian temple dance, Odissi, based on the path of the devadasis.

Yet my womb and all the spiritual omens kept pointing me back West—to Christianity and to Mary Magdalene, Mother Mary, and the Mary priestesses.

Back home, in the soft light of ancient churches, I also found myself inside a spiritual womb, a hand-created cave, a temple designed for a second birth. I looked around and saw female saints, the Mother of God, the priestess Apostle of Apostles, whose words had been silenced, but whose presence was still radiating out from these places of worship.

As I opened up to the tantric possibilities of a mystical Christianity of the "Mary Path," life began to share the secrets of my coming-of-age vision with me— received at an age that indigenous traditions say a person receives the "download" that will guide their life. As the veil was peeled away, it revealed that Mary Magdalene was a spirit keeper of the Womb, and that she was returning to help us awaken our holy center, symbolized by the Black Madonna.

I knew we had to heal the Motherline—personal, ancestral, and cosmic, and create a new cosmology. This is the work of the great restoration and return. Inside our mother's womb, we are encoded for our life, on biological and spiritual levels. It becomes the Womb of God.

If this connection is broken or disrupted, our connection with Source is lost, fractured, or distorted. The womb of the mother forges our perception of the universal reality, which is either filled with coldness, disconnection, despair, and separation, or with the joy of life, connection to a nourishing source, and union. We then go on to replicate this "womb world" in our life.

There is a Divine Mother wisdom within the consciousness of the body of the Cosmos, and the Earth, and our own sacred bodies that we can awaken to "remother" ourselves and heal toxic imprints. Mystics call this the Holy Spirit. There is a dazzling love that birthed us, with an umbilical cord connected to our spiritual center—called the holy of holies, the womb of our soul, by gnostics. When we heal the Motherline to restore the Red Thread, we are born again in love.

Through the guidance of Mary Magdalene I realized that I needed to remember how to come alive as a woman again; and how to *become a force of nature*. I needed to reunite my feminine source, my womb-soul, with the center of Earth, the heart of Gaia.

Return of the Moon Colleges

Magdalene was a presence rooted in the landscape of the earth and the landscape of the body; she called me inward to meet the elemental powers of creation. This was her holy gospel—sung across the winds, and spelled out on wildish seascapes. It was wild and innocent, love drenched and ecstatic, the shimmer of the Holy Spirit.

She called me to a goddess path, whose track lines had been walked on for thousands of years by priestesses who were not only legends and myth, but who were once living, breathing women, who had experienced everything I also faced. I could hear them whisper to me with encouragement, and I felt the imprint of their path lighting up inside me. Their legacy was rebirthing through modern-day women across the world.

It sounded fantastical to the logical, everyday thinking self. But it was utterly real. Emerging from an ancient mist, the temples of the goddess were awakening. The feminine arts of the moon colleges were returning; with sacred music, ritual adornment, ceremonial living, temple dance, herbal lore, sacred anointing, water baptism, lustral ritual, oils, scents, love poetry, and sexual magic. In this sacred realm, a woman's body power was bold, ensouled, and wildly ravishing, and this expression of sexual allurement was not only safe but was revered as holy.

This was the soul embodiment of Sophia—*Wisdom*—a rapturous, enchanted feminine energy; a cosmic multidimensional mistress of the mystery of dark matter, the weft and warp of all life. All the great mystics who entered the mystery agreed: the universe is vibrating like a strummed harp, singing like choirs of angels, weaving, dancing, and celebrating like a cosmic allurement of temple priestesses. I also came to learn this: that many of the places and sacred sites that legend and folklore link to Mary Magdalene were once important goddess lairs and mystery schools.

These threads of legend, when woven together, begin to form a curriculum—an education of sorts, a telluric apprenticeship in the Rose Line, for her pilgrims.

Glastonbury
Lady of Avalon

MEETING THE LADY OF AVALON
And did those feet in ancient time
Walk upon England's mountains green?

And was the holy Lamb of God
On England's pleasant pastures seen?
And did the countenance divine
Shine forth upon our clouded hills?

WILLIAM BLAKE (1757–1827)

I was first called to the pilgrimage site of Glastonbury—the sacred Isle of Avalon. This sacred place of fairy lore and lost myths is an important key in the Celtic weave of the Magdalene Mysteries. Not only is it the site of the first Christian church in Britain, folklore also says Mother Mary and Jesus visited, as did Mary Magdalene.

Glastonbury, with its mystical red and white springs and chalice well, is a place of sacred union that has been sacred to the goddess for thousands of years, and is an important pilgrimage site to this day. There is wild magic in this land. The Lady of Avalon, who resides there, is guarding the chalice of the Holy Grail and its mysteries. An ancient goddess worship site, it was probably also the seat of an ancient feminine mystery school, which drew Magdalene and many of her priestess line.

Glastonbury was a key to this Magdalene memory, as if her footsteps had left a map.

Legends say that after the crucifixion, Joseph of Arimathea arrived in Glastonbury with twelve disciples to establish the first Church of Christ on British lands. It was said that he was also carrying the Holy Grail, a sacred cup that had collected the blood of Christ as it flowed out from the wound in his side. This myth could also be interpreted to mean that he was escorting Mary Magdalene and her holy bloodline.

This original Church of the Grail was founded in 63 CE by Joseph of Arimathea, becoming one of the first churches in the world built on the goddess's holy land. Everything about this *primera* church speaks to a legacy of Marian worship, an ancient memory of the mermaids of Mary, the priestesses of the Divine Mother.

According to twelfth-century historian William of Malmesbury in *De Antiquitate glastoniensis,* Joseph and his circle of refugees from Palestine received a vision from the angel Gabriel, who told them to build a church in honor of the Holy Mother of God, presumed to be the Virgin Mary, in her role as the Divine Mother. The special site for the church came in a heavenly revelation, and was located by a sacred spring, dedicated to the goddess, which was then housed as a Holy Well.

Built from traditional wattle and daub, this early place of Christian worship of the Mother was built in small circular form, honoring the sacred womb. This specific style of church design was later emulated by both Templars and Freemasons, who made it clear in their sacred texts that the dimensions symbolized the feminine and the regenerative womb of rebirth.

Glastonbury Abbey was eventually built on the site of this archaic church, with a Mary Chapel and crypt containing Saint Joseph's Well being constructed directly over this original sacred site, known in local lore as the "vagina of the birth goddess." The Mary Chapel, within the Glastonbury Abbey complex, is still renowned for its spiritual potency, and its design is based on the *gematria,* or sacred geometry, of the vesica piscis, where two circles come together in sacred union to form a yoni portal, or mandorla, also representing the Christ child that births from this union.

Architect and mystic Frederick Bligh Bond, who recognized and studied this sacred womb geometry back in 1908 during his excavations of the abbey, also discovered an omphalos stone, a large egg stone, which was universally sacred to the goddess—and which still resides on the grounds of the abbey, just behind the Abbot's Kitchen.[1]

According to priestess Kathy Jones, founder of the Glastonbury Goddess Temple, this sacred Avalonian womb-stone has a depression in it where the priestesses and oracles of the goddess would sit while menstruating to issue their prophecies. She says: "Here the menstruating Oracle of the Goddess would sit, her holy blood collecting as she gave voice to the Word of the Goddess. This was the blood of Charis, the Goddess of sexual love, from which the word *Eucharist,* meaning communion, comes."[2]

The moon blood was believed to give wisdom, blessings, and healings to devotees—literally "giving charis," or giving the charity of the Divine Mother's womb wisdom.

Sisters of the Bride

For all the magic of the famous abbey, there was another thread to be woven.

It was a different site in Glastonbury where Magdalene's spirit called me to her; a dragon lair and goddess navel called Bride's Mound—a small, neglected, yet wild mound on the outskirts of the town that was rarely visited and not celebrated.

It was as if Mary and her priestess lineage had veiled themselves, then sunk deep into the sacred earth, allowing the grass and wildflowers to grow over her memory. Asleep she may have been, but not dead, because in the dark fertile soil of the below, as she measured out her tenure in the Underworld, her power was gathering force.

With a small map in hand, from a fellowship of Avalonians who were trying to preserve the site, I set out to find this place;* it was hamartolos—an outsider, unseen. I walked the dragon's spine of Wearyall Hill, passing the holy thorn tree high on the hill, garlanded with bright ribbons, waving their vibrant magic, fluttering in the wind. The holy thorn is a tree native to Magdalene's land, ancient Palestine, and was

---

*This journey was in 2009 when it was more difficult to find. It is now easier to access thanks to the Friends of Bride's Mound who are custodians of the site.

said to have miraculously grown from the spot where Joseph of Arimathea rooted his shamanic pilgrim's staff in the earth. It flowers twice a year, in spring and winter, bringing plant spirit medicine of the Christ-gates of Easter and Christmas.

The atmosphere of Glastonbury has a curious effect, as if the landscape has been stretched like a drumskin across many times, and a subtle music from many worlds is playing across its surface for those who listen deep. I felt my feet tapping out rhythms across this ancient drum, as if each footstep were knocking on a doorway.

The Mother's presence was palpable, shimmering just beneath the pale powder-blue sky and the white clouds once thought to be the overspill of the celestial breastmilk. Greenery adorned the land, and yet there was also an immense sadness in me. She was here, but the bridge was broken, the connection disbanded; her songs no longer resounded across the green and merry lands, war blood had soaked her soil, rather than the life-giving moon blood of her daughters; her dancers had turned to stone.

I was walking the Motherline, bearing my offerings of wildflowers and bitter tears.

With sad symbolism, this sacred Magdalene site was located near the sewage works, where the fast rise and slow decay of industrialization squatted on the land like a trauma built brick-by-brick from hard granite into a tall, abandoned factory tower.

Descending down the dragon tail of Wearyall, I stood and waited to cross a busy road that dissected Her body in half, like a precise surgeon's scalpel. I looked out at fields ahead of me, seeing no obvious clue to any sacred site hiding away. Just ravens cawing above, laughing mischievously at my plight; speaking to me in tongues. I found my way to a small stream and walked along its banks, cutting through farmers' fields, looking through scrublands of grass, trying to see my way. Often the pilgrimage to the adytum of the goddess unfolds in this way, along forgotten, abandoned lines, scattered with the trash and dead ends of civilization. Yet she is singing from that black grave, menstruating within her womb of rebirth.

Examining my map, I searched for the site where the holy well had once taken pride of place, and finally found a plaque and a tumble of bricks and a hole in the earth. I carefully lay down some of my offerings, collected flowers, berries, and crystals; aware that I was offering her body back to her as a blessing and prayer of return. Continuing on my walk, the soft silence of the land was reaching out to me. The breeze felt warm and encouraging, and the sadness had mellowed out into hopeful longing. Seeing red ribbons fluttering off the branches of an old tree, gnarled and bent double with the greenings of many seasons, I knew I had arrived at the doorway.

I stopped and said prayers, and passed my hands across her wise wizened bark. Then I struggled across a bramble, and a once-stone wall, into the grassy mud of a field. A distinct grass mound rose before me, perfect in its small compact swelling. It was the budding belly of a pregnant mother, taut and round, filled with secret life.

A gentle wind was ruffling the grass as if her hair was being gently, playfully tussled. I slowly walked up the hill, embraced by the shimmering, silent spirit of Sophia. At the top the landscape opened out, and I saw the Tor rising high in the distance. From this angle it was as if I were looking across the legs and pregnant womb of the goddess, and seeing the swell of her magnificent breast and nipple rise before me.

With some searching I found a small spot that marked the epicenter of this sacred site, a small circle ringed in the earth, marked out with small pebbles from the nearby land and layered inside with small offerings from dedicated Avalonians. I placed my offerings inside the small womb circle, and then lay upon her body. The sky opened up above me, and I felt myself descend downward to meet her.

The vision of Mary I had received in St. Marie Cathedral at the age of thirteen was again reactivated, catalyzing a translation process, etched into in the landscape of my body.

Her Christed priestesses and saints were still singing from inside the soil.

Who could imagine the many secrets of Magdalene this place was still holding?

Bride's Mound, Brigit's Throne

Bride, Bride, come in!
Thy welcome is truly made,
Give thou relief to the woman,
And give thou the conception to the Trinity.[3]

BIRTHING INVOCATION TO BRIDE,
PATRONESS OF MIDWIVES

Bride's Mound is located in Beckery, to the west of Glastonbury town, and was also known as Brigit's Island. The name *beckery* may come from an Irish phrase meaning "Little Ireland," referring to the number of Irish pilgrims, or it may also come from an old English word meaning "beekeeper's island." Either way, the area was an ancient processional way of the goddess of Brigitania, known as Bride or Brigit, and was later known as the "women's quarters," denoting it as a sacred feminine space.

Its ritual role was as the gateway to Avalon, a womb portal where one could enter the dreamlands of the *Sidhe,* and the otherworld of the fairy queen of the mists. After the goddess was banished, Mary Magdalene rose up to carry on her flame, and to take guardianship of the portal and the old wisdom that was encoded in the land.

Excavations at Bride's Mound have revealed an early chapel dedicated to Mary Magdalene, which formed part of a greater Mary Magdalene hermitage and housed a spiritual community of women—likely where Saint Bridget stayed in Glastonbury in 488 CE, when legends say she left Ireland to make a pilgrimage to this sacred site.[4]

She is said to have left sacred relics in the Magdalene Chapel, including a spindle and a bell—both items traditionally associated with priestesses and female shamans. The chapel was later dedicated to Saint Bridget, the ruins still visible in the 1790s. In line with secret traditions of the left-hand path of the Feminine Christ lineage, the Magdalene Chapel was a place to "menstruate" old energies and emerge cleansed. John of Glastonbury, in his chronicles of Glastonbury, recorded in the fourteenth century, describes how there was a hole in the south wall of the chapel through which people would crawl for forgiveness of their sins; a purification for pilgrims.

These menstrual rituals to cleanse sin belonged to the old, prehistoric womb religion, where ritually enacting a journey through a womb space, as a symbolic menstruation and rebirth of the spirit, was recorded in spiritual traditions across the world—invoking the mystical powers of the goddess to cleanse and resurrect. This symbolic act of passing through a "vulvic hole" for blessings and healing was a continuation of the ancient Neolithic customs of the goddess. Christian pilgrims of the Celtic lands still enacted these rites in the chapel of Mary Magdalene.

This site also housed an old well, once dedicated to the goddess Brigid, which was believed to rise from the *olmbec* of the goddess, the Holy Womb of Mother Earth. In Celtic lore, a feminine sacred site always included a holy well or spring, a sacred tree, such as a yew, oak, or thorn, and a pregnant mound or standing stone circle. According to tradition, this spring, named Saint Bride's Well, existed as late as the 1920s, marked by a thorn tree where women would tie ribbons, rags, or clouties. In the old religion, these ribbons would be blessed with spit or menstrual blood.[5] Worshippers and pilgrims would also sip Bride's Well waters at midnight on midsummer's eve, later dedicated to the water-blesser, John the Baptist, and on the eve of her wedding, a bride would visit the well with her bridesmaids, who would enact a water ritual and baptism to bathe the bride's feet and body with holy water.

Celtic lore dedicated sacred wells to the Matronae, the three mothers of the trinity.[6]

Eventually these wells came under the stewardship of Sophia, and the Mary priestesses.

Arthur and the Moonastery of Holy Virgins

Connections with the left-hand of Christianity and the Grail myths were abundant. John of Glastonbury also reported that there had been a "monastery of Holy Virgins," priestesses of Christ, on Wearyall Hill where legends say King Arthur once stayed. During his stay with the holy ladies, he received a prophetic dream over three consecutive nights, where he was told to visit the Magdalene Chapel at Beckery.

According to legend, King Arthur arrived at the Magdalene Chapel on Ash Wednesday the day after festival time, when lent—preparation for Easter—begins. Brimming with hidden menstrual symbology, King Arthur arrives to find the door of the chapel guarded by fiery swords, to protect the adytum from unworthy visitors. Inside, an aged priest is saying mass. The Virgin Mary appears with Jesus in her arms, and the baby is given as the holy sacrament, and his flesh and blood is eaten. Miraculously, the Christ child reappears, whole and uninjured.

At the end of the ceremony the Virgin Mother gives King Arthur an equal-armed elemental womb cross of crystal, which was said to be a great treasure kept in Glastonbury Abbey for years. Arthur then changes his standard from the dragon to a silver cross on a green field, in honor of this vision and gift from Heaven's Queen.

For initiates with gnosis and who journeyed with the Grail Mysteries, this was a communion of Dragon's Blood, the ancient Eucharist of the Divine Mother—the womb blood that could both form a child from its wisdom and flow out as a blessing. The gruesome symbology of "eating the Christ child" was to protect the revelation of the older ritual of menstrual blood sacraments, a secret rite that was a highly forbidden and heretical part of the Grail legacy, still being persecuted by the church. Arthur changes his standard from the dragon to the moon cross to veil this secret. King Arthur, who legends say is buried in Glastonbury, is steeped in the Magdalene Mysteries, and the legends of the Holy Grail and the pilgrimage into the Grail Castle.

In those days the River Brue was close to Bride's Mound and often flooded, creating a mystical, blessed island of sacred women, which could only be reached by boat. Pilgrims would arrive at the Magdalene Chapel by boat, and in another legend told in the Grail romances, King Arthur arrived at Beckery by barge, mortally wounded, seeking the healing of the ladies of the island, who were devoted to Mary Magdalene. It was here that the supernatural sword, Excalibur, was thrown into the River Brue. These legends and stories later became retold and enshrined in the *Mists of Avalon*.

Underneath the fables, there is a very clear tradition of Mary Magdalene worship, rooted in ancient Celtic traditions of the Holy Grail, followed by "sub rosa" pilgrims.

For me, the ribbons on the trees seemed to wave with quiet promise—and a plea. There was living herstory under my feet, rising in a kundalini of remembrance. Who could imagine that such a rich legacy of Magdalene lay almost forgotten?

I could feel the presence of the Christian priestesses, spiritual women devoted to Christ, whose essence still illuminates the island, rising from the shrouds of the mist.

I longed to read their secret gospels, now turned to dust and bone.

Lost Scrolls of the Feminine

I couldn't stop dwelling on the name for the area of Bride's Mound in Glastonbury, the "women's quarters," a description whose meaning it was said had faded into obscurity, but which sounded uncannily like a code for the women's mysteries—also known as the moon, womb, or blood mysteries, the cycles of birth and rebirth.

Had they really vanished into obscurity? Somehow, I doubted it. But, like the legends of Inanna's descent, they had most certainly taken refuge down in the Underworld. I was reminded of certain plant species, priestesses in their own right (now named as weeds), who not only grow but thrive in areas of disturbed and desecrated land. These plant mistresses emerge through the broken cracks of concrete pavements, to bring their wild medicine to the wasteland, and to regenerate our sick, ravaged soil.

The teachings of Magdalene's Mysteries and the Rose Line had this power, too. It flourished amid persecution, it veiled itself as needed to survive, and it secretly thrived, administering the medicine of the Divine Mother where it was most needed—audaciously hidden, even in pious churches, priesthoods, and in holy sacred texts. For the Grail mysteries to truly die out, humankind would have to become extinct, because every woman's womb is a lost scroll, inscribed with the hidden teachings. Like nature's wisdom, it emerges again, as if from nowhere, yet more alive than ever and imbued with the vast greening power of creation and the living goddess.

My own womb had called out to me, with my diagnosis of endometriosis, and the more I listened, the more a calligraphy of wisdom started to write itself out through me, a lost wisdom that my mind could not fathom, but that my womb remembered.

Mary Magdalene was calling to me from the secret chambers of my own womb—she was a guide of the underworld, a barque lady of the bardo realms, sailing on gossamer threads.

Isle of Iona

Dove of Sacred Union

Magdalene is also contrary and unfathomable at times, in the merry dance she leads.

After this immersion in the Magdalene Mysteries of Glastonbury, an important wisdom thread of this book was next handed to me in my ancestral lands of Scotland, near where my maternal great-grandmother had once hailed from.

Magdalene communicated to me that I had to visit a remote island in the inner Hebrides called Iona—a sacred island of the Celtic Christian tradition and the fae. Iona's old Gaelic name *Innis nan Druidhneach* also means "Island of the Druids," whose famed motto of spiritual courage was *Y Gwir Erbyn Y Byd,* or "truth against the world."

Iona lies out in the Atlantic Ocean, beyond the Isle of Mull, accessible by ferry only. The island is famous as the spiritual place of Saint Columba—the Dove—who traveled from Ireland, along with twelve companions, and built his ministry and a famous monastery there in 563 CE, which later became the abbey built in 1200 CE.

It is also renowned for the strange fact that kings and queens across Europe are interred there, as if it is a secret Blessed Isle of the Dead for the lost Grail lineage. Further back in time, the island was believed to be sacred to the male orders of the Druids—and before even that, in the mists of time, it was a blessed isle of women. Legends say that Iona is the residence of the Lady of the Lake, who greets all great warriors who come to her after death to give up their sword of war to be reborn.

The nunnery, the oldest building on the isle, still bears a faint etching of a

Sheela-Na-Gig, a name harkening back to the Sumerian priestesses called the holy nu-gig—and the regal stamp of the womb religion, with its blessing of the wonderous vulva. Legends suggest that this sacred island was once a thriving feminine mystery school, where priestesses and wise women practiced their oracular arts and psychic sciences, and often folklore confirms this connection with feminine wisdom ways.

Brighid was the resident Celtic queen of the Hebridean islands—as the holy Bride of the fairy faith. And it is said that originally the island was a shrine to a goddess who was an ancient feminine moon divinity and hence sacred to women. Though later on in Christian times, all women, except nuns, were banned from residing on the island.

On the nearby island of Staffa is a powerful black basalt sea cave, a primeval cathedral, shaped from stone as the dragon womb of Tiamat. It was said the Druids only entered the cave for the most important initiate rites, such as soul resurrection.

Author Fiona Macleod, writing in 1900, says, "When I think of Iona, I think too of the old prophecy that Christ shall come again upon Iona . . . now as the Bride of Christ. A young Hebridean priest once told me how, 'as our forefathers and elders believed and still believe, that Holy Spirit shall come again which once was mortally born among us as the Son of God, but, then, shall be the Daughter of God. The Divine Spirit shall come again as a Woman. Then for the first time the world will know peace.'"[7]

Once again, I discovered that wherever a legacy of goddess lore lived—tales and stories of Mary Magdalene and Christ would surely follow closely behind it. Some legends say that Mary Magdalene was buried in a cave on Iona, while others say she birthed her child in a cave there—mirroring the rite of divine birth. Other myths say that in the future a Divine Woman from the isle of Iona will redeem the world, as if Magdalene has planted light-seeds of the Divine Feminine Christ here.[8] Professor Hugh Montgomery, in *The God-Kings of Europe,* reviews these oral traditions, writing that "John Martinus was believed in the early Christian Period to be the last son of Jesus by Mary Magdalene. In some versions he was born on Iona."[9]

Similar to magical lore across Celtic Britain, the legends of Magdalene were closely entwined with that of the Celtic goddess Brighid, and the later Christian Saint Bridget—who was said to be the daughter of a Druid priest, raised both in Ireland and Iona. Bride became known as the beloved "Mary of Gael," and one of her most popular Gaelic names is *Muime Chriosd,* or "Foster-Mother of Christ,"

and oral legends say she flew like an angel from Iona to become a midwife to Mary as Jesus was born.

In Celtic tradition a foster-parent was a very sacred role, usually alluding to a spiritual mentor who was charged with a child's spiritual initiation and learning. Could this refer to an oral tradition that Jesus came to Iona for spiritual tutelage, to receive a druidic education, maybe during the wandering years of his youth? Bride was also known as *Brighid nam Bhatta,* or Saint Bride of the Mantle, from legends of her wrapping the newborn baby Jesus in her mantle during Mary's time of need.

In other Hebridean traditions told in the *Carmina Gadelica,* Christ is named "the Shepherd of the flocks," and Saint Bride is called "the Shepherdess of the flocks," intuitively linking her to the legacy of Mary Magdalene and the Feminine Christ.

Hill of the Dove

I set out on my solitary pilgrimage, booked to stay at a Catholic prayer house on *Cnoc a' Chalmain,* the "hill of the dove," which is run by a sweet old nun who bakes cakes for afternoon tea and then prepares a cooked feast every evening, while bustling about in her nun's habit. My room is small and sparse, but comfortable, with a window looking out over a beautiful view of the wild gray-blue ancient ocean.

If Glastonbury is the birthing body of the goddess, then this is her untamed soul. Around the table in the evening, all the pilgrims of the prayer house gather together to break bread—often from different denominations of the Christian faith, from Anglican to Catholic, and of course to my own forbidden faith, a Magdalene heretic. Everyone's particular brand of faith is welcomed without question here, and over dinner red wine and conversation flows, along with the true spirit of Christianity.

One day, on my return from a windswept walk on the beaches, I find a portly Catholic priest and an elderly Anglican vicar risking their knee joints to scour the bottom shelves of the bookcase, trying to find Mary Magdalene books for me to read, exclaiming with enthusiasm. Their innocence and good faith touch me deeply, and reminds me that for every story of persecution, there are countless others of charity.

The land is majestic, streaming with the crowning light of the Feminine Christ. I feel at home here, literally as if these were my homelands—not just my ancestral lands, but the home of a very ancient spiritual lineage I belong to.

Upon arriving on Mull, a thick, swirling mist had descended as we drove through sweeping hills and rugged lands, moving ever closer to Iona. I weep as if the mist shrouded a long-forgotten family, who chide me for not returning sooner, and embrace me dearly.

Many heretical Celtic Christian traditions, such as those in Iona, were outlawed because of either the implication that Jesus had not been crucified or had survived the crucifixion or that Mary Magdalene had been the natural heir to their ministry.

There are strong folk traditions that place the family of Jesus in Scotland. Scottish oral folk tradition says that Pontius Pilate was actually from a Scottish family, and some say even Jesus was from a Celtic-Jewish background, explaining some of the druidic elements of Christianity. Other legends say that Jesus spent time in Scotland with his uncle visiting Iona, South Uist, and the Isle of Skye—known as the Isle of Isa (a name for Jesus). In 1933, Henry Jenner, formerly a keeper of manuscripts of the British Museum, described a trip he took to the Hebrides where he found that, "there are a whole set of legends of the wanderings of the Holy Mother and Son in those Islands."[10] So folk memory reveals their mythic presence.

A powerful oral tradition in Scotland also tells how Jesus and Magdalene visited Scotland after their escape from Palestine, in order to birth their children on Iona. Supporting these folktales, a nearby church on the neighboring Isle of Mull depicts a happy family portrait of a clearly pregnant Mary Magdalene holding hands with Jesus. Set in a small village called Dervaig, Kilmore Church features this highly heretical and remarkable stained-glass window (plate 16), which was designed in 1908. In case there is any doubt this is a pregnant Mary Magdalene, a quote from the Gospel of Luke is included below that directly quotes Christ discussing Mary of Bethany. It reads: "Mary hath chosen that good part, which shall not be taken away from her." This window, created over a hundred years ago, shows these heresies are not new. There appears to have been a revered, yet hidden, legacy of Mary Magdalene.

More confirmation of this Magdalene heresy arises back over in Iona, at the graveside of Anna MacLean, the last prioress of the old nunnery, who died in 1543. On her tombstone, there is an effigy of a woman with child, with an inscription dedicated to "Saint Maria." The woman has long hair and is positioned between twin towers, both medieval symbols of Mary Magdalene and the high priestess, mirroring similar heresies that were common in Europe, especially in France and Flanders.[11]

Once Magdalene's family is safely birthed, other legends and folktales place them living out their lives near Rennes Les Chateau in the South of France, where they continue their ministry of sharing the feminine teachings of love, and baptizing people in the nearby river Sals at a place now known as the "fountain of lovers." Other folktales say they made their permanent home in the Celtic heartlands of Glastonbury, which is why the legends of King Arthur and the Grail arose there.

I percolate all these possibilities as I walk the land, divining Magdalene's footsteps. Honoring her priestess legacy of adornment, on my final day I visit a gift shop attached to a local museum. I am browsing the beautiful displays of hand-crafted island jewelry, when a ring, or rather the unique design of a ring, catches my eye. It is a silver *Claddagh,* an Irish sacred marriage ring—with two hands clasping a crowned heart, symbolizing true love and faith, and also the Holy Trinity—described in Christian lore as Jesus, the Holy Spirit, and God. Yet in the hidden symbology of the Magdalene Mysteries path, it also depicts the left-hand path of Mary Magdalene and the right-hand path of Yeshua, united and crowned within the Holy Womb of God.

I knew I had to have this ring, without knowing why at that point—but my instinct said this would be a talismanic symbol to wear. As I took the ring to the lady at the counter, she held it in her hands and examined it, looked up at me, as if to size me up, took a deep breath, then started to share local folklore about the ring.

"Are you single?" she asked me, somewhat directly, with a penetrating gaze.

I answered in the affirmative, as she watched me put the ring on my finger.

"Folks say that if you wear this Celtic sacred union ring, you'll be married within a year," she told me, breaking out into a huge smile, as if she had just cast a blessing.

I couldn't help but laugh out loud. She looked at me quizzically.

"There is absolutely no chance of me getting married in the next year," I told her firmly, explaining that I had been single for many years, and that relationships were not my forte.

I left the shop, still shaking my head at the ridiculous suggestion. I also felt my heart shimmer, as if a slight chink of light had opened in a previously firmly closed door. I told myself to shake it off, and come back to reality. There was not any possibility.

The next day I left the island, forgetting the prophecy, but wearing the ring.

Within almost a year to the day, I returned to Iona, married and on my honeymoon.

The Great Swan, Cosmic Mother

It appeared the sacred lands of Iona had graced me with a touch of the Magdalene magic, and now the pilgrimage path had expanded to two, thanks to Magdalene's matchmaking. So together we began to explore the next MM threads calling to us.

In September 2012, just after our honeymoon, Azra and I drove all the way down the spine of Albion, visiting Avebury stone circle, passing back into Glastonbury, then driving over the invisible line into the south country, down into Cornwall. First, on our wandering path, we paid our courtesy visit to Avebury, one of the great stone circles of England, the largest known in Europe, which was built starting 3000 BCE. The womb circle of Avebury has a distinctly feminine spirit, and spiritually, the site holds the imprint of worship of the ancient womb religion, and is known colloquially as the Swan Circle—linking it to the old womb priestess cults.

In one custom, the villagers of Avebury would climb the earth mound of Silbury Hill on sacred days to eat fig cakes—a ritual coming all the way down from Sumerian worship of Inanna, where fig cakes were eaten to celebrate the Queen of Heaven, ritually enacting receiving the nourishment and transmission of her Holy Vulva.[12] In the 1960s, professor Alexander Thom, who specialized in discovering lunar and stellar alignments at megalithic stone-circle cathedrals, established that Avebury was aligned to Cygnus, the constellation known as the Swan or the Cosmic Vulva.[13]

In this ancient religion, probably originating in prehistoric times, many of the stone circles were aligned to the constellation of Cygnus—the Great Swan in the sky. The magic of this particular constellation is that it sits in the vulvic rift of the Milky Way, and was considered to be a sacred gateway into the galactic womb of the goddess. Avebury is steeped in the swan lore of the ancient feminine mysteries; one of the standing stones features a carved head and neck of a swan, and the marshes surrounding Avebury welcome migrating swans, returning home each winter.

We felt the flutter of celestial swan wings with us as we circled the stones, finding our way to the serpentine swan neck of the processional way, which leads into the sacred womb circle of the stones. The stones were speaking, in a faint whisper, as if they were thirsting for respite from the energetic severed artery of the road that cuts the womb of the swan goddess in half, slicing her creative powers apart.

Something peculiar was playing on my mind as we sat quietly with the stones.

On our way to the site, we had stopped by at our lyre maker—an old gnome-angel who was crafting us a womb-shaped lyre, tuned to the sacral chakra resonance. At the back of his craft studio, sitting regally, was a half-finished swan lyre. The body was carved into a fulsome shape of a swan, with a strong neck leading up to her beautiful head. Never before had I had such a strange sensation that an instrument was actually alive, pulsating with energy and spirit. She was an ensouled being, and seeing her part-formed in the embryo of the studio was humbling and mesmerizing.

I knew immediately that we had to have her. She belonged with us. As a storyteller, harpist, and spirit keeper of the feminine ways, I could feel Brigit's presence with me, as guardian of the old bardic traditions, calling out to her poet-priestesses to birth out new "swan songs" to re-enchant the soul of the world.

It was uncanny, because swan lyres—instruments similar to harps and shaped or adorned with swans—were once used by ancient priestesses in their ecstatic rites. But this ancient art had died out, and the swan lyres had disappeared from the world. All that remained were archaeological findings from feminine-centric cultures, including an alabaster lyre styled with a swan's head on each side from Knossos on Crete, as well as Minoan seals depicting bird lyres and vases from seventh-century Smyrna showing a swanlike bird above a lyre. Plus, the beautiful "Swan Goddess of Ephesus," a fragment of a musical instrument played in cult worship, featuring an adorned goddess standing on a sphinx with a swan emerging above her, as the cosmic goddess, was believed to represent the soul of universe.

Initiates of the mysteries were often called Swans, particularly if they had achieved "resurrection," such as in the Dionysus or Christ mysteries.

Now, sitting in the Circle of the Swan at Avebury, it felt like something was brewing.

Sisterhood of the Swan

Born in the wild moors of Yorkshire, in the north of England, the goddess whom my ancestors served was named Brigantia—a variant of Brighid, Brigit, and later Bride. She is the patroness of poetry, or *filidhecht* in Gaelic, and the gift of tongues, divination, and prophecy that belonged to the *bansidhe* and *filidh*—seer women of the fairy hills. Her symbolism is kept in the form of Brighid's crosses, a four-armed widdershins swastika woven from rushes, which is traditionally set over doorways to protect the home from harm, and honors the left-hand pathways of the feminine.

The Swan goddess of Ephesus (Turkey), a fragment of a swan lyre played in cultic rituals, ca. 650 BCE.

Brigit is known as the White Swan. Her feast day is Imbolc, February 1, which marks the approaching departure of swans migrating to the Arctic; they return to England again in November, a time celebrated by pagan swan feasts, later known as Martinmas. In legends, priestesses of Brigit are depicted as shapeshifting swan maidens, famous for wearing magical, ceremonial swan cloaks, the disguise of fairy women. They are associated with womb temples such as Newgrange in Ireland, a terrestrial doorway between the worlds, where the mystic swan queen has her throne. Swan priestesses presided over sacred death and rebirth rites, coaxing souls here, and taking them back home. Many of Bride's symbols are identical to those of the Egyptian goddess Isis, who also bears magical otherworldly swan wings.

The totem animals of Bride were the serpent and swan, symbols of the feminine. Ancient images of the mermaid priestess lineages, the sacred womb shamans of the Divine Mother, had either a dragon or serpent tail, and wings like a swan or a dove. These totem animals revealed the wisdom of the embedded womb world of creation, the dragoness Earth Womb, and the swan spirit of the Celestial Womb.

The legacy of the swan priestesses and their ancient rites of swan worship are written, in secret braille, across the entire landscape of Britain. In fact, the name *Britain* itself may be a variant of the name Brighid, meaning the "bright one," and closely connected to the old name for England—*Albion,* meaning "shining white."

As I searched for the spirit of Mary Magdalene, she arrived in a swan barge. What was the connection? What did old stones and swans have to do with the infamous heroine of the Bible, who was carrying a secret jar of whore wisdom? As always, the secrets were inside the stones and the land, and my own bones and ancestral DNA, as long as I remembered to dial in with the right "heart-womb codes."

The constellation of Cygnus, the Swan, was the gatekeeper to the celestial mysteries of the Holy Whore of Heaven, and her galactic womb portal—the very same mysteries encoded throughout the world in a veiled reference to a universal religion or "womb cult," tracing down from the time of Inanna and Isis, as the goddesses who sailed the Cygnus gateway and Milky Way in their "heavenly boats." According to some researchers, even the famous pyramids in Egypt are actually aligned to the constellation of Cygnus, each pyramid serving as a sacred womb.[14]

It was a long-forgotten form of feminine shamanism, the way of the Grail, that was the revered path of the priestesses, and the forbidden legacy of Mary Magdalene. In fact, the stellar mysteries of the Swan are deeply and secretly rooted in Christian tradition, as the Milky Way, or Via Lactea, was seen as "the Road to the Virgin Mary in Heaven," explaining why primordial goddesses such as Brigid in the Celtic traditions and Isis in Egypt became synonymous with Mary, the mother of Jesus.[15]

And of course, it is no coincidence that the angels of Christianity are depicted with swan wings (usually white, but also red or black at times—colors of the lunar cycle), and that these white wings symbolize their holiness and ability to travel between heaven and earth, as messengers, protectors, and blessers, like the shamans of old.

In a deeply veiled, but enchanting way, Christianity had a magical form of ancient swan shamanism nested within it, connected to the ancient womb wisdom of the Sumerian, Egyptian-African, tantric, Greek, and Celtic priestess traditions, showing there is a sisterhood of Sibyls, a sisterhood of the swan, across the world, whose traditions are connected and congruent, and whose path can be globally expressed as Sophia: *Divine Wisdom.*

Mary Magdalene is part of this Holy Spirit of Sophia, who expresses through various tutelary goddesses, each holding dragon keys of different lands and traditions. The stories from each tradition repeat the same symbolic motifs, such as sacred marriage. Every Bride has a sacred lover; from Inanna and Dumuzi, to Ishtar and Tamuz, to Isis and Osiris, King Solomon and Sheba, right through to Jesus and Magdalene.

In Celtic lore, Bride—like Isis—also has a brother-lover she laments and rebirths. In one particular story, Brighid is known as *Banmorair-na-mara,* the Lady of the Sea—similar to Isis's appellation as Isis Pelagia, Isis of the Seas, with her sacred barque. As Lady of the Seas, she belongs to the mermaid folk of old, the divine fairy race. As the tale goes, she goes weeping across the earth because she has lost her brother, Manan the Beautiful. Eventually after her lamenting and searching she finds him at last, and woos him with enchanting fairy songs and exquisite, otherworldly flowers.

The magical power of her feminine enchantments brings him back home again.

Ballads honor her divine feminine journey, for walking the Mary Path:

> *And with you for guidance be*
> *The fairy swan of Bride of flocks,*
> *The fairy duck of Mary of peace.*[16]

In places like Avebury, I can almost hear Bride's laments still humming on the wind. And I'm also reminded of Magdalene, lamenting in the garden of Gethsemane for her sacred lover, and singing her magical songs of resurrection to bring him back to life, just as Isis before her had resurrected Osiris with her holy mermaid ministrations.

I wanted to learn these laments, soul-weaving spells, and incanted enchantments of rebirth and remembrance, which were once the prized and holy practicum of the ancient feminine temples, and the whore-priestesses who resided and studied there.

Scholars and their books may tell me there is no connection, no swan songs streaming down a shared spiritual line, no threads to be woven together; only disconnected facts. But my womb says otherwise, and her voice is stronger.

Cornwall

The Lost Swan Priestesses

Next on our Rose pilgrimage we entered the old lands of Lyonesse—in wildish Cornwall. Here in the far southwest of the Celtic tip of England, we discovered more swan secrets, hinting of covens of swan priestesses, practicing an archaic form of wombcraft, dedicated to Bride. Intrigued, I read about a mysterious sacred site called Saveok, in Cornwall, where remnants of ancient swan worship have been found, including ceremonial offerings of swan wings, swan feathers, crystals, and other fetishes associated with witchcraft.

A few days later, a friend had recommended a musical-instrument maker who lived on the beautiful and rugged coast of Penwith near St. Michael's Mount. Within half an hour of arriving at the musical-instrument maker's house, gazing out onto the wild sapphire sea, lashing with white-tipped wings, I mentioned Saveok.

"Oh, my sister-in-law is custodian of that site," he said amiably. "Shall I call her?"

Within minutes we were speaking on the phone, and had agreed to visit the archaeological site that weekend—in time for the last dig before it closed for winter. Our visit to the land felt like a homecoming. I still remember it clearly . . .

2012: It's late in the afternoon, and the light is softening, preparing to greet the dusk. The bushes are lush and green and there is a foggy dampness to the air; not quite rain, but as if the mystery of the mermaids is kissing us with a whispering sea breeze. I can sense something moving behind the veils, as if the feminine spirit is gathering herself up to greet us. This is not a civilized goddess of ancient religion, or a sun-soaked Mediterranean fertility muse, this is a Lady of the Old Stones, wild and witchy, canny, full of spells and enchantments, who weaves between the mists and fogs. She is beyond a Celtic goddess, she is older, hag-mistress of the lost fairy folk.

Traveling through the narrow country lanes in north Cornwall, near the artist town of Falmouth, I am trying to calm down my rising anticipation. We are traveling to a little-known archaeological site of a lost cult of swan priestesses, whose forgotten faith has been practiced in modern time by Cornish witches. These wise women carried on practicing their rituals right under the watchful eye of the Inquisition, going until the 1970s, in a witchcraft line probably passed from mother to daughter.

We make the sharp turn into an off-road muddy country lane, and without our volition, the iPod switches on and "Song of the Siren" starts to play, melancholy and haunting, as if providing a magical soundtrack to our first impression of the land. I take my first look at the gentle rolling hills, the river running to the right-hand side, drinking in the wild essence of the place, as the music continues to play, and a female voice croons: *"Til your singing eyes and fingers, Drew me loving to your isle . . ."*

There is some wild ancient magic that I did not know I had been thirsting for so deeply, until this moment, until this meeting, at the home of the swan priestesses.

Our first glimpse of the site revealed a chocolate-box cute old white cottage, sitting above the archaeological site, which was nearer to the riverbanks in the valley. The custodian of the site gave us a private tour of the ritual pits, some of which had once been lined with swan wings, and were most recently used by local witches. It felt surreal to be there, the veils were so thin, I could almost see the eyes of the witches upon us, gently chastising us in case we got too close to their magical spells.

A secret coven of Cornish witches had first dug the ritual witch pits back in the 1640s, and excavations had shown that the ritual pits were used in recent times. Digging a womblike hole in the earth and placing sacred offerings—including feathers, crystals, hair clippings, and menstrual blood—harnesses the power of earth's life force for creative purposes. Swan feathers, crystal eggs, and other offerings had been discovered in these pits, including special stones brought from the beaches of Swanpool, over fifteen miles away. As we have seen, the swan is a symbol of the goddess and a spiritbird of the priestess and native shamanic witch traditions. Similar ritual pits for wombcraft are also used in Africa and across the world.

Most fascinating for me was seeing the two ritual pools also found at the site, created in an ovarian formation, with a birth canal leading to the waters of the river. The pools may have been used for initiation, prophecy, or even childbirthing. Both pools mirror each other, with stone seats carved in the bottom for ritual purpose.

The priestess rites were not only in faraway temples, but right here, in my homelands, and it felt as if every local ancestral incarnation of the goddess and her clans of womb shamans added a different spice, a different flavor, to the Rose legacy.

Descent into the Underworld

Rituals of Inanna-Sophia

I am in the blood of my becoming.

SEREN BERTRAND

Often, when we touch this ancient magic, we must also bear an initiation into a deeper level of wisdom to earn the knowledge—this is a *descent into the underworld*. The ancestral wise witches started to call me *downward*, as I held on to that shining swan light for dear life. Many ancient myths speak of a descent journey into the underworld, and in the oldest versions, this is a journey to heal the lunar mitochondrial DNA of the Motherline.

In the story of Demeter and Persephone, it is the separation of the mother and daughter, and the initiation of the maiden into her fertility and womanhood. It speaks to the incredible bond between a mother and daughter, and the complex navigation of interwoven ancestral feminine souls, once merged, now individuating into two.

In Inanna's journey, perhaps the older myth, she is descending to meet her dark sister, Ereshkigal, the forbidden and lost underworld parts of her own soul. She is removing the adornments of power and defense mechanisms she has protected herself with, in order to make herself whole in the black womb of the Earth Mother.

I related to both tales, meeting the grief of my outer mother, and the pain of my own inner sister, and how these stories were internalized, dismembering my own soul. The descent into the underworld is a psychic menstruation process—a journey of release on a cosmic and soul level. Inanna-Sophia's is a cosmic journey, a falling down into embodiment and matter. Ereshkigal is the dark Earth Womb goddess. She is also Lilith. She is the instinctive, feminine consciousness, lunar, cerebellar. The underworld is deep and primordial, the abyss; associated with snakes, dragons, birth, sexuality, and shadow.

The journey can also be described as Eve descending down to meet Lilith. Eve is the bright feminine, the cerebral consciousness, the fertile plants and pretty flowers shooting up into the light, into the upperworld. Yet without Lilith, she has no roots, and she will wither. Without Lilith, Eve's legacy is a wasteland. Magdalene is described as becoming the New Eve—but what the church forgets to mention is that she does this by descending down into hell to bring the sisters together again, to merge Snake and Swan.

Lilith is claw-footed, wily, cunning, sexually voracious, humorous, a double dealer. Just as Eve is about to float off into the heavens, Lilith reaches out to grab her ankles and pull her back down again; back into a dark lake of menstrual blood, dirt, sweat, and sex.

Ereshkigal was the female goddess of the Earth Womb, until she was displaced or raped by the male gods. In early versions, when a male god goes down to visit her, she seduces him and has sex with him for six days—she has an insatiable sexual appetite, a feature of the Underworld. She is Inanna's elder sister: Inanna is queen of heaven and earth, and Ereshkigal is Queen of the Underworld. Their separation into a disconnected heaven and earth is part of the incomplete, dismembered feminine, who no longer spans from root to crown, and whose queendoms are no longer whole. This is the Magdalene path, to make this descent, to unite the queendoms again, and to sanctify the wild sexuality of the untamed feminine with the heart.

As I discovered, you do not choose the underworld, it chooses you.

Ereshkigal calls.

During the time of my descent into the underworld, I meet my own inner disfigurement and dismemberment, the parts of me lost, incomplete, cut off. As

I descended, spiraling down into the roots, I have a surgery to remove a fibroid. At the same time, my mother is hospitalized, processing a deep pain in body and soul, catharting her own lineage trauma. I trust that this black tunnel I am walking through is also a divine birth canal. On the night before the surgery I have a dream of the magical "panther body," a feminine form that is brimming with erotic power, dressed like a Mae West in a tight black dress and furs. Madame Lilith comes to greet me, and like Inanna, she is "dressed to the nines." She invites me into the wild sexual power of the underworld, the dark feminine diva. This is the lost part of the feminine soul, wild and free, dark and deep, coming to greet me.

The surgery leaves a scar on my body, over my womb space; I am afraid to look, afraid that it is ugly or has somehow disfigured me. But when I see it, I instantly accept it with love and honor. I wear it proudly. I feel it is a shrine or memorial to all the womb wounds of my lineage, now made visible across my flesh, a scar but also a liminal healing gateway. The scar is red. In fact, the word *scar* is an old word for "red." I see it not as a mark of shame, or ugliness, written across my body, but as the sacred red thread. It is a shrine of Sophia.

MAGDALENE ORACLE
THE DESCENT—MIRYAI OF THE NASURAI

I was born into an ethno-religious minority group in Iraq, the Nasurai Mandai (Nasoraean Mandaeans), who are the last surviving gnostic group from antiquity. This group fled from the Jordan Valley about two thousand years ago and ultimately settled along the lower reaches of the Tigris, Euphrates, and Karun Rivers in what is now Iraq and Iran. After the 2003 invasion of Iraq, many of us fled once again and now reside in small numbers around the world. Full-immersion baptism in fresh water is our principal ceremony.

After a near-death experience, and having to let go of much of what I had known and was attached to, I was finally led to a descent and rebirth. During that time, I found myself overcome with an overwhelming desire to know the feminine face of god and for the first time I began the deeper exploration of the Nasoraean Mandaeans and my lineage.

I understood that my relationship with Life could only go as deep as I was willing to go within myself—I had spent much of my life outwardly seeking that which could only be found by first descending down to my roots, acknowledging my ancestors, and honoring my blood. It was with an unexplainable joy and peace that I found Her, within my roots.

As I began the deeper exploration of the Nasoraean Mandaeans, I discovered the feminine in Simat Hiia, Ruha d-Qudsha, and Miryai (sometimes also spelt as Miriai). In Mandaic (a dialect of Aramaic), Simat Hiia translates to "Treasure of Life," Ruha d-Qudsha to "Holy Spirit," and Miryai is a hypocoristic form of "Miriam" or "Mariam."

In Simat Hiia, I discovered the Divine Cosmic Mother of All, who is described as the Great Wellspring and the Mother of Kings (she is often invoked alongside the Cosmic Father, Yawar-Ziwa, who is described as the Great Date Palm). Together they are praised for their divine cosmic marriage. Ruha, as the Great Earth Mother, is described with words identical to those in the gnostic poem "The Thunder, Perfect Mind"; and Miryai, who is their embodiment and the name of a great high priestess, almost forgotten today, appeared as the equivalent of the gnostic Miriam Magdala—Mary the Magdalene.

One of the many treasured parts from the scroll of Miryai describes the feminine light: "I, Miryai, am a vine, a tree which stands at the mouth of the Living Stream. The tree's leaves are sweet and the tree's fruit are pearls. The tree's branches are radiance and its tendrils are light. Its prized scent spreads among the trees and goes out into all worlds."

When Miryai speaks about radiance and light she is referring to solar and lunar principles. In Mandaic, the word for masculine light is Ziwa; feminine light is Nura or Noorah—the translation for Ziwa is "radiance" or "radiant light" (solar light), Nura is "light" or "luminous light" (lunar light). Ziwa is the yang, Nura is yin.

Alongside these Divine Feminine faces, I also found the words Womb and Cosmic Womb capitalized and mentioned frequently. In the Mandaic scroll, "Alf Trisar Suialia" (the Thousand and Twelve Questions), it is written "for the Womb is a great world, there is nothing greater or more powerful than it." These discoveries felt like coming across pearls and treasure in the Great Sea of the Mother and it was as if I had been born anew in receiving them; perhaps this is why Her name translates to "Treasure of Life."

Baptism is key to our tradition, and it is interesting to note that the origin of the word Jordan, the river Yeshu (Jesus) was baptized in and the word for all "Living Waters" (considered the holiest of holies to the Nasoraean Mandaeans), is derived from the Hebrew Yarden and the Mandaic-Aramaic Yardna, which means "to flow down, descend." The ceremony of baptism allows us to be spiritually reborn through the act of descending. To descend down is often associated with feminine wisdom traditions.

However, it is not necessary to be baptized, or to have a near-death experience like I had, to experience this rebirth; we need only descend internally and connect with the "Living Waters" within our Inner Realms to receive the treasures that are waiting for us there.

With my descent, I received the Nura (Lunar Light) from the Great Womb of the Cosmic Mother, the Earth Mother, and a Magdalene of my ancestors. It is my knowing that they are deeply present, honored, and celebrated within the roots of all lineages and traditions across time, space, and all dimensions, and are always with us. We need only to descend to meet them and, through this, we come to discover the most sacred parts of ourselves.

ROSE SIGER, ORACLE OF MIRYAI, 2018

Stations of the Womb Cross

In Christianity the descent into the Underworld is translated into the Crucifixion and Resurrection event—formed into a pilgrimage of the fourteen Stations of the Cross, featuring a cosmic transfiguration over three days in the womb of Christ's tomb.

It is known as the *Mystery of Golgotha*—the stations of death and rebirth within the skull, also symbolic of the feminine "skull," the pelvis with its instinctive cosmic intelligence. The Resurrection Mystery begins on the morning of Maundy Thursday with Chrism Mass, where the holy anointing oils that will be used throughout the year are blessed. Maundy Thursday commemorates the Last Supper, and Maundy is the rite of foot washing. This ancient ritual is explained by Jesus in the Gospel of John, where he says: *"Mandatum novum do vobis ut diligatis invicem sicut dilexi vos,"* or "A new commandment I give unto you: That you love one another, as I have loved you." During Chrism Mass priests are called to renew their ministry by reaffirming their vows.

In Britain this mystical day of the Last Supper and initiation of the Resurrection ritual was called Royal Maundy and coins were given out in red and white purses. Across in India, pilgrims and entire families traditionally visited fourteen churches, one for each station of the cross, traveling across the lands in devotional caravans.

I asked myself, for what or whom do we need to perform this ritual of love? What do we stand for fullheartedly, that we need to renew our dedication and commitment to? What love calls us? It felt like a preparation ritual, this symbolic

Last Supper, before the descent begins, where we sustain ourselves with acts of love and strengthen our faith, like our ancestors who feasted so they could withstand the oncoming famine.

In the goddess Inanna's descent, she prepares herself with the rituals and adornments of feminine power, makeup, turban, wig, dress, and lapis jewelry. At every station of the Underworld, which has seven gates, she has to lose one item. Eventually she is stripped naked, and strung up as a corpse on the underworld tree.

In the rebirth mysteries of Jesus, he also descends into hell where he is "strung up." In their rebirth and resurrection rituals, Templars would go underground into a round womb church, for a descent into the underworld. Likewise, in the early Irish church, Saint Patrick was lowered down into a cave for three days, in a death and rebirth ritual. This cave is called Saint Patrick's Purgatory, and was used by pilgrims who would also be lowered on ropes down into the dark womb of the cave for their rebirth. There is also a cave under the holy sepulcher in Jerusalem, the womb cave of the mother, whose powers can rebirth the soul into its resurrection.

High initiates of Pythagoras would descend into a dark, earthly womb chamber, where they would take sacred entheogens to midwife their visionary resurrection.

For modern pilgrims, this womb-tomb power can still be found in the church womb.

Church of Rebirth

So, on one Easter weekend, we pilgrimage to the Cathedral of St. John the Baptist in Savannah, first founded by those fleeing the Huguenot persecutions in France. The cathedral is like a huge cosmic womb, a temple of Isis that has traveled across time.

The whole cathedral is a ritual landscape devoted to rebirth and resurrection; at the entrance is an octagonal baptismal womb font, flowing with the sacred waters, adorned with sacred feminine symbology of downward pointing triangles and Celtic crosses. The grand ceiling arcs up above painted in deep royal blue with constellations of starry golden fleur-de-lys, as if the queenly heavens of the cosmos are arrayed above us.

As we approach the birth canal of the central aisle, we are surrounded by fourteen Stations of the Cross, with statues of Jesus, each depicting and marking his soul disrobing. At the heart of the cathedral we are greeted with a huge marble altar, housing the Cosmic Cross, and rich red velvet thrones decorated with the

Maria, by Alfons Mucha, from *Le Pater,* 1899.

alpha and omega, and the pelican, the Christ, feeding her children from the substance of her body's blood.

We see Our Lady—the Lady of Sorrows, the Lady of Mercy—and to her we bow.

Sorrow of the Motherline

I percolate on the last few years, the death of my father, and my mum's sickness, not just in body, but in mind, inherited through the maternal line. Little do I know that during this descent, my mother is also preparing for her death. It is as if my world is dissolving.

It feels as if I am navigating Inanna's descent for my entire maternal lineage. This is the emotional and spiritual cauldron that I am in during our Easter pilgrimage. A deep grief has floated close to the surface, and I feel the lamentation cry sounding within me.

Savannah is turned out for Easter Saturday, and the Stations of the Cross service, wearing their best clothes and best faces. I do not think they have heard a woman cry out her wild lament for Jesus; where the pain of his time inside the tomb is vocalized. They hear one now, as I surrender into this great mystical rite of Isis. At each station I mourn for Jesus, and for my own "cruxed" soul fragments. I lament his pain and my own, and that of the world.

I pray feverishly, weeping out loud, calling out within my heart: *"Jesus I am in the tomb with you, please grant me my resurrection."* At each station we turn to face the next station of his suffering. It is in the turning I feel the power of the mandala, the "facing" of whatever it is we don't wish to see or feel or let go of, but that needs completion.

Under the starry canopy of the blue cathedral dome, praying and weeping during Stations of the Cross, ritually undergoing Inanna's descent journey, it feels as if I have been transported back in time. The polite faces fade, and the priestesses arise. I can hear the lamentations of the Marys, and the rich timbre of the Magdalene's cry.

The Holy Mother's presence is vast, as if the world opens and expands to fit into her. I am astounded at the continuity of the rituals of Sophiology, still being enacted—even if their origins are somewhat obscured. I conjure up the texts that tell of Inanna's descent, and how at each station of the Underworld, the womb cross, the crux of life, the center of earth, she has to peel off one more layer of her worldly self.

I also call to mind the fourteen pieces of Osiris that Isis had to remember and reassemble so she could impregnate herself and give birth to the new child of consciousness, for a new cycle. I feel the magical power of the numerology, the power of the seven, doubled to power of the fourteen, symbolizing sacred union and the unified celestial birth womb.

I surrender into the great mystery of Virgin Mary Isis, who presides over this shamanic journey of dismemberment and reconstitution, to refertilize the world.

I weep with gratitude to Jesus and Mary Magdalene, shamanic guides of this rebirth.

For you formed my inward parts; you knitted me together in my
mother's womb. I praise you, for I am fearfully and wonderfully
made. Wonderful are your works; my soul knows it very well.
My frame was not hidden from you, when I was being made
in secret, intricately woven in the depths of the earth.

PSALM 139:13–16

Creating the New-Birth Womb

I had gone out searching for Magdalene, but she had circled me back to my own roots, to explore my own ancestral line, and the family mandala that birthed me. We cannot have our second birth without descending to heal our first birth.

This was the Rose Key Magdalene was most wishing to share with all of us; to find the gifts that come from remembering the ancestral magic within our own blood lineages, which live within us as entire realms of wisdom and support, waiting for our arrival.

There is an Ancestral Soul of our lineage and an Ancestral Soul of the land. It is a genetic Grail that holds parts of us together, and weaves with the missing parts of those who went before. Our entire lineage is a vast web being spun across time. Our healing comes from stitching these timelines back into wholeness. We do not leave anyone behind. Our Ancestral Web spans back to the start of time, and laces forward into the very end of time. Our stories, our past, need to be rethreaded.

Even if the lines are broken, within our body intelligence the thread remains strong. I had to face my broken Motherline, with love and wisdom, in order to become a mother to myself, so I could birth out into the world the woman I was meant to be.

From this divine birth of my true self, I could then be a mother to my lineage. *I was to call into being the birth womb of my own becoming . . .*

Return of the Witches

Wisdom of the Ancestors

I have dreamt in my life, dreams that have stayed with me ever after,
and changed my ideas; they have gone through and through me, like
wine through water, and altered the color of my mind. And this is
one: I'm going to tell it.

EMILY BRONTE, *WUTHERING HEIGHTS*

Even though the hints were there, even though in dreams I walked through dark landscapes carrying the frail body of my mother, when she died, I wasn't prepared.

And now I know that nothing *can* prepare you for the loss of your mother—the woman who birthed you, the body who was a bridge from heaven, the womb that wove you. Despite any failings, any flaws, any personality clashes, all the deep wounds, our mother is our foundation. Without her we would not exist. And then she leaves the world. She takes her world with her, and leaves you standing naked, reborn, in your own.

It can be, at moments, strangely liberating. Yet mostly it was a shocking and crushing grief and loss, and a sudden knowing, a soul-level gnosis, of all she had built, created, given, that in my struggle to individuate, like a wriggling caterpillar, I had not always appreciated. As I mourned, the words *"thank you, I love you,"* wept out of me.

Ancestral Wise Witches

As soon as I was on the motherland again to be with my mum in her death journey, the doorway into the forgotten women of my ancestral lineage opened. I began to commune with the witches, chantresses, cunning folk, seers, and medicine women of the British lands; those whose many-thousand-year-old native feminine wisdom had been burned alive.

It was time for them to return, they told me, as esteemed and honored ancestors.

Of course, the timing was uncanny—we were approaching Samhain, the Hallowed Eve, when the veils between the world are thinnest, and the ancestral witches roam the land.

Procession of Witches, **Arthur Rackham (1867–1939)**

Mrs. Pendle

The scene was set when I discovered a beautiful purple witch's hat in my mother's wardrobe, sat perfectly upright, like it had lifted off Professor McGonagall's head and had flown itself over from Hogwarts. To say it seemed peculiar was an understatement. I lifted it out, feeling a talismanic power emanating from it, as if my mom had left a coded wink. I had always told the story of my mom's solidarity with the witches of the old ways, and how she had berated our local vicar, but I suddenly felt a deeper resonance.

As a teenager I had been a little embarrassed of her loud defense of the witches, wise women as she had called them, with her proclamations that nature was her church, and her distaste for state religion, and her refusal to go near a church, not even for carols. As a young woman, I had sat with her, percolating over a cuppa, and discussing the courage of the witches. She told me their history, and she spoke of them with reverence and shared her deep sadness at what they endured. I never asked how she knew of them, or why she felt so connected to them, and their plight. Now it made sense: *she was of the witch lineage.*

The next day we headed out to the ancestral valley where my dad was buried, to visit his green-grave, a living tree, and to see *Mam Tor,* our ancestral Mother Mountain. As always, we stopped in the local village for a cup of tea and cake, and to browse the shops. We were looking around my favorite shop, named *The Toll Bar,* when something caught my eye. It was a band of flying witches, beautifully made spirit dolls, hanging in the corner.

I had seen them before, on other visits, but had not lingered too long looking at them. I realized, with a sharp shame, that part of me had wanted to look the other way. I was still scarred by their stories in some deep part, still afraid of the fire that had consumed them.

Now I walked over to behold them properly, gingerly touching their soft velvet skirts, and feeling the sharp bristle of their brooms, and the pursed lips on their porcelain faces. As a coven, suspended on thin gossamer strings from the ceiling, they seemed to come alive and speak to me, chiding me, calling me, and reminding me: *they were my kinfolk.*

Turning over a label to read about them, I saw that they were called the "Witches of Pendle," referring to local medicine women who had been accused of witchcraft in 1612, and who had lived near and practiced at Pendle Hill, a famous pagan Bronze Age site. Eleven of them had been put to trial, nine women and two men. Nine had been executed.

Likewise, over in the next village, the Witches of Bakewell, two local women, had been tried and killed on spurious charges in 1607. Even now, the tales are told as a local curiosity, like a fantastical ghost story for Halloween, rather than given due respect.

One of the spirit dolls twirled on her string, as I contemplated their story with an ache welling inside my heart. She had a beautiful purple velvet dress, and a tall purple witch hat, with purple netting—almost identical to the purple witch hat I'd found in my mother's closet. I got close to her, rubbing her feet, and feeling the magic of my lineage. As I rubbed her feet, I instinctively promised her, "it's safe to walk on this earth again."

The store assistant saw me take her down, and smiled broadly. "Beautiful, isn't she?" I nodded. "You know what that is don't you?" She said, pointing toward the wall behind the witches. Looking closer I could see it was some kind of old blackened brick alcove. "It was an old toll gate where they paid for the dead bodies to pass through," she told me. The alcove, now blocked up, looked over a narrow alley leading to the church graveyard.

With this information, my eyes adjusted and I saw that the witch dolls were hung up all around this old toll gate where dead bodies passed through. *They were guardians of the dead, and guides to the passageways between the worlds.* I remembered that in Egypt, spirit dolls were buried with people, as they were believed to guide the dead across the bardo realms of the Underworld. Similarly, in local witch traditions, crafting spirits dolls as talismans of protection and guidance was common, most famously in "bridie dolls."

I knew this spirit doll of my ancestral witch-kin was here to help me as my mother transitioned, and also to connect me with a deeper soul memory of my bloodline.

At home, I created an altar with her on it, and my mom's purple witch hat. I place them near the window, with the view over the wild moors in the distance, their spiritual home. Every day I light candles on the altar, making sure to blow them out when we leave the house. On Hallows Eve we return to the house to find it illuminated by candles. They have reignited of their own accord, creating an uncanny candlelit cathedral illuminating the witch doll in the darkness.

Later, on this powerful Samhain, the trick-or-treaters are going strong, and Azra has made three runs to the local shops for more sweets. Once the holiest night of the ancestral fairy-witch traditions, now, for most, it is more of a festival or spectacle than a spirit doorway.

But as one little girl, about six years old, dressed to perfection as a witch with her tall pointy hat and black dress walked away from our door clutching her sweeties, I shouted out "Happy Samhain" into the dark, cold night, using the old name for the holy day. I see her mother bend down and whisper into her little girl's ear, *this is our New Year's Eve.*

Bailey's Hill

Bailey Hill at High Bradfield, near Dungworth Storrs, is at the line between the Yorkshire moors and the Derbyshire Dales. *It feels ancient here.* It was just a short bicycle ride away from my mother's birthplace, Loxley—also said to be the birthplace of Robin Hood—and it was her favorite place as a young girl.

After visiting my mom in hospital on the full moon, I knew we had to visit the church at Bradfield, and the mysterious Bailey Hill that loomed behind it—an ancient Bronze Age sacred witch mound, an original place of worship, a high place of the old religion.

High Bradfield is believed to stand on the site of an Anglo-Saxon place of worship, and the church holds an old Saxon Cross—which may have been the original church meeting point. It is also an old Bronze Age site, and was a ritual and burial site at least four thousand years ago. In the surrounding area there are old stone circles, known as lady of the rings, and the prehistoric cairn Apronful of Stones overlooks Loxley valley.

In archaeological terms, Bailey Hill is a thirty-four-foot-high, man-made conical mound, surrounded by a deep trench, measuring 504 feet. It also has a processional man-made long mound that leads up to the hill, and the site is a Scheduled Monument, meaning that it has been designated a historic site of national importance. One historian says, "It seems to me, these two strange mounds were 'church' to the primitive inhabitants of this place. They formed the local seat of religion and justice."[17] This is a sacred place; known as clan hills, witch hills, or fairy hills; home of the ancestors, the "Old Uns." It is where witches gathered for festivals and local councils, a place later connected to the Templars and Robin Hood.

My mother's family lived nearby, seven sisters who lived alongside each other—including my grandmother—and who most likely would have practiced the old ways, using herbs for healing, and following the native traditions alongside being good Christian godfearers. My grandma saved my cut hair in a box so it couldn't be used for spells. Mom said they practiced folk herbalism for common ailments, and visited local female "psychic" seers.

With this in mind, we open the gateway to the old church and walk through the pathway. On a yew tree to the right I see a baby's pacifier dangling from the branches, alongside ribbons. This is the old custom of honoring a Mother Tree and tying clouties—rags and ribbons, and even dolls and baby wares, if fertility is needed—into her branches for luck. It goes back to the old traditions, as far back as Sumeria, that tell of a Tree of Life. I'm amazed to see that the old ways are still being practiced, for all to see, in the church grounds. The offerings flutter against the wild sky, politely ignored by religious folk.

Inside the church I go to light a candle as a prayer for my mom. But perfectly, there are no candles. Instead there is a small crafted "Mother Tree" with hand-cut pieces of paper, on which to write prayers and petitions, and brightly colored ribbons to tie them onto this prayer tree. Choosing a red ribbon, I smile to myself. Even here, inside the sanctuary of the old church, I find the old goddess rites of tying ribbons and prayers into a holy tree.

Brigit Heads—Genius of the Clan

When I deepened my quest to discover more about Mary Magdalene, she had circled me back to my own homelands and heritage, and her forgotten imprint there.

Now it was as if she had opened the gates of the earth, to go down even deeper.

Mary Magdalene is famously depicted often holding a skull, which symbolizes wisdom in many traditions, and some people connect it to the beheading of John the Baptist. Indeed, the Templars are said to worship a mysterious head, said to be John's. But the tradition of a skull or magical head is far older than Christianity, and abounds in Celtic tradition and British native witch lore. Jewish folk legends even say that the first man, Adam, was buried at Golgotha, the place of the skull, to protect Jerusalem.

Sacred heads were believed to be supernatural conduits for the Old Uns, the mysterious prehistoric gods of the lands and the ancestors who were the "Genius of the Clan." They were guardians of gateways or thresholds, either physical or non-physical, and they were charms to protect against evil, and to protect clan homesteads and lineage wisdom.

Bradfield church abounded with talismanic stone heads, a practice connected to the goddess tradition. "The head represents the *animus loci* of the clan and the building the ancestral spirit protects. They are guardian talismans in British folk tradition. The heads are often called 'Brigantian heads' referring to the Brigantes, followers of the Goddess."[18]

Under the fierce gaze of the "clan heads," we finally made our way through the graveyard and up beyond the safe confines of the church grounds, ascending up to old Bailey Hill. Walking past a sign for Robin Hood's grave, and through the narrow old stone gate, a subtle portal way, we stopped to pay our respects to the land. Nearby we saw another sacred tree, adorned with clouties and ribbons. First we made our way there to offer our gifts and to ask permission to enter.

Slowly, silently, we began to walk across the long mound, approaching the high conical peak of Bailey Hill. The trees are old and groaning, heavy with leaves and memory. This *nemeton,* this sacred grove, is ancient. It is a wood-and-bone elevator to the earth's core. As we reach the circular mound, it is as if we have been ushered into a primeval womb. Silence is heavy upon us, and the light is dim, as if the trees have closed their arms around us and we are now in *their* world; an older world than time can even dream of. From the roots of this primeval darkness of dank green, rich with memory, a small song arises within me; clear and simple and insistent. It is a clan song that belongs to my mother, every note a stone step on the pathway of her lineage, going back through time.

Nearby a huge tree has toppled over, and her vast roots are pushed up into the sky. Where she has fallen, a huge gaping cavity into the earth has appeared, dark black with soil. As we reach Bailey's Mound and begin to circumambulate it, with the vision of the tree-door still in me, without thinking, I say out loud: "The gateway to the Ancestors has opened."

Circling the mound, I "sing the gateways" of the Earth Womb open for my mom to enter. I receive a message . . .

VISION OF THE ANCESTORS

They are walking up from the dark center of the earth.
Carrying torch flames in their hands, spiraling upward.
Somehow, I have summoned them, and they have answered.
It is rare, nowadays, for the clan to surface in this way.
They know all the paths of the Underworld, they know the way.
Slowly, surely, their footsteps beat out a processional drum rhythm.
They are coming to collect my mother and to take her back home.
Without them, she may not find her way through the labyrinth.
But with the Light of the Ancestors she will be escorted safely.
As they reach the surface a searing light pierces through the dark.
The doorway is being opened; between soil and soul, world and womb.
I keep chanting even though the opening door is pulling me apart.

> *Only feet moving, tongue moving, sounds rolling keep me bound.*
> *The Ancestors with eyes of black cave crystals stare into me.*
> *I, who have called them from their deep abyss to the world of light.*
> *They tell me with no words of the two souls within one body.*
> *One earth soul, and one star soul. One descending soul; one who rises.*
> *One primordial soul made of flesh, bone, blood, memory, who stays.*
> *Rests here in the earth's core, as body-of-earth, as Ancestor, still alive.*
> *Yet invisible, unseen, without a birth-body, but still made of dark matter.*
> *Still part of this great evolution of earth, still bound and entangled.*
> *One celestial soul made of stardust, sound and light, who leaves.*
> *Flys upward across dimensions, across rivers of time, to shining lands.*
> *Who leaves its earthbound body, who casts off memory and time.*
> *Back to who-knows-where heavens and worlds we meet only in dreams.*
> *It is this star soul who we lose and leave, and this earth soul we keep.*
> *The Ancestors, the Old Uns live on within earth, dreaming with us.*
> *Without their wisdom, we are unraveling the very fabric earth is made of.*
> *Not just soil and plant and stone, but river, memory, blood, and bone.*
> *Our short memory, our short lives, are not enough to live a true life.*
> *Only a threading, a great weaving across time, can create a human being.*

Then the silence enshrouds me again; thick and damp, misted and veiled. The vision throbs inside me; I keep it silent for a while so it can "take."

Later on, back "in the world" I remember a line from the Gospel of Magdalene, enquiring on the nature of matter, and what happens to the body when it is separated from the soul:

"Will matter then be utterly destroyed or not?" The Saviour replied, "Every nature, every modeled form, every creature, exists in and with each other. They will dissolve again into their own proper root. For the nature of matter is dissolved into what belongs to its nature."[19]

Our body has a soul: it returns to the living soul of earth, to become an Earth Ancestor.

For too long we have forgotten this primordial soul; this earthly Soul of Sophia.

Losing My Mother

After arriving home from Bailey Hill a sorrowful peace had descended upon me, as if my heart had sunk to the bottom of a strange and forgotten ocean that I once belonged to.

Standing in my childhood bedroom, I watched the sun setting over the Yorkshire moors, with a soft peace spilling across the horizon in peach pinks and burnished oranges, as if oceans of love were flowing across the land. Time was suspended on rays of light.

Then the phone rang, and Azra answers. He comes to tell me, simply, *"she's gone."* It was as if she had followed the magic pathway of the setting sun in the west, and now her soul was flying along silver pathways, as the Taurus full moon rose up into the sky. We raced to the car to go and be with her, and to bless and anoint her earth body. It was as if time had shattered just like glass. Something once solid had disappeared into dust.

A luminous full moon was hung in the sky, watching over the hospital as we arrived. I sat with her dead body and sang lullabies to her as I anointed her, while the moon mother shone through the hospital window and across her bed. I could have sat and sung to her forever. Leaving, and saying goodbye, was the hardest thing I've ever done.

Speaking to the nurses, we discovered she had passed away at *almost the exact time* that we had been at the ancestral witch mound, Bailey Hill, singing the gateway open for her. Sensing the Ancestors, I had said, "This is my mum's place—deep, wild, and witchy." I had received the spirit power of my mother's lineage beyond her own lifetime. An otherworldly ancestral embrace then descended to hold my grief. Death can be a very gentle being; She is like a thousand fluttering swan feathers and long-forgotten sorrowful songs. She is perfect stillness. The presence of death is identical to the light at birth.

As the mother of our birth womb reunites with the cosmic womb, we are catapulted into the vast spaciousness of the Void, as She becomes our new mother. This experience is disorienting, overwhelming, devastating, and an unexpected psychic dissolution. We are also simultaneously pulled down into our roots, into the forgotten world of our origins. But, like a Russian doll, suddenly my mother was *within me,* as an Ancestor. A love that I once perceived as *outside* me was now flowering with immense beauty *inside.*

With sorrow and love, I also wept with gratitude and shame to the precious Earth Mother, She whose body we live within. How little we appreciate what she shares, and how little we comprehend the magnitude of what we will lose if we deplete her and she goes.

Priestess and Death Doula

To prepare for my mother's funeral, I created a womb pouch containing secret knitted spells, made in the old way of the ancestral medicine women, using glass knitting needles. Knitting, sewing, weaving, and embroidery were not just crafts, *they were magic.* I placed this talisman in the wicker coffin alongside other "grave goods" for her journey.

There was no way a vicar or priest could officiate at her funeral—she might actually rise from the grave to protest over that, I explained to the undertaker. Instead, it was agreed that I would lead a simple graveside service for her, and priestess her back into the earth. Because the weather was cold and threatening rain in the lead up to the funeral, I ended up buying a vintage big black cape to wear, along with my mom's black witch boots.

Under a gray sky, on a November new moon in Scorpio we gathered around her graveside, a womblike space dug in the sacred earth, next to my dad's resting place. Mam Tor loomed in the distance, her long dragon tail curling down to the graveside. I could not help but remember a dream I had months earlier, where my mother had told me: *"we are Scorpios."*

I spoke a few words about her returning home to the earth, and celebrated her life. Rather than long sermons, we had time to be in silence with the land and the spirit of my mom. Each person was then given a red rose to place on her coffin, as they made their personal prayers, and said goodbye. Some old friends had brought their own white Yorkshire roses, a nod to the War of the Roses and the balance of white and red rose united again, bringing peace.

As my mother's womb had birthed me into this world, now I midwived her back into the womb of Mother Earth, for her rebirth into Spirit world. A powerful cycle was complete, of mother birthing daughter, and daughter rebirthing the mother back home.

Neanderthal "Robin Hood" Caves

Something profound had shifted within me, as if the ancestors had consecrated me into a gathering space for all the deep-soil-blood-wisdom of their lineage. Doorways to secrets of the land kept opening; pointing to witches, Robin Hood, Mary, and the Neanderthals.

There was a place, only about thirty minutes' drive from my childhood home, that suddenly began to call out to us. We weren't sure if we would have time to visit, but the message was coming through with "urgent" stamped all over it. We *had* to visit Cresswell Crags.

Cresswell Crags, on the borders of Yorkshire, Derbyshire, and Nottinghamshire, is a stunning old limescale gorge that feels as if you just stepped back into prehistory. It has a number of preserved caves that were first inhabited by Neanderthals over 40,000 years ago, then used by modern humans over 20,000 years ago, and also—as local legends say—became the hideout of Robin Hood and his merry men in medieval times. Containing Britain's only examples of Upper Paleolithic cave art, predating the pyramids by 10,000 years, the caves are a cathedral of the prehistoric Mother religion.

Red ochre has been found there, symbolic of menstrual and birth blood, used in shamanic rebirth and death ritual. There are also a number of "bird" figures, which are considered to be female anthropomorphs, highly stylized magical female forms, plus drawings of red deer, who were animal familiars of female fairy shamans, women who were between the worlds, as guardians and keepers of Otherworld. Over in Starr Carr in Scarborough, in the county of Yorkshire, shamanic deer antler headdresses have been found—a sign of the old deer priestesses who were crowned with the feminine wisdom of earth. The cave art also contains several downward pointing triangles, which archaeologists suggest symbolize vulvas, making it a classic site of the old womb religion.[20]

Most unbelievably, this sacred site has a cave named *Robin Hood's Cave*. I could almost feel Robin Hood and the merry men dancing behind us, urging us on, as if inviting us to a Magdalene Sabbath—*where the merry women of Maid Marian meet*. Did Robin Hood, as the grand master of the Magdalene Mysteries, preside over this Mary worship, originating from prehistoric times, as the local witches had said? Without meaning to, we were circling around the sacred lairs of the Templar merry men.

Since my quest to discover more about Mary Magdalene had begun, I had often wondered why I felt so drawn to her, and why—in Yorkshire of all places!—I had received my vision of her in the St. Marie Cathedral when I was thirteen years old. Now it made more sense, Magdalene *was* connected to the lands of my birth, through a red thread of Robin Hood lore and Templar worship. Those who walked the Grail Path had walked alongside my own ancestors, and may have even been connected to them.

Witch Marks

Upon entering Cresswell Crags, we try and get our bearings to find the right path, and bump into a member of the Heritage staff who is leading a group of children to the Robin Hood Cave for an educational tour. He is a jovial man who is very helpful, and we walk along and chat to him about the site before our paths part, so we can take the left-hand path that circles around the gorge.

After an hour of walking the land, we circle around and reach the Robin Hood Cave—just as the Heritage guide is leaving it. We stop and talk for a while, and we ask why it's called Robin Hood's Cave—he tells us it was named in Victorian times, after legends that say Robin Hood came here. He then tells us proudly that they have *just* made a new discovery in the cave only last week, around the time of Samhain. Excited, we ask what they have discovered, imagining some more early Ice Age art that the caves are famous for. Instead he leans forward, and he replies: "Witch marks."

We can't believe it. Robin Hood, the witches, and Mary Magdalene are always interlinked, both hiding and revealing the magic of the old faith through myth of place and past. Now when I read "Robin Hood's well" or "Robin Hood's Cave" I know it is a place of feminine womb worship, somewhere sacred to the ancestral witches, and those of the cult of Magdalene. Robin Hood is the Pan, the witch king, the Christ of the Circle.

The devil—or "Robin" as the witches called him—was thought to mark a person at the end of a nocturnal initiation rite. This became the famous witch's mark, which is also linked to talismanic feminine goddess symbols, even ritually scribed onto churches. It is very likely that the "merry" goddess worshippers were holding their sacred Sabbaths in this cave in medieval times, knowing it was sacred to the Neanderthal Old Uns.

It turns out that the public had been asked to create a record of these ritual carvings, known as witch marks, by the heritage agency Historic England, to coincide with the celebration of Halloween. The BBC had even reported on the news story, saying:

> The symbols, also known as apotropaic marks, can be found on medieval houses, churches and other buildings, most commonly from around 1550 to 1750. They took many forms, but the most common type was the "Daisy Wheel," which looked like a flower drawn with a compass in a single endless line that was supposed to confuse and entrap evil spirits. They also sometimes included letters,

such as AM for Ave Maria, M for Mary or VV, for Virgin of Virgins, scratched into walls, engraved on wooden beams and etched into plasterwork to evoke the protective power of the Virgin Mary.[21]

A group of witch-mark hunters had discovered them etched into the Robin Hood Cave, once a haunt of the ancient Neanderthals, who had also etched out their own vulvic witch marks, and images of shamanic shapeshifting magical women, who were witches of sorts.

The findings have hardly been made public, and no pictures of the witch markings have been shared yet. The Heritage guide pulls out his phone and asks, "Do you want to see them?" As we peer over to look, he scrolls through his phone to find them. He then shows us distinctive etchings on the cave wall of stylized *W*s and door marking, all consistent with the womb religion and the symbols for the sacred gateway of the feminine, the Doorway of Life, later adopted in Mary Magdalene and Marian worship.

He remarks on the feminine connection, sharing with some embarrassment that the symbols are of "female anatomy." And he also references the evidence for art depicting female shamans and magical female *V*s—symbol of the vulva— elsewhere in the site. He says, mistakenly, that the newly discovered witch markings are to protect people from witchcraft, and to ward off the "gateway of hell." This is a sadly common misconception of most people, still perpetuated from the witch persecution times. In fact, the carvings are sacred symbols of the witches, drawn to invoke blessing and protection of the feminine in the sacred womb cave. The gateway to "hell" was in fact the gateway to the ancestors and the gateway of the goddess and the sacred Earth Womb.

Over at Runswick Bay, by the North Sea, it is said women would carry their children into a cave at night for cures, believing that a powerful spirit inhabited the womblike cave. As with many places in England, people have still energetically drawn a veil over the old ways, which are everywhere and clearly apparent to see, but not mentioned or overtly referenced. On Ilkley Moor there is a stone circle a thousand years older than Stonehenge, and the area has over 250 cup-and-ring markings (symbols of the grail womb); on Haworth Moor—where Emily Bronte based Wuthering Heights and the wild love story with the "heathen" Heathcliff— there are standing stones of the witches, sacred to generations of native worship for thousands of years. St. Helen's church in Doncaster, near Robin Hood's Mary Magdalene church, has a beautiful Sheela-Na-Gig opening her legs and touching her vulva, displayed inside the church, and a dragon image on an outside stone.

This was the parish of the *Mayflower* pilgrims. To cover up the blatant goddess and womb religion symbols, people say these symbols are to ward off evil or a reminder of the devil or not to sin. Nonsense! Everyone knew what these symbols meant, and touched upon their power in reverence, knowing them as the mark of the goddess.

Witch Marks, Magdalene Marks

Witch marks derive from a long tradition of sacred feminine symbology, used by wise women, womb shamans, and practitioners of magic since time immemorial. The most common forms are the Tree of Life symbol, also called the daisy wheel or hexafoil, as well as pentagrams, hexagrams, W's, M's, V's, gateways, and crosses. The V's, W's, and M's first appear as symbols of the vulva of the goddess beginning in the time of the Neanderthals, and were then used as icons of the cults of Virgin Mary and Mary Magdalene. The witch marks, such as the cross and Flower of Life patterns, are also found in the Sumerian and Babylonian religions, placed as talismans on their temples. Pentagrams trace the path of Venus, the Star of Love, through the sky, and the hexagram was King Solomon's seal, inherited from an ancient tradition of Mesopotamian magic.

The recent surge of interest in witch marks and their rediscovery by modern archaeologists shows that the practice of folk magic, or practical witchery, was extremely widespread in medieval Europe. Witch marks are talismanic symbols engraved on wood and stone, used to call in magical power—for protection, for blessings, to ward off evil, to navigate a threshold, or for various magical spells. They were carved and recarved over hundreds of years into all manner of public, private, and sacred sites, ranging from old churches, caves, and historic buildings, to Shakespeare's birthplace and the Tower of London. The Wookey Hole cave of Somerset, England, is an example of a large number of witch marks found in a cave, a traditional site of worship by Druids and witches as the yoni passageway into the womb of the earth. The caves at Cresswell Crags have the most witch mark carvings anywhere in Britain. Caves were understood to be "birth and death" gateways of the earth goddess used in magic ritual and rebirth.

Witch marks can also be found in the Cistercian monastery, Saint Bernard of Clairvaux Church, founded in the twelfth century in the name of the spiri-

Stone carvings and witch marks of the former Saint Bernard of Clairvaux monastery. Clockwise from top left: Cross similar to Cathar and Templar crosses, surrounded by patterns similar to the flower of life design: pentagram, stylized cross, and MM sign.
(Photos by A. and S. Bertrand)

tual father of the Templars. It has since been removed from Spain, stone-by-stone, transported across the Atlantic Ocean by William Randolph Hearst, and rebuilt in Miami. It is littered with carvings of witch marks, with V's, M's, flowers of life, and other feminine talismans (see photos above).

In the book *Hidden Charms,* English folklore experts say that the W or VV sign is the most popular symbol used as a ritual protection mark, "by a ratio of nearly 2:1."[22] The V and W, and the M, symbolize the vulva and the birthing mother.

One of the main features of witch marks is the *vulvic* nature of their magic. They appear at liminal thresholds such as holes, doors, or entry points that represent the vulva, the vaginal gateway that is the threshold between life and death or Otherworld.

As a birthing mother and her attendants know, birth—and by association the vulva as gateway of sexuality and birth—is both auspicious *and* dangerous. It is a gate of new life, but it also requires careful protection, sanctification, and prayer and ritual to bring forth the blessings. Used improperly, or without protection and respect, it can also be a passageway for negative or traumatized energies to enter or leave, bringing chaos.

In a greater sense, the homestead, hearth, cave, sanctified building, temple, or church is a womb space that requires careful tending and ritual protection and sanctification. The womb space is, after all, the place that births, nurtures, and sustains the family and community. It actively needs to court the forces of bounty and benevolence, and to ward against the natural energies of dissolution that are associated with such a sacred space. Womb spaces, as portals between the worlds, are also natural gathering places for supernatural, cosmic, and elemental forces that need to be contained and navigated.

Caves have an extra significance as portals that lead down into the womb of the earth, with spiral paths down through the dense cold darkness of soil, of bones and rock, until reaching the center, brimming with the red "hell fires" of creative power and potential.

In Sophiologic terms, the womb space creates, fructifies, births, *and* also menstruates, dismantles, releases, and destroys, following the dark/light cycle of the moon. This is the essence of knowledge that witchcraft or rather *wombcraft* employs. Ancient folk practice is aimed at fertilizing and protecting the ritual womb space, and warding off any negative energies that might enter into it or be conjured up within it.

Cunning folk in the native English tradition often cited the "Red Sea" in their exorcisms, banishing energies "back to the Red Sea," referencing Lilith and the wild, uncontrollable menstrual sexuality of the primordial feminine goddess, which could bless or smite. This is similar to the Wrathful Red and Black Dakinis of Tibetan Buddhism, used in magical practice. For those who were initiated into true wombcraft, these energies were protective deities who were imbued with a deep primordial power to guard and purify. Over time, with patriarchal and superstitious frameworks, this energy became feared.

Sophia's Return

The Waxing Moon

My own mother was gone, but I could feel the Great Mother with me, in all her guises.

From Bride and Cailleach in the Celtic lands to Isis and Hathor in Egypt, and Yemoja and Oshun in central Africa and White Buffalo Calf Woman and Rainbow Woman in the Americas to Saraswati and Kwan Yin in Asia, I could feel a global sisterhood of Sophia, united under the universal motherhood of god, calling to us—whose shared rites and symbols tell of a prehistoric indigenous religion that covered the entire world, until it was suppressed and forgotten.

Divinity is immanent and transcendent. It is exactly like a child in the womb. The mother's blood and presence is within the child, and the child is within the mother. Yet there is also an aspect of the mother that is outside, or greater than the womb world of the child—while still connected to it. The Mother creates the womb world, *is* this world, lives within this world, yet is also transcendent, outside this world. That is her Mystery.

There are universes upon universes, mother-worlds within worlds, multi-wombs, each giving birth from within and beyond the great Mystery of the

Mother, the Magdalene Mysteries. Universes themselves are both child and mother, merged, and individuating. Each of our personal births and soul rebirth individuation journeys mirror the universe.

> When you come to know yourselves, then you will be known and you will realize that you are children of the Living Mother. But if you do not come to know yourself, then you live in poverty and you are poverty. (Gospel of Thomas, verses 3–4)

In Kabbalah, the Jewish mystic tradition that Yeshu and Magdalene came from, there is a story, or midrash, called the Diminishing Moon, which may well be the original source of the Fallen Sophia mythic cosmogenesis story that was taken up by gnostics, drawing from oral traditions of Kabbalah, passed down from the early roots of time.

The story tells of the key role the feminine plays in the evolution of the cosmos, and places the ascension of the feminine at the center of a great cosmic redemption. It is based on the lines in Genesis: "And God made two great lights. . . . The great light to rule by day and the small light to rule by night." It explores the clear paradox that the two lights are originally great and equal, but that somehow the moon becomes diminished. In these interpretations the sun and moon also represent male and female, and the masculine and feminine energy.

The story begins with the Moon and the Sun as two equal lights, who "share a crown together." However, the Moon complains to God that it is difficult to share a crown. He suggests that she step down and diminish herself to a lesser light. She, of course, refuses. However, God persuades her that by becoming cyclical—waning and waxing—in the end, not only will she return to her equal position, her wisdom and power will be greater.

Similar to the Sophia myth, and the later Magdalene story, there is also a suggestion that redemption after a fall, or love chosen from free will and experience, will be a deeper and brighter love than has ever been known, and will evolve every aspect of consciousness.

So the Moon, our lunar Sophia and soul of the cosmic feminine, begins her great descent, her journey as a diminished light, tumbling down into the embodiment of great cycles. As she falls into the cyclical feminine, she also begins to menstruate, as dark energy gathers within the dark side of the moon and requires a monthly "sin" purification. Paradoxically, in the feminine mysteries, this cyclical nature grants her immense fertility, wisdom, and creative power.

This "fall" of the Moon, or Sophia, has vast cosmic consequences. Because the universe is holographic, there is not one part of existence where the feminine is not diminished, and this disturbs the equilibrium of creation and brings evil into the world. Therefore, every part of creation and the entire universe is devoted to the return of the feminine light. The whole cosmos desires the return of the feminine and the "waxing of the moon." In this formula, the role of the masculine is to support the ascension of the feminine principle, until eventually they are reunited "wearing one crown" in a perfect state of love.

The story goes: "When she attains her completion, every piece of the universe will realize its own perfection, for the moon, in all her far-flung places, will finally wax full."[23] This grand cosmic reunion of the feminine and masculine principle, in a mature union, which is enacted in every dimension and particle of the universe, is considered to be the *coming of the Messiah* or the *Messianic age,* rather than any one person or relationship. Although, it is believed individual humans can hold important archetypal blueprints for the collective that can advance this union and lay seeds of possibility in consciousness.

One Kabbalist scholar describes this reunification of the Moon and Sun, the feminine and masculine, and the very creative fabric of the universe, as an event that will make them "Crowned by the 'heart center' of the Mother and her prayerful vision for her children."[24]

The Hasidic saint the Baal Shem Tov puts it this way: "When the moon shall shine as bright as the sun, the Messiah will come." In Kabbalah there is the idea that god is becoming through us. That god is not static and completed, a remote mystery outside of our world, but is also within it, coevolving with us; that the god/dess needs us, that our transformation is transforming her/him, that s/he is woven into this great experiment of love returning back to love; Sophia's Return.

"For the possibility of perfecting to exist within Divinity, some portion of absolute perfection had to forfeit its noble origins and descend into the depths."[25] This is the Moon/Sophia's journey of descent to "grow good." This journey of perfecting is inherently feminine (cyclical, not linear or static) and is a labor of love that the soul longs for as it brings soul growth and amazing bounty. It is the Great Work of perfecting or soul rebirth that the mystic alchemists speak of.

Our redemption is not just personal, it is ancestral—and ultimately it is cosmic.

Womb of Sophia—Rebirthing the World

This journey of Sophia's return can be midwifed by rebirthing ourselves through the divine love story of Jesus and Magdalene, as the archetypal world parents, the *anthropos of union,* to heal the fragments of our soul that came through already broken in our individual birth stories. This is an act of spontaneous soul retrieval and calling on an act of grace.

We are rebirthing ourselves directly from the Womb of Sophia, the Holy Spirit.

The feminine way is an erotic religion. At its root *eros* is the desire to "join together," with lover, with land, with mother, with cosmos, with self. It is salty, earthly, and soaked in the liquids of love; tears, blood, semen, breastmilk, vulvic elixirs, rain, mud. Salt is the feminine soul, and Mary Magdalene is described as the salt of the earth, as vessel of the world soul. Jung writes in *Mysterium Conjunctionis* about salt: "it represents the feminine principle of Eros, which brings everything into relationship in an almost perfect way . . . its most outstanding properties are bitterness and wisdom." The flowing salt of our tears are sermons of love etched on bare faces, grief and praise for this grand "weaving and unweaving."[26]

Before we can experience "two become one," we must first heal and repair the imprints of when "one became two" and our original womb-birth into separation consciousness. It is important to do our own soul-healing work; yet how can we piece together a bowl that has been shattered into a million pieces? Only She who created us, who holds the original birthing templates, can make this miraculous restoration now. We must call upon her grace. We must surrender ourselves into her fertile dark-birth womb.

We must engage in the process, like the birthing child, shifting to the right position, working with the mother's body, but we must trust in the birth wisdom of the Mother. We must surrender to the dark tunnel and welcome the dazzling light. Mother Earth, incarnate Sophia, is asking us to *listen to her,* and be part of the birth. She is calling us to her side, as her most trusted midwives of a new consciousness.

She who lovingly created our souls, who is with us always, is now in divine labor.

She is menstruating, flowing with the deep release of her purification.

She is birthing the new cycle, and our restored primordial humanity.

We are Sophia; we are that mother-father of a renewed earth.

This great love is the fabric of our universe, and who we are.

When Sophia falls, she is falling in love.

When Sophia returns, she perfects her love.

The Moon wanes, the Moon waxes. Cycles complete.

> *Our Savior is our true Mother in whom we are endlessly born and out of whom we shall never come.*
>
> Julian of Norwich

MAGDALENE ORACLE
Birthing New Earth

The Magdalenes came and encircled me. Together they were softly humming a gentle lullaby. They asked me to lay down and they began to anoint my body with menstrual blood, as if to awaken my senses. The blood was brimming with magic and opened up a portal within and I felt myself traveling down and down, through the tree roots and the earth's dark, rich soil. I was taken into the middle of the earth where a wild, wild woman was sitting.

As I looked at her I thought she was giving birth but when I tuned in I realized that she was in fact menstruating the "pain body" of humanity. The Magdalenes asked me to tune in to this woman's womb lining and the frequency that she was menstruating and I felt it to be a frequency that most women carry inside of their wombs. The Magdalenes then asked me to feel into the frequency "behind" what I was currently feeling and I experienced the most beautiful energy! In fact, the word beautiful is not even enough to begin to capture the essence of that experience. It felt as though Sophia was pregnant with her true essence. In her fertile womb a new earth was gestating, birthed from within, pregnant with more love and life than our minds could even begin to imagine.

As I listened to the song of the Magdalenes I could hear them sing about the earth as a flower and how when woman attunes to the flower of the center of the earth, she can begin to embody more of that energy herself.

At the end of my journey I was taken to a magical tree that towered up into the sky with its branches and leaves gently dancing in the wind. It felt as if I stood in front of a living church. My eyes gazed over a beautifully carved door; above it was a shimmering rose church window. Farther up, the tree trunk branched out into two, and the two were embracing each other and itself; it was the very visual of a couple rooted in oneness.

Slowly, slowly the door on the tree began to open ajar, until languidly disappearing. In its place was a radiant, mystical rose and I could hear Sophia's words whispering to me; the door has never been closed.

NATVIENNA HANELL, 2018

CHAMBER 30

THE WAY OF LOVE
Awakening the Feminine Soul

So we grew together,
Like to a double cherry, seeming parted,
But yet an union in partition,
Two lovely berries moulded on one stem.

WILLIAM SHAKESPEARE,
A MIDSUMMER NIGHT'S DREAM

JESUS AND MARY MAGDALENE SHARED a path of love often described as "mercy." This cosmic love is an outpouring of womb consciousness, marrying the compassion of the heart with primordial creative womb power. Neil Douglas-Klotz says, "This love was derived from the old Hebrew word for womb [*rachem*] and is related by root to 'Hokmah.' *Hokmah* is the Hebrew word for Wisdom—the Divine Sophia."[1]

This love is not a thinking love or sentimentality; it is full-bodied and deeply rooted. It is a love that *births itself out* from a communion with the womb of Creator. It is a practical, ethical magic that harnesses the forces of creation and our personal creative power, in service to love—birthing enlightened wizards and witches of cosmic wisdom.

Hokmah is the "Whore Mother," the Womb Mother who creates the first cosmic womb of emptiness; a multidimensional, holographic, universal womb space, the Womb of God that can gestate realms and birth them into reality and being. She is the Ain Sof, the Sophia, from which the infinite mystery poured into form. Birthed from her womb, she is also entangled and embodied in her child of creation.

The mystery teaching of Jesus and Magdalene was a soul embodiment that unified the higher and lower dimensions of cosmos and consciousness. This al-*chem*-y (recall ra*chem*) is the soul work done within the dark of the womb, as the reweaving of the psyche, with the reinstallation of the primal templates, to be born again in Divine Mother's image.[2] This is the queendom of heaven that is living within us, always at our very core.

Queendom is the feminine template of creation, the mother root. Imagine yourself in the womb at a few weeks old. You are in a feminine template, held in a feminine womb, being woven into form by a feminine creative process, through moon blood. Yet the sacred father, the masculine principle, has contributed by activating this process. Until ten weeks old we are bi-gendered, we hold the potential for both male and female form, and so at this time we are an embodiment of both possibilities.

In the queendom, we are fluid, oceanic, infused with the active spark of the masculine, and immersed in the deep, primal dark waters of the womb mother. Womb is our creative power, our Shakti, our primal, energizing, birthing, life force. Rachem is a compassion that pours from our "inner womb—the province of Hokmah."[3]

On the path of love, Jesus and Magdalene lead us into the mysterium of the soul, the inner moonlit dimension within each being that is actually a vast infinite womb of consciousness, weaving within form, yet formless as a dark, starlit night skywomb. In the New Testament the Aramaic word that describes this womb-soul is *napsha*, variously described as self, soul, or "life."[4] It could also be described as our feminine soul, or the hidden realms of the subconscious or unconscious. In ancient times this occulted, hidden aspect was compared to a womb.

Exegesis on the Soul, a gnostic text from Nag Hammadi, describes the soul (*napsha*) as feminine, and compares it to a woman who has fallen into prostitution. With this understanding, the soul *is* Sophia, who is on an epic journey of restoration from unreflective unconsciousness into the magical wisdom of womb consciousness. This deep soul healing and awakening is the ministry of the Feminine Christ. The text says, "The sages who came before us gave the soul a feminine name. She is also feminine in nature, and she even has a womb. When the womb of the soul . . . turns to the inside, she is baptized . . . the soul is cleansed so that she may regain what she had at first, her former nature, and she may be restored. That is her baptism."[5]

In gnostic mystery teachings, the soul was also the microcosm of heaven on earth within our body. Sethian gnostics explained how the universe was a womb and said, "heaven and earth have a shape similar to the womb . . . examine the pregnant womb of any living creature, and . . . discover an image of the heavens and earth."[6]

The feminine soul, our napsha, is a somatic and cerebellar consciousness. It is a feminine dimension consciousness that is circular and spiral, not linear. It responds to stories, symbols, veiling, art, poetry, myth, dance, feeling, riddles, sound, scents. The word *napsha,* feminine soul, is used 200 times in gospels—revealing the state of consciousness that the Christ path is pointing us toward.[7]

In this way of being, one does not *have* a soul, one *is* a soul. The soul is pre-eminent, the birther, the center. There is a womb of the soul that we live inside, so the soul is not inside us, but instead we live inside the soul, which contains, feeds, and nurtures us. If we diminish or starve our feminine soul, we actually destroy our source of life.

This soul-womb is in many ways a mother to us, and is similar in conception to the "daemon," an angel or a guide who is part of us, yet also bigger than our individuality.[8] On a practical level, it could also compare to the morphic field that Rupert Sheldrake describes—an invisible energy field that guides our form and consciousness. This soul-womb energy field holds the memory of all our lives. It also holds the perfected image of humanity, and can restore our original blueprint.

Motherline Meditation

+ Breathe into your own spiritual womb inside you (any gender); feel the container of energy. Now expand into the energy of your mother's womb who conceived you. Breathe and feel the container of energy pulsing.

+ Now expand into your grandmother's womb, which formed and held the eggs that became your body. Breathe and feel the container of energy pulsing.

+ Now expand out into your ancestral lineage womb, containing your entire bloodline. Breathe and feel the container of heart-womb energy pulsating.

+ Now expand into the womb of the Ancient Mothers that contains the entirety of all human souls. Breathe and feel the container of energy pulsing.

+ Now expand into the womb of Gaia, that contains all life on earth. Breathe and feel the container of energy pulsing.

+ Now expand out into the womb of the solar system. Breathe and feel the container of energy pulsing.

+ Now expand out into the womb of the galaxy. Breathe and feel the container of energy pulsing.

+ Now expand into the womb of the universe. Breathe and feel the container of energy.

+ Now expand into the womb of emptiness, the pregnant fullness of all possibility.

+ Now allow yourself to expand and melt into the wombs within wombs, into the infinity of the womb of creation, that womb of the great mystery, beyond All, who births creation. Sit in this spaciousness for as long as you feel called.

You can also repeat the meditation in reverse, returning to your centerpoint, here on Earth, in present time, in your body, including everything you are, all your ancestors, all your memories, all your desires, all your pain, all your beauty, as a living part of the web of infinite wombs, emanating from the heart of creation.

Transformation of the feminine soul is the realm of Hokmah, wisdom, the Sophia.

Tucked into the anatomical structure of our limbic, emotional brain and nestled close to the cerebellum, the governess of our deep feminine mother consciousness, lies the anatomical amygdala, so-named because of its almond, mandorla-like, shape. The function of the amygdala—with its integral connection to fragrance, scent, and powerful emotional and sex responses—is to be a spiritual conduit for our love, desire, passions. This is the brain center that, like Mary Magdalene, "loves much."

This cerebellar power of the *instinctive brain* and its primal consciousness is connected to the miracles that Jesus and Magdalene were able to embody, and why they gathered great crowds as they traveled village to village as healers. This gift was not theoretical or philosophical, it was a practicum of magic and miracles. It was embodied, real, the *power of the Sophia*. This came from being awakened from the alchemical laboratory of cerebellar and deep feminine brain consciousness.

We can open rose petals of inner transformation, nurturing a new seed of love from within our womb-soul, so we can birth and manifest new realities and behaviors.

Let us journey into our napsha, the womb of our feminine soul, to reveal the dazzling petals of possibility, as we awaken our Feminine Christ Consciousness.

MAGIC DOORWAY

There is a secret place.
A radiant sanctuary.
As real as your own kitchen.
More real than that.
Constructed of the purest elements.
Overflowing with the ten thousand beautiful things.
Worlds within worlds.
Forests, rivers.
Velvet coverlets, thrown over featherbeds,
Fountains bubbling beneath a canopy of stars.
Bountiful forest, universal libraries.
A wine cellar offering an intoxication so sweet
You will never be sober again.
A clarity so complete
You will never again forget.

This magnificent refuge is inside you.
Enter.
Shatter the darkness that shrouds the doorway.
Be bold. Be humble.
Put away the incense and forget
the incantations they taught you.
Ask no permission from the authorities.
Close your eyes and follow your breath
to the still place that leads
to the invisible path
that leads you home.

SAINT TERESA OF AVILA, "INTERIOR CASTLE"

CHAMBER 31

MAGDALENE MANDALA

The Wheel of the Witches

God is a circle whose centre is everywhere and whose circumference is nowhere.

SAINT AUGUSTINE

WE NOW OPEN THE MAGIC DOORWAY into the mandala of the Feminine Soul to discover and walk upon the Rose Path of love. We are calling in the energies of MM that live inside of us, that are not far away in a biblical land, or far away in someone else's idea of who she is. What we are really calling in is the essence of MM that belongs *inside you,* that has made a home inside you, and is *your* unique connection with her.

Before we begin to peel away the rose petals of this wisdom, place one hand on your heart, and one hand on your womb space (all genders, beneath the navel). As we have discovered, in ancient Sumeria, there was an actual word for the heart-womb, referring to the unification of the heart and womb, and it was *Sha,* a root sound from which we get words like *Shakti,* a tantric feminine power word. This word, used by the priestesses, was a sacred word that referred to the primordial life-force energy that is in the heart and the womb—which comes from the same source. What this tells us about the left-hand path of MM is that our power and our love flow from the same holy well. Our power is full of love, and our love is full of power.

Take a moment to breathe into your *Sha* energy before we begin to move around the Magdalene Mandala. You may sense an infinity loop flowing between the heart and womb. We can perceive it as Mother Mary, the Great Mother, within our heart, and the Magdalene within our womb. With this energy unification, they become one.

On a tantric level we can vision Yeshu in the heart and Magdalene within the womb.

Cosmic Magdalene—Mary the Mandala

The mandala—a circular map or medicine wheel—has been used in traditions across the world, including Indian Shakti traditions with the famous Kali Yantra and Sri Yantra, the tantric Tibetan dakini mandalas, and the elemental mandalas of the alchemists of medieval mystical Christianity and the esoteric old Judaic traditions.

Indigenous traditions of the Americas also use mandalic or cross formations as maps of the world, the subtle worlds, and the dimensions of consciousness, as do the native Celtic and Awenydd traditions, with their spirals and labyrinths. At its basis the mandala or cross represents the four directions and elements that create the world, plus the center of emergence.

The power of the Magdalene Mandala is that it gives us a technology to unify the major archetypes of the sacred feminine, which are often fragmented or separated from each other. It allows us to embody and understand relationships between different aspects of feminine power and wisdom, and to weave them together. This creates a constellated feminine mandala that becomes a spiritual womb of rebirth. It helps us understand the ministry of Mary Magdalene as a spiral path, drawing pilgrims into a sacred circling around the divine center of creation; the birth portal.

MM is not linear; she does not come to us in a straight line, but in a mandala, a circle, and that is how she shares her energy with us. Every time we connect to MM, she asks that we open into this mandala consciousness. And of course, mandala means moon doorway, in the way that MM's name means magic doorway—they are the same. The name *Magdalene* is another word for mandala. She is Mary the Mandala.

A mandala is a dimensional portal; it is an initiatory map, it is a journey. It is not something that is presented as a done deal. At its heart is *elemental Shakti*; primordial creativity. Apuleius, a mystery school initiate from two thousand years

ago, and author of the book *Metamorphoses,* described his initiatory process to become a priest of the goddess Isis as a flow through the elements.

Philosopher, and one of the founders of modern psychology, Carl Jung also describes the importance of the elemental archetypes and energies in the alchemical transformation process. He says, "We have reached the symbol of the quaternitas, the synthesis of the four elements, the quinta essentia in the mandala."[1] Each of us *potentially* has all four of the psychological functions (or elements)—fire (intuitive), earth (sensation), air (thinking), water (feeling)—at our disposal.

The ancient feminine traditions were centered on awakening, alchemizing, and unifying the primordial elements, and understanding that these primal powers *in both substance and potentiality* reside with all of us, as wells of energy to draw upon. These primordial elements, described as witches and the offices of Magdalene here, and as dragons in our *Womb Awakening* book, are the dakinis in Tibetan Buddhism. They live within us, yet they are vaster and older than us—they are our *birthers*. They can also be described as angels or archangels and daemons, guardian spirits. This wisdom springs from inside us as our own *inner oracle* that guides us wisely, and allows us to draw upon a vast, ancient power of knowing called "gnosis."

So, in this Magdalene Mandala, we are working with the four elements of nature, and the root that births those elements into being: earth, air, fire, water, and ether, or spirit. These elements are the building block for all of creation and our bodies. They are full of Magdalene magic. MM teaches us the mysteries of incarnation, the mysteries of form, the mysteries of matter, the Mother Mysteries. She can be transcendent, but she is more classically a teacher of immanence—showing us how we can live in this world in a deeply rooted, mystical, passionate, and awakened way.

Elemental Christ—Fire and Water

Christianity is an elemental religion. With John the Baptist we see the water and air elements, with baptism in the water of the river as the holy dove of spirit descends from the sky. Jesus ministers with the elements of fire and earth, with the eucharist of blood, the "fire of the moon," and through rebirthing deep in the womb-tomb cave of Mother Earth.

With its core sacraments of the eucharist of holy blood and baptism of living waters at its root, Christianity is a tradition of blood and water. It describes the ritual technology of healing through the power of blood and the cleansing of water. It may draw upon an ancient knowing, now forgotten by most, of the biological capacities of blood as the regenerator of life force, or *prana,* and the transmitter of ancestral and species memory, promising the possibility of cellular remembrance and rebirth.

Similarly, a growing fetus is created and nourished by the placental blood, drawn from the original womb lining, and the amniotic waters inside the mother's womb. This explains our spiritual relationship to the life-giving properties of blood and water, as the placenta, known as a "mother," feeds us her eucharist of blood and nourishment, and the amniotic rivers of the womb break and baptize us for birth.

In mystical Christianity these powers are called upon for a second birth of spirit.

Color Alchemy

Mary Magdalene often speaks to us through the vibration of sound and color, through the primary transmission of resonance and instinctual cerebellar gnosis. The wavelengths of reflected light determine what color we see, and the transmission of color is a *perceptual process* of the deep feminine back brain.

Color magic is a significant part of ancient elemental alchemy and mystical practice. Psychologist Carl Jung says, "This synthesis of the four is often symbolized in Hermetic Philosophy by the synthesis of the many colors in the cauda pavonis (the peacock's tail). The totality is manifested in the fullness of colors. This always has a symbolic meaning and the unfolding of the colors, the feeling values, means an unfolding of the personality, in which positive and negative feelings are united."[2]

Each element is also associated with a color, as MM works with color alchemy and symbolism. That is one of her most clear ways to communicate. The colors of the Magdalene are a way to understand the different archetypes of the Magdalene.

Traditionally in the Magdalene Mysteries, color instantly told pilgrims or initiates everything they needed to know. Usually in medieval art we see pictures of MM wearing either a red cape or a green cape: the fire and earth elements, associated with primal dragon energy. The Virgin Mary is usually connected to the celestial realms: heavenly white and blue, the elements of air and water. Virgin Mary Isis is also known as the goddess of the seas, the primordial oceans of spirit and water. Churches and cathedrals devoted to Mary Isis often have blue-domed ceilings, punctuated with silver or gold stars, and some have naval or ship themes.

Symbolically, in this Mandala of Mary, red/green is Mary Magdalene and white/blue is Mother Mary and black is the Divine Mother, the Great Black Madonna, or Void.

Although it helps to visualize the higher and lower Sophia this way, where we see one version of Mary who is in the heavens, or in the sea, and another aspect of Mary that resides in the greening of the earth, or the passions of fire, *they are interwoven.* We all have the red/green and white/blue magic within us. When we work with the Mary mandala, we are stirring the Marys in our cauldron so they become unified within the *black rose* of creation.

This Rose Key is that the Magdalene Mandala is in us all, and we have all of it—this is the unified potential of who we are. But for some people there is a gift quality, or there is a time in their life when one element comes forward to help or to teach. Or one element is needed to balance us. The mandala can help us take a snapshot of where we are—we may say: "the red priestess is calling me, but it's difficult to embrace." That gives us a clue to where our challenge is, where our growth edge is.

What we see through the elemental Mandala of Magdalene is she is not just an isolated woman, who came from nowhere. She is not just a big lonely question mark. She is actually deeply connected to earth, deeply connected to spiritual, mystical traditions, and deeply connected to lineages of priestesses and wise women who passed their traditions down to her, as she passed them forward. In her spirit, and in her name, Magdalene holds a great continuity of the red thread of Sophia. This is why so many people who don't identify with Christianity and monotheistic religions, or the biblical story of MM as a redeemed sinner, suddenly find Magdalene calling to them. They feel her presence, she comes to them in dreams or synchronicities, books present themselves, pictures catch their eye. It is the call of the Magdalene.

Consult Your Inner Oracle

If you need to answer a question or make a decision in your life, consult with your Inner Oracle, who can guide you with a full body knowing that helps clear your path.

YOUR PREPARATION

+ Have a journal or paper and pen nearby to write in during the session,
+ Sit on a chair or in a cross-legged posture, feeling relaxed with a straight spine,
+ Connect with the earth under your feet and the heavens above your head,
+ Take four deep breaths to anchor and root into your body and the elements,
+ Bring a question or decision you have into your awareness for an answer.

YOUR THINKING MIND

+ First bring your awareness to your head and connect to your thinking mind,
+ Ask yourself—"What do I *think* about this issue?"
+ Let your logical mind weigh up all the aspects and arguments and write them down in a clear linear list.

YOUR FEELING HEART

+ Next bring your awareness into your heart and connect to your feelings,

+ Ask yourself—"What do I *feel* about this issue?"
+ Let your feelings—or fears and sadness—flow and write them down without judging them as illogical or wrong.

YOUR KNOWING WOMB

+ Then bring your awareness to your womb/hara and connect to your knowing,
+ Ask yourself—"What do I *know* about this issue?" This knowing is your intuitive, gut instinct, which will speak to you in direct and simple terms.
+ From this knowing write down any actions you need to take or consider.

By honoring each aspect of our perception—mind-soul-body—and all our feelings and thoughts, we can reach the deep inner knowing of situations arising in our life.

Tripleworld Goddess—The Holy Trinity

When we understand the Mandala of the Magdalene, and the magic doorways she is opening to lineages of feminine wisdom, we realize that not only is she connected to our roots and ancestry and the past of our feminine wisdom, she is actually becoming the doorway to the future, the rebirth of our feminine wisdom traditions.

She is a very important doorway and presence. She is an incredible guide, an introducer or connector. She can open the doorway to the Cathars and the green witches. She can take you through a magic doorway to the priestesses of Hathor and the sacred sexual witches. She can open the door to the mermaids, and to the lineages of Africa and Sumeria, and to tantric and Celtic lands. She can open the doorway to the galactic womb and all the celestial female shamans who brought prophecy and vision down from the place that birthed our galaxy. That is how we develop our relationship with MM, she is so much more than one woman, she is a gateway to many women, many lineages, many streams of wild feminine wisdom.

There is also a "Holy Trinity" within the Mandala of Magdalene, which was known in ancient times as the Triple Goddess and as the Tree of Life, expressed as the Upperworld, Middleworld, Lowerworld. By remembering ourselves as multi-dimensional and elemental beings, we claim our destiny. And we can call upon an incredible wisdom tradition, so that we are no longer fragments floating along in a capitalistic world that wants us to close down our wisdom, and close down our bodies, so we can be a productive cog in a wheel of consumerism. Suddenly we are calling upon a powerful tradition of wisdom, the *Wheel of Witches*. We can receive gnosis, we can embody it, and we can practice it. We can become a practical witch, a living Magdalene. We can bless ourselves and our community with *Sophia;* wisdom.

Entering the Mandala

As we circle the Magdalene Mandala, we meet the different aspects of the Magdalene as wisdom streams of the sacred feminine. These elemental aspects of Magdalene can be seen as "offices" or homes of the Magdalene. What you will discover is that you may have a special connection with a certain office of the Magdalene, a certain lineage, a certain aspect, a certain elemental quality. Within each office lives a whole lineage of teachings and priestesses, available for you. By working closely with that office, title, element, doorway, a whole lineage of priestess wisdom is waiting to download into you. You may also feel drawn to a certain aspect of the Magdalene that can give you guidance about your life and future journey.

As we circle the mandala, write down any impressions that come to you, and which aspects of the Magdalene offices you feel embodied in, as your elemental gift, or what office you feel very attracted to. Ask which one you have felt called toward, or flirted with, though you may be holding yourself back because it feels daunting to take that leap into a new office of the Magdalene. Ask yourself what color witch you feel most naturally connected too. Make altars to her, wear her colors, draw her, make an oracle card or shrine image of her. What color witch brings up discomfort or challenge for you? Journey with her—what deep medicine does she bring? What does she have to teach you? Often what disturbs us can also bring great treasure.

Visualize each elemental witch, and ask for a message from each aspect of Mary.

Aramaic—Language of the Goddess

During our journey around the Magdalene Mandala we will also receive an Aramaic wisdom word for each of the rose petals we are exploring. These words are doorways for us to open so we can explore the path of love more deeply. There will also be ritual, prayer, or meditation to help us put into practice this Aramaic wisdom.

The sacred language of Aramaic is one of the oldest living languages in the world, and was once the language of the worshippers of Ishtar-Inanna-Sophia. It originated in the lands of Syria (Assyria) by at least the tenth century BCE, but became the common language across all of the ancient Near East. Aramaic spread as far west as Cyprus, to the Caucasus Mountains in the north, to Egypt and Arabia in the south, and east all the way to India.

For more than a thousand years it was the primary language of Babylon, whose magical word weaving was the language of Ishtar's Tree of Life mysteries. It also came to be the most common language of Middle Eastern Jews, the seed language of mystical Kabbalah as well as Sufism. It is a magical living language, with many layers and feminine doorways of wisdom, for *Sophia* to pour through.

Stations of the Mandala

Working with the Magdalene Mandala invokes the original Tree of Life, the ancient map of the subtle dimensions and directions of the multidimensional universe.

First, we call in the seven directions; the vertical axis of the tree, expressing as an Upperworld, Middleworld, and Lowerworld, the holy trinity of worlds (also embodied in the Cosmic Womb, human womb, and Earth Womb), and then the horizontal axis of the tree, expressing as the four elements, body of Mother Earth.

We then call upon and honor our Motherline, the grandmothers and foremothers of our ancestral lineage, and the Ancient Dragon Mothers of our spiritual lineages.

We also honor our forefathers, and the divine masculine who has been a guardian and gardener to the feminine mysteries throughout time, holding space for the mandala to flourish.

Lastly, we bow down to the Great Divine Mother, the central portal of all creation.

With this invocation of feminine wisdom, we acknowledge the spherical womb-shape of creation, and the debt we owe to our ancestors, both past and future.

The vertical subdivisions of the Magdalene Mandala contain the triple Marys, who hold the triple-womb worlds within them, circled in the unity of the Holy Sophia. These represent the three worlds or levels within the Tree of Life; the roots that descend down into the Underworld or Otherworld of the ancestors, and the womb of earth, and the crystal queendoms of memory and ancient genetic lineages. The trunk or middle gateway of the tree unites the collective wombs of all women and mothers, the plant and flower queendoms and the animal queendoms, rising then into the great branches that reach up into the

UPPERWORLD

MIDDLE

WORLD

LOWERWORLD

celestial heavens of the Cosmic Womb, where the Divine Mother emanates all the worlds as Ain Sophia.

The horizontal emanations of the Magdalene Mandala revolve (or revulva) around the four elemental homes or offices of the creative powers of Magdalene's ministry. Each branch of the elemental cross holds specific powers and gifts related to priestess and witch lineages who have walked the path of the Feminine Christ. This includes the green witch, the red witch, the white witch, and the sea witch, who lead to the black witch who dances us into the spiral.

Within the center of the cross is the *quintessence,* the fifth element and Mystery of the Black Magdalene, known as the Black Swan or Black Rose, the apocalyptic revealers, initiators, and soul doulas, who bring souls into the world, and who escort them home, who channel the power of the Void, the Cosmic Womb, to rebirth consciousness and resurrect love.

The Magdalene Mystery is often split up into two feminine aspects: Lilith and Eve. Symbolically they form the visible and invisible spectrum of primordial Black Light. Like the yin/yang symbol—the Black Lilith and White Eve are entwined, co-creative and inseparable, manifesting symbolically as a White Swan of illumination and a Black Swan of revelation; the black hole of dissolution, where we are magnetically drawn back to the womb center, and the white hole that births us out into the light. Spirit keepers call this the mysterious "dark-bright."

In MM we see a woman who understood how to heal with the medicine of earth, and the medicine of her body, and the medicine of her soul. During the Resurrection Mystery, Mary Magdalene worked with all five offices of the cross of Life in order to complete the tantric rite of initiation and resurrection. As a mistress of the elements, hailing from a lineage of women who trained in each office to harness and claim each elemental power, she was able to bless, anoint, initiate, and rebirth to achieve the descending/ascending resurrection, unifying consciousness with the triple worlds of the Holy Sophia: "I and the Mother are One."

> *Humanity, take a good look at yourself. Inside, you've got heaven*
> *and earth, and all of creation. You're a world—everything is*
> *hidden in you*
>
> HILDEGARD OF BINGEN

Rose Petal 1—Being Rooted

Underworld

Underworld/Lower Sophia/Marie Salome
Guardians: Crones/Ancestors/Dragons
Gifts: Wisdom/Rebirth/Rooting/Ancestral Healing

Our first station on the womb cross of the Magdalene Mandala roots us into the realms of the ancestors, those whose lives our own existence stands upon, right down to the very first ancestral Grandmothers who birthed the human species.

Beyond that we descend into the realms of the nonhuman ancestors, often called the Old Uns, and bed our roots into the womb of earth, who herself was birthed from the galactic womb and the Cosmic Mothers, connecting us all to sky and soil.

This world-womb vibration is often conceived of as a cauldron, where crones, grandmothers, and wild witches stir the ancient wisdom of our genetic memory. It allows us to be fully *remembered* beings who understand our ancestral heritage.

On the *Ghent Altarpiece* we see it as the fountain leading to the Underworld, where every wise wo/man has descended for initiation into the mysteries.

Aramaic Wisdom of the Underworld
Abwoon—Primordial Goddess
Aramaic: Abwoon (Ahh-wooo-nn)
Meaning: Birthing, generating, vibrating.

Abwoon is the Aramaic word that became "Father" in the Lord's Prayer, "Our Father, in Heaven." The common translation uses the Latin word *pater,* meaning "father." When Yeshu spoke this prayer, he would have used an Aramaic word, not Latin.

In Aramaic, *abwoon* means the "birther" or "creator," suggesting the great mystery, the Nameless One, who is a mystical Womb beyond gender, yet containing both. Of course, creating and birthing is often expressed as feminine or womb-centric. Likewise, heaven is described using a feminine word meaning "queendom." So this powerful name of god, in its essence, calls upon the *Divine Birthing Queendom.* In Celtic tradition the word for the Underworld (Earth Womb / Primordial Womb) is *Annwn,* and is pronounced as anoon—which is very similar to abwoon. The elongated "ooo" sound is common for birthing mothers who are in labor with child.

Abwoon is the generator, the parent portal of genesis, or the *Divine Birther*. It is also through abwoon that we receive *regeneration,* which is our second birth, or rebirth. It is in the image of abwoon that we are created and generated, through the original birth template that is divine, primordial, and whole. In the power of abwoon we can rebirth back into the temple of Original Innocence, which in the gnostic Gospel of Mary Magdalene is described as becoming "the child of true Humanity," the blueprint of a new human consciousness.[3] Abwoon is a womb name for god. It is the primordial aspect of creator, the Great Womb, that generates, gestates, and gives birth to her creation and imbues that creation with her "cosmic or spiritual DNA," an alchemical, quantum cosmogenesis.

Take a moment to tone or chant the word *abwoon.* Where in your body do you feel the sound vibrate? This resonance moves through the throne, our root and womb. It connects us into the Mother Father Creator, the Great Womb, who births and renews everything in her unconditional love; birthing us anew in each moment.

It is also an aspect of the Divine Ancestor, the Antecedent, who protects and nourishes us and our lineage. It is the red thread that unites our bloodlines. It speaks to the magical knowing that every human, in the legacy of abwoon vibrating within them, echoes with the first moments of the universal creation, the Big Birth. This is a key concept in the mystical Jewish Kabbalah of *Tikkun Olam,* which means the "restoration of the world," or the reweaving of the Motherline and Sophia's Return or descent into the throne of creation, illuminating the heart of all matter.

Each human contains a shard of golden light of the original creation within them, which may be buried or hidden. In rebirth/resurrection this divine light is restored.

Rose Ritual
Womb Time Healing

If you wish to develop a mystic prayer-womb for your *second birth* within the Womb of the Divine Mother, the mystical abwoon realm of regeneration, you can combine Mary's Prayer of Love (shared in Rose Petal 2) as a rebirth prayer with this powerful ritual, which contains spell weaving used in the feminine folk and witch traditions.

Your Magical Tools

- A Womb Pouch—a small purse or pouch with a drawstring, made from fabric of your choice; you may be drawn to a color that holds specific magic, or to a pattern. Your *feeling* is what imbues the pouch with birth magic. Ideally you can craft this womb pouch yourself, or you can buy a ready-made one.

❧ A 13-inch length of red yarn, ideally naturally dyed, symbolizing the red thread.

Your Rebirth Ritual

+ Tie nine knots into the length of red yarn; each one represents nine moons in the womb. With each knot you tie, imagine each of the nine moons you spent in the womb. This rebirth red thread is your spiritual umbilical cord to Divine Mother.

+ Sit in a comfortable position for your rebirth prayer ritual. If you wish you can light a candle or burn incense.

+ Make an intention to heal and rebirth each of your nine moons in the womb.

+ Hold the rebirth red thread in your hands; feel a body-sense connection.

+ Touch the first knot/moon in your rebirth red thread and hold it. Say the rebirth prayer of love to heal this first moon in the womb. Or say a prayer, mantra, intention, or invocation of your choosing.

+ Repeat this process with all nine moons/knots, repeating the prayer nine times.

+ Afterward, store your rebirth red thread in your womb pouch. Keep your womb pouch either on your altar or in a safe and sacred place.

+ At any time you feel the red thread needs releasing, you can offer it to the fire, or bury it in the earth near or under a mother tree to root you into the Earth Mother.

Rose Petal 2—Birthing Reality

Middleworld

Middleworld/Earthly Sophia/Mary Magdalene

Guardians: Ancient Mothers/Priestesses/Lions

Gifts: Moon Wisdom/Sacred Union/Radiance/Manifesting

The next station on the womb cross of the Magdalene Mandala brings us the creative power that emanates from being rooted, so we can manifest in the world.

We are in a web of life, an intricate and interconnected grid that connects all life-forms together with a frequency of creativity. This connection within us, laced from womb to womb, human to human, being to being, particle to particle, holds the vital power to birth our dreams into reality, birthing us into being in every moment with the power of our breath that mirrors the beating heart and womb pulse of creation.

This station of the cross is relational, interconnected, entangled—it is the power that determines how successful we will be in creating a life that we dream of, with thriving relationships, supportive community, and expressing our creative purpose, our *moonshine*. It energizes us to be abundant, alive, intuitive, embodied, engaged, and empowered, and holds our sacred power as co-creators, manifestors, and agents of intention, transformation, and change.

On the *Ghent Altarpiece* this is the sacred altar in the center of the painting, holding the red throne and the menstrual chalice of the Holy Grail; symbolic of our creative womb power.

Aramaic Wisdom of Middleworld
Maryah—Spiritual light
Aramaic: Maryah (Maa-ree-ahhh)
Meaning: Spiritual light, holy, honored

The name of the famous Lord's Prayer comes from a medieval translation in the King James Bible where the words *spiritual light* or *honored one* become "Lord" in the more feudal sense of the word, implying secular power or ruling over people. The Aramaic word, *Maryah* can be applied to any gender, and means a "light bearer."

Originally the Lord's Prayer was a *rebirthing prayer,* from the Rebirth Mystery school of John the Baptist, which may have been drawn from the goddess temples.

The Gospel of Luke 11:1 describes how Yeshu shares this prayer with his circle, who asked him to teach them what he has learned from John the Baptist: "One day in a place where Jesus had just finished praying, one of His disciples requested, 'Lord, teach us to pray, just as John taught his disciples.' So Jesus told them, 'When you pray, say: Abwoon D'Bwashmaya' [Aramaic]." The meaning is Our Birthing Mother, the queendom of creation, the outpouring sound and light waves of Shakti.

> *You pay God a compliment by asking great things of Her**
> SAINT TERESA OF AVILA, WOMB MYSTIC

---

*The quote has been re-envisioned to have a feminine-gendered god.

In the Rebirth Mysteries, prayer is imbued with womb power—it is primordial and creative, it contains a mysterious communication with the womb within our souls. God answers our prayer, not from separation, from far away, but from within the infinite womb source that lives inside us, and is magical, generative, and full of love.

Prayer is a feminine form of communion; mysterious, otherworldly, it bridges all realms. It is our umbilical cord back to our Creator that can never be broken or lost. Prayer is a way of communicating through the feminine back brain, the cerebellum, the unconscious—the place out of time and space, where miraculous possibilities abound. Prayer is the language of Love. True prayer is not a mental asking or talking to an external deity; it is a natural waveform of feeling that flows through the heart, containing the essence of your deepest heart's desires. It communicates, communes, and activates the "god" particles held within your own cells. It floods every atom with pure love, awakening this cellular memory of love from the inside, dissolving all barriers to merging with the love perceived as outside. It attunes your own transceiver mechanism so you can receive great wisdom, insight, and intuition, reconnecting you to the web of life—the vast biological internet of all existence.

More than words, prayer is communicated through our *bhava*—our deep desires, feelings, dreams. It expresses through our broken-open hearts and our passionate, fire-born womb dragon. Prayer lives deep inside the feeling feminine dimension.

True prayer expresses through our *primordial soul template,* which is still held in original innocence in the deepest core of our being, and in our womb. It calls for that which you do not even know you want or need; it plants creative seeds that awaken you and blossom into a destiny you could barely conceive of; it heals the places in you so lost in shadows you are barely aware of them; it opens you to infinite magical possibilities, it bestows the benevolent power of grace; it can transform anything in a moment of miracle, even that which you thought would take forever to heal.

It also opens us to receive Holy Spirit or Holy Shakti, which flows like Divine Nectar from the Great Womb of our Creatrix—and as this golden light of Love floods our beings, we remember we *are* this love, we were never truly separated or set apart.

Our prayers can be cries for help, or silence or bursts of deep gratitude or ecstasy. Our every moment is a prayer, and the Great Mother is always listening. This is our lifeline to the knowing that we are not alone, even if we think so, and that we are held in an infinitely intelligent and loving web of life, which always supports us.

We can also pray from our sexual and creative power within our womb and root, not just the love of the heart. Experiment with praying from the abwoon underworld.

Rose Ritual

Mary's Prayer of Love—The Mermaid's Prayer

This beautiful prayer from the Grail lineage, as taught by Yeshu and Mary Magdalene in their Sacred Union, was the prayer to Mother-Father Creator—the Great Womb.

It was a daily prayer of the heart for those following the path of love, along with walking the labyrinth—symbolic of the Great Womb—weaving through the twists and turns of the spirals of life, with all paths leading home to the Womb of Creator. Magdalene is the Lady of the Labyrinth, who represents the Grail Rose at the center.

The Prayer of Love spoken in ancient Aramaic, a sacred seed-sound language, is an extremely powerful way to open the paths of love within your being. The English version of it we now know as the Lord's Prayer is believed by many to be a more limited translation that does not capture the true feminine essence of the prayer.

Some say this prayer originated in the temples of Isis as a birthing-prayer to the Mother of Creation. This is our midrash—an inspired interpretation—of the prayer.

> *Abwoon d'bwashmayah*
> Our Prime Creator, who births all from the Great Womb,
> *Nethquadash shmakh*
> I am full of the awe of Love's presence in All.
> *Teytey malkoothakh*
> May the Feminine power of creation birth Love within me.
> *Nehway t'sebyahnakh*
> May I merge with the flow of Shakti,
> *Aykanna d'bwashmayah Ahp b'arhah*
> So we may create heaven on earth.
> *Habw lan lahkma d'soonqanan yaomanah*
> Give us the gifts of Love's beauty and abundance.
> *Aykanah daph khnan shbwoqan l'khayyabayn*
> Let forgiveness rebirth All into Innocence.
> *Wolah tahlan l'nesyuna*
> Bring me the wisdom of true knowing.

Aela patzan min bishah
Help me feel and release all that is not Love.
Metol d'dilak hee malkothah
For the Power of Love is the only Truth.
Woahaylah wahteshbookhtah
Our hearts are strong with faith and trust.
L'ahlameen almeen
For Love is eternal.
Ahmeyn
By the Great Womb may it be so.

Rose Petal 3—Cosmic Vision

Upperworld

Upperworld/Higher Sophia/Virgin Mari Isis
Guardians: Star Mothers/Cosmic Angels/Swans
Gifts: Illumination/Prophecy/Life Purpose/Teachers

This station on the womb cross of the Magdalene Mandala brings us into the Upperworld realms, the celestial heavens of the sky world and our star kin. This is a visionary space that leads us beyond our everyday human concerns, and stretches out a timeless vision hung like a tapestry across the constellations of stars.

We can take feminine shamanic journeys to these celestial star realms for wisdom, prophecy, insight, and visions of the future and the past, as they weave together. This is a transcendent realm beyond the limitations of the body or even time and space.

In ancient Egyptian tradition, inherited from the indigenous African Grandmothers, this vibration was perceived as the goddess Nuit, whose body stretched out across the universe. Every day the sun returned into her dark womb and every morning she birthed the light back out again. Later on, the goddess Isis and Virgin Mary—who we call Virgin Mari-Isis—became the Queen of Heaven and Queen of the Universe.

This station brings us gnosis and wisdom, and makes us able to rise above the narrow vision of our current life or perspective and to remember our cosmic self. In the *Ghent Altarpiece* this is the Cosmic Dove, clothed in dazzling golden light who descends down from the heavens to illuminate the world with her amazing grace.

Aramaic Wisdom of Upperworld
Da'ath—Doorway of Gnosis and Radiance

Hebrew: דעת

Da'ath (daat)

Meaning: Knowledge, mystical threshold, related word is *Daleth,* doorway.

Power of the Magic Doorway: "Ask, and it shall be given you; seek, and you shall find; knock, and it shall be opened unto you: For every one that asks receives; and he that seeks finds; and to him that knocks it shall be opened" (Matthew 7:7–8).

Da'ath, or Daleth, is another distinctly feminine aspect of Christ Consciousness. It awakens a feminine soul-knowing, somatic body wisdom, and womb gnosis; it is a knowing that activates our cerebellar consciousness, beyond words and ideas. When we have an experience of gnosis, we discover realms within ourselves, unknown, that are beyond the cerebral mind's ability to think, understand, or perceive. It is a journeying into, and coming to know, these wild inner realms that transforms our normal consciousness, or rather it reunites us with our true cosmic consciousness.

In mystical lore this gnosis is equated with the Tree of Knowledge within the Garden of Eden. Another way of saying it: Da'ath represents our deep lunar consciousness. Lunar cycles and moon time have long been associated with visionary, oracular knowing and wisdom. A second sight that can "see in the dark"—these are the *witch eyes* of the power of Da'ath, the nonlogical and magic of the seer and prophetess. This knowing does not come through thought, logic, or reason, but comes in lightning bolts of awareness and vision, felt throughout the soul—an alive cosmic creature whom we live within, and who in startling moments makes its presence known to illuminate us with the vastness of who we are and our place in the cosmos.

In Kabbalah, Da'ath is the abyss, the dark womb of the Void that unites the left-hand and right-hand of God into a scintillating radiance of awakened consciousness. This is the Great Work of alchemy, uniting Chesed, and its higher aspect of Hokmah, wisdom, with Gevurah and its higher aspect of Binah, a womb of pregnant potential. This is the sacred work of forging the Two into One, and catalyzing an ecstatic, generative, shining darkness of awakened womb consciousness that descends down the chakra spheres of the human form and soul in primordial innocence.

Daleth is the number four in gematria, the elemental cross of light, the womb doorway between the worlds, where all beings enter this realm and leave this realm. It is the doorway of both life and creativity and death and dissolution. It is a two-way door.

The knowledge that Da'ath brings us is also a frequency of *pleasure.* Indeed, the Hebrew for Eden, עֵדֶן, also means "bliss and pleasure." This directs us to the forbidden gnosis of the Magdalene and the ancient priestess lineages. It is the gnosis of the Rose, which is bestowed through somatic, ecstatic beauty and sacred sexual bliss. This vibration of sacred pleasure, beauty, bliss, and radiance literally *enraptures* the body and soul on a vibrational level, uniting us with the frequency of the Creator— which is coded with cosmic orgasmic bliss, as worlds climax in and out of being.

A doorway of pleasure opens in our napsha when we open to the joy, love, and sensuality of life, not as a way to avoid our feelings or the truth of our soul, but as a sacred pathway to *feel more deeply* the truth and wild love within our feminine soul. Our soul is crafted from the dark matter of sexual energy, the primal kundalini force; Da'ath births through us in a blissful, conscious awakening of our cosmic sexuality. This is the sensual salvation of Shakti, the goddess energy at the root of existence.

It is a *feeling dimension,* full of the softness, stillness, silence, slowness, and kindness that lives at the doorway-heart of matter, in the mystical queendom of the Sophia.

When this Rose Petal unfolds, we embody our feminine soul into the magic of *beingness,* the timeless doorway of radiance that is available to us in every moment.

Rose Ritual
Blue Rose Meditation
+ Bring your awareness down into the body.
+ Feel the presence of the Magdalene essence within you.
+ Feel your body gently vibrating and humming with energy.
+ Feel a soft light emitting from the core of your cells.
+ With every breath feel your body vibrate more deeply.
+ With every breath feel the light in your cells glow brighter.
+ Allow the breath to wash all the way through your body—down to your feet, and up through your body into your arms and hands.
+ Feel the pulse of life within you, breathing through you, in and out.
+ Surrender to the flow of life.

Take a long pause.

+ Bring your awareness into your heart.
+ Tune in to how your heart feels—notice colors, sensations, or impulses.
+ Allow yourself to drop deeper down into the secret chamber.
+ Begin to visualize a beautiful, deep red rose.
+ Feel and see this deep red rose slowly unfold her petals.
+ At the center of the rose a beautiful fragrance is emitted. Feel this divine fragrance, this unguent of the feminine begin to spread through your heart.
+ Now allow this fragrance to spread through your body like a warm fire.
+ Now allow this anointing fragrance to flow out into the world like a healing balm.
+ You are the myrrhophore of love.

Take a long pause.

+ In the floor of the secret chamber of your heart, visualize a spiral staircase going down.
+ You light a torch of fire, and holding it aloft in your hand, you begin to descend downward . . . going deeper and deeper into the darkness, holding the light to guide you.

Take a long pause.

+ You enter the holy of holies, the Cave of the Womb.
+ Tune in to how your womb feels—the colors, sensations, impulses.
+ There is a circle traced at the center, and with your torch you light a fire.
+ You watch and feel this fire gently warm and illuminate the Womb Cave.
+ The fire transforms into a dazzling blue rose.
+ Begin to visualize this blue rose slowly unfold her petals.
+ As the Blue Rose opens, a scintillating blue light begins to infuse your womb,
+ Now this shimmering blue light spreads throughout your body.
+ Now visualize this blue light surrounding earth.
+ Feel the celestial doorway of Virgin Sophia open, and receive her wisdom.

Take a long pause.

+ It is time to return to the present, bearing the light of the Grail, offering your vision in service.
+ You are the Illuminatrix—the light bearer.
+ May your gifts bless the world.

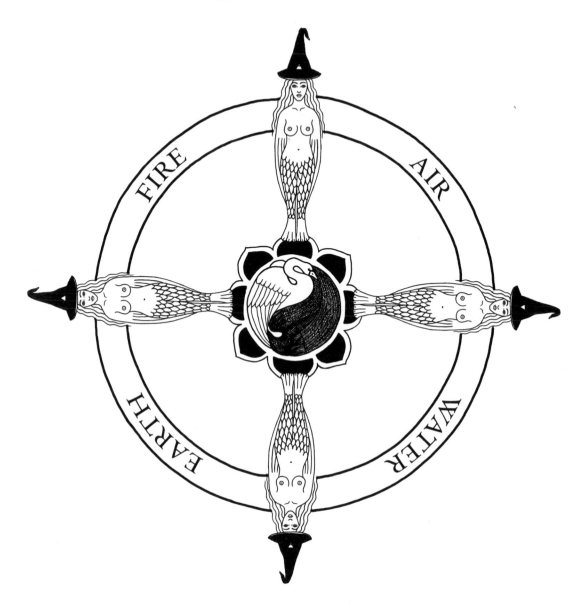

Rose Petal 4—Gaia Magic

Earth: Green Witch

Office of the Green Magdalene / Green Rose

Element: Priestess of earth, green robes
Ministry: Herbalism / Healing / Midwifery
Archetypes: Wise Woman / Antlered Goddess / Curandero
Color Codes: Vibrant green, rich earthy brown, warm sunlight
Sigil: Green fleur-de-lys or web of life / Celtic knot

Glance at the sun. See the moon and the stars. Gaze at the beauty of
earth's greenings. Now, think. What delight God gives to humankind
with all these things. All nature is at the disposal of humankind. We
are to work with it. For without we cannot survive.

HILDEGARD OF BINGEN

The first office on the elemental stations of the womb cross of the Magdalene Mandala is the Green Magdalene, representing earth. It could also be called the path of the green witch, also known as a hedge witch or an herbalist or a midwife. The Green Magdalene is a potion priestess and a wise woman. She is earth based and knowledgeable about the medicine within the earth and within the body. She wears a green mantle to illustrate that she is at one with the greening power of earth.

We find our hints of MM as a green witch expressed through the witch traditions of native medicine women throughout the world, including the native Christ-priestesses of Mary. The Magdalene path of the green witch harnesses the wisdom of Sophia, the serpent force, as it lands in telluric hot spots on the earth, helping us to ride, amplify, and imbue ourselves with the creative power rising from the ley lines of earth energy—the Dragon Chalices of power. With this earth magic a priestess or womb shaman becomes a conduit, oracle, and vessel for the vast intelligence of Gaia. This wisdom also includes aligning and flowing with the powers of the cycles and seasons, earthly, lunar, solar, celestial. It is not about manipulating earth to get what you want, but riding the energy to be the greatest possibility of who you can be.

At the heart of working in the office of the Magdalene green witch is developing a relationship with the soul of the earth, and the spirit of the plants, as well as the minerals, rocks, the rivers, streams, and lakes, and the animal and elemental beings.

Like with any relationship, if you communicate with plant and elemental beings, listen to them, and take care of them, a deep bond of understanding and relationships develops. Then if you need help with spiritual healing, for yourself or others, you can call on them and they will be there. But if you have never had a relationship with earth and her plant and mineral people, or her animal spirits, if you don't know them, if you've spent no time with them, if you've never listened to them, and never tended to them, they may still help you—but not with the same power and depth as a being who considers you to be like a family member. The wombcraft of MM as a green witch is a devotional relationship with earth, connecting to the Sophianic spirit of the plants—the goddess power living in them.

We can name this Magdalene path of the green witch as *whorticulture*—the wisdom of nature and the cycles of earth informed with the sacred sexual powers and practices of the ancient high priestesses, the Holy Whores of the Great Mother. The Magdalene witch-priestess lineage holds the ancient knowledge of healing and subtle awakening with plant medicine, flower essences, lunarized water, crystals, plant remedies, tinctures, poultices, aphrodisiacs, flower mandalas and blessing ceremonies, and Womb healing and awakening with steams and herbs. This wisdom was encoded in matrilineal grimoires, alchemy texts, and herbiaries.

MM's symbol of the anointing jar, with its distinguished lineage in the temples of Inanna, announces her as a potion priestess. We know that she is carrying a jar full of healing oils. Clearly, she is working with medicinal plants. In some of the apocryphal stories, MM goes to the tomb of Christ with her healing unguents and she applies her healing salves to his deep wounds, and helps resurrect him back to life. This alabaster jar filled with the healing unction of the feminine is the Holy Grail, flowing with the nature-infused memory of the Rose lineage.

In feminine consciousness, stories and myth are like a concertina, they can stretch out into many levels. We can see the stories of Magdalene and her healing unguents on a symbolic level, but we can also see it very practically—she is a medicine woman and herbalist. Taken literally, the heretical myths say Jesus didn't die. They took him off the cross, and brought him to a safe space, and the priestesses of Mary actually came with herbal remedies and applied them to his physical wounds to heal them.

In this reading of the story, we vision MM and the priestesses of Mary as herbal wise women, participating in a Living Resurrection ritual, with their herbs and spells. This is not something we usually hear about her, and to create this deep healing in someone who had been so injured, Magdalene would have to call upon the spirit of the plants, not just the biological properties. She would have called on the soul of Sophia embodied in earth and her plants to create this deep regenerative healing.

As we have read previously, vervain, which was an important herb all across Europe, was considered to be connected to the way Isis had regenerated Osiris, and the way MM regenerated Jesus. What these stories tell us is that MM was a green witch, she was a plant priestess. Just as we might stir our pots, making our salves,

Magdalene likely did this too. This is a lineage of her wisdom we can draw upon.

The green witch office is a treasury of old wisdom, held within the practical library of knowledge often passed from mother to daughter, as one of the green gifts of the Motherline. Not only is wisdom transmitted but important relationships and alliances between family bloodlines and spirits of place and plant species on earth. Certain plants, flowers, and stones are also renowned worldwide as allies and transmitters of this green office of the Magdalene, such as Rose and Lily in the flower realm, and Chrysocolla, the beautiful earth-jewel known as the "Goddess Stone," famed for its feminine consciousness and its energy of heart-womb magic.

In order to embody this office we must connect with the ensouled nature of earth, the living Goddess, the Earth Womb of creation, without whom we would not exist.

> *Holy Spirit, the life that gives life: You are the cause of all movement. You are the breath of all creatures. You are the salve that purifies our souls. You are the ointment that heals our wounds. You are the fire that warms our hearts. You are the light that guides our feet. Let all the world praise you.*
>
> HILDEGARD OF BINGEN

Aramaic Wisdom of the Earth
Makikhe—Mystical Surrender

Aramaic: Makikhe (Maa-kee-key)
Meaning: Meekness/surrender, to be "down to earth."

> *Blessed are the meek for they shall inherit the earth.*
> BEATITUDE 3, SERMON ON THE MOUNT

This is a word of wisdom that allows us to inherit the power and blessing of the earth element. It is a humbling; literally meaning *humus,* of being "down to earth."

We often perceive *meekness* as a word that implies subservience or weakness; yet it is actually a feminine, flowing word that evokes the softness and fluidity of nature. What the Beatitudes are whispering to us is the power of the feminine dimension.

In modern times, we are told that to succeed we have to push, force, or work hard. Makikhe, or meekness, tells us to let go, soften, open to the flow, return to earth. This meekness is to accept the complete humility of love; to let go of control, to let go of all agendas, expectations, and goals of what you want to get from a person or situation. This is an inner softening, a liquidity, an earthing. It allows all stuck emotions to soften, flow, and pass through your system, in trust and deep surrender.

This emotional softening and release allows us to connect with the power of earth, of being humble, grounded, rooted, and connected to the vast intelligence of life. In body prayers we evoke this feeling by bowing down, touching the earth, expanding our "I" with gratitude and a smallness that dissolves us into the vastness of the universe, where our humility is the door to infinity. This is also a catharsis, a feminine root word for descending into the feminine dimension—letting down liquid, like tears, menstrual blood, breast milk, and also letting down into liquid love.

Often grief can bring us into this state of humility and a softening into love, which is the natural state of our body. When we hold on to grief and emotion, it becomes stuck in the body, making us rigid, tense, and hard—the opposite of makikhe. This is why grief rituals and lamenting were so important in the feminine priestess traditions, as this connection to and expression of grief allowed flow and softness.

Similarly, when a baby is born it lets go and releases down into the birth canal, after being baptized by the flowing womb waters, to enter into the realm of Gaia. It passes through a mystical gateway into the earth world. During this descent down the birth passageway, the child falls backward and surrenders into a new life in the light.

The spiritual state of makeekay is deeply connected to the states of surrender experienced during birthing, deep grief, soul rebirthing, and sacred sexual union. Gratitude and giving thanks also bring us into deep states of humble peace.

With this Rose Petal we enter the organic light at the heart of creation, which radiates out through the natural world, and our deep instinctual feminine essence.

Rose Ritual—Gratitude for Life
Prepare for the Ritual
Create a simple Elemental Earth Bowl:

+ Choose a pot or glass bowl (not plastic).
+ Consecrate it for sacred use (cleansing with water and prayer will work).

+ Fill it with organic soil about an inch from the top.
+ Place a green candle in the center, held in the soil.
+ Place flowers around the candle on the soil.
+ You can also place crystals or herbs in the four corners.

Write a Gratitude List
+ On a sheet of paper write the *M* talisman at the top.
+ Then write either eleven things you are grateful for today or twenty-two things you are grateful for this year or thirty-three things you are grateful for in your life.
+ The number of "gratitudes" denotes the number of minutes (for example, eleven gratitudes make the ritual eleven minutes long). This can be done as a daily morning or evening practice. The twenty-two- and thirty-three-minute ritual can be done on auspicious dates.

Begin Your Ritual
+ Place your earth bowl in front of you (at least three feet away), on top of your talismanic gratitude list.
+ Light your candle and invoke the Feminine Christ light.
+ Sit with enough space to bow forward.
+ Place your hands in the womb "Venus mudra" (see illustration on page 445). Bow down to earth resting your Venus mudra on the floor.
+ Feel your gratitude to earth for all the gifts you receive.
+ Return to the original sitting pose with a womb Venus mudra.
+ Keep repeating this Venus mudra bow at a slow pace. Or, sit and meditate, pray, or just be in presence for eleven, twenty-two, or thirty-three minutes.

Complete Your Ritual
+ Finish by bowing once again to earth with the Venus mudra on the floor.
+ Blow out your candle thanking the Holy Trinity of Sophia and Earth.
+ In silence and gentle reverence empty the soil out onto the land. Make it an offering back to earth, planting your gratitude.
+ Wash your bowl out, visualizing that you are cleansing your chalice. Connect into the knowing that your chalice is open to receive.

Magdalene Moonistry: For menstruating women, you can also offer moon blood back to earth in gratitude, creating a bioenergetic mother-daughter bond with the Earth Mother. This Sophia sacrament celebrates the divinity of creation. As you make the offering, affirm: "I give back this life to she who gave me life. May my blood be rooted into the earth, flowing with her wisdom."

Note: Nonmenstruating women can practice this ritual using an herbal tea blend, including hibiscus for its beautiful red color. Prepare in a cup or chalice and offer on a dark moon.

Rose Petal 5—Embodied Shakti

Fire: Red Witch

Office of the Red Magdalene
   Element: Priestess of fire, red robes
   Ministry: Tantric Sex/Allurement/Manifestation
   Archetypes: Madame Pele/Red Tara/Scarlet Woman
   Color Codes: Vivid scarlet, and soft rose light
   Sigil: Downward-pointing red triangle

> *I, the fiery life of divine wisdom, I ignite the beauty of the plains, I*
> *sparkle the water, I burn in the sun, and the moon, and the stars.*
>
> HILDEGARD OF BINGEN

We next move around to the Red Magdalene, home to the element of fire. Other names for the Red Magdalene are the red witch, the Holy Whore, the Scarlet Woman, the Lady in Red, the sexual priestess. This is often summed up in the archetype of the sacred prostitute, the aspect of Magdalene that is high mistress of kundalini Shakti, whose sexuality is awakened and initiatory, and whose sensuality brings transformation both to herself and to others. The biblical word for this fire element transfiguration was *horasis,* a Greek word that means "womb enlightenment." Interestingly, it was said that Christ came to "baptize through fire."

The red priestess presides over the sexual and menstrual mysteries—she is the kundalini Shakti, the fire, the volcano, the lava, the heat that brings transformation and awakens our dragon power. If you watch the Hawaiian fire goddess Pele menstruating her lava, you see what is at the core of our Earth. It is fiery and wild, it destroys and creates, but it is also soft and flowing and brings new land and new worlds. This kundalini fire at the center of the Earth Womb also lives within the center of women's wombs. Menstruating women flow "lava" every month with the cycle of the moon, partaking in the incredible menstrual mysteries of the earth and moon. If we were to just meditate on that alone we would awaken our fiery core.

Because the fire element is perceived as wild and uncontrollable, it has often been dampened or suppressed in women—both individually and collectively. The red witch is not just a metaphor for kundalini, it actually represents a true office: lineages of real women, in real times, who practiced the feminine arts of the fire.

Throughout time, women who worked with fire both as a physical element and as psychic and energetic kundalini fire wore red to symbolize their awakened Shakti. In Sumeria, when a priestess was initiated, she wore a red turban; in the temples of Isis and Hathor in Egypt, the priestesses wore red robes and veils. In the native traditions of Britain, in places such as Devon and Cornwall, witches wore red shawls or headscarves to identify themselves. Red was the sign of a witch and female shaman. It was considered to be an alluring and dangerous color, like the women.

Of course, MM took the red robes of the priestesses and the initiation into the red rites, and received her inauguration and red robes. In medieval art Magdalene is often pictured wearing the red robe of the witch priestess. In the modern world, we don't necessarily see the significance of this connection unless it is pointed out, but five hundred years ago, if you saw artwork in a church with MM wearing a huge red cape, you would know the artist was communicating to you that MM was part of the witch tradition. And of course, red was also the color of menstrual blood, and gnostics used to mark a red cross on the forehead, another sign of the red witch.

The reputation of the "Lady in Red" lives on to this day, with associations of seduction, enchantment, sexual allurement, and witchcraft, harkening back to the sexually empowered priestesses of ancient times, who were then persecuted. The archetypal power of this office is full of intense magic, because all around the world, wearing red was a sign that not only were you a witch but you were a sacred sexual witch, a harlot. And a women's sovereign sexual power was forbidden.

What patriarchy feared more than anything was the fiery sexual power of an awakened woman in full command of her magic, who had the power to initiate.

There were many kinds of witches spoken about in the Inquisition, but what the church patriarchs raged against most was the "sexual licentiousness" of some witches. It was their fiery sexual power that really angered the establishment.

The sexual kundalini power of the fire element is analogous to volcanoes, each individual portal—be it human or earthly—channels a central fire within the earth. The source is shared and inexhaustible. You cannot put a volcano out. Its fire will flow again. It is linked through a network of energy, and rivers of primal magma, to volcanoes across the world. So it is with the office of the red priestess; her sexual fire power is eternal—even if it is suppressed, it may go underground and remain inactive for a while, but the essence and source of the fire is not extinguished, and it will return and rekindle.

When women connect their individual womb fires together in circle, and invoke its power with clear intentions, they generate an incredibly strong energy for change. The fire element, and the sexual kundalini energy, is a mediator and bridge between heaven and earth. It is the serpent that provides a ladder for consciousness to climb and ascend. Sexual energy is a sensual aliveness embodied in an awakened form. Although it can awaken or be gifted through physical sexual exchanges between people, it is not necessarily connected to sexual activity or sexual relationships.

Primarily, the kundalini fire reflects your connection to earth and the Spirit of Sophia, and how easily this can express and illuminate in your body and soul. Both men and women cultivated this sensual, serpentine sexual current as a solo practice. It was essential that a person had a good grounding in ethics and was evolving and purifying their consciousness before they worked with the power of kundalini fire. The fire element without discernment or maturity can burn or be destructive. Ideally, the fire element is balanced with water, and held between earth and air in the mandala, which requires rooting into the deep, organic, ancient wisdom of earth, rising into the visionary perspective and experience of air, with its clear, nonattached principles.

A Mistress of Fire is flowing with the power of her purified desire, a magnetic force that manifests everything that is in her highest purpose, and that illuminates her. When the fire element is awakened, a person becomes a lamp who can light others.

Be who God meant you to be and you will set the world on fire.
SAINT CATHERINE OF SIENA

Aramaic Wisdom of the Fire Element
Rachem—Holy Shakti of the Womb

Aramaic: Rachem (Rah-chem, with a breathy "ch," as in "challah")
Meaning: Mercy, womb, related word is *Rakhma,* unconditional love

> *Blessed are those filled with womb-light:*
> *for they shall find mercy.*
> GOSPEL OF MATTHEW 5:7

Rachem comes from the word root R-Ch-M and is present in different versions in Aramaic, Hebrew, and Arabic. It means a love that pours from the womb, and evokes the essence of a creative light, a radiating compassion pulsing in soft flames. Neil Douglas-Klotz says this about it in his translation, "From the old Hebrew word for 'womb' . . . the roots suggest the radiating forth of light and heat (RA) from an interior place (ChM)."[4] This rachem, love-mercy, which lives at the heart of the Feminine Christ teachings, is comparable to the love of a mother for a child. Hence it is also a word for womb; the magical portal of the Divine Mother mysteries.

This is the deep and unconditional love and mercy of the Great Mother, the Womb of God, who enfolds all in her arms, and creates, nurtures, sustains, and feeds them. It is the dynamic loving actions of womb consciousness, and the womb space that rests in the feminine dimension of *being;* the pulsing peace of the merciful essence of life.

It is this Womb of Love that Yeshu and Magdalene lead us to in their teachings of love, upon the path of Love. Because the word for love is a root word for womb, their teachings could also be called womb teachings, or the path of the womb—returning to our Source. Everyone has this Womb of Love within them, and is immersed in this Divine Womb.

We often associate the word *mercy* (a mermaid word) with softness, compassion, and a gentle, cradling love full of forgiveness and understanding; it is all of that, *and* it is also brimming with warmth, light, heat, and radiance: the flow of Cosmic Shakti. This mercy is wild as well as soft; it is fierce and pulsating with primal power. It is the love of a mother lioness, a tigress, a panther of the feminine, it is the Divine Mother's love in action, watching over her brood with wisdom and compassion.

The Holy Womb of Shakti is also scented with sensual elegance, because this love is not disconnected from the eros of existence, it is an embodied and ensouled love. It is a love that pours and flows upon rivers of desires and inspired creative audacity. Within the Womb of Love, we are asked to *come fully alive,* for our love to be fully lived, fully felt, fully expressed, fully initiated. It is also from this root word that we get the word *alchemy,* which speaks of a transformation or transfiguration of the very substance of the human soul, of a journey to divinize and resurrect our Shakti.

How are you creating this Womb of Love within your life, within your body, within your soul? Can you feel the spark of life, the fire of Shakti, within your sacred center?

This energy of rachem is not passive; it is *fully ignited.* When you feel this mercy, this Divine Shakti within you, what does it ask of you? Your womb knows the path of love. Tune in to this deep love, this holy fire, and ask it to guide you in your life.

Behold, the Queendom of the Goddess is within your womb.

LUKE 17:20–21

Rose Ritual
Holy Fire: Womb of Christos Ritual

Gather the following:

- ❧ 1 red tea light, organic
- ❧ A glass bowl of water, purified (if possible)
- ❧ Rose geranium anointing oil

Optional: hold or wear a red ruby
Space: dark, private, no noise (nighttime is ideal)
Ritual: Twenty minutes

For women/the feminine aspect of self:

+ Fill the bowl with the purified water.
+ Sit in a dark room with the bowl and light the candle. Place the red tea light in the bowl of water (it will float).
+ Anoint yourself with the oil on your forehead, heart, and womb.
+ Chant "Mar-ee-yah" three times across the water.
+ Pray for the Feminine Christ to bless the water.

✦ Meditate on the flame in the bowl of water for five minutes.

✦ Close your eyes and visualize the flame in your womb.

✦ Pray to receive the Christ light into your womb.

✦ Sit for ten minutes allowing the Christ flame to illuminate your womb.

✦ Close the ritual—blow the candle out in the name of the Holy Spirit. Pour the water in your garden, in the name of the Earthly Sophia. Ask that your womb be rooted in heaven as it is on Earth.

For men/the masculine aspect of self:

✦ Complete the same ritual, replacing the womb with the heart.

Rose Petal 6—Star Wisdom

Air: White Witch

Office of the White Magdalene/White Rose

Element: Priestess of air, white robes

Ministry: Psychic/Energy Worker/Visionary

Archetypes: Blessing Witch/Virgin Mary/Swan Priestess

Color Codes: Shimmering white light, and soft golden or silver glow

Sigil: White or gold crown

Rising out of the flames, we enter the celestial realms of the White Magdalene, who is emissary of the element of air or wind. She is known as a white witch, and also represents the high office of the Virgin Mary and the goddess Isis. In Celtic traditions she is called a blessing witch, a priestess who gives blessing and protection, and who presides over rituals and ceremony that celebrate rites of passage. This aspect of the Magdalene is also connected with psychic gnosis, prophecy, and visionary knowing—either through those who channel the upperworlds to predict the future or those who receive apparitions, such as the visitations of Mother Mary to Bernadette of Lourdes and the children at Medjugorje in Bosnia. Similar visions have been reported in Ireland and across the world, and the Blessed Virgin is often described as radiant, wearing white robes and shimmering with otherworldly light, similar in countenance to the Fairy Queen.

This office of the Magdalene is a heavenly doorway between the worlds. It is the portal of conscious conception and energy blessings, where white witches, midwives of consciousness and soul doulas, bring incarnating souls and visionary star wisdom through cosmic portals. It is also the home of the elemental gift of those who can give energy transmissions of light, such as reiki, hands-on healing, or long-distance healing. This gentle energy is purifying, uplifting, and inspiring. A famous archetype of this is the swan priestess lineage, the benevolent blessing witch who uses her vision to illuminate, bless, and protect others and to bring wisdom, inspiration, and support to herself and her community, invoking the Swan Mother.

Within the element of air, a key archetype of the white witch comes from the Egyptian and Celtic traditions. The goddess Hathor, in Egypt, is more often connected with the red witches, and with sacred sexuality and the priestess rites. Whereas Isis, as the Queen of Heaven, is a goddess of the stars and a goddess of the seas, more connected with the magic of starlight and the celestial realms. In the Celtic traditions, MM is strongly connected to the goddess Brighid or Bride, and there is long tradition of sacred sites, sacred wells, sacred legends being passed on to MM or to Saint Brigit, so that they are almost interchangeable. Brighid's feast day is Imbolc, February 1, which marks the returning light in the northern hemisphere.

The office of MM as the *Stella Maris* is also represented by the priestesses of Isis. Isis is depicted with white swan wings. The tradition of Bride and Isis is identical in many aspects, as they are both goddesses of the galactic womb and Milky Way. The powers of the white witch often originate in the celestial wisdom of the Milky Way and galactic womb, which is the holy seat and breast milk of the Cosmic Mother.

When a white witch takes shamanic journeys to collect wisdom and boons from these celestial realms it has a very distinct quality: it awakens them as a shining one, it is glittering with starlight. It is like flying through the universe on swan wings. There were whole schools of priestesses and womb shamans who would psychically travel to the galactic womb and travel down the Milky Way to receive prophecy and visionary wisdom that they would bring back to their community—this was classical feminine shamanism. They would fly with their animal familiar, a swan, for example, down the Milky Way to the constellation of Cygnus, which was believed to be the vulva of the galactic goddess. In the Gospel of Mary Magdalene, Magdalene was called sky walker or space conqueror, because she, like the dakinis of Tibet and the frequency of White Tara or Kwan Yin, held this role and this energy transmission of bright light.

If you are drawn to this office you will be attracted to travel with your spirit body to celestial realms. It will be easy for you to leave your body and

to access other worlds and information from other dimensions or star ancestors. This high swan magic holds a very refined subtle quality, as if starlight
is raining down on you. It is filled with the elegant power of air, which uplifts
us with a power that is transparent but potent. Those who are gifted in the air
element can often receive deep guidance for humanity from a very visionary, big
perspective—beyond all limits of time or space.

Whereas the green witch is very rooted, very down to earth, very practical,
the swan priestess is "up high in the clouds," drawn to the timeless and formless,
cultivating a consciousness that can receive the big visions that put everything into
perspective. This archetypal energy is dreamy, ethereal, enchanting, and refined. It
often needs to balance out with the grounding warmth of earth and fire elements.

Mary Magdalene, as the White Swan, could open doors to celestial realms,
she could bring through souls, and she could guide energy back home to the
Divine Mother. This office is a classic aspect of the Feminine Christ as light
bearer or Savioress.

This archetypal energy is also closely related to the Moon Mysteries, and
the way that the celestial body of the moon up in the heavens affects us down
here on earth. The moon herself is a celestial white witch who blesses, heals, and
purifies us. She was known as a lunar white swan as she waxed to full moon and
as she emerged as a new moon.

Aramaic Wisdom of the Air Element
Tahorah—Moon Mother/Soul Cleansing

Hebrew: טהרה
Tahorah (ta-whore-ah)
Meaning: Ceremonial purification

> *Then she shall remain in the blood of her*
> *purification for 33 days.*
>
> LEVITICUS 12:4

Related word in Arabic: *Harama.* Tahorah is consecrated for holy use, banned
from secular use, with the power to purify. A womb *whore/har* word related also
to harem—a sacred gathering of women; originally refers to a moon temple of
menstruating priestesses.

The wisdom of the moon, the celestial *Stella Maris,* was believed to be held in
women's wombs and their lunar cycles, giving them the power to bless and heal,

and also to practice purification rites for their own soul and the soul of their community. The bright light of the full moon was a blessing, and the dark moon was a cleansing.

Menstruation was first a divine ritual of purification granted by the blessings of the womb, following the mysterious lunar cycle, that could initiate a physical *and* soul cleansing—not only of the menstruating women, but for her entire community. Menstruation was a spiritual purification at a deep soul level in the form of release. It was the prototype of all forms of ritual exorcism, cleansing, and purification.

Menstruating women were considered to be the "holy of holies" as they purified the collective soul of the *anima mundi,* within the world womb, as well as their own personal womb. Such were their powers of purification it was forbidden for them to participate in secular activities, as their sacred powers were so strong at this time. During ovulation, a gift of the full moon, a woman was invested with radiant creative powers, where she could receive and impregnate with the heavenly light.

The moon is our teacher; sin is our spiritual power to cycle with the phases of birth/death/rebirth, which are so beautifully elucidated for us by the Moon Mother. We learn of the dark moon and the letting go into the spaciousness of the womb of emptiness; then the magic of the first light of the new moon, born from the womb of dark. We learn of our waxing, gestating, creative power as the moon grows into her shining radiance, until we receive the astounding heavenly glory of her fullness giving itself to all life at the peak high moon. Then the descent begins, waning, letting go, pouring the light of the sun down into the dark womb of Mother Earth. We understand the nonattachment of the natural creative cycle.

The cosmic mystery school of the moon and lunar consciousness teaches us about *timing,* and the process of initiating, gestating, ripening, and then releasing and clearing. It is one of the most important feminine practical arts that is very much connected to embodiment and the laws of form and nature, the immanent Sophia. Although womb shamans have traditionally been celebrated as mistresses of this art, *all* human beings are children of the moon and flow with the lunar cycles.

The high vision of air asks us to understand where we are in the cycle of our souls, and the cycle of our bodies and emotions, and to trust and honor that cyclical embodiment. It makes us ask not *if* but *when,* as we consult our inner guidance and star wisdom. For there are no fixed possibilities, or certainties in life, but there are certain flows, moments, and timings that we can cleverly ride, calling on the cosmos as our ally. We can know when to conceive and when to menstruate energetically.

When we do not flow or cycle, we become stuck and stagnant, we make mistakes, and act out of line with the harmony of the universe. We come "out of the flow." In some cases, this creates the need for an exorcism, a menstruation of trapped energy.

The practice of astrology, and reading tarot and oracles, comes from this practicum of reading the signs presented to us in high vision to give guidance and direction.

> *To every thing there is a season, and a time to every purpose under*
> *the heaven:*
> *A time to be born, and a time to die; a time to plant, and a time to*
> *pluck up that which is planted;*
> *A time to kill, and a time to heal; a time to break down, and a*
> *time to build up;*
> *A time to weep, and a time to laugh; a time to mourn, and a time*
> *to dance.*
>
> ECCLESIASTES 3

Rose Ritual
Anointing of the Moon Ritual

> *She is come; the return of the feminine is at hand*

> *Repent ye: for the kingdom of heaven is at hand*
>
> MATTHEW 3:2

✦ Anoint with red ochre on the palms of the hands, the tops of the feet, and on the third eye gateway, the place between the eyebrows. You can mix in moon blood with your ochre.

✦ Pray with your hands in a wide V shape above your head, the universal "drawing down the moon" position, which has been depicted since Paleolithic times.

✦ After raising your arms and greeting the moon, bring your hands into a Venus mudra above your head, so that your hands are creating a triangle shape. Gaze at the moon through this pyramid, channeling lunar power into your body.

✦ Feel the power of the moon and the celestial cycles.

+ Ask for cosmic divine wisdom to flow into you from the Divine Mother, and for the shining light of the moon to illuminate you.
+ Visualize radiant starlight and moonlight circulating around your body before settling into the chalice of your womb, which gathers the moon rays.
+ Complete by bringing your arms down and placing the Venus mudra as a downward pointing triangle over your womb, infusing the energy.

In a womb circle gathering, you can anoint each other and pray, meditate, sing, or chant, feeling the womb power of the original harem of holy moon priestesses, as you channel the power of the moon and star systems as they waltz round the sky.

Magdalene of the Mystery—Incantation

Ask the Moon and Stars to transmit wisdom of the great cycles of life and cosmos.

> *Magdalene of the Mystery*
> *Magdalene of the Ring*
> *Magdalene of the Mystery*
> *To you this song we sing*
>
> *Magdalene of the Doorway*
> *Magdalene of the light*
> *Magdalene of the Doorway*
> *Shine on us so bright*
>
> *The grail cup is pouring*
> *Down into my heart*
>
> *The Grail Cup is calling*
> *Deep within my womb*
>
> *Anoint us with your love*
> *Anoint us with your light*
> *Anoint us with your wisdom*
> *Turn us toward the good*
>
> *Magdalene of the Mystery*
> *Doorway of the Soul*
> *To you this song we sing*

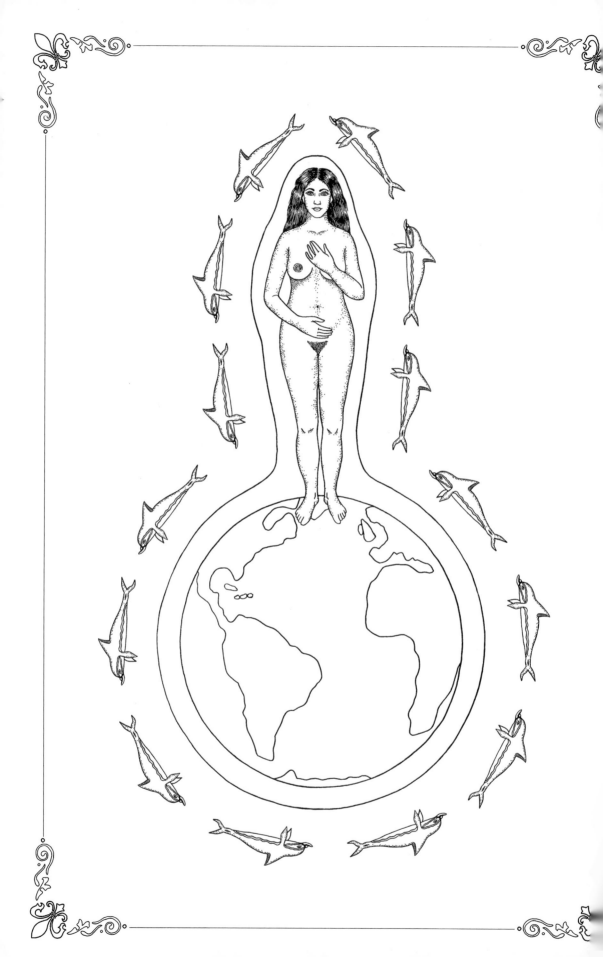

Rose Petal 7—Mermaid Rituals

Water: Sea Witch

Office of the Blue Magdalene / Blue Rose

Element: Priestess of water, blue robes
Ministry: Cleansing/Anointing/Spiritual Beauty
Archetypes: Mermaid/Aphrodite/Lady of the Lake
Color Codes: Bright aqua and turquoise, deep sea greens
Sigil: Comb and mirror, *M* pictograph, chalice

As we move around the mandala to our next office of the Magdalene, we come to the Blue Magdalene in the element of water. This is a very specific blue, not midnight blue, but vivid turquoise, azure, or aqua. It brings the deep healing frequency of the ocean and the restorative powers of the waters of life. The feminine shamans in this element are often named as a sea witch, or mermaid, or temple priestess, or lady of the lake. They are great healers, bringing medicine through harmony, beauty, purification, and baptism. Visualize a tired or overwhelmed aspect of yourself or the world being bathed in beautiful aquatic blue waters and cleansed with gentle waves of energy. The water element is deeply feminine, attuned to our most precious and vulnerable feelings, and holds a very uplifting vibration, filled with purity of heart.

In Mesopotamia there was a true and historic lineage of water priestesses that specialized in the elemental medicine of water that heals, restores, and rebirths. In ancient Sumeria there were two female water divinities that the priestesses worked with. One is Tiamat, who is the goddess of the deep, the great water dragon of the ocean. The other was Nammu, the spirit of fresh water, lakes, rivers, and wells. The priestesses of Nammu were known for carrying an alabaster jar. And of course MM also carries an alabaster jar, a symbol that reveals her lineage as a mermaid priestess. In their public ministry, Jesus, Magdalene, and the apostles worked around the Lake of Galilee, in the lands that were home to the Jewish mermaid goddess Asherah, who bears the epithet: "She who strides across the waters."

John the Baptist, whom Jesus was once a student of, performed baptism rituals in the River Jordan—a tradition that originated with the water priestesses of Sumeria. The Bible describes how Jesus's disciples baptized even more people than John did. This suggests a foundational elemental magic within the spiritual life of Mary Magdalene, who was a priestess of Sophia and cultivated a deep connection with the great world soul of earth, and this beautiful natural magic of land and water. We can close our eyes and go back in time to when she and

Yeshu were being baptized in the River Jordan, under the divine sigil of the goddess—the Dove—also calling upon the lineage of the mermaids and honoring the spirit of water goddess Nammu.

We can vision that when they were doing their water rituals at the Lake of Galilee, they were honoring the great water divinity of the goddess in the full knowledge that without that water of life, both physically and spiritually, we would not be alive. In the Christian tradition there is a great celebration of water—from the fountain of life, the baptismal font, to the numerous mentions of the living waters in the gospels, and in sayings attributed to Jesus, including: "Whoever believes in me, as the Scripture has said, out of his heart will flow rivers of living water" (John 7:38).

In Celtic traditions, the sacred oral traditions recount stories of the Well Maidens, revered women who were guardians and priestesses of the springs, rivers, wells, and lakes that were believed to be holy and a gateway to Otherworld and the gods. The concept of the fountains, wells, and living waters that give redemption and spiritual sustenance originated in the traditions of the mermaid priestesses and ancient womb shamans. They were so connected with the divinity of earth that they understood that water was holy and sacred, and that water is encoded with cosmic memory and possibility, so when we baptize with it, or anoint or submerge ourselves in water, we are creating new quantum possibilities in our body and soul.

There is a powerful vibration of harmony, beauty, peace, and bliss in the water element, channeled by those who are drawn to this office of the Magdalene. The healing and purification of water is not the intense, cathartic experience of fire; instead it flows with a profound softness of love that is gentle, restorative, and regenerative. If you have ever had a really difficult time, you may have felt this pull to go to the water to help yourself heal and integrate the experience. Mother Ocean and her beautiful aqua water is visualized as a deity and goddess across the world.

This archetype is very connected with Aphrodite, who is often pictured emerging naked from the sea, held within a great scallop shell, the symbol of the divine yoni.

Often the sea witch, the Blue Magdalene, is an essence we call upon when we are feeling quite depleted or overwhelmed. It is a regenerative vibration, filled with beautiful and auspicious healing energy. We reconnect with the flow of life again.

Aramaic Wisdom of the Water Element
Maryah Alaha—Devotion of the Heart
   Aramaic: Maryah Alaha (Maaa-ree-ah Aal-aa-haa)
   Meaning: Light within Creation, related word is *Elohim* (birth goddesses)

The Aramaic name for god is Alaha—the living breathing presence of the Great One. The translation of the tetragrammaton, YHWH, is Maria/Morio, usually transliterated as *Mary-ah,* meaning "Honored One." *Mar/Mor* is a feminine womb word referring to the great oceans of the original Womb of Creation, also embodied within the sacred womb of woman, the shamanic seascape and gateway to heaven that births every human being into this world. Mari/Mar was originally a titular name for the great goddess, and eventually became an honorific prefix for persons of any gender who held a high position of respect and power. Jesus and Mary Magdalene called their god Maryah Alaha in their spiritual work. Speaking, incanting, or chanting this name opens the womb-heart into god's love.

Living the Path of Devotion

Maryah Alaha is the unity of the great ocean of womb consciousness that births us into being as an individual drop of water or light particle. It is the Great Mermaid, who also brings us the remembrance that there is a unified reality we all come from that is our true substance, and which we can always return to and live from within. The love within this vibration is liquid, flowing, dissolving our "self."

By remembering the truth of Maryah Alaha within us, we invoke the power of sacred duality, where form and formlessness, visible and invisible, light and dark are married together in an ecstatic, devotional union. When we feel the cosmos make love within Maryah Alaha we revoke the negative spell of separation, where we forget our origins. The great "Mar" calls us back to the ocean of vibration that lives within.

The name *Alaha* resonates in the chambers of the sacred heart and opens us to love. This oceanic love awakens our sacred heart-womb into pure devotion. We can take time every day to stop for a few moments, and place one hand on the heart, and one hand on the womb, and whisper to ourselves "Maryah Alaha"—and for a moment we can release our body and soul back to the ocean of union, exhale, and merge back into the vast primordial birth waters within Divine Mother's womb. On the next inhale we can gather this energy back into our current incarnation, into our body.

Our bodies are made of almost 70 percent water, and we are aquatic beings. Opening ourselves to this waveform of energy within, and the waterways of blood and lymph in our bodies, feeling our breath as great oceanic tides, helps us relax. In breathing with this magical tidal pulse of life, we remember we are both human and mermaid, primal and celestial, finite and infinite, formless and embodied.

We belong to the earth and we also belong to the great deep—the tehom—of the Divine Mother. Before we walked on earth, we swam inside the oceanic womb.

Rose Ritual
Mermaid Incantation—Eleven Minutes

Awakening the vibration of the voice with incantation and ceremonial sound was a key of the priestess healing arts. Sound shamanism helps us to literally become enchanting. With magical incantation our voice can transform into a powerful shamanic musical instrument. Sacred sound helps restore the body's cellular resonance, and encodes dimensional doorways into psychic realms, which enchant the soul back home. Incantation takes many forms, from prayer, invocation, toning, singing, and chanting, to yoga nidra, guided shamanic journeys, and regression. Sound is often described as oceanic or moving in waves and opens us to the flow.

Magical Items
- Crystal glass filled with water
- A stop clock if you prefer to time your ritual

Temple Preparations
- Place your glass on an altar you are facing, or in front of you if you do not have an altar.
- Sit in a comfortable position, cross-legged or kneeling.

Ritual Body Prayer
+ Gaze into the water in the crystal glass, invoking the lineage of holy mermaids,
+ Contemplate the liquid water,
+ Contemplate the crystal container. One's nature is to flow, and expand. One's nature is to hold, and contain.
+ Bring your hands into prayer position in front of your heart (see illustration).
+ Chant the name "Maryah," feeling the energy kiss of your hands. Feel the power of attraction for union and embodiment.
+ Move your hands into the Orans position (see diagram) as you chant "Alaha." Feel your heart opening and expanding and flowing outward.

Prayer mudra of the heart   **Orans position**

Venus mudra

✦ Bring your hands back to prayer mudra and chant "Maryah,"
✦ Then open your hands out into the Orans mudra and chant "Alaha."
✦ Continue this for eleven minutes, feeling love flow through you and embody in you.
✦ Complete by moving your hands into the Venus mudra (see illustration). Infuse the warm healing energy into your womb space.
✦ Visualize the water infused with the sound vibration of love you have generated. You can sip the water as a sacrament and then give the rest as an offering back to earth.

> *Great Mother, I have never ceased hymning your name.*
> *I have heard your call.*

Place of Refuge—Closing Prayer

In this place of refuge

I met my soul

I came home

Womb of God

I take refuge

I am safe here

Seashore calls

Waves of peace

Wash my heart

In this place of refuge

I met my soul

I came home

Ancient Mothers

Ancient Mermaids

Your Refuge is my home

In this love I take refuge

Your waves carry me home

Rose Petal 8

Spirit Door—Black Witch

Office of the Black Magdalene/Black Rose

Element: Cosmic Womb/Earth Womb, black robes

Ministry: Rebirth/Initiation/Soul and Death Doula

Archetypes: Black Madonna/Kali/Cailleach

Color Codes: Midnight black, deep purple, and deep blue light

Sigil: Raven, four-armed cross, or ouroboros

> *[S]he made darkness Her secret place; Her pavilion round about
> her were dark waters and thick clouds of the skies.*
>
> PSALM 18:11

> *I said to my soul, be still, and let the dark come upon you
> Which shall be the darkness of God.*
>
> T. S. ELIOT, "FOUR QUARTETS"

We know the Black Magdalene in mystical Christianity as the Black Madonna. In Tibet, she is also known as Troma Nagmo, the Black Dakini, or Black Tara. She is also the Cauldron of Cerridwen, the Egyptian Nuit, and the black goddess of ancient India, Kali Ma. In the Magdalene traditions she is also linked to Sara-le-Kali. She is the Cosmic Womb. In this aspect she is the origin of where everything is birthed. She is the deep black Void from which all life emerges and to which all life returns. Her Divine Mystery is the great infinity of god, called the "deep dazzling darkness."

In churches and cathedrals, we often find the Black Madonna located down inside the crypt, symbolizing the deep, dark womb underworld that is her black throne. We can return to her womb while living to be rebirthed. All the great mystics and initiates called upon this return to the womb for a second birth. While our birth mother forges our body and brings it into the world, the second birth forges our divinity from within the Cosmic Mother's womb, to rebirth our awakened soul. Everyone who undergoes deep transformation experiences this death and rebirth.

This can be a very deep and overwhelming and disorienting experience. The Black Magdalene chooses us, when we are ready. As a culture, we are experiencing this rebirth as collective consciousness now descends into the Void, the Womb of Kali. It requires surrender; the more afraid and overwhelmed we are, the more surrender helps the process. Going through the death and resurrection is rarely a fully conscious choice. When we are dancing with the Black Dakini it is normal to feel disoriented, isolated, afraid, depressed, anxious, losing a sense of self, because you are actually being dissolved; the old you is being dismantled. In the mystery traditions this prepares us for our real-life death, because at the time of death, we dissolve our human form. We leave this world. And if we have done it while we are alive, we are more familiar with it, so it makes that transition easier. It makes it easier to step between different dimensions, and to travel the underworld realms of the bardo.

The office of the Black Magdalene facilitates a profound purification, to meet and heal our soul wounds, so that we can emerge empowered by the vastness of the Divine. Traditionally, in mystery initiates, this experience removes the fear of death.

What we discover in the depths of darkness is a love so spacious and embracing that it permeates the fabric of all life, interwoven with every aspect of our worldly lives. At the very heart of darkness, a ray of light births out, from the depths of this love. It is like a black hole/white hole: when you descend into the Void it appears as if you are being sucked into a magnetic black hole, but when you are coming out the other side, you are "seeing the light." In physics, on the other side of a black hole is a white hole that is birthing out new energy into a different universe or dimension. The divine portal of the black hole transmutes and transforms all our sorrow and suffering, rebirthing it out again as a new ray of light, a new dawn of consciousness.

In Christianity, when we peel away all the dogma, it speaks of an amazing shamanic transformation process that is at the very heart of humanity and our deepest experiences: gestation, birth, bliss, and bereavement, grief, then rebirth of hope. Most people have times when they enter the cave of darkness, the tomb of Christ, the womb of Kali. It feels like there is no light, as if all hope is being sucked out. It can be terrifying; we plead, "I don't want to go in!" And then you are in, and it is lonely and overwhelming. It feels like everything is falling apart and nothing is working. In the Christ Mysteries, it is at this point that even Jesus cries out in confusion and despair, feeling that God has abandoned him. He calls out *Eli Eli lama sabachthani?*—which means, "My God, my God, why have you forsaken me?"

But then comes the moment when the door opens, and that first shaft of light comes, and you see the light. You emerge from the womb-tomb. This is also the first experience we have here on earth, traveling from a dark womb, down a dark passageway, until finally we emerge into a startling light that reveals an entirely new world, a vast new dimension of being.

It encodes the cycles of life, and the cycles of rebirth, which is why the Christ Mysteries are so relevant and have endured over thousands of years. They speak to us at such a primal level of this womb experience of being in the dark, gestating, journeying, and then being rebirthed out into a new dimension—born into the light.

Black Magdalenes are called to this office to act as soul midwives, assisting people through this death and rebirth process, much like a doula supports a woman at birth. Only the person birthing their soul can complete the process, but they can be supported, especially by those who are experienced in how to navigate the journey. In the divine darkness, if we can withstand the journey, we discover our wisdom, our power, and our treasures of soul and spirit and the gifts of our ancestral lineage.

When we are in that rebirthing space, we need to be really gentle with ourselves, and call upon allies. In the Christ Mysteries, the Mary priestesses come into the tomb and minister to Jesus while he is in his death/resurrection transition space. It is completely dark, but the Marys are carrying torches. They arrive at the tomb as his allies; they are the midwives of consciousness. They find Christ in his initiatory journey, battered and bruised, and they come with their medicines on every level.

These traditions are very real, they map the deep individual psychological, spiritual, and cultural and collective transformation process. We know it will feel like the womb-tomb experience will last forever and that we will never see the light again. We need to call upon allies, so we don't have to do it alone. No one ever came out of that tomb without a midwife. That is the heart of the story, and that is the heart of the Magdalene Mysteries. The Feminine Christ is always with us and within us.

> *O guiding dark of night!*
> *O dark of night more darling than the dawn!*
> *O night that can unite*
> *A lover and loved one,*
> *Lover and loved one moved in unison.*
>
> "THE DARK NIGHT OF THE SOUL,"
> BY SAINT JOHN OF THE CROSS
> (TRANSLATED BY A. Z. FOREMAN)

Completing the Mandala

We can see in the different offices of the Magdalene all aspects of how she created an alchemical container of transformation. The herbs and green wisdom of earth, the activation of kundalini fire, the blessing and protection of the higher realms, the healing balm of water, and the death and rebirth initiation that resurrects our love.

This is the mandala of Magdalene and her key elemental offices, which are aspects of her soul, and *our* soul and the collective feminine soul, present in everyone on earth.

These medicines of the Magdalene are gifted through this resurrection mandala. In our journey, first we call upon it as a resource to ourselves. Otherwise we can't minister to anyone else. We are calling on the medicine of the Magdalene that we ourselves need. And only after that can we be a medicine for other people. With the offices of the Magdalene there is a gift to receive, but also the question, "What can I give?" Your wisdom is needed in the world, and that is the greater purpose of this Vision Quest, to hear the call of the Magdalene and to come into one of her offices, one of her ministries. She will give resources, gifts, and soul healings so you can share wisdom with the world as part of the greater ministry of the Magdalene.

The Magdalene Mandala is about recognizing the archetypes and unifying them, uniting them, recognizing how the sacred feminine, or the template of the whole woman, has been fragmented. It is the unification of the feminine archetypes that creates the most profound effect, transmitting out the divine feminine essence. It creates the "whole womb," the whole woman.

CHAMBER 32

SACRED UNION

Entering the Bridal Chamber

THE CENTER OF THE ROSE of the Feminine Christ teachings is at-one-ment with the radiating, pulsing, loving heartbeat of all creation, divinized and embodied on earth.

In classic gospel teachings it was described with the Aramaic words *malkutha shamayim,* which have often been translated as the prophetic "kingdom of heaven." Yet this name contains the seed of a beautiful, blooming flower of the Magdalene Mysteries. If this word vibration is to be our alchemical map, where does it point?

Malkutha, the word translated as "kingdom" in the gospels, which is at the heart and center of the ministry of Jesus, is actually a feminine noun, making it more accurately a "queendom." In the Jewish mystical tradition, Malkuth is also the throne of the Shekinah, and the queendom of the Lower Sophia of the Sephiroth. The word *Malkutha* was originally the name of the ancient Great Goddess and expresses the embodied and immanent divinity of the feminine root of creation.

Shamayim, the word translated as "heaven," is not a distinct place or city above and outside of the world but is instead a state of divine consciousness that permeates all creation. It is a frequency of love and a dimension of being, as well as a subtle realm. It is the vibrating flow, play, and pulsing spanda of Divine Shakti, the shimmering light and sound waves vibrating through all of creation in harmonic resonance.

It is this shimmering queendom that the Magdalene Mysteries invite us into.

The name Jesus calls god is feminine, and the heaven he seeks is a queendom already here on earth, the realm of Sophia, fully unified and embodied. This feminine queendom is a vibration of such exquisite beauty and harmony that few can actually feel it or tune in to it or exist within this fairy queendom of the "living goddess." The priestess lineage of Magdalene was devoted to this embodiment.

We cannot return to the queendom without returning to the womb, and our state of original, undivided womb consciousness (with a childlike heart, as Jesus describes), from where we can have our second birth into alchemical, individuated adulthood. Heaven is our interconnectedness, the unified quantum energy soil at the root of everything, whereas earth or creation is the individual flowering of that root. Everything grows from the invisible darkness to the visible light (in druidic thought this is expressed by an upside-down tree with its roots in the air). Creation is the flowering, the spontaneous, fluorescent budding of the Divine Source into millions of expressions, each unique, beautiful, belonging to the flowering of consciousness; each one with its own colors, textures, sounds, light forms, yet all rooted in love.

Heaven on earth is Sophia's journey to bring illuminated wisdom from the root to blossom out into the flower, in new manifestations of love and consciousness. It is an experiment in Divine Mothership, to allow the cosmic individuation of creation through free will, while still remaining sourced and connected into the root Mother.

In Eastern mystical traditions (Kabbalah) earth/creation can influence heaven; just as a birth mother is always psychically connected to her children, and her love or experience is passed onward to them, *also* their healing, love, or experience feeds back to her. Divine Mother and her creations (children) are in a "becoming" together.

DAWN OF THE RESURRECTION

He is Risen,
She is the Light of the World.

Vision: *It is early morning on the day of the resurrection, before the dawn has risen. It is complete darkness. Mary Magdalene and the Marys are walking in procession across the land to the tomb—they are each bearing a torch, held high against the dark night sky. Theirs is the only light visible across the land, the flame of the*

torches they are bearing. They are walking over a hill and silhouetted with this light.
It is like a funeral march or a procession, but it is soft and determined, each foot
like a prayer in front of the other, walking with perfect knowing, through the deep
night. Jesus lay in the tomb enshrined in darkness, heavy like black velvet around
him. The resurrection is not yet come. But the myrrh bearers are on their way to
find him and bring the balm.

Mary Magdalene, and the Mary priestesses, reach the garden, the tomb is
in view, and suddenly on the horizon, the first ray of light appears . . . as the sun
begins to rise up.

When Christ is in the tomb, he is in the Womb-Cave of the Divine Mother—through the Magdalene Doorway he has accessed the multidimensional gate of creation, where all opposites are unified. Its origin is Inanna's descent into the Underworld. To descend into this place of pure harmonic resonance also requires traveling through the fractured aspects of personal and collective consciousness to heal them.

In doing so, it was believed that his union with Sophia, marrying heaven and hell again, had reopened the cosmic door between the worlds, deep in the world womb, and set free trapped souls—creating a cosmic redemptive pathway for humankind.

The Bible describes this shamanic journey: "What does 'he ascended' mean except that he also descended to the depths of the earth? He who descended is the very one who ascended higher than all the heavens, in order to fill the whole universe" (Ephesians 4:9–10).

In the crucifixion story of Jesus, those with the eyes to see can understand the feminine descent symbolism hidden in the story. Jesus was crucified on "the Living Cross" or the "Cross of Calvary," which was a representation of the feminine Tree of Life—a parallel story to Odin's hanging on the Norse Yggdrasil tree of life, as well as images of the mystery school saviors, Dionysus and Orpheus, hanging on a cross or tree of life. The flow of Christ's blood into the earth, and his three-day entombment in a womb cave enacts the shamanic "menstrual" descent and merging into the body and consciousness of Mother Earth, paralleling the ritual journeys once practiced by almost every culture across the earth for thousands of years.

The alchemical map of this process is the outer limbs of the Tree of Life/Elemental Cross merging into the center still point, where the diverse creative powers are activated and completed into awakening, and then unified into a central "eye" of One.

It can also be expressed as the alchemical marriage of the Dragon and the Dove, or Serpent and the Swan—the union of masculine and feminine, and spirit and matter.

When this alchemical union is achieved within the psyche, we unite the cerebral consciousness with the cerebellar feminine dreamtime consciousness, and awaken our innate capacity for co-creation and co-dreaming with the world soul of Sophia.

Rose Ritual
Dragon and Dove

> *Be as wise as the serpent and as a pure as the dove.*
>
> MATTHEW 10:16

The Dove/Cosmic Womb/Holy Spirit
The Dragon/Gaia Womb/Primordial Shakti

When the two become one, heaven on earth is birthed

Dove/Swan Elements: Purity, devotion, surrender, descending, lunar
Mantra: "I am birthed by the power of creation, as a child of the Cosmos, I am above nothing in creation and surrender to the innocence of love."

Dragon/Serpent Elements: Power, passion, creation, ascending, solar
Mantra: "I am a vessel to birth the power of creation, as a primal generator of the Cosmos, I am beneath nothing in creation and I manifest bliss."

Dragon and Dove Movement Meditation

We can imagine our body as the alchemical container for this process, as the Tree of Life, with our legs and womb as the roots, and our arms and head as the branches.

Visualize the Tree of Life, expressed as an elemental cross within the human body. The head is upperworld, the feet are lowerworld, and each outstretched arm is a side of the cross. From our womb, the roots snake downward into the earth through our legs, connecting us to the Earth Womb; from our heart, the branches expand us upward and outward through our arms and head, out into the Celestial Womb. We are rooted with wings, serpents, and doves.

We can visualize a serpent of kundalini Shakti emerging from the fiery core

of earth, winding itself around the trunk of the tree, our thirty-three-vertebrae spinal column, charging our body with life force. This is the elemental power of life gifted to us by Mother Earth, the lower Sophia. When we die and cross to spirit world, this serpent life force returns back to Gaia's Womb. This serpent or dragon energy is part of our holographic embodied feminine soul.

We can also visualize a spirit bird, such as a dove or swan, resting up high in the branches of the Tree of Life/Womb Cross, which is our spirit or divine soul. This aspect of us is a subtle consciousness that can "fly out" outside the body and journey. This is the aspect of our feminine soul connected to the Higher Sophia and the cosmos that can journey through multiple dimensions before returning to the body to roost in the upper branches. At death this aspect returns back to the stars.

+ Visualize the spine becoming a serpent.
+ Visualize the spine stretch out and undulate.
+ Notice any places in the spine where the serpent feels restricted. Allow the serpentine energy to keep flowing.
+ Breathe up from the base of the spine.
+ Raise your arms, allow wings to unfold from your back/shoulder. Feel your wings open your chest and the heart chakra.
+ Breathe to the root of your serpent tail and the tip of your wings.
+ Sit or stand in meditation, breathing with this awareness for eleven minutes.

You can also practice this with your beloved.

+ Sit or stand back to back and merge the spinal serpents.
+ Allow the swan-angel wings to unfold together.

Descending into the Womb of the World
Tantric Union, Two Become One

Mary said, "There is but one saying I will speak to the Lord concerning the mystery of truth: In this have we taken our stand, and to the cosmic are we transparent."

FROM THE GNOSTIC DIALOGUE OF
THE SAVIOR, NAG HAMMADI

This journey of descent and resurrection also takes place in sacred sexual union. This unfolds inside the crucible of the womb, when the magnetic gravitational pull of attraction between the complementary poles of male and female, or the inner masculine and feminine, or any magnetic configuration of love, is completely surrendered to. In the mystical center point of this meeting, souls and bodies merge; a perfect union and spaciousness unfolds that dissolves all polarity and transcends them into pure bliss consciousness. The lovers become the archetypal world parents, rebirthing and fertilizing the world.

"Thy kingdom come" has a hidden tantric meaning when translated as "her queendom comes," referring to the orgasmic bliss of the queendom of Shakti that is "coming" into existence, delighting creation with pulse waves of quantum

pleasure. This queendom of Shakti lives within all people transfiguring the body into bliss.

A sexual descent into the womb for the purposes of spiritual awakening and deepening into love has been practiced over thousands of years by the tantric, gnostic, Taoist, Hermetic, and mystery school lineages. This archetypal story of Jesus and Magdalene's redemptive sexual union is part of this Grail tradition.

In the Indian tantric traditions, the Baul songs say: "In the Muladhar is the mother of the world, and in the Sahasrar is the father. If the two are united, you won't die or be born again." Philosopher and psychologist Carl Jung says of this alchemy of opposites meeting in the *conjunctio:* "The meeting of two personalities is like the contact of two chemical substances: if there is any reaction, both are transformed."

In the Christ teachings of inner alchemy, it also refers to the deep spiritual power of "two becoming one." In the canonical gospels it says of marriage, "So they are no longer two but one flesh. What therefore God has joined together, let not man separate" (Matthew 19:6). And in the apocryphal Gospel of Thomas, Jesus goes deeper into the tantric teaching on unification, saying: "When you make the two into one, and when you make the inner like the outer . . . and the upper like the lower, and when you make male and female into a single one, so that the male will not be male, nor the female be female . . . then you will enter [the queendom]."[1]

This tantric merging of the left hand and right hand, representing the solar and lunar currents of the creative forces, is also discussed in the Acts of Peter, where Peter explains why he is being crucified upside down: "Concerning this the Lord says in a mystery, 'Unless you make what is on the right hand as what is on the left and what is on the left hand as what is on the right and what is above as what is below and what is behind as what is before you will not know the [queendom].'"[2]

In the Gospel of Philip, a gnostic text found at Nag Hammadi, it says that light and darkness, life and death, right and left "are brothers of one another, they are inseparable," again illuminating the doctrine of the "two as one" through unification.

This alchemical unification process can take place in any sexual union, where the polarities of left and right, solar and lunar, deep and high are becoming married.

Doorway of Sacred Union

This sacred marriage of opposites is at the heart of the Christ Mysteries, taking place within the Bridal Chamber of womb consciousness. Our everyday relationships also evoke this initiatory chamber. Placing our intimate relationships at the center of our spiritual altar creates a paradigm shift. Our everyday life becomes the practice. The details of our relationships become a rosary bead to meditate and pray with, bringing deep alchemical potential. Our heart's longing to be deeply touched by a soulful love that is embodied and lived here in the flesh becomes a beacon of light. We enter the Bridal Chamber. Mary Magdalene was known as the woman who loved much. On this path, we are not measured by how enlightened we are, or how perfected we are. Rather, we are called to live the question: "How much can I open my heart to love?"

It doesn't matter if you are madly in love, or happy alone, or desperately lonely, or if you have "failed" in love many times, or if you are in deep union, or if you are afraid of commitment, or who you love, or what your gender or sexual orientation is—this Great Love accepts all pilgrims, and anoints all who answer onto the Path of Love.

The Magdalene Mysteries are about *how to open the Magdalene, the magical doorway*—or said another way, *how to open the heart-womb as a gateway to love*. For the feminine, it is about becoming the Magdalene, becoming the chalice—sensual, radiant, magnetic, embracing, open, vulnerable, powerful, radically alive. For the masculine it is about recognizing that the woman is the Magdalene, that her body and soul holds the keys of magical nectar of life—and through his love, he has the power to bloom her open, so they may both step across the threshold together into the mystery. This can be practiced as an outer or inner alchemy by anyone.

This was known as horasis in ancient times, and was the secret of the mystical "crucifixion" within the great round of the elemental womb cross—the physical, spiritual, sexual awakening through the portal of the activated Magdalene womb-heart. It is the key to awakening a multidimensional sexuality rooted in pure love.

It is a co-creative process in which the door is inside of us, and we need only remember how to open up this doorway and step through—and by doing this we step into a different dimension, and our own personal evolution and the evolution of humanity takes a quantum leap forward. We begin to activate at the next level what we might call our magical powers: telepathy, extrasensory perceptions, the ability the shift the energetic fabric of life, to have positive effects on the quantum field. It is the deepest magic, and the deepest power that can only be accessed through love.

Not only is it a portal of awakening, a portal of mystical union and multidimensional sexuality, it is a direct portal into the Cosmic Womb as well as the Gaia Womb. In order to birth your star-body on earth, you must enter the dreaming of the Lower Sophia, and help her to dream a new dream, filled with ecstatic love.

In this there is an incredible joy, lightness, an incredible flow and freedom—an incredible movement of Shakti. It is where the Dragon meets the Dove, where the most beautiful sacred heart and purity and sense of expanded and refined energy meets life-force energy, Shakti, and sexuality, descending like lightning into earth.

MAGDALENE ORACLE

True Earth, Tree of Life, Troubadours

There was an important task to be done—a quest.

There was a time limit and we were nearing the end of the allotted time, and there was a very focused, intense energy that happens just as time is about to run out.

Before us were a number of colored boards, all being brownish, and a ridge of canvas that each had to be painted in the identical color to one of the boards. Only one of the boards/colors was the correct one—the color of the true earth.

It was our task to identify which one was true earth, and paint its identical color.

We had completed the task, so we thought, and identified and painted the correct one. Nearing the last moments, we realized it was not the correct one—all the boards were synthetic copies of the color of earth, not the true color. The correct one suddenly appeared as if it had only just materialized before our eyes.

Rather than a color board it was actually soil and earth, but the plants were so withered and dying it was difficult to detect the earth and her color. There was one last tree on the earth, which was depleted, but still alive. It had a deep red root that spiraled down into the center of earth. From this one last tree, and its red root, we could detect the true color of earth.

As we completed the task successfully, a message arose from the tree. It said the message was from the troubadours. Yet in the dream the name that was given for the troubadours was trouvere *(Northern French for troubadour). The trouvere said that Love, especially in its form of erotic love, was an actual earthly substance filled with magic, which is incredibly precious and very sensitive and can be damaged if not honored or revered in its true spiritual essence.*

They had hidden it for safekeeping, disguised as something else, waiting for the time that it was safe for this precious substance of love to emerge on earth again.

Seren Bertrand, Dream 2016

Divine Father—Sons and Lovers

The word *Christ* literally means the "Anointed One"—it is an initiatory term for the one who was anointed by the Magdalene, the living vessel and embodiment of the sacred feminine, by the Divine Mother. The woman is the anointer; she is the Shekinah.

For many thousands of years across the world, male leadership or kingship was granted by the blessing of the feminine, through the sovereignty of the land, and her appointed priestesses, either the holy bride, the lady of the lake, or the grandmothers.

Womb births both man and woman, in union, into the Resurrection Body. It is a Grail Light Body—a cascade of living light that pours through every cell, awakening the stem cells. This process happens through the Womb, because the Womb holds the blueprint of Original Innocence, and every true creation, those that hold the seed of new life, must come through the energies of the Womb. The Womb holds the blueprint of the Christed Being. She is only waiting for sunlight to shine upon it, so it can bloom. The woman is the Eve, the carrier of the potential of new life.

The path of the Feminine Christ is to place the whole, restored, complete vision of Divine Feminine and Divine Masculine side by side, equal in importance, both honored and respected, both with a place at the table, in union together—who can birth the divine child of consciousness, created from a holistic template of unity.

In ancient tantric and indigenous cultures, men were rooted deeply into the feminine as "sons of the goddess," as a "clan member," and from this secure place, he was connected to nature, to his body, to his feelings, to his instincts, to his love, and to his relationships with others. From this rooted place he could then bloom out into his true masculine identity and become a "lover of the goddess," taking the throne as an equal consort and father to her creations. He did not separate from the Mother principle, or the Feminine principle within himself. Instead his seed of wild masculinity bears fruit from deep within this fertile feminine soil. No longer an adolescent, he takes up his role as an inner king, bringing the maturity and depth of his masculine gifts to the world. From this blooming of masculine consciousness, rooted in the Motherworld—no longer as a dependent, but as a co-creator—the Mother/Father, Goddess/Lover fertilized the world with their alchemical marriage.

This is the Bridal Chamber where the quantum love affair of divine matter consummates itself in mystical sexual union, and where man and woman, and complementary twin pairs of creation, meet again to merge back into the love void.

The tantric heart of the Jesus/MM story is about our journey of resurrection through love and unity, as opposed to the negative spell of death, separation, and suffering. By birthing a new child of humanity from the template of their union, they lay the spiritual seeds of redemption and a new story of human consciousness and potential. We see this in the *Ghent Altarpiece,* which can open to divide and separate Adam and Eve from each other, and from God, or it can close and bring them back together again, with an image of a New Eve pregnant with New Earth.

DEAR LOVER,

I do not need you to be anything,
Other than a human man on the pilgrimage path,
For love, and embracing all that emerges.
I do not expect you to be the Savior on a white horse,
Or the spiritual messiah of conscious relationship.
I know who you are, and I am here with you.
Let us walk together in the crucible of wounds,
Where dark nights are lit by the stars of our love.
I look inside my womb-eye through time,
I see you have been many things—
King, Priest, Prophet,
Warrior, Scholar, Scientist,
Pioneer, Provider, Protector,
Even a "God" at times. . . .
Let us lay these heavy robes down . . .
And enter the Garden of Eden within,
Where we can meet in innocence, you and I,
Man and woman, naked, humbled in ecstasy,
Where Lover's eyes are Magic Doorways.
I invite you into my holy chamber. . . .
There is wine and succor here,
And space for your needs, your weakness, your grief. . . .
I have a sacred fire where your anger and pain can burn,
I know you worry, and I have no words,
Only the soft prayers of my touch.
When we lay, skin by skin, breathing,
I feel something greater breathing us
In the darkness—
A Womb of Love,
That holds us together,

Even when we have forgotten how to hold ourselves,
And each other.
I will meet you here,
In this sacred place
Where the Two become One.

SEREN BERTRAND

Living Resurrection

A Star Is Reborn: Sacred Geometry of the Feminine Christ

I and the Mother are One.

The geometry of resurrection is the stellated dodecahedron—the twelve-pointed star. Hidden within is the mystical thirteenth point, the center point of union at the heart of matter—the throne of thirteen, the "perfected soul." This geometry can also be expressed as "Christ and twelve disciples."

This represents the merging of sacred union, and the collapse or enthronement of sacred duality back into One, through the unity of the gateway of the Cosmic Womb/Ain Sof with the gateway of the Earth Womb/Malkuth—creating the restoration and unified divinity of Sophia in all dimensions simultaneously.

It is the sacred geometry of the stargate within the womb, which is a direct "wombhole" into the Womb of Creation and the dimension of infinite love. When the two become one and descend (catharsis) into the holy of holies, the light bodies of the merkabas unify into the zero-point, *where a new star is born.*

Scientists now believe this sacred geometry describes the shape of the universe. Professor George F. R. Ellis, who coauthored *The Large Scale Structure of Space Time* with renowned physicist Stephen Hawking, suggests the possibility that, not only is the universe finite, but it is shaped as a dodecahedral sphere, saying, "If confirmed, this is a major discovery about the nature of the universe."[3]

French cosmologists also conclude that the universe is round and finite, shaped as a dodecahedral sphere—resembling a universal womb—rather than flat and infinite. Jean-Pierre Luminet, an astrophysicist who specializes in the phenomena of black holes, reported in a prestigious journal about the dodecahedral shape of the universe, which he also visions as "non-infinite." Reflecting pentagonal faces of the dodecahedron give the illusion of an infinite universe when in fact it is finite.[4]

Star of Christ: stellated dodecahedron
(By Tomruen, CC BY 4.0)

Dodecahedral space, which represents a mandala of perfected creation, is not a modern discovery of scientists, but was elucidated by Kabbalists and philosophers. Kabbalist mystics visioned the Tree of Life as being dodecahedral in shape, knowledge of which was given to Abraham by angels. Later, Kabbalist mystic Leonora Leet "described the regular dodecahedron as the geometric symbol of the Earth and also that of 'Perfected Malkuth,' or the realm of matter in general."[5]

The famous Greek mathematician Pythagoras, who was a student of the female Dragon Oracle of Delphi, the Pythia, described the dodecahedron as the "geometry of heaven," representing the etheric substance that the constellations were made from. He believed that each element formed a crystalline sphere around the earth, which rotated to create marvelous "harmonic sounds of the spheres," comparable to angelic lyres and harps heard by those in resonance with the "Divine Sophia."

Philosopher Plato (fourth century BCE) also described the dodecahedron as the quintessence of the cosmos, representing the "fifth" element of ether, the cosmic womb mandala. He called it the sacred geometry that god used for arranging the whole heavens. Plato tells how Timaeus of Locri thought of the universe as being enveloped by a gigantic dodecahedron containing the four solids of the elements of fire, air, earth, and water. He also believed time had a beginning, conceived along with the universe—just like a human lifespan begins, in finite form, as the soul arrives in the womb.

Luca Pacioli (1445–1517) devotes the second part of his book *De Divina Proportione,* published around 1509, to the Platonic solids. He writes:

> As God brought into being the celestial virtue, the fifth essence, and through it created the four solids . . . earth, air, water, and fire . . . so our sacred proportion gave shape to heaven itself, in assigning to it the dodecahedron . . . the solid of twelve pentagons, which cannot be constructed without our sacred proportion.[6]

As above, so below: As the dodecahedron represents the womb of the universe, so it contains the perfected womb of the human soul transfigured into a "celestial star" shining with the radiance of love, in harmony with the infrastructure of the cosmos.

To raise your energy vibration, meditate on an image of this "soul star" of the Feminine Christ, feeling its magical structure awaken inside you. Place images or models in your home or temple, and create crystal healing grids of the geometry.

CHAMBER 33

MINISTRY OF THE MAGDALENE

Return of the Wild Feminine

I don't know if it was the sudden rush of unwatered wine into my
bloodstream or the Middle Eastern rhythms, or the flickering lights,
or the flash of stars overhead, but I let myself go. As we danced,
swaying back and forth, circling each other, our hips switching, our
arms moving as if we held live serpents, I heard the sistrum . . .
I smelled the sweet smoke of the Temple of Isis or Venus.
I saw all the Temples that had come before, in all times and
places . . . skin after shed skin revealing what pulsed beneath, the
colors and patterns brighter and bolder each time. Then at last there
were no more temples, only rock and earth and a chasm
where stars spilled through.

ELIZABETH CUNNINGHAM,
THE PASSION OF MARY MAGDALEN

MAGDALENE IS A WILD, WILD WOMAN—whirling with Shakti, pas-
sion, and the primordial forces of creation. She is soft. She is powerful. She is soft
power. We so often connect to the soft, loving side of this feminine energy, but we
forget, leave out, or deliberately avoid her enraptured, wild side. Magdalene is also
an enchantress, in its truest sense, pulsing with a sensual, magnetic energy.

She is the Lady in Red, full of passion, power, ecstatic womb enlightenment, wisdom, fierce devotion. She sings the Song of Songs with joyful abandon. She comes bearing a gift—the sexual serpent of life, wild, free, radical, ecstatic. When we have had our pure sexual energy, our Grail Light, stolen, used, abused, or crushed, the light of the Feminine Soul of the world dims. We lose our life force, our Christ force. The Feminine Christ returns to anoint us once again in the magical balm and elixir of our sacred sexual energy, the primal living liquid light.

This dynamic, Wild Feminine is not limited to the story of one person or priestess—it is a living, vibrant frequency within everyone, calling to be remembered and embodied. It is the Holy Spirit. The Spirit of the Holy Whore of Wisdom.

Magdalene means "magic doorway," at its deepest levels it is a frequency of womb consciousness beckoning us within.

The Grail Light returns, Womb Consciousness rebirths.

The Magdalene Manifesto

All transformation and change comes from the roots up, it is an emerging energy that moves up from deep within us, and can often be unexpected to the conscious mind. It is as if the heart has decided something before the mind knows.

The essence of Mary Magdalene returns in this roots-up way.

Suddenly we cannot live in the ways we have anymore.

Take time to percolate: What can you not live with anymore?

Take time to tune in: What can you not live *without* anymore?

Your desire for the way of beauty and love is full of transformative power.

Trust this Call of the Magdalene.

In this wave of breathtaking love, she allows us to let go of conditioned psychic, spiritual, and emotional programs of scarcity, fear, and control; to allow the imprinted notion that pain, suffering, and sacrifice are the highest offering to be brought back into the cosmic Cauldron of Renewal to be dissolved into love.

She whispers into our souls, our cells, our hearts to share the eternal knowing that to be Christed means to embody the pure and wild flow of Shakti, life force. When we surrender to the very foundational forces of Life herself, and soften to allow the oceans and rivers of love to flow through us, we reach at-one-ment.

The Feminine Christ invites us into this Cradle of Union, rebirthing the wisdom teachings of the ancient feminine mystery schools for a new era, for a New Earth, so we can once again find balance within ourselves and our world.

MAGDALENE'S PRAYER

I pray with the primordial Rivers of Life flowing through my awakened Sexuality.

I pray as a mystical Doorway opens in my inner Womb, leading out into a vaulted cathedral of Feminine consciousness flowing infinitely from Divine Mother's Womb.

I pray as my Body begins to transform into a cosmic gateway for my beloved, and the Void dissolves us both, and touches us with her starlit fingertips of Love.

I pray as my Womb becomes a bridge for all that has left to return.

I pray with my grief, with my sorrow, with my heart shattered open into a million fragments, as if the first primordial burst of Creation is still reverberating inside.

I pray with my Heart, even when it is closed, frightened, confused, and afraid.

I pray because I am fragile. I have been broken. I cannot do this alone.

I pray because I am immeasurably strong and ferocious. I pray with howls for the suffering of the world. I pray with the fury of forgotten wrath.

I pray when I have no more prayers left and hopelessness is with me.

I pray when it is all smashed on the floor and cannot be fixed.

I pray with fangs and claws and the power of fire-forged volcanic ash. I pray to digest all the pain deep into the soil of my belly and birth out wildflowers.

I pray because there is a Fire in me that cannot go out, which lights every dark night.

I pray with beauty and I pray with the ugliness of all that is unsaid.

I pray with laughter, and birdsong, and forest floors. I pray with the softness.

*I pray with tree roots, and earthworms, and fur. I pray with the
rain and the snow.*
*I pray with my Touch and I pray with my Love. I pray with my
consecrated Womb.*
*I pray with the Blood that floods from the inner luminosity of my
celestial mansion.*
*We are the Whores and the Holy Ones, Honored and Scorned,
Wild and Unborn.*
Our prayers are the song of the Universe calling us home.

SEREN BERTRAND

The Feminine Christ is returning, as prophesied, to unite in Sacred Marriage the spiritual Divine Love from the subtle realms of spirit, with eros, the sensual, primordial Love of the embodied realm of matter—both are complementary expressions of the infinite Source of Creation and Love.

The Feminine Christ comes to rebirth the Way of Love, a path of redemption and resurrection within our sacred bodies, within our hearts and souls. She reminds us that the highest and deepest sacrament is pleasure, ecstasy, love. She brings the healing salve, *salvation,* to our wounds of separation and suffering—to the mistaken idea that we are set apart from the infinite love and mercy of our Creator, or the magical co-creative weave of the Web of Life that supports us.

In her Shining Womb of renewal, the Feminine Christ dissolves our psychic wounds that have pitted man against woman, humankind against Mother Gaia, dark against light. She reminds us of our connection, our interweaving, our longing for Union.

The Feminine Christ unveils her bridal face so that we can remember who we truly are and celebrate a world of life, renewal, communion, collaboration, and creativity. When the world around us feels full of suffering and wounded actions, it can be easy to collapse into fear or to become frozen. The Gospel of Mary Magdalene tells the story of how the disciples are too afraid to spread the teachings of love, until Mary Magdalene speaks up with courage and compassion and inspires them into action.

She calls us to embrace the qualities of kindness, compassion, intimacy, pleasure, joy, beauty, passion, giving, receiving, tolerance, nurturance, wildness, sacred sexuality, sacred family, friendships of the heart; to remember we are all brothers and sisters in "Christ."

What would Mary Magdalene teach about our current world situation?

Can you ask for her earthy-divine advice, support, and inspiration?

How can you anchor more of these qualities in your life—and the world?

Then Mary stood up. She greeted them all, addressing her brothers and sisters. "Do not weep and be distressed nor let your hearts be irresolute . . ." When Mary said these things, she turned their hearts toward the Good.

GOSPEL OF MARY OF MAGDALA,

TRANSLATED BY KAREN KING

⋘౭౩⋙

Completing the Rose Path

PRAYER OF THE MAGDALENE

Holy Spirit, Shekinah,
Holy Sophia, Mother Earth,
Holy Mother, Mari-Isis,
Great Grandmother Ocean,
Cosmic Mother of Creation—
We are your vessels of life.
Pour through us into the world.
Make our waters flow crystal clear.
Make our voices sing for all to hear.
Make our wells run deep and true.
Make us the rainbow bridge back to you.
We invoke the light within matter,
Birthing heaven here on earth.
Give us the courage and the grace
To be the Grail of healing balm,
To give the Eucharist once again,
That anoints our hearts with love.
In the mystery of the Dove,
Ah-Moon.
May it be rooted in the earth,
And birthed through the womb.
Kadosh, Kadosh, Kadosh

SEREN BERTRAND

⋐౦౩⋑

ACKNOWLEDGMENTS

THIS WORK STANDS ON THE SHOULDERS of scholars who have dedicated their lives to specific areas of study, and we wish to acknowledge and share our appreciation for several key people. Please understand that our conclusions do not necessarily reflect their opinions or views. Gratitude to: Betty De Shong Meador, Samuel Noel Kramer, Diane Wolkstein, Raphael Patai, Morton Smith, Karen King, Elaine Pagels, Margaret Starbird, Neil Douglas-Klotz, Sarah Schneider, G. R. S. Mead, Jean-Yves Leloup, Susan Haskins, Margaret Murray ("debunked" by academia, but still a legend), and Jane Schaberg, an oracle of Magdalene and woman of courage.

Much appreciation to the contributors of the art and oracles: Especially to Natvienna Hanell (@holywomanholygrail) and Helen Claira Burt (@hellies .goddess) for their beautiful illustrations and inspirations, to Rose Siger and Natvienna Hanell for the oracles that share their wisdom and insight, and to Stéphane Beaulieu (mytras@hotmail.com) for his archaeological illustrations and art. Thank you also to Mermaid Anabel Vizcarra and Welsh Witch Louisa Williams, for all their help in creating and holding beautiful spaces for the "Magdalene Magic" to flow, and to Linda Go and Catherine Shead for their support.

Personal thanks: Joy Barber-Hua (for our lifelong friendship and our magic Magdalene Mystery tours together to France). To our parents, Margaret Bertrand, Scott and Diane Bertrand on Azra's side, and Jean and Andrew Astill (now ancestors) on Seren's side. Merlin and Lyra, our feline companions and rogue book editors, who entertained us by paw-typing and adding or deleting words on a regular basis.

Many thanks to our publisher Inner Traditions: to Grail Knight Jon Graham, and to the "holy trinity" of word witches, Jeanie Levitan, Nancy Yeilding, and Jamaica Burns Griffin. Plus, thank you to Erica Robinson, Ashley Kolesnik, and the rest of the ITI team. A special thanks to "Mama" Jeanie for her wisdom, understanding, and humor.

Gratitude to Rose Siger, whose email about her heritage as an Iraqi-born Nasoraean Mandaean, with personal words of support and encouragement for me (Seren), arrived "out of the blue" at just the perfect moment, which I took as a magical "Magdalene wink." Thank you Rose, your divinely inspired timing meant everything.

NOTES

Introduction.
Visions of the Rose—
Left-Hand Path of the Feminine Christ

1. Origen, *Against Celsus*, 570.
2. Muss-Arnolt, "On Semitic Words in Greek and Latin," 106–7; Shaw, *Sketch of the Religions of the World*, 317.
3. Jeff A. Benner, "Hebrew Found in English Words," Ancient Hebrew Research Center website.
4. Muss-Arnolt, "On Semitic Words in Greek and Latin," 106–7. See also discussion in Nicholas King, "Gnosticism: An Investigation," 295.
5. John A. Halloran, *Sumerian Lexicon, Version 3.0*, 24, 48. Available at Sumerian.org website.
6. Laura Geggel, "540,000-Year-Old Shell Carvings May Be Human Ancestor's Oldest Art," LiveScience website, December 3, 2014.
7. Jung, *Aion*, 54; see also discussion in Freke and Gandy, *Jesus and the Lost Goddess*, 286.
8. Mead, *Did Jesus Live 100 B.C.?* 175.

Our Love Letter.
Rose Pilgrims—Sacred Masculine Vision

1. Ehrenreich and English, *Witches, Midwives, and Nurses*, 53.

Magdalene—Holy Whore of Sophia

1. Haskins, *Mary Magdalen*, 188.
2. Haag, *The Quest for Mary Magdalene*, 280.
3. Walker, *Woman's Encyclopedia of Myths and Secrets*, 820.
4. Orr, *Kissing the Hag*, 119, "The Whore."

5. John Lamb Lash, "She Who Anoints," March 2004. Available at Bibliotecapleyades webpage.

6. Bertrand and Bertrand, *Womb Awakening*, 111.

7. Julian of Norwich, *Revelations of Divine Love*, 60.

8. Julian of Norwich, *Revelations of Divine Love*, 60.

9. Julian of Norwich, *Revelations of Divine Love*, 60.

10. Bourgeault, *The Meaning of Mary Magdalene*, 113.

11. Haag, *The Quest for Mary Magdalene*, 37.

12. Sanhedrin 107b and Sota 47a from Laible, "Jesus Christ in the Talmud," 41.

Chamber 1.
Dragon Mothers—
Ancient Elemental Magic

1. Michael Greshko, "World's Oldest Cave Art Found—And Neanderthals Made It," *National Geographic* website, February 22, 2018; John Noble Wilford, "In African Cave, Signs of an Ancient Paint Factory," *New York Times* website, October 13, 2011; Snow, "Sexual Dimorphism in European Upper Paleolithic Cave Art," 746–61.

Chamber 2.
Mermaid Priestesses—
Chalice of Holy Waters

1. Hyde, *Paganism to Christianity in the Roman Empire*, 57–58.

Chamber 4.
Divine Whore—
Inanna, Mistress of the Vulva

1. Excerpt from Meador, *Princess, Priestess, Poet*, xi.

2. Excerpt from "Holy Song," translated in Meador, *Uncursing the Dark*, 60.

3. Excerpt from "The Sacred Marriage Ritual," translated in Meador, *Uncursing the Dark*, 59–60; see also Hillel, *The Redemption of the Feminine Erotic Soul*, 10–11.

4. Meador, *Inanna, Lady of Largest Heart*, 11.

5. Wolkstein and Kramer, *Inanna Queen of Heaven and Earth*, 12–13.

6. Wolkstein and Kramer, *Inanna Queen of Heaven and Earth*, 12–13.

7. Wolkstein and Kramer, *Inanna Queen of Heaven and Earth*, 12–13.

8. Leick, *Sex and Eroticism in Mesopotamian Literature*, 96.

9. Translated by Meador in *Inanna, Lady of Largest Heart*, 11; see also Samuel Noah Kramer's translation in "Cuneiform Studies and the History of Literature," 505–6.

10. Leick, *Sex and Eroticism in Mesopotamian Literature,* 129.

11. Leick, *Sex and Eroticism in Mesopotamian Literature,* 52.

12. Meador, *Inanna, Lady of Largest Heart,* 159.

13. Leick, *Sex and Eroticism in Mesopotamian Literature,* 97.

14. Leick, *Sex and Eroticism in Mesopotamian Literature,* 97.

15. Leick, *Sex and Eroticism in Mesopotamian Literature,* 98.

16. Leick, *Sex and Eroticism in Mesopotamian Literature,* 129.

17. Leick, *Sex and Eroticism in Mesopotamian Literature,* 152.

18. Leick, *Sex and Eroticism in Mesopotamian Literature,* 182.

19. Wolkstein and Kramer, *Inanna Queen of Heaven and Earth,* 41.

20. Leick, *Sex and Eroticism in Mesopotamian Literature,* 84.

21. Jacobsen, *Treasures of Darkness,* 30–34.

22. Jacobsen, *Treasures of Darkness,* 34.

23. Jacobsen, *Treasures of Darkness,* 34.

24. Jacobsen, *Treasures of Darkness,* 32–33.

25. Leick, *Sex and Eroticism in Mesopotamian Literature,* 180.

26. Meador, *Inanna, Lady of Largest Heart,* 7.

27. White, "The Earliest Images," 38.

28. Meador, *Inanna, Lady of Largest Heart,* 62.

29. Meador, *Princess, Priestess, Poet,* 12.

30. Leick, *Sex and Eroticism in Mesopotamian Literature,* 126–27.

31. Wolkstein and Kramer, *Inanna Queen of Heaven and Earth,* 151.

32. Wolkstein and Kramer, *Inanna Queen of Heaven and Earth,* 153.

33. Wolkstein and Kramer, *Inanna Queen of Heaven and Earth,* 153.

34. Wolkstein and Kramer, *Inanna Queen of Heaven and Earth,* 152.

35. Levy, *Gate of Horn,* 101.

36. Kramer, *The Sumerians,* 51.

Chamber 5.
Goddesses of Galilee—
Temple of Asherah, Wisdom of Lilith

1. Nala Rogers, "Israeli Cave Offers Clues about When Humans Mastered Fire," *Science Magazine* website, December 12, 2014.

2. Michael Balter, "Humans and Neandertals Likely Interbred in Middle East," *Science Magazine* website, January 28, 2015.

3. Hovers, Ilani, Bar-Yosef, and Vandermeersch, "An Early Case of Color Symbolism," 491–522; Vandermeersch, Arensburg, Bar-Yosef, and Belfer-Cohen, "Upper Paleolithic Human Remains from Qafzeh Cave, Israel," 7–21.

4. Edgar and Kinney, *The Vulgate Bible,* translation of Exodus 34:29.

5. Josephus, *Jewish Antiquities,* 78–79.

6. Seligsohn, "Star-Worship Among the Israelites," 527–28.

7. Owen Jarus, "Massive 5,000-Year-Old Stone Monument Revealed in Israel," *Live Science* website, September 15, 2014.

8. Ran Shapira, "Discovery of 9,000-year-old Cultic Sites Changes Our Understanding of the Evolution of Worship," *Haaretz* website, April 1, 2015.

9. Sharon et al., "Monumental Megalithic Burial and Rock Art Tell a New Story about the Levant Intermediate Bronze 'Dark Ages.'"

10. Sharon et al., "Monumental Megalithic Burial and Rock Art Tell a New Story about the Levant Intermediate Bronze 'Dark Ages.'"

11. Jeremiah 4:30; 2 Kings 9:30; Hosea 2:13 (New International Version).

12. Stol, *Women in the Ancient Near East,* 38, 399, 405.

13. 2 Kings 17:10–12 and 17:16–17 (NIV).

14. Beaulieu, "Eve's Ritual," 149.

15. Rast, "Cakes for the Queen of Heaven," 167–70.

16. Rast, "Cakes for the Queen of Heaven," 174; Maier and Sharp, *Prophecy and Power,* 83.

17. Bentley, *Sisters of Salome,* 30–36.

18. Judges 11:34; I Samuel 18:6–7 (Westminster Leningrad Codex).

19. Song of Solomon 7:1–8 (New Living Translation).

20. Judges 21:20–22 (WLC); Ta'anit 4:8 (William Davidson edition).

21. Cia [Cynthia Sautter], "Searching for Biblical Roots of Belly Dance," *The Best of Habibi* 16, no. 1 (Winter 1997). Available at TheBestofHabibi.com webpage.

22. Budin, *The Myth of Sacred Prostitution in Antiquity,* 27.

23. Budin, *The Myth of Sacred Prostitution in Antiquity,* 30.

24. Budin, *The Myth of Sacred Prostitution in Antiquity,* 31.

25. Budin, *The Myth of Sacred Prostitution in Antiquity,* 31.

26. Budin, *The Myth of Sacred Prostitution in Antiquity,* 43.

27. Budin, *The Myth of Sacred Prostitution in Antiquity,* 33.

28. Budin, *The Myth of Sacred Prostitution in Antiquity,* 34.

29. Beaulieu, "Eve's Ritual," 135.

30. Beaulieu, "Eve's Ritual," 138–39.

31. Ackerman, "Queen Mother," 385–401; Bin-Nun, *The Tawananna,* 54, 256, 268; Beaulieu, "Eve's Ritual," 62.

32. 1 Kings 2:19 (NIV).

33. Ackerman, "Queen Mother," 386–89; I Kings 2:19 (NIV).

34. Beaulieu, "Eve's Ritual," 136.

35. De Vaux, *Ancient Israel,* 118; Ackerman, *Warrior, Dancer, Seductress, Queen,* 140.

36. Dijkstra, "El, the God of Israel," 81–126.

37. Davies, *In Search of "Ancient Israel,"* 149–50.

38. Patai, *The Hebrew Goddess,* 30.

39. Morton Smith, *Jesus the Magician,* 158.

40. 1 Kings 11:4 (NIV).

41. Niehr, "Israelite Religion and Canaanite Religion," 23–36.

42. Dever, *Did God Have a Wife?* 317.

43. Grahn, *Blood, Bread, and Roses,* 9.

44. Patai, *Hebrew Goddess,* 76.

45. Patai, *Hebrew Goddess,* 84.

46. Patai, *Hebrew Goddess,* 85.

47. Patai, *Hebrew Goddess,* 94.

48. Bledstein, "Tamar and the Coat of Many Colors," 65–85.

49. John A. Halloran, *Sumerian Lexicon, Version 3.0,* 30. Available at Sumerian.org website.

50. Patai, "Lilith," 305.

51. Patai, *Hebrew Goddess,* 231–46.

52. Patai, *Gates to the Old City,* 455.

53. Zohar i. 148a–b, Sitre Torah.

Chamber 6. Motherline of Christ— Son of the Goddess

1. Jerusalem Talmud Megillah 15a.

2. Schaberg, *The Illegitimacy of Jesus,* 92–95.

3. Schaberg, *The Illegitimacy of Jesus,* 92–95.

4. Luke 1:46–52 (International Standard Version).

5. Lambdin, *The Gospel of Thomas,* verse 105.

6. Schaberg, *The Illegitimacy of Jesus,* 45.

7. Stol, *Women in the Ancient Near East,* 400.

8. Shabbat 104b and Sanhedrin 67a, authors' adaptation of translation quoted in Schäfer, *Jesus in the Talmud,* 16. See also discussion 16–19.

9. Shabbat 104b and Sanhedrin 67a in Kessler, *An Introduction to Jewish-Christian Relations,* 76.

10. Schaberg, *The Illegitimacy of Jesus,* 153.

11. Kallah 51a as quoted in Schaberg, *The Illegitimacy of Jesus,* 150. See also discussion on pages 149–51.

12. Kallah 51a as quoted in Schaberg, *The Illegitimacy of Jesus,* 151.

13. Schäfer, *Jesus in the Talmud,* 25–30.

14. Schaberg, *The Illegitimacy of Jesus,* 147; Origen, *Against Celsus* 1.28–30.

15. II Maccabees 6:7 (KJV).

16. Mead, *Did Jesus Live 100 B.C.?* 174.

17. Jorunn Jacobsen Buckley, *Mandaeans,* 4, 49.

18. Protoevangelium of James 7:1–2.

19. Babylonian Talmud Kethuboth 106a (William Davidson edition).

20. 2 Baruch 10:19 (Charles, "II Baruc," 486); Mishna Shekalim 8:5–6 (William Davidson edition).

21. Exodus 38:8 (KJV).

22. Pesikta Rabbati 26:6 (William Davidson edition).

23. Revelation 11:19 to 12:1 (NIV).

Chamber 7. Apostle of Ecstasy— Magdalene, the Female Pope

1. John Lamb Lash, "She Who Anoints," available at Bibliotecapleyades webpage, March 2004.

Chamber 8. Divine Prophetess— Ancestry and Origins of Magdalene

1. De Voragine, *The Golden Legend,* 72–88 (as to Mary Magdalene), 135–40 (as to Martha).

2. Lucotte, "The Mitochondrial DNA Mitotype of Sainte Marie-Madeleine," 10–19.

3. Picknett, *Mary Magdalene,* 121–48.

4. Scott, *Hatshepsut, Queen of Sheba.*

5. Haskins, *Mary Magdalen,* 155–56.

6. Haskins, *Mary Magdalen,* 155–56.

7. Haskins, *Mary Magdalen,* 157.

8. Gold, *Monsters and Madonnas,* 154–59.

9. Schaberg and Johnson-Debaufre, *Mary Magdalene Understood,* 148–50.

10. James McGrath, "Miriai is a Vine," chap. 35 in *The Mandaic Book of John* webpage, June 13, 2012.

11. Jorunn Jacobsen Buckley, *Mandaeans,* 54.

12. Jorunn Jacobsen Buckley, "The Mandaean Appropriation of Jesus' Mother, Miriai," 185–91.

13. James McGrath, "Miriai is a Vine," chap. 35 in *The Mandaic Book of John* webpage, June 13, 2012.

14. James McGrath, "Miriai is a Vine," chap. 35 in *The Mandaic Book of John* webpage, June 13, 2012.

15. James McGrath, "Miriai is a Vine," chap. 35 in *The Mandaic Book of John* webpage, June 13, 2012.

16. James McGrath, "Miriai is a Vine," chap. 35 in *The Mandaic Book of John* webpage, June 13, 2012.

17. Philip Myers, *Ancient History,* 147.

18. Goodrich, *Priestesses,* 221; Bernal, *Black Athena,* 118–19.

19. Goodrich, *Priestesses,* 236, referencing Aeschylus.

20. Goodrich, *Priestesses,* 199.

21. "Delphic Oracle's Lips May Have Been Loosened by Gas Vapors," *National Geographic* website, August 14, 2001.

22. John Collins, *Seers, Sibyls, and Sages in Hellenistic-Roman Judaism,* 185, quoting Pausanias, *Descriptions of Greece,* 10.12.9.

23. F. W. H. Myers, *Essays,* 21; see also Goodrich, *Priestesses,* 205.

24. Tertullian, *Ante-Nicene Fathers,* 142.

Chamber 9.
The Circle of Marys—
Feminist Ministry of Jesus

1. Allione, *Prajnaparamita Recordings*; see also Young, *Courtesans and Tantric Consorts,* 4–5, 123, 129.

2. Morton Smith, *Jesus the Magician,* 209.

3. Jennifer Viegas, "Earliest Reference Describes Christ as 'Magician,'" *Discovery News,* NBCnews website, October 1, 2008.

4. Booth, *Hypatia,* 128.

5. Bertrand and Bertrand, *Womb Awakening,* 50–55, 57–66, 70, 81–87, 90–92, 94, 106–8, 115.

Chamber 10.
Holy Matrimony—
Were Jesus and Mary Married?

1. Meyer, "Gospel of Philip," 171.

2. Meyer, "Gospel of Philip," 171.

3. Karen King, *Gospel of Mary of Magdala,* 15.

4. Karen King, *Gospel of Mary of Magdala,* 17.

5. Love, *Mirror of the Blessed Life of Jesu Christ,* 153; see also Haskins, *Mary Magdalen,* 195.

6. Haskins, *Mary Magdalen,* 197, paraphrasing Nicholas Love, *Mirror of the Blessed Life of Jesu Christ,* chap. 72.

7. Haskins, *Mary Magdalen,* 199.

8. Jacopone Da Todi, "The Crucifixion," in *The Oxford Book of Italian Verse, 13th Century–19th Century,* edited by St. John Lucas (Oxford: Clarendon Press, 1910), 65; translation by authors. See also discussion in Haskins, *Mary Magdalen,* 197–98.

9. Love, *Mirror of the Blessed Life of Jesu Christ,* 256; see also discussion in Haskins, *Mary Magdalen,* 213.

10. Epiphanius, *Panarion,* 117.

11. Mead, *Simon Magus: His Philosophy and Teachings,* 67.

12. Parashat Lech Lecha, verse 346, in the Zohar.

13. Leloup, *Gospel of Philip,* 67.

14. Leloup, *Gospel of Philip,* 47.

15. Gospel of Thomas in Robinson, *Nag Hammadi Library in English,* 148–52.

Chamber 11.
Resurrection Mysteries—
The Crucifixion and Divine Rebirth

1. Haskins, *Mary Magdalen,* 191.

2. Haskins, *Mary Magdalen,* 210.

3. Wolkstein and Kramer, *Inanna Queen of Heaven and Earth,* 40–47.

4. Wolkstein and Kramer, *Inanna Queen of Heaven and Earth,* 40–47.

5. Wolkstein and Kramer, *Inanna Queen of Heaven and Earth,* 40–47.

6. Powell, *The Most Holy Trinosophia,* 51.

Chamber 12.
Bishops of Sophia—
Female Spiritual Leaders

1. Origen, *Commentary on the Epistle to the Romans,* 291.

2. Epiphanius, *Panarion,* 637.

3. Epiphanius, *Panarion,* 637.

4. Origen, *Against Celsus,* 426.

Chamber 13.
Gnostic Magdalene—
The Salvation of Sophia

1. *Pistis Sophia,* 80.

2. Parpola, "Assyrian Tree of Life," 174.

3. *Pistis Sophia,* 13–14.

Chamber 14. Tantric Temple—
Ecstatic Mystics on the Path of Love

1. Mason, *In Search of the Loving God,* chap. 4.

2. Swami Vivekananda, "The Sages of India," in "Lectures from Colombo to Almora."

From "The Complete Works of Swami Vivekananda," vol. 3. Compiled by Wikisource contributors. Available at Wikisource.org website.

3. Yogananda, *Autobiography of a Yogi*, chap. 32.

4. Bertrand and Bertrand, *Womb Awakening*, 411.

5. Bertrand and Bertrand, *Womb Awakening*, 137.

6. Marglin, *Wives of the God-King*, 180.

7. Marglin, *Wives of the God-King*, 110.

8. Marglin, *Wives of the God-King*, 109.

9. Marglin, *Wives of the God-King*, 110.

10. Marglin, *Wives of the God-King*, 171.

11. Haroonuzzaman, "Understanding Baul language," *Daily Star* website, May 14, 2011.

12. Bauman, Bauman, and Bourgeault, *The Luminous Gospels*, 66.

13. Osho, *The Beloved*, 45.

Chamber 15. Heretic Queen— Magdalene's Escape to Europe

1. Pistis Sophia, as quoted in Ehrman, *Peter, Paul and Mary Magdalene*, 209.

2. De Ville, *Tziganes*, 72.

3. As quoted in Haskins, *Mary Magdalen*, 126.

4. Starr, *Teresa of Avila*, 223.

5. Starr, *Teresa of Avila*, 225.

6. John of the Cross, *Complete Works*, 8.

7. Heriz, *Saint John of the Cross*, 69–70.

8. Lea, *A History of the Inquisition of Spain*, 29–33.

9. Baroja, *World of the Witches*, 135.

Chamber 16. Magdalene Order— Cathar Priestesses of the Dove

1. Stoyanov, *The Other God*, 278–79.

2. Coppens and Douzet, *Secret Vault*, 55–58.

3. Bertrand and Bertrand, *Womb Awakening*, 354, 365, 367.

4. Malcolm Barber, *Crusaders and Heretics*, 109.

5. Malcolm Barber, *Crusaders and Heretics*, 110.

6. Malcolm Barber, *Crusaders and Heretics*, 109–10.

7. Malcolm Barber, *Crusaders and Heretics*, 111.

8. Malcolm Barber, *Crusaders and Heretics*, 112.

Chamber 17.
Red Witch—
Scarlet Saint of the Wise Women

1. Bonwick, *Irish Druids and Old Irish Religions,* 238.
2. Baroja, *World of the Witches,* 86, 101, 119.
3. Baroja, *World of the Witches,* 91.
4. Bertrand and Bertrand, *Womb Awakening,* 149.
5. As quoted in Hatsis, *Psychedelic Mystery Traditions,* 189–90.
6. Baroja, *World of the Witches,* 60.
7. Picknett, *Secret History of Lucifer,* xiii.
8. Baroja, *World of the Witches,* 52–53.
9. Manilius, *Astronomica,* 333.
10. Robson, *Fixed Stars and Constellations in Astrology,* 54, 208.
11. Gary, *Silent as the Trees,* 28.
12. Gary, *Silent as the Trees,* 28.
13. Gary, *Silent as the Trees,* 16.
14. Gary, *Silent as the Trees,* 30.
15. Gary, *Silent as the Trees,* 41.
16. Gary, *Silent as the Trees,* 41.
17. Gary, *Silent as the Trees,* 40–45.
18. Gary, *Silent as the Trees,* 41–42.
19. Baroja, *World of the Witches,* 42.
20. Picknett, *Secret History of Lucifer,* 59.
21. Baroja, *World of the Witches,* 101.

Chamber 18.
Templar Wizards—
Robin Hood and Maid Marian

1. Drake, *Shakespeare and His Times,* 78.
2. John Matthews, *Robin Hood,* 156.
3. "A Gest of Robyn Hode," ballad 117, stanza 440, in Child *English and Scottish Popular Ballads.* See also discussion in Davis, *Robin Hood,* 111.
4. John Matthews, *Robin Hood,* 148.
5. Davis, *Robin Hood,* 32.
6. Roberts, *The Legendary Ballads of England and Scotland,* 582.
7. John Matthews, *Robin Hood,* 112.
8. John Matthews, *Robin Hood,* 99.

Chamber 21.
Templars of Burgundy—
Alchemists of Mary

1. Schonfield, *Essene Odyssey,* 162–65. See also Picknett and Prince, *Templar Revelation,* 109, 121.
2. Picknett and Prince, *Templar Revelation,* 109, 121–22, 194.
3. Andressohn, *The Ancestry and Life of Godfrey of Bouillon,* 5–15. Silva, See also *First Templar Nation,* 46, 123; Baigent, Leigh, and Lincoln, *Holy Blood, Holy Grail,* 107.

Chamber 22.
The Lady in the Landscape—
Body of the Goddess

1. Power, "Women in Prehistoric Rock Art," 86; see also Bertrand and Bertrand, *Womb Awakening,* plate 10.

Chamber 23.
Magdalene and the Sibyls—
Prophetesses of Sophia

1. Ramon K. Jusino, "Mary Magdalene: Author of the Fourth Gospel?" Beloved Disciple website, 1998.

Chamber 24. Red Throne—
The Original Sacred Altar

1. "Bright Friday," available at the website of the Orthodox Metropolitanate of Hong Kong and Southeast Asia.
2. "Bright Friday," available at the website of the Orthodox Metropolitanate of Hong Kong and Southeast Asia.
3. De Meaux, "An Exposition of the Doctrine of the Church of England," 60.
4. Bertrand and Bertrand, *Womb Awakening,* 51, 53, 64, 72, 102, 117, 181, 285.
5. Bertrand and Bertrand, *Womb Awakening,* 50–98.
6. Edersheim, *The Life and Times of Jesus the Messiah,* 185–87.

Chamber 25. Feminine Eucharist—
The Primeval Sacrament

1. Lewy, "The Late Assyro-Babylonian Cult of the Moon," 431; see also Key, "Traces of the Worship of the Moon God Sîn," 24.

2. Singer, *The Jewish Encyclopedia,* s.v. "Sinai, Mount."

3. Athenaeus, *Deipnosophistae,* vol. 2, book 3, chap. 109f, 17; Athenaeus, *Deipnosophists,* vol. 1, book 3, chap. 73, 180.

4. Bertrand and Bertrand, *Womb Awakening,* 292, 299.

5. Acts of Thomas, chap. 50, as quoted in Spinks, *Do This in Remembrance of Me,* 40; see also Attridge, *Acts of Thomas,* 53.

6. Acts of Thomas, chap. 133, as quoted in Spinks, *Do This in Remembrance of Me,* 40; see also Attridge, *Acts of Thomas,* 101.

7. Irenaeus, *Against Heresies,* 1.13.2.

8. Saxon, *The Eucharist in Romanesque France,* 205–7.

Chamber 27. John the Baptist— Waters of Life

1. Picknett and Prince, *Templar Revelation,* 41, 157.

2. Meador, *Inanna, Lady of Largest Heart,* 40.

3. Leick, *Sex and Eroticism in Mesopotamian Literature,* 45, 280.

4. Hippolytus's *The Apostolic Tradition,* 21:1–38, as quoted in González, *Resources in the Ancient Church,* 170.

5. Cyril of Jerusalem, "Lecture XX," 147.

6. Picknett and Prince, *Templar Revelation,* 194.

Chamber 28. Divine Sophia— Return to Love

1. Gospel of Mary 10:8 in King, *Gospel of Mary of Magdala,* 17.

Chamber 29. Honoring the Motherline— Walking the Red Path

1. Jones, "The Goddess in Glastonbury," In the Heart of the Goddess, the Website of Kathy Jones.

2. Jones, "The Goddess in Glastonbury," In the Heart of the Goddess, the Website of Kathy Jones.

3. Carmichael, *Carmina Gadelica,* 166.

4. Jones, "The Goddess in Glastonbury," In the Heart of the Goddess, the Website of Kathy Jones.

5. Linda Iles, "St. Brigid of the Wells," *Mirror of Isis—An Official Fellowship of Isis Publication* (website), vol. 5, no. 3, Samhain 2010.

6. Linda Iles, "St. Brigid of the Wells," *Mirror of Isis—An Official Fellowship of Isis Publication* (website), vol. 5, no. 3, Samhain 2010.

7. Macleod, *Divine Adventure*, 98–101.

8. Macleod, *Divine Adventure*, 208–9.

9. Montgomery, *God-Kings of Europe*, chap. 12, n 2.

10. Henry Jenner, "Was Christ in Cornwall?," a letter to *The Western Morning News and Daily Gazette* on April 6, 1933, Plymouth, UK; see also discussion in Eedle and Eedle, *Albion Restored*, 69–70.

11. Barry Dunford, "Were Jesus & Mary Magdalene on the Isle of Iona?" Sacred Connections Scotland website, 2019; also "Grave slab—Prioress Anna MacLean." Historic Environment Scotland website.

12. Johnson, *Byways in British Archaeology*, 194.

13. Andrew Collins, *Cygnus Mystery*, 86–89.

14. Andrew Collins, *Cygnus Mystery*, 137–60, 176–79.

15. Andrew Collins, *Cygnus Mystery*, 99–101.

16. Fiona Macleod, *Winged Destiny*, 243, quoting incantation no. 114, "Beannachadh Seilg," from Alexander Carmichael's *Carmina Gadelica*, 310–11.

17. Addy, *The Hall of Waltheof*, 40.

18. David Clarke, "Head Cult," 22, 282.

19. Karen King, *Gospel of Mary of Magdala*, 13.

20. "Paleolithic Art and Archaeology of Creswell Crags, UK," Research project of Department of Archaeology, Durham University website.

21. "Public Asked to Record 'Witch' Markings on Halloween," *BBC News* website, October 31, 2016.

22. Linda Wilson, "By Midnight, By Moonlight," 42, quoting Lee Prosser from the *Guardian*.

23. Schneider, *Kabbalistic Writings*, 76.

24. Schneider, *Kabbalistic Writings*, 74–75.

25. Schneider, *Kabbalistic Writings*, 177, quoting R. Kook's *Orot HaKodesh*, "Perfection and Perfecting."

26. Koltuv, *Weaving Woman*, 47, quoting Carl Jung.

Chamber 30. The Way of Love— Awakening the Feminine Soul

1. Douglas-Klotz, *Hidden Gospel*, 143.

2. Douglas-Klotz, *Hidden Gospel*, 143.

3. Douglas-Klotz, *Hidden Gospel*, 117.

4. Douglas-Klotz, *Hidden Gospel*, 115.

5. Bertrand and Bertrand, *Womb Awakening*, 211.

6. Bertrand and Bertrand, *Womb Awakening,* 1.

7. Douglas-Klotz, *Hidden Gospel,* 115.

8. Douglas-Klotz, *Hidden Gospel,* 116.

Chamber 31. Magdalene Mandala— The Wheel of the Witches

1. Jung, "Lecture III, 12th May, 1939" in *Modern Psychology,* 112–15.

2. Jung, "Lecture III, 12th May, 1939" in *Modern Psychology,* 112–15.

3. Karen King, *Gospel of Mary of Magdalene,* 60.

4. Douglas-Klotz, *Hidden Gospel,* 195.

Chamber 32. Sacred Union— Entering the Bridal Chamber

1. Gospel of Thomas, logion 22, in Barnstone and Meyer, *Gnostic Bible,* 51.

2. Acts of Peter, The Vercelli Acts, c.38 in Schneemelcher, *New Testament Apocrypha,* 213.

3. Ellis, "The Shape of the Universe," 566–67.

4. Belle Dumé, "Is the Universe a Dodecahedron?" *Physics World* website, October 8, 2003.

5. Iona Miller, "The Dodecahedral Universe & the Qabalistic Tree of Life," *Green Egg Magazine,* no. 151 (June 2010) (digital magazine available on website of Iona Miller).

6. Richter, *Rhythmic Form in Art*, 42, quoting from Luca Pacioli and Leonardo da Vinci's *De Divina Proportione.*

BIBLIOGRAPHY

Ackerman, Susan. "The Queen Mother and the Cult in Ancient Israel." *Journal of Biblical Literature* 112, no. 3 (1993): 385–401.

———. *Warrior, Dancer, Seductress, Queen: Women in Judges and Biblical Israel.* New Haven, Conn.: Yale University Press, 2009.

Addy, Sidney Oldall. *The Hall of Waltheof.* London: David Nutt, 1893.

Allione, Tsultrim. *Prajnaparamita Recordings.* Recorded lectures in CD format. Pagosa Springs, Colo.: Tara Mandala, 2016.

———. *Women of Wisdom.* Ithaca, N.Y.: Snow Lion Publications, 2000.

Andressohn, John C. *The Ancestry and Life of Godfrey of Bouillon.* Bloomington: Indiana University, 1947.

Angus, Samuel. *The Mystery-Religions: A Study in the Religious Background of Early Christianity.* Mineola, N.Y.: Dover Publications, 2011.

Ashby, Muata, and Karen Vijaya Ashby. *Egyptian Yoga.* Miami: Cruzian Mystic Books, 2005.

Ashe, Geoffrey. *The Virgin.* London: Routledge and Kegan, 1976.

Athenaeus. *The Deipnosophistae.* Vol. 2. Loeb Classical Library edition. Cambridge, Mass.: Harvard University Press, 1928.

———. *The Deipnosophists, Or Banquet Of The Learned Of Athenaeus.* Vol. 1, translated by C. D. Yonge. London: Henry G. Bohn, 1854.

Attridge, Harold W. *The Acts of Thomas.* Edited by Julian V. Hills. Salem, Ore.: Polebridge Press, 2010.

Baigent, Michael, Richard Leigh, and Henry Lincoln. *Holy Blood, Holy Grail.* New York: Dell, 1983.

Barber, Elizabeth Wayland. *The Dancing Goddesses: Folklore, Archaeology, and the Origins of European Dance.* New York: W. W. Norton, 2014.

———. *Women's Work, The First 20,000 Years: Women, Cloth and Society in Early Times.* New York: W. W. Norton, 1996.

Barber, Elizabeth J. Wayland, and Paul T. Barber. *When They Severed Earth from Sky: How the Human Mind Shapes Myth.* Princeton, N.J.: Princeton University Press, 2011.

Barber, Malcolm. *Crusaders and Heretics, 12th–14th Centuries.* London: Variorum, 1995.

Baring, Anne. "Rebalancing the Masculine and the Feminine." Seminar available at AnneBaring.com. (Accessed July 27, 2019.)

Barnstone, Willis. *The Other Bible: Jewish Pseudepigrapha; Christian Apocrypha; Gnostic Scriptures*. New York: HarperCollins, 1984.

Barnstone, Willis, and Marvin W. Meyer. *The Gnostic Bible*. Boston: New Seeds, 2006.

Baroja, Julio Caro. *The World of the Witches*. Phoenix, Ariz.: Phoenix Press, 2001.

Bauman, Lynn C., Ward J. Bauman, and Cynthia Bourgeault. *The Luminous Gospels: Thomas, Mary Magdalene, and Philip*. Telephone, Tex.: Praxis, 2008.

Beaulieu, Stéphane. "Eve's Ritual: The Judahite Sacred Marriage Rite." Master's thesis, Department of Religion, Concordia University, Montreal, Canada. 2007.

Begg, Ean. *Cult of the Black Virgin*. Wilmette, Ill.: Chiron Publications, 2015.

Bell, Shannon. *Reading, Writing and Rewriting the Prostitute Body*. Bloomington: Indiana University Press, 1992.

Bentley, Toni. *Sisters of Salome*. Lincoln: University of Nebraska Press, 2005.

Bernal, Martin. *Black Athena: The Afroasiatic Roots of Classical Civilization*. Vol. 1. London: Free Association Books, 1987.

Bertrand, Azra, and Seren Bertrand. *Womb Awakening: Initiatory Wisdom from the Creatrix of All Life*. Rochester, Vt.: Bear & Company, 2017.

Billingsley, John. *Stony Gaze: Investigating Celtic & Other Stone Heads*. Chieveley, UK: Capall Bann, 1998.

Bin-Nun, Shoshana R. *The Tawananna in the Hittite Kingdom*. Heidelberg: Winter, 1975.

Black, Jeremy A., Anthony Green, and Tessa Rickards. *Gods, Demons, and Symbols of Ancient Mesopotamia: An Illustrated Dictionary*. Austin: University of Texas Press, 2014.

Bledstein, Adrien Janis. "Tamar and the Coat of Many Colors." In *A Feminist Companion to Samuel & Kings,* 2nd ser., edited by Athalya Brenner. Sheffield, UK: Sheffield Academic Press, 2000.

Bloch, Ariel A., and Chana Bloch. *The Song of Songs: The World's First Great Love Poem*. New York: Modern Library, 2006.

Bohak, Gideon. *Ancient Jewish Magic: A History*. Cambridge: Cambridge University Press, 2011.

Bonwick, James. *Irish Druids and Old Irish Religions*. London: Griffith, Farran & Co., 1894.

Booth, Charlotte. *Hypatia: Mathematician, Philosopher, Myth*. London: Fonthill Media, 2017.

Bourgeault, Cynthia. *The Meaning of Mary Magdalene: Discovering the Woman at the Heart of Christianity*. Boston: Shambhala, 2010.

Brand, John. *Observations on the Popular Antiquities of Great Britain*. Vol. 1. London: H. G. Bohn, 1848.

Breasted, James Henry. *A History of Egypt: From the Earliest Times to the Persian Conquest*. Cambridge: Cambridge University Press, 2015.

Buckley, Jorunn Jacobsen. "The Mandaean Appropriation of Jesus' Mother, Miriai." *Novum Testamentum* 35, no. 2 (1993): 181–96.

———. *The Mandaeans: Ancient Texts and Modern People.* Oxford: Oxford University Press, 2002.

Buckley, Thomas, and Alma Gottlieb. *Blood Magic: The Anthropology of Menstruation.* Berkeley: University of California Press, 1988.

Budge, E. A. Wallis. *Books on Egypt and Chaldea.* Vol. 2, *Egyptian Magic.* London: K. Paul, Trench, Trübner & Co, 1899.

Budin, Stephanie. *The Myth of Sacred Prostitution in Antiquity.* New York: Cambridge University Press, 2008.

Buonaventura, Wendy. *Belly Dancing.* London: Virago Press, 1983.

———. *Serpent of the Nile: Women and Dance in the Arab World.* London: Saqi Books, 1989.

Butler, Alan. *The Goddess, the Grail, and the Lodge: Tracing the Origins of Religion.* New York: Barnes & Noble Books, 2006.

Carmicheal, Alexander. *Carmina Gadelica: Hymns and Incantations with Illustrative Notes on Words, Rites, and Customs, Dying and Obsolete.* Vol. 1. Edinburgh: Printed for the author by T. and A. Constable, 1900.

Charles, R. H. "II Baruch." In *The Apocrypha and Pseudepigrapha of the Old Testament in English,* volume 2, 481–524. Oxford: Oxford University Press, 1913.

Charney, Noah. *Stealing the Mystic Lamb: The True Story of the World's Most Stolen Masterpiece.* New York: Public Affairs, 2012.

Child, Francis James. *English and Scottish Popular Ballads.* Edited by Helen Child Sargent and George Lyman Kittredge. Boston: Houghton Mifflin Company, 1904.

Chilton, Bruce. *Mary Magdalene: A Biography.* New York: Doubleday, 2005.

Churton, Tobias. *Gnostic Mysteries of Sex: Sophia the Wild One and Erotic Christianity.* Rochester, Vt.: Inner Traditions, 2015.

———. *The Mysteries of John the Baptist: His Legacy in Gnosticism, Paganism, and Freemasonry.* Rochester, Vt.: Inner Traditions, 2012.

Clarke, David. "The Head Cult: Tradition and Folklore Surrounding the Symbol of the Severed Human Head in the British Isles." Ph.D. diss., University of Sheffield, 1998.

Clarke, Robert B. *An Order Outside Time: A Jungian View of the Higher Self from Egypt to Christ.* Charlottesville, Va.: Hampton Roads, 2005.

Collins, Andrew. *The Cygnus Mystery: Unlocking the Ancient Secrets in the Cosmos.* London: Watkins Publishing, 2006.

Collins, John J. *Seers, Sibyls, and Sages in Hellenistic-Roman Judaism.* Boston: Brill Academic Publishers, 2001.

Coppens, Philip, and Andre Douzet. *The Secret Vault: The Secret Societies; Manipulation of Sauniere and the Secret Sanctuary of Notre-Dame-de-Marceille.* Amsterdam: Frontier, 2006.

Cordovero, Moses Ben Jacob, and Ira Robinson. *Moses Cordovero's Introduction to Kabbalah: An Annotated Translation of His Or Ne'erav.* New York: Michael Scharf Publication Trust of Yeshiva University Press, 1994.

Cort, Andrew. *The Sacred Chalice: Women of the Bible; The Inner Spiritual and Psychological Meaning of Their Stories.* Self-published, Createspace, 2013.

Crashaw, Richard. *The Complete Works of Richard Crashaw.* Vol. 1, edited by Alexander B. Grosart. London: Robson and Sons, printed for private circulation, 1872.

Cunningham, Elizabeth. *Magdalen Rising: The Beginning.* Rhinebeck, N.Y.: Monkfish Book, 2010.

———. *The Passion of Mary Magdalen: A Novel.* Rhinebeck, N.Y.: Monkfish Book, 2007.

Cyrino, Monica Silveira. *Aphrodite.* Oxon, UK: Routledge, 2010.

Cyril of Jerusalem. "Lecture XX." In *A Select Library of Nicene and Post-Nicene Fathers of the Christian Church: Second Series.* Vol. 7, edited by Philip Schaff and Henry Wace, 147–48. New York: Christian Literature Company, 1894.

Dalley, Stephanie, ed. *Myths from Mesopotamia: Creation, the Flood, Gilgamesh, and Others.* Rev. ed. Oxford World's Classics. Oxford: Oxford University Press, 2000.

Davidson, Sean. *Saint Mary Magdalene: Prophetess of Eucharistic Love.* San Francisco: Ignatius Press, 2017.

Davies, Philip R. *In Search of "Ancient Israel": A Study in Biblical Origins.* Sheffield, UK: Sheffield Academic Press, 1992.

Davis, John Paul. *Robin Hood: The Unknown Templar.* London: Peter Owen, 2009.

De Meaux, Monfieur. "An Exposition of the Doctrine of the Church of England." In *A Preservative Against Popery, in Several Select Discourses Upon the Principal Heads of Controversy Between Protestants and Papists.* Vol. 3, edited by Edmund Gibson. London: H. Knaplock, 1738.

De Sarzec, Ernest. *Découvertes en Chaldée.* Vol. 2. Paris: Ernest Leroux, 1912.

De Vaux, Roland. *Ancient Israel: Its Life and Institutions.* Translated by John McHugh. New York: McGraw Hill, 1961.

De Ville, Frans. *Tziganes: Témoins des Temps.* Preface by José Pirnay. Brussels: Office de publicité, 1956.

De Voragine, Jacobus. *The Golden Legend or Lives of the Saints.* Vol. 4, Temple Classics, translated by William Caxton, edited by F. S. Ellis. London: J. M. Dent & Sons, 1900.

Debus, Michael. *Mary and Sophia: The Feminine Element in the Spiritual Evolution of Humanity.* Edinburgh: Floris Books, 2013.

Dee, Jonathan. *Chronicles of Ancient Egypt.* Toronto: Prospero, 1998.

Dennis, James Teakle. *Burden of Isis: Being the Laments of Isis and Nephthys.* Classic Reprint. N.P.: Forgotten Books, 2015.

Dever, William G. *Did God Have a Wife? Archaeology and Folk Religion in Ancient Israel.* Grand Rapids, Mich.: Eerdmans, 2008.

Dijkstra, Meindert. "El, the God of Israel—Israel, the People of YHWH: On the Origins of Ancient Israelite Yahwism." In *Only One God? Monotheism in Ancient Israel and the Veneration of the Goddess Asherah.* Edited by Bob Becking, Meindert Dijkstra, Marjo C. A. Korpel, and Karel J. H. Vriezen, 81–126. London: Sheffield Academic Press, 2001.

Doresse, Jean. *The Secret Books of the Egyptian Gnostics: An Introduction to the Gnostic Coptic Manuscripts Discovered at Chenoboskion.* New York: MJF Books, 1997.

Douglas-Klotz, Neil. *Desert Wisdom: Sacred Middle Eastern Writings from the Goddess through the Sufis.* San Francisco: Harper Collins, 1995.

———. *The Hidden Gospel: Decoding the Spiritual Message of the Aramaic Jesus.* Wheaton Ill.: Quest Books, 2008.

Drake, Nathan. *Shakespeare and His Times.* Paris: Baudry's European Library, 1843.

Drob, Sanford L. *Kabbalistic Visions: C. G. Jung and Jewish Mysticism.* New Orleans: Spring Journal Books, 2017.

Durdin-Robertson, Lawrence. *The Goddesses of Chaldaea, Syria and Egypt.* Enniscorthy, Ireland: Cesara Publications, 1975.

Edersheim, Alfred. *The Life and Times of Jesus the Messiah.* Vol. 1. New American Edition. New York: E. R. Herrick and Co., 1886.

Edgar, Swift, and Angela M. Kinney. *The Vulgate Bible: Douay-Rheims Translation.* Cambridge, Mass.: Harvard University Press, 2010.

Egan, Harvey D. *An Anthology of Christian Mysticism.* 2nd ed. Collegeville, Minn.: The Liturgical Press, 1996.

Eedle, Arthur, and Rosalind Eedle. *Albion Restored: A Detective Journey to Discover the Birth of Christianity in England.* Self-published, Lulu, 2013.

Ehrenreich, B., and Deirdre English. *Witches, Midwives, and Nurses: A History of Women Healers.* 2nd. ed. Old Westbury, N.Y.: Feminist Press, 2010.

Ehrman, Bart D. *Peter, Paul and Mary Magdalene: The Followers of Jesus in History and Legend.* Oxford: Oxford University Press, 2006.

Ellis, George F. R. "The Shape of the Universe." *Nature* 425 (October 9, 2003): 566–67.

Emmerich, Anna Katharina. *Mary Magdalen: In the Visions of Anne Catherine Emmerich.* Rockford, Ill.: TAN Books, 2005.

Epiphanius. *The Panarion of Epiphanius of Salamis Books II and III. De Fide.* 2nd rev. ed. Translated by Frank Williams. Boston: Brill, 2013.

Faraone, Christopher A., and Laura McClure. *Prostitutes and Courtesans in the Ancient World.* Madison: University of Wisconsin Press, 2006.

Ferber, Sarah. *Demonic Possession and Exorcism: In Early Modern France.* London: Routledge, 2004.

Forrest, M. Isidora. *Isis Magic: Cultivating a Relationship with the Goddess of 10,000 Names.* St. Paul, Minn.: Llewellyn Publications, 2001.

Freke, Timothy, and Peter Gandy. *Jesus and the Lost Goddess: The Secret Teachings of the Original Christians.* New York: Three Rivers Press, 2001.

———. *The Jesus Mysteries: Was the Original Jesus a Pagan God?* New York: Element, 2003.

Frohlich, Ida. "The Female Body in Second Temple Literature." In *Religion and Female Body in Ancient Judaism and Its Environments,* edited by Géza G. Xeravits, 109–127. Berlin: Walter de Gruyter, 2015.

Gardner, Laurence. *The Grail Enigma: The Hidden Heirs of Jesus and Mary Magdalene.* London: Harper Element, 2009.

Gary, Gemma. *Silent as the Trees: Devonshire Witchcraft & Popular Magic.* London: Troy Books, 2017.

Geyer, John. *Mythology and Lament: Studies in the Oracles about the Nations.* Aldershot, UK: Ashgate, 2004.

Ginzburg, Carlo. *Ecstasies: Deciphering the Witches Sabbath.* Translated by Raymond Rosenthal. New York: Pantheon, 1991.

Glazebrook, Allison, and Madeleine Mary Henry. *Greek Prostitutes in the Ancient Mediterranean, 800 BCE–200 CE.* Madison: University of Wisconsin Press, 2011.

Goff, Beatrice Laura. *Symbols of Prehistoric Mesopotamia.* New Haven, Conn.: Yale University Press, 1963.

Gold, Judith Taylor. *Monsters and Madonnas.* Syracuse, N.Y.: Syracuse University Press, 1999.

González, Catherine Gunsalus. *Resources in the Ancient Church for Today's Worship AETH.* Nashville, Tenn.: Abingdon Press, 2014.

Goodrich, Norma Lorre. *Priestesses.* New York: HarperPerennial, 1990.

Goodrick-Clarke, Nicholas, and Clare Goodrick-Clarke. *G. R. S. Mead and the Gnostic Quest.* Berkeley, Calif.: North Atlantic Books, 2005.

Grahn, Judy. *Blood, Bread, and Roses: How Menstruation Created the World.* Boston: Beacon Press, 1993.

Grant, Robert M. *Gnosticism and Early Christianity.* New York: Columbia University Press, 1969.

Graves, Robert. *The White Goddess.* London: Faber & Faber, 1961.

Graves, Robert, and Raphael Patai. *Hebrew Myths: The Book of Genesis.* New York: McGraw-Hill, 1966.

Graves-Brown, Carolyn. *Dancing for Hathor: Women in Ancient Egypt.* London: Continuum, 2010.

Green, Joel B., Jeannine K. Brown, and Nicholas Perrin. *Dictionary of Jesus and the Gospels.* Downers Grove, Ill.: InterVarsity Press, 2013.

Grenn-Scott, Deborah. *Lilith's Fire: Reclaiming Our Sacred Lifeforce.* N.P.: Universal Publishers, 2000.

Grey, Peter. *The Red Goddess.* Dover, UK: Bibliothèque Rouge/Scarlet Imprint, 2011.

Haag, Michael. *The Quest for Mary Magdalene.* New York: Harper, 2016.

———. *The Tragedy of the Templars: The Rise and Fall of the Crusader States.* London: Profile Books, 2014.

Hammer, Jill, and Taya Shere. *The Hebrew Priestess: Ancient and New Visions of Jewish Women's Spiritual Leadership.* Teaneck, N.J.: Ben Yehuda Press, 2015.

Harrison, Jane Ellen. *Prolegomena to the Study of Greek Religion.* 3rd ed. London: C. J. Clay and Sons, 1922.

Hart, George. *The Routledge Dictionary of Egyptian Gods and Goddesses.* London: Routledge, 2005.

Haskins, Susan. *Mary Magdalen: Myth and Metaphor.* New York: Riverhead Books, 1993.

Hatsis, Thomas. *Psychedelic Mystery Traditions.* Rochester, Vt.: Park Street Press, 2018.

Heartsong, Claire, and Catherine Ann Clemett. *Anna, the Voice of the Magdalenes: A Sequel to Anna, Grandmother of Jesus.* Austin, Tex.: S.E.E. Publishing, 2010.

Heriz, Paschasius. *Saint John of the Cross.* Whitefish, Mont.: Kessinger, 2010.

Hillel, Rachel. *The Redemption of the Feminine Erotic Soul.* York Beach, Maine: Nicolas-Hays, 1997.

Hippolytus. *The Refutation of All Heresies.* Translated by J. H. Macmahon. Edinburgh: T & T Clark, 1870.

Hornung, Erik. *History of Ancient Egypt.* Edinburgh: Edinburgh University Press, 1999.

———. *The Secret Lore of Egypt: Its Impact on the West.* Ithaca, N.Y.: Cornell University Press, 2001.

Hornung, Erik, and David Lorton. *The Ancient Egyptian Books of the Afterlife.* Ithaca, N.Y.: Cornell University, 1999.

Houston, Jean. *The Passion of Isis and Osiris: A Union of Two Souls.* New York: Ballantine Books, 1995.

Hovers, Erella, Shimon Ilani, Ofer Bar-Yosef, and Bernard Vandermeersch. "An Early Case of Color Symbolism: Ochre Use by Modern Humans in Qafzeh Cave." *Current Anthropology* 44, no. 4 (2003): 491–522. doi:10.1086/375869.

Hyde, Walter Woodburn. *Paganism to Christianity in the Roman Empire.* Eugene, Ore.: Wipf & Stock, 2008.

Irenaeus. *Against Heresies.* In *The Ante-Nicene Fathers: The Writings of the Fathers Down to A.D. 325.* Vol. 1, translated by Philip Schaff. Edited by Arthur Coxe. Buffalo, N.Y.: Christian Literature Company, 1885.

Jacobsen, Thorkild. *The Treasures of Darkness: A History of Mesopotamian Religion.* New Haven, Conn.: Yale University Press, 1976.

John of the Cross. *The Complete Works of Saint John of the Cross.* Translated by David Lewis. London: Spottiswood, 1864.

Johnson, Walter. *Byways in British Archaeology.* Cambridge: University Press, 1912.

Jolly, Penny Howell. "Jan Van Eyck's Italian Pilgrimage: A Miraculous Florentine Annunciation and the Ghent Altarpiece." *Zeitschrift Für Kunstgeschichte* 61, no. 3 (1998): 369–94.

———. *Picturing the "Pregnant" Magdalene in Northern Art, 1430–1550: Addressing and Undressing the Sinner-Saint.* Burlington, Vt.: Ashgate Press, 2014.

———. "Rogier Van Der Weyden's 'Pregnant' Magdalene: On the Rhetoric of Dress in the 'Descent From the Cross.'" *Studies in Iconography* 28 (2007): 209–80.

———. "The Wise and Foolish Magdalene, the Good Widow, and Rogier Van Der Weyden's 'Braque Triptych.'" *Studies in Iconography* 31 (2010): 98–156.

Jones, Kathy. *The Goddess in Glastonbury.* Somerset, UK: Ariadne Publications, 1990. Available online at Kathy Jones's website, "In the Heart of the Goddess."

Josephus. *Jewish Antiquities.* Vol. 2: *Books 4–6,* translated by H. St. J. Thackeray and Ralph Marcus. Loeb Classical Library. Cambridge, Mass.: Harvard University Press, 1930.

Julian of Norwich. *Revelations of Divine Love.* Translated by Elizabeth Spearing. London: Penguin, 1998.

Jung, Carl. *Aion: Researches into the Phenomenology of the Self.* London: Routledge, 1959.

Jung, Carl, E. Welsh, and B. Hannah. *Modern Psychology: Notes On Lectures Given At the Eidgenössische Technische Hochschule, Zürich.* Vols. 3–4. 2nd ed. Zurich: K. Schippert, 1959.

Keel, Othmar, and Christopher Uehlinger. *Gods, Goddesses, and Images of God in Ancient Israel.* Minneapolis, Minn.: Fortress Press, 1998.

Kenyon, Tom, and Judy Sion. *The Magdalen Manuscript: The Alchemies of Horus & the Sex Magic of Isis.* Boulder, Colo.: Sounds True, 2006.

Kessler, Edward. *An Introduction to Jewish-Christian Relations.* Cambridge: Cambridge University Press, 2010.

Key, Andrew F. "Traces of the Worship of the Moon God Sîn among the Early Israelites." *Journal of Biblical Literature* 84, no. 1 (1965): 20–26.

King, Karen L. *The Gospel of Mary of Magdala: Jesus and the First Woman Apostle.* Santa Rosa, Calif.: Polebridge, 2003.

King, Leonard W. *Babylonian Magic and Sorcery.* Classic Reprint. London: Forgotten Books, 2016.

———. *Enuma Elish: The Seven Tablets of the History of Creation.* N.P.: Filiquarian Publishing, 2007.

King, Nicholas. "Gnosticism: An Investigation into the Possible Origins of Some of Its Salient Features." Ph.D. diss., University of Leicester, 1990.

Knight, Chris. *Blood Relations.* New Haven, Conn.: Yale University Press, 2013.

Koltuv, Barbara Black. *Weaving Woman.* York Beach, Maine: Nicolas-Hays, 1990.

Kramer, Samuel Noah. "Cuneiform Studies and the History of Literature: The Sumerian Sacred Marriage Texts." *Proceedings of the American Philosophical Society* 107, no. 6 (1963): 485–527.

———. *History Begins at Sumer.* Philadelphia: University of Pennsylvania Press, 1988.

———. *Sumerian Mythology: A Study of Spiritual and Literacy Achievement in the Third Millennium B.C.* Philadelphia: University of Pennsylvania Press, 1997.

———. *The Sumerians: Their History, Culture, and Character.* Chicago, Ill.: University of Chicago Press, 2008.

Labat, René. *Manuel D'Épigraphie Akkadienne*. 5th edition. Paris: Librairie Orientaliste Paul Geunther, 1976.

Laertius, Diogenes. "Pythagoras." In Book 8 of *Lives of Eminent Philosophers* vol. 2, 320–66, translated by R. D. Hicks. Edited by E. Capps, T. E. Page and W. H. D. Rouse. New York: G. P. Putnam's Sons, 1925.

Lahr, Jane. *Searching for Mary Magdalene: A Journey through Art and Literature*. New York: Welcome Books, 2006.

Laible, Heinrich. "Jesus Christ in the Talmud." In *Jesus Christ in the Talmud, Midrash, Zohar, and the Liturgy of the Synagogue,* 1–100. Translated and edited by Rev. A. W. Streane. Cambridge: Deighton Bell & Sons, 1893.

Lambdin, Thomas O., trans. *The Gospel of Thomas.* The Gnostic Society Library website.

Lash, John Lamb. *Not in His Image: Gnostic Vision, Sacred Ecology, and the Future of Belief.* White River Junction, Vt.: Chelsea Green, 2006.

Lea, Charles Henry. *A History of the Inquisition of Spain.* Vol. 4. New York: MacMillan, 1922.

Legrain, L. *Ur Excavations.* Vol. 3, *Archaic Seal-Impressions.* Oxford: Oxford University Press, 1936.

Leick, Gwendolyn. *The Babylonians: An Introduction.* London: Routledge, 2007.

———. *Sex and Eroticism in Mesopotamian Literature.* London: Routledge, 2003.

Leland, Charles Godfrey. *Alternate Sex: Or the Female Intellect in Man, and the Masculine in Woman.* Classic Reprint. N.P.: Forgotten Books, 2015.

Leloup, Jean-Yves. *The Gospel of Philip: Jesus, Mary Magdalene, and the Gnosis of Sacred Union.* Rochester, Vt.: Inner Traditions, 2004.

———. *The Sacred Embrace of Jesus and Mary: The Sexual Mystery at the Heart of the Christian Tradition.* Rochester, Vt.: Inner Traditions, 2006.

Leloup, Jean-Yves, and Joseph Rowe. *The Gospel of Mary Magdalene.* Rochester, Vt.: Inner Traditions, 2002.

Lesko, Barbara S. *The Great Goddesses of Egypt.* Norman: University of Oklahoma Press, 1999.

Levack, Brian P. *The Devil Within: Possession Et Exorcism in the Christian West.* New Haven, Conn.: Yale University Press, 2013.

Levy, G. Rachel. *The Gate of Horn: A Study of the Religious Conceptions of the Stone Age, and Their Influence upon European Thought.* London: Faber and Faber, 1948.

Lewy, Julius. "The Late Assyro-Babylonian Cult of the Moon and Its Culmination at the Time of Nabonidus." *Hebrew Union College Annual* 19 (1945): 405–89.

Love, Nicholas. *The Mirror of the Blessed Life of Jesu Christ.* London: St. Catherine Press, 1926.

Lubicz, Isha Schwaller De, and Lucie Lamy. *Her-Bak: The Living Face of Ancient Egypt.* New York: Inner Traditions International, 1978.

Lucotte, Gerard. "The Mitochondrial DNA Mitotype of Sainte Marie-Madeleine." *International Journal of Sciences* 2, no. 12 (2016): 10–19.

Lumby, Lauri Ann. *Song of the Beloved: The Gospel According to Mary Magdalene.* Oshkosh, Wisc.: Authentic Freedom Press, 2014.

Lumpkin, Joseph B. *The Books of Enoch: The Angels, the Watchers and the Nephilim, with Extensive Commentary on the Three Books of Enoch, the Fallen Angels, the Calendar of Enoch, and Daniel's Prophecy.* Blountsville, Ala.: Fifth Estate, 2011.

Luria, Isaac Ben Solomon, and Eliahu Klein. *Kabbalah of Creation: Isaac Lurias Earlier Mysticism.* Berkeley, Calif.: North Atlantic, 2005.

Mackey, Albert, Edward L. Hawkins, and William James Hughan. *An Encyclopedia of Freemasonry and Its Kindred Sciences, Comprising the Whole Range of Arts, Sciences and Literature as Connected with the Institution.* Vol. 2. New York: Masonic History Company, 1912.

Macleod, Fiona [William Sharp]. *The Divine Adventure, Iona: By Sundown Shores.* 2nd edition. London: Chapman and Hall, 1900.

Macleod, Fiona [William Sharp]. *The Winged Destiny: Studies in the Spiritual History of the Gael.* London: Chapman and Hall, 1904.

Magdalena, Flo Aeveia. *I Remember Union: The Story of Mary Magdalena.* Putney, Vt.: All Worlds, 1992.

Maier, Christl M., and Carolyn J. Sharp. *Prophecy and Power: Jeremiah in Feminist and Postcolonial Perspective.* London: Bloomsbury, 2015.

Mair, Victor. "Ancient Mummies of the Traim Basin: Discovering Early Inhabitants of Eastern Central Asia." *Expedition Magazine* 58, no. 2 (2016): 24–29.

Malachi. *St. Mary Magdalene: The Gnostic Tradition of the Holy Bible.* St. Paul, Minn.: Llewellyn, 2006.

Malvern, Marjorie M. *Venus in Sackcloth: The Magdalen's Origins and Metamorphoses.* Carbondale: Southern Illinois University Press, 1975.

Mama Zogbé. *The Sibyls: Demystifying the Absence of the African Ancestress; The First Prophetess of Mami (Wata).* Martinez, Ga.: Mami Wata Healers Society, 2007.

Manilius, Marco. *Astronomica.* Edited and translated by George Patrick Goold. Cambridge, Mass.: Harvard University Press, 1977.

Mann, A. T., and Jane Lyle. *Sacred Sexuality.* London: Vega, 2002.

Marglin, Frédérique Apffel. *Wives of the God-King: The Rituals of the Devadasis of Puri.* Delhi: Oxford University Press, 1985.

Markale, Jean. *The Church of Mary Magdalene.* Rochester, Vt.: Inner Traditions, 2004.

Marshall, Taylor. "Did Jewish Temple Virgins Exist and Was Mary a Temple Virgin?" Available at Taylormarshall.com (blog). (Accessed July 27, 2019.)

Mason, Mark. *In Search of the Loving God.* Eugene, Ore.: Dwapara Press, 1997.

Massey, Gerald. *Ancient Egypt: The Light of the World.* New York: Cosimo Classics, 2007.

Mathers, S. L. MacGregor. *The Kabbalah Unveiled: Containing the Following Books of the Zohar: The Book of Concealed Mystery; The Greater Holy Assembly; The Lesser Holy Assembly.* London: Routledge & K. Paul, 1951.

Matthews, Caitlin. *Sophia Goddess of Wisdom, Bride of God*. Wheaton, Ill.: Quest Books, 2013.

Matthews, John. *Robin Hood*. Glastonbury, UK: Gothic Image Publications, 1993.

McGowan, Kathleen. *The Book of Love*. New York: Simon & Schuster, 2010.

———. *The Expected One*. New York: Touchstone, 2006.

Mead, G. R. S. *Did Jesus Live 100 B.C.?* London: Theosophical Publishing Society, 1903.

———. *The Gnostic John the Baptizer: Selections from the Mandæan John-book*. Erscheinungsort Nicht Ermittelbar: Kessinger, 1997.

———. *Gnosticism: Fragments of a Faith Forgotten*. N.P.: Forgotten Books, 2008.

———. *Pistis Sophia: A Gnostic Text*. Blacksburg, Va.: A & D Publishing, 2009.

———. *Simon Magus: An Essay on the Founder of Simonianism Based on the Ancient Sources with a Re-evaluation of His Philosophy and Teachings*. Chicago: Ares, 1974.

———. *Simon Magus: His Philosophy and Teachings*. Edited by Paul Tice. San Diego, Calif.: Book Tree, 1999.

Meador, Betty De Shong. *Inanna, Lady of Largest Heart: Poems of the Sumerian High Priestess Enheduanna*. Austin: University of Texas Press, 2006.

———. *Princess, Priestess, Poet: The Sumerian Temple Hymns of Enheduanna*. Austin: University of Texas Press, 2010.

———. *Uncursing the Dark: Treasures from the Underworld*. Asheville, N.C.: Chiron Publications, 2013.

Metzger, Deena. *The Woman Who Slept with Men to Take the War out of Them*. Culver City, Calif.: Peace Press, 1981.

Meyer, Marvin, ed. "The Gospel of Philip." In *The Nag Hammadi Scriptures*, 161–86. New York: Harper One, 2007.

———. *The Nag Hammadi Scriptures*. New York: HarperOne, 2009.

Meyers, Carol L., Toni Craven, and Ross Shepard Kraemer. *Women in Scripture: A Dictionary of Named and Unnamed Women in the Hebrew Bible, the Apocryphal/Deuterocanonical Books, and the New Testament*. Boston: Houghton Mifflin, 2001.

Montgomery, Hugh. *The God-Kings of Europe: The Descendants of Jesus Traced through the Odonic and Davidic Dynasties*. San Diego, Calif.: Book Tree, 2006.

Morgan, Giles. *A Brief History of the Holy Grail*. London: Robinson/Running Press, 2011.

Morrow, Susan Brind. *Dawning Moon of the Mind: Unlocking the Pyramid Texts*. New York: Farrar, Straus & Giroux, 2016.

Muhl, Lars. *The Law of Light: The Secret Teachings of Jesus*. London: Watkins, 2014.

———. *The O Manuscript: The Seer, the Magdalene, the Grail*. Aarhus: Lemuel Books, 2008.

Murdock, Maureen. *The Heroines Journey*. Boston: Shambhala, 1990.

Murray, Margaret Alice. *The God of the Witches*. New ed. London: Faber & Faber, 1952.

Muss-Arnolt, W. "On Semitic Words in Greek and Latin." *Transactions of the American Philological Association (1869–1896)* 23 (1892): 35–156.

Myers, F. W. H. *Essays: Classical*. London: Macmillan, 1883.

Myers, Philip van Ness. *Ancient History.* 2nd rev. ed. Boston: Ginn and Company, 1916.

Nahmad, Claire, and Margaret Bailey. *The Secret Teachings of Mary Magdalene: Including the Lost Gospel of Mary, Revealed and Published for the First Time.* London: Watkins, 2006.

Niehr, Herbert. "Israelite Religion and Canaanite Religion." In *Religious Diversity in Ancient Israel and Judah.* Edited by John Barton and Francesca Stavrakopoulou, 23–36. London: A&C Black, 2010.

Origen. *Against Celsus.* In *The Ante-Nicene Fathers: Translations of the Writings of the Fathers Down to A. D. 325.* Vol. 4, edited by Alexander Roberts and James Donaldson. New York: Charles Scribner's Sons, 1913.

Origen. *Commentary on the Epistle to the Romans, Books 6–10.* The Fathers of the Church. Translated and edited by Thomas P. Scheck. Washington, D.C.: Catholic University of America Press, 2002.

Orr, Emma Restall. *Kissing the Hag: The Dark Goddess and the Unacceptable Nature of Women.* Hants, UK: O-books, 2009.

Osho. *The Beloved.* Vol. 1. Pune, India: Rebel Publishing House, 1999.

Owen, Lara. *Her Blood Is Gold: Awakening to the Wisdom of Menstruation.* Wimborne, UK: Archive Publishing, 2008.

Ozaniec, Naomi. *Daughter of the Goddess: The Sacred Priestess.* London: Aquarian/ Thorsons, 1993.

Pagels, Elaine H. *Beyond Belief: The Secret Gospel of Thomas.* London: Pan, 2005.

———. *The Gnostic Gospels.* New York: Random House, 2004.

Parpola, Simo. "The Assyrian Tree of Life: Tracing the Origins of Jewish Monotheism and Greek Philosophy." *Journal of Near Eastern Studies* 52, no. 3 (1993): 161–208.

Patai, Raphael. *Adam ve-Adama* [Man and Earth]. Jerusalem: Hebrew Press Association, 1941–42.

———. *Gates to the Old City: A Book of Jewish Legends.* Detroit, Mich.: Wayne State University Press, 1981.

———. *The Hebrew Goddess.* Detroit, Mich.: Wayne State University Press, 1968.

———. "Lilith." *Journal of American Folklore* 77, no. 306 (1964): 295–314.

Pausanias. *Description of Greece.* Vol. 5, edited and translated by Sir James Frazer. London: Macmillan, 1913.

Phillips, Graham. *The Chalice of Magdalene: The Search for the Cup That Held the Blood of Christ.* Rochester, Vt.: Bear & Co., 2004.

Picknett, Lynn. *Mary Magdalene: Christianity's Hidden Goddess.* New York: Carroll & Graf, 2004.

———. *The Secret History of Lucifer: The Ancient Path to Knowledge and the Real Da Vinci Code.* Philadelphia: Da Capo, 2005.

Picknett, Lynn, and Clive Prince. *The Templar Revelation: Secret Guardians of the True Identity of Christ.* New York: Touchstone, 1997.

Pinch, Geraldine. *Egyptian Mythology: A Guide to the Gods, Goddesses, and Traditions of Ancient Egypt*. Oxford: Oxford University Press, 2004.

———. *Magic in Ancient Egypt*. Austin: University of Texas Press, 2010.

Pistis Sophia. Translated by George Horner. Introduction by F. Legge. London: SPCK, 1924.

Plutarch. *Of Isis and Osiris*. N.P.: Theophania Publishing, 2011.

Pomeroy, Sarah B. *Goddesses, Whores, Wives and Slaves: Women in Classical Antiquity*. London: Bodley Head, 2015.

Powell, Robert. *The Most Holy Trinosophia: And the New Revelation of the Divine Feminine*. New York: Anthroposophic Press, 2001.

———. *The Mystery, Biography & Destiny of Mary Magdalene: Sister of Lazarus John & Spiritual Sister of Jesus*. Great Barrington, Mass.: Lindisfarne Books, 2008.

Power, Camilla. "Women in Prehistoric Rock Art." In *New Perspectives on Prehistoric Art*, 75–103. Edited by G. Berghaus. London: Praeger, 2004.

Prophet, Elizabeth Clare, and Annice Booth. *Mary Magdalene and the Divine Feminine: Jesus' Lost Teachings on Woman*. Gardiner, Mont.: Summit University Press, 2005.

Qualls-Corbett, Nancy, and Marion Woodman. *The Sacred Prostitute: Eternal Aspect of the Feminine*. Toronto: Inner City Books, 1988.

Quillan, Jehanne De. *The Gospel of the Beloved Companion: The Complete Gospel of Mary Magdalene*. Foix, France: Éditions Athara, 2011.

Quirke, Stephen. *Ancient Egyptian Religion*. London: British Museum Press, 1992.

Rast, Walter E. "Cakes for the Queen of Heaven." In *Scripture in History & Theology: Essays in Honor of J. Coert Rylaarsdam*, edited by Arthur L. Merrill and Thomas W. Overholt, 167–80. Eugene, Ore.: Pickwick, 2009.

Redgrove, Peter. *The Black Goddess: And the Sixth Sense*. London: Paladin, 1989.

Riachi, Shmuel Meir. *The Elucidated Tomer Devorah*. Nanuet, N.Y.: Feldheim Publishers, 2015.

Richter, Irma. *Rhythmic Form in Art*. Mineola, N.Y.: Dover Publications, 2005.

Roberts, Alexander, and James Donaldson, eds. *The Ante-Nicene Fathers: Translations of the Writings of the Fathers Down to AD 325*. Vol. 4. Buffalo, N.Y.: Christian Literature, 1885.

Roberts, Alison. *Hathor Rising: The Power of the Goddess in Ancient Egypt*. Rochester, Vt.: Inner Traditions, 1997.

Roberts, John S. *The Legendary Ballads of England and Scotland*. London: Frederick Warne and Co., 1890.

Robins, Gay. *Women in Ancient Egypt*. Cambridge, Mass.: Harvard University Press, 1993.

Robinson, James M., ed. *The Nag Hammadi Library in English*. San Francisco: Harper Collins 1990.

Robson, Vivian. *The Fixed Stars and Constellations in Astrology*. London: Cecil Palmer, 1923.

Roe, Dinah. *The Rossettis in Wonderland: A Victorian Family History*. London: Haus, 2011.

Sasson, Jack M. *Civilizations of the Ancient Near East.* New York: Charles Scribner's Sons, 1995.

Saxon, Elizabeth. *The Eucharist in Romanesque France: Iconography and Theology.* Rochester, N.Y.: Boydell, 2006.

Schaberg, Jane. *The Illegitimacy of Jesus: A Feminist Theological Interpretation of the Infancy Narratives.* Sheffield, UK: Sheffield Phoenix Press, 2006.

———. *The Resurrection of Mary Magdalene: Legends, Apocrypha, and the Christian Testament.* New York: Continuum, 2004.

Schaberg, Jane, and Melanie Johnson-Debaufre. *Mary Magdalene Understood.* New York: Continuum, 2006.

Schäfer, Peter. *Jesus in the Talmud.* Princeton, N.J.: Princeton University Press, 2007.

Schaup, Susanne. *Sophia Aspects of the Divine Feminine: Past & Present.* York Beach, Maine: Nicolas-Hays, 1997.

Schneemelcher, Wilhelm. *New Testament Apocrypha.* Vol. 1, rev. ed., translation edited by R. McL. Wilson. Louisville, Ky.: Westminster John Knox Press, 2003.

Schneider, Sarah. *Kabbalistic Writings on the Nature of Masculine and Feminine.* Lanham, Md.: Jason Aronson, 2001.

Scholem, Gershom Gerhard. *On the Kabbalah and Its Symbolism.* New York: Schocken, 1996.

Schonfield, Hugh. *The Essene Odyssey.* Shaftesbury, UK: Element Books, 1984.

Schumann-Antelme, Ruth, and S. Rossini. *Sacred Sexuality in Ancient Egypt: The Erotic Secrets of the Forbidden Papyrus; A Look at the Unique Role of Hathor, the Goddess of Love.* Rochester, Vt.: Inner Traditions, 2001.

Schussler Fiorenza, Elizabeth. *Jesus, Miriam's Child, Sophia's Prophet: Critical Issues in Feminist Christology.* New York: Continuum, 1994.

Scott, Emmett. *Hatshepsut, Queen of Sheba.* New York: Algora Publishing, 2012.

Seligsohn, M. "Star-Worship Among the Israelites." In *The Jewish Encyclopedia.* Vol. 11, edited by Isidore Singer, et al. New York: Funk and Wagnalls, 1905.

Sharon, G, A. Barash, D. Eisenberg-Degen, L. Grosman, M. Oron, and U. Berger. "Monumental Megalithic Burial and Rock Art Tell a New Story about the Levant Intermediate Bronze 'Dark Ages.'" *PLoS ONE* 12, no. 3 (2017): e0172969.doi .org/10.1371/journal.pone.0172969.

Shaw, Robert. *Sketch of the Religions of the World.* 8th ed. St. Louis, Mo.: Becktold & Co., 1904.

Shepsut, Asia. *Journey of the Priestess: The Priestess Traditions of the Ancient World; A Journey of Spiritual Awakening and Empowerment.* London: Aquarian Press, 1993.

Silva, Freddy. *First Templar Nation.* Rochester, Vt.: Destiny Books, 2017.

Singer, Isadore, ed. *The Jewish Encyclopedia.* Vol. 11. New York: Funk and Wagnalls, 1905.

Smith, George. *Chaldean Account of Genesis, Containing the Description of the Creation.* N.P.: Nabu Press, 2010.

Smith, Morton. *Jesus the Magician: A Renowned Historian Reveals How Jesus Was Viewed by People of His Time.* Charlottesville, Va.: Hampton Roads, 2014.

Snow, Dean R. "Sexual Dimorphism in European Upper Paleolithic Cave Art." *American Antiquity* 78, no. 4 (2013): 746–61.

Spinks, Bryan D. *Do This in Remembrance of Me: The Eucharist from the Early Church to the Present Day.* London: SCM Press, 2013.

Stagg, Evelyn, and Frank Stagg. *Woman in the World of Jesus.* Edinburgh: Saint Andrew, 1981.

Starbird, Margaret. *The Goddess in the Gospels: Reclaiming the Sacred Feminine.* Rochester, Vt.: Bear & Company, 1998.

———. *Magdalene's Lost Legacy: Symbolic Numbers and the Sacred Union in Christianity.* Rochester, Vt.: Bear & Company, 2003.

———. *The Woman with the Alabaster Jar: Mary Magdalen and the Holy Grail.* Rochester, Vt.: Bear & Company, 2006.

Starr, Mirabai. *Teresa of Avila: The Book of My Life.* Boston: New Seeds, 2007.

Stavrakopoulou, Francesca. "Popular Religion and Official Religion." In *Religious Diversity in Ancient Israel and Judah.* Edited by John Barton and Francesca Stavrakopoulou, 37–60. London: A&C Black, 2010.

Stol, Marten. *Women in the Ancient Near East.* Translated by Helen and Mervyn Richardson. Boston: De Gruyter, 2016.

Stone, Merlin. *Ancient Mirrors of Womanhood: A Treasury of Goddess and Heroine Lore from around the World.* Boston: Beacon Press, 1991.

Stoyanov, Yuri. *The Other God: Dualist Religions from Antiquity to the Cathar Heresy.* New Haven, Conn.: Yale University Press, 2000.

Talbot, Alice-Mary Maffry. *Holy Women of Byzantium: Ten Saints Lives in English Translation.* Washington, D.C.: Dumbarton Oaks Research Library and Collection, 1996.

Teresa of Avila. *The Interior Castle (The Mansions).* Translated by E. Allison Peers. London: Sheed & Ward, 1999.

Tertullian. *The Ante-Nicene Fathers: Translations of the Writings of the Fathers Down to A.D. 325.* Vol. 3, *Latin Christianity: Its Founder, Tertullian,* edited by Rev. Alexander Robert and James Donaldson. Revised by A. Cleveland Coxe. New York: Charles Scribner's Sons, 1918.

Teubal, Savina J. *Ancient Sisterhood: The Lost Traditions of Hagar and Sarah.* Athens, Ohio: Swallow Press / Ohio University Press, 1997.

———. *Sarah the Priestess: The First Matriarch of Genesis.* Athens, Ohio: Swallow Press, 1986.

Thompson, R. Campbell. *The Devils and Evil Spirits of Babylonia: Being Babylonian and Assyrian Incantations against the Demons, Ghouls, Vampires, Hobgoblins, Ghosts, and Kindred Evil Spirits, Which Attack Mankind.* Whitefish, Mont.: Kessinger, 2007.

———. *Semitic Magic: Its Origins and Development*. York Beach, Maine: S. Weiser, 2000.

Tomberg, Valentin. *Christ and Sophia: Anthroposophic Meditations on the Old Testament, New Testament & Apocalypse*. Translated by William Baxter Philalethes. Great Barrington, Mass.: SteinerBooks, 2011.

Tyldesley, Joyce Ann. *Daughters of Isis: Women of Ancient Egypt*. London: Penguin Books, 2005.

Vandermeersch, Bernard, Baruch Arensburg, Ofer Bar-Yosef, and Anna Belfer-Cohen. "Upper Paleolithic Human Remains from Qafzeh Cave, Israel." *Journal of the Israel Prehistoric Society* 43 (2013): 7–21.

Vere, Nicholas De. *The Dragon Legacy: The Secret History of an Ancient Bloodline*. San Diego, Calif.: Book Tree, 2004.

Vital, Ḥayyim Ben Joseph, and Isaac Ben Solomon Luria. *The Tree of Life*. Vol. 1, *The Palace of Adam Kadmon,* translated by Donald Wilder Menzi and Zwe Padeh. Northvale, N.J.: Jason Aronson, 1998.

Walker, Barbara G. *The Woman's Encyclopedia of Myths and Secrets*. San Francisco: Harper Collins, 1983.

Ward, Benedicta. *Harlots of the Desert: A Study of Repentance in Early Monastic Sources*. London: A. R. Mowbray, 1987.

Warner, Marina. *Alone of All Her Sex: The Myth and the Cult of the Virgin Mary*. Oxford: Oxford University Press, 2016.

Watterson, Barbara. *Women in Ancient Egypt*. Stroud, UK: Amberley, 2013.

Webb, Mary. *Precious Bane*. London: Jonathon Cape, 1924.

Welburn, Andrew. *The Beginnings of Christianity: Essene Mystery, Gnostic Revelation and the Christian Vision*. Edinburgh: Floris, 2004.

West, John Anthony. *Serpent in the Sky: The High Wisdom of Ancient Egypt*. Wheaton, Ill.: Quest Books, 1993.

White, Randall. "The Earliest Images: Ice Age 'Art' in Europe." *Expedition: The Magazine of the University of Pennsylvania* 34, no. 3 (1992): 37–51.

William Davidson digital edition of the Koren Noé Talmud, with commentary by Rabbi Adin Steinsaltz Even-Israel. Sefaria.org, by Koren Publishers.

Williams, H. Noel. *The Pearl of Princesses: The Life of Marguerite, D'angoulême, Queen of Navarre*. London: Eveleigh Nash, 1916. Classic Reprint, N.P.: Forgotten Books, 2018.

Wilson, Linda. "By Midnight, By Moonlight: Ritual Protection Marks in Caves beneath the Mendip Hills, Somerset." In *Hidden Charms: Transactions of the Hidden Charms Conference, 2016,* edited by Jeremy Harte and Brian Haggard. Hebden Bridge, UK: Northern Earth Books, 2017.

Wilson, Stuart, and Joanna Prentis. *Power of the Magdalene: The Hidden Story of the Women Disciples*. Huntsville, Ark.: Ozark Mountain, 2009.

Witt, R. E. *Isis in the Ancient World*. Baltimore: Johns Hopkins University Press, 1997.

Wolkstein, Diane, and Samuel Noah Kramer. *Inanna Queen of Heaven and Earth*. New York: Harper & Row, 1983.

Woolley, Charles Leonard. *Ur Excavations Vol. IV, The Early Periods: A Report on the Sites and Objects Prior in Date to the Third Dynasty of Ur Discovered in the Course of the Excavations*. London: Joint Expedition of the British Museum and of the Museum of the University of Pennsylvania, 1955.

Yogananda. *Autobiography of a Yogi*. Los Angeles: Self-Realization Fellowship, 1993.

Young, Serenity. *Courtesans and Tantric Consorts: Sexualities in Buddhist Narrative, Iconography, and Ritual*. New York: Routledge, 2004.

INDEX

Numbers in *italics* preceded by *pl.* indicate color insert plate numbers.

ABOUT THE AUTHORS

AZRA AND SEREN BERTRAND are award-winning authors, dedicated to remembering the earth-honoring wisdom traditions of the sacred feminine lineages across the world. Through storytelling, spiritkeeping, Sophiology, music, and visionary journeying, they create space for the emergence of our radiant, embodied ecology of love.

Their first book together, *Womb Awakening: Initiatory Wisdom from the Creatrix of All Life,* won five awards in its first year of release, including the Nautilus Silver Award in the category of women.

Azra Bertrand, M.D., graduated from Duke University School of Medicine, and has a degree in biochemistry. He has been a pioneering doctor and mystic for twenty years, helping more than 20,000 people to heal on a physical, emotional, and spiritual level. He was born into a lineage of healers, including physicians to the German royal court in Renaissance Europe, and is deeply connected to the Sophia earth wisdom.

Seren Bertrand is a storyteller, author, and energetic midwife to the wave of feminine consciousness that is bringing balance back onto our planet. She has immersed herself in the Magdalene Mysteries for over fifteen years, especially within the Celtic and Christian spirit keeper traditions of Awen—the Holy Spirit.

Visit the website: www.SerenBertrand.com

Books of Related Interest

Womb Awakening
Initiatory Wisdom from the Creatrix of All Life
by Azra Bertrand, M.D., and Seren Bertrand

The Gospel of Mary Magdalene
by Jean-Yves Leloup

Return of the Divine Sophia
Healing the Earth through the Lost Wisdom Teachings
of Jesus, Isis, and Mary Magdalene
by Tricia McCannon

The Healing Wisdom of Mary Magdalene
Esoteric Secrets of the Fourth Gospel
by Jack Angelo

The Woman with the Alabaster Jar
Mary Magdalen and the Holy Grail
by Margaret Starbird

The Healing Power of the Sacred Woman
Health, Creativity, and Fertility for the Soul
by Christine R. Page, M.D.

Healing Journeys with the Black Madonna
Chants, Music, and Sacred Practices of the Great Goddess
by Alessandra Belloni
Foreword by Matthew Fox

The Heart of the Great Mother
Spiritual Initiation, Creativity, and Rebirth
by Christine R. Page, M.D.

INNER TRADITIONS • BEAR & COMPANY
P.O. Box 388
Rochester, VT 05767
1-800-246-8648
www.InnerTraditions.com

Or contact your local bookseller